Uncle John's
GREAT
BIG

AUSTRALIAN
BATHROOM
READER®

The Bathroom Readers' Institute

Ashland, OR
&
San Diego, CA

UNCLE JOHN'S GREAT BIG AUSTRALIAN BATHROOM READER®

For information, write
The Bathroom Readers' Institute
5880 Oberlin Drive, San Diego, CA 92121
unclejohn@advmkt.com

Cover design by Michael Brunsfeld
San Rafael, CA (*brunsfeldo@attbi.com*)

National Library of Australia
Cataloguing and Publication data

ISBN: 1-57145-815-8

1. Wit and humor 2. Anecdotes 3. Curiosities and wonders 4. History–Miscellanea 5. Science–Miscellanea 1. Title: Uncle John's bathroom reader.

828.07

Printed in Australia by Griffin Press
First printing: January 2002

10 9 8 7 6 5 4 3 2 1 02 03 04 05

Project Team: Portable Press
Allen Orso, Publisher
JoAnn Padgett, Director, Editorial & Production
Allison Bocksruker, Project Manager
Cindy Tillinghast, Staff Editor
Georgine Lidell, Inventory Manager
Laurel Graziano, International Sales Director
Project Team: Bookwise International
Rod Davis, Managing Director
Robert Sarsfield, Publisher
Rosemary McDonald, Australian Project Editor

THANK YOU

Jeff Altemus
Ask Janis Editorial
Claudia Bauer
Bloomsbury Books
Casey Bourgeois
Shelley Brigman
Steve Brummett
Michael Brunsfeld
Jeff Cheek
Lisa Cooper
Faye Courtenay
Bill Crawford
Scott Dalgarno
John Darling
Carol Deane
John Dollison
Kathy Dratch
Susan Elkin
Bill Eriksen
Andrea Freewater
Debra Gates
Abby Granach
Janet Harris

Tim Harrower
Valerie Hendel
Sharilyn Hovind
Jay Ingram
Gordon Javna
John Javna
Jesse & Sophie,
B.R.I.T.
Mary Kaufman
Béla Keenan
Erin Keenan
Stephanie Keenan
Douglas Keeslar
Lonnie Kirk
Lenna Lebovich
Jennifer Lee
Erik Linden
Jim McCluskey
Jenny McCracken
Peter McCracken
Jack Mingo
Richard Moeschl
Arthur Montague
Jeanette Murray

Jay Newman
Jeff Painter
Barb Porshe
Sherry Powell
Paul Protter
Julie Roeming
Chris Rose-Merkle
Sam and Sarah
Mike Schuster
Melissa Schwarz
Lorien Sekora
Jill Sheridan
Douglas Sigler
Bennie Slomski
Dee Smith
Andy Sohn
Rich Stim
David Sugar
(Prof. Pear)
Uncle Edgester
Tessa Vanderkop
Dale Vidmar
David Wallechinsky

CONTENTS

*Extra-long articles suitable for an extended sitting session
are marked with an asterisk.*

INTRODUCTION

G'day! Uncle John's *Bathroom Reader* may be new to Australia, but it's a tradition in America—and one we're proud to share. We at the Bathroom Readers' Institute are flushed with pride to find ourselves writing for a second generation of bathroom readers! "I can't believe that this series is older than my kids," Uncle John says. "It's been 15 years and more than 2 million books since the very first *Bathroom Reader*."

This book marks a momentous occasion in the history of bathroom literature: the first time that Uncle John and the Bathroom Readers' Institute have crossed the Big er, Pond...to share our wit and wisdom with citizens of another nation. And what a nation! We are thrilled to share the *Bathroom Reader* with the folks who nickname flies "dunny budgies" and who actually have *toilet races*. (If you think we're joking—obviously you don't live in Winton, Queensland—look at the article on page 273.) We could hardly believe it ourselves. Uncle John got all misty-eyed at the thought. Any nation that combines its love of sport with such an astounding sense of humour deserves the very best in lavatory reading material, and we're proud to provide it.

We invite you to add to our repository of quality lavatory literature. If you have bits of weird trivia, strange-but-true history, or ideas to share with the Bathroom Readers' Institute, your gems have a chance to appear in future editions of the *Bathroom Reader*. Contact us at our website, *www.bathroomreader.com*. The website also has samples from other *Bathroom Reader* books, discussions of upcoming projects, polls, and contests. (For inquiries about this book in particular, email us at *unclejohn@advmkt.com*.)

Thanks so much for your support. We are always delighted—and astonished—by your enthusiasm for our work. That's what keeps us going through the long months of research and writing. We love knowing that someone out there is waiting for it.

Go with the flow!

—*Uncle John and the Bathroom Readers' Institute*

OUR LAST OUTLAW

Ned Kelly was the most famous Australian bushranger of them all.
Was he an innocent victim just trying to protect his family?
Or was he really just a crook? Whatever your point of view,
he's as good as you get to a national hero.

PICK OF THE LOT

Most countries seem to have at least one criminal folk hero. America has a pile of them—Jesse James, Billy the Kid, Baby Face Nelson. England has Robin Hood and more recently, the Great Train Robber Ronald Briggs. Even the ever-polite, staid Canadians have managed to come up with a couple—bank robbers Paddy Mitchell and Edwin Boyd, although Paddy's a bit of a stretch because, although Canadian, most of his exploits were in America.

In Australia, we have a doozy. We can afford to be selective as we have a lot of people to choose from. After all, our country was originally colonised by transported convicts and thieves — all top blokes I'm sure but none must have had the right mixture of charisma, youth, imagination, and daring, which is a must to become legendary. Then along came somebody with all the right credentials — Ned Kelly.

19TH CENTURY ROBIN HOOD

Ned came from a poor Irish immigrant family. His parents were transported from Tipperary to Tasmania as petty convicts. Ned was born in Victoria in 1854. He had seven siblings and life was tough for the Kelly family, especially after his father died and Ned became the head of the family.

Ned had gainful, legitimate employment as a lumberjack, fence builder and stockman, but in order to make ends meet he took 'other employment' i.e. cattle rustling and horse stealing. He was first convicted for horse stealing when he was 16 (Ned said he had only 'borrowed' the horse), but records show he was a late starter—his younger brother Dan was accused of horse stealing at the tender age of five! How he even managed to get on a horse at that age is anybody's guess, but it just goes to show those Kelly boys were certainly resourceful!

Ned was released from jail in 1874, but four years later he and his mother were accused of attacking a policeman and shooting him in the wrist. Ned swore it was because the officer had assaulted his sister, however, the officer said otherwise. Mrs Kelly was sent to jail for three years but Ned escaped and went bush with his brothers and several friends. From then on, Ned and the Kelly gang were on the run and wanted by the police. A reward of 100 pounds was offered for the capture of Ned.

Family was important to Ned Kelly and his belief that his mother had been wrongly convicted meant that he now wanted revenge. In 1878, he and his gang stumbled across police camped at Stringy Bark Creek and during a subsequent shootout, three of the four policemen were killed. The reward for Kelly and his gang rose to two thousand pounds and would subsequently rise to an amazing eight thousand pounds — the equivalent today of two million dollars!

Being on the run wasn't cheap, so the Kelly gang soon took up bank robbing. Their first effort netted them two thousand pounds! These robberies were important in the making of the Kelly legend. By defying authority, by robbing the rich and by not taking any more lives, the gang fitted the popular image of brave and bold bushrangers. At each robbery Ned Kelly gave one of his hostages a letter to be passed on to the government where he defended his innocence and explained how he'd been persecuted by police. He also composed an autobiography and a manifesto for a new independent state. The authorities were worried—not only was Ned a successful robber, he now seemed to have political aspirations! It was time to put him in his place.

KNIGHT IN ARMOUR

The showdown came in June 1880 when the gang was at the Glenrowan Hotel in country Victoria. They were surrounded by police, so the gang members donned armour suits and started to fight. During the shootout, Ned escaped through the police lines but returned several times to try and rescue his brother and friends. The other three gang members were killed but, remarkably, Ned Kelly survived—with 28 bullet wounds. He was a sentimental chap, our Ned. Beneath his armour he wore a green sash which he had been given years earlier for saving the life of a drowning boy.

Ned was taken into custody and when he recovered was convicted of murder. When sentenced, Ned's comment to the much-hated magistrate was, "I'll see you where I'm going." Despite protests by thousands of supporters, he was sentenced to death and on 11th November 1880, Ned Kelly was hung at Melbourne Goal aged 25 years old. The magistrate dropped dead in his chambers twelve days later!

Ned Kelly's final words before hanging were, "Such is life." Mother Kelly was still in prison when Ned was hung. Her last words to him were, "Mind you die like a Kelly, son." She lived on to be 92, dying in 1923.

Ned Kelly's legend lives on. For some he was no more than a criminal but for others he was seen as brave and daring, and a bit of a larrikin — someone distinctly Australian!

* * *

THE DEATH OF NED KELLY

Ned Kelly fought the rich men in country and in town,
Ned Kelly fought the troopers until they ran him down;
He thought that he had fooled them, for he was hard to find,
But he rode into Glenrowan with the troopers close behind.

"Come out of there, Ned Kelly," the head zarucker calls,
"Come out and leave your shelter, or we'll shoot it full of holes."
"If you take me," says Kelly, "that's not the speech to use:
I've lived to spite your order, I'll die the way I choose!"

"Come out of there, Ned Kelly, you've done a lawless thing:
You've robbed and fought the squatters, Ned Kelly you must swing."
"If those who rob," says Kelly, "are all condemned to die,
You had better hang the squatters; they've stolen more than I."

"You'd best come out, Ned Kelly, you've done the government wrong,
For you've held up the coaches that bring the gold along."
"Go tell your boss," says Kelly, "who lets the rich go free,
That your bloody rich men's government will never govern me."

"You talk all right, Ned Kelly, your tongue is slick, I own;
But I have men to help me and you are all alone."

More babies are born in the month of September than in any other month.

They burned the roof above him, they fired the walls about,
And head to foot in armour Ned Kelly stumbled out.

Although his guns were empty he took them by surprise;
He wore an iron breastplate and armour on his thighs.
Although his guns were empty he made them turn and flee,
But one came in behind him and shot him in the knee.

And so they took Ned Kelly and hanged him in the jail,
For he fought them single-handed although in iron mail.
And no man single-handed can hope to break the bars;
It's a thousand like Ned Kelly who'll hoist the Flag of Stars.

—**John Manifold:** *Selected Verse*, **London, 1948**

* * *

ZAPPA'S LAW & OTHER FACTS OF LIFE

You know Murphy's Law: "If someting can go wrong, it will." Here are some other immutable laws of the universe to consider.

Zappa's Law: "There are two things on Earth that are universal: hydrogen and stupidity."

Lowe's Law: "Success always occurs in private, and failure in full public view."

Todd's Law: "All things being equal, you lose."

Thompson's Theorem: "When the going gets weird, the weird turn pro."

Vac's Conundrum: "When you dial a wrong number, you never get a busy signal."

The Unspeakable Law: "As soon as you mention something...
• if it's good, it goes away.
• if it's bad, it happens."

The Queue Principle: "The longer you wait in line, the greater the likelihood that you are standing in the wrong line."

Issawi's Law of Progress: "A shortcut is the longest distance between two points."

FOREIGN FUNDS

As many countries change over to the Euro, Uncle John thought it was important to capture why different kinds of money are called what they are. Why is a franc called a franc, for example? We put together a list of various currencies and how they got their names.

DOLLAR. (American). Silver coins from the Joachimsthaler valley in Germany were common in Europe before America was founded. The name went from "Joachimsthalergroschen" to "thaler," which became "dollar" and was used to refer to any large silver coin. The colonists adopted the term. (See more about the dollar on page 62.)

LIRA. (Italy). From the Latin word libra, or "pound."

DRACHMA. (Greece) Means "handful."

RUPEE. (India) Comes from the Sanskrit rupa, which means "beauty" or "shape."

KORUNA. (Czechoslovakia) Means "crown."

GUILDER. (Netherlands) From the same root as "gilded," the guilder was originally a gold coin. It was first introduced from Florence in the 13th century.

ROUBLE. (Russia) Means "cut-off," a term that dates back to the days when portions of silver bars were literally "cut off" from the bars and used as coins. The rouble was first issued as a silver piece in 1704.

PESO. (Mexico) Means "weight." It was introduced by Spain in 1497, then adopted by Mexico and other Latin American countries in the late 19th century.

PESETA. (Spain) Means "little peso," and was created in the 18th century as a "companion" coin to the Spanish peso (no longer in circulation.)

FRANC. (France) First issued in 1360, as a gold coin. Gets its name from its original Latin inscription, Francorum Rex, which means "King of the Franks," the title given to kings of France in the 1300s.

RIYAL. (Saudi Arabia) Borrows its name from the Spanish real, meaning "royal."

ESCUDO. (Portugal) Means "shield," referring to the coat of arms on the original coin.

YEN. (Japan) Borrowed from the Chinese yuan, which means "round," and describes the coin. First issued in 1870.

Vitamin rule of thumb: The darker green a vegetable is, the more vitamin C it contains.

OOPS!

Everyone's amused by tales of outrageous blunders—probably because it's comforting to know that someone's screwing up even worse than we are. So go ahead and feel superior for a few minutes.

HAPPY BIRTHDAY!
"Matt Brooks of Cheshire, England, a furnaceman, thought he was 63 years old in 1981. When he applied for early retirement, he learned that he was really 79 and should have retired 14 years earlier."

—Encyclopedia Brown's Book of Facts

BLIND JUSTICE
"Judge Claudia Jordan caused panic in her court in Denver when she passed a note to her clerk that read: 'Blind on the right side. May be falling. Please call someone.' The clerk rang for help. Informed that paramedics were on the way, the judge pointed to the sagging Venetian blinds on the right side of the room. 'I wanted someone from maintenance,' she said."

—The Fortean Times

HIGH WIRE ACT
"During a parade through Ventura, California, a drum major twirled his baton and threw it high into the air.

"It hit a power cable and melted. It also blacked out ten blocks, put a radio station off the air and started a grass fire."

—The World's Greatest Mistakes

AMEN
"Warren Austin, U.S. ambassador to the United Nations in 1948, expressed the wish that Arabs and Jews would settle their differences 'like good Christians.'"

—Not A Good Word About Anybody

FLOUR POWER
"After great expense and preparation, British climber Alan Hinkes attempted to scale the 7925-metre [26,000-foot] high Nanga Parbot mountain in Pakistan. He got about halfway up and was

eating a Pakistani bread called chapati, which is topped with flour, when the wind blew the flour in his face, causing him to sneeze. It resulted in a pulled back muscle that made further climbing impossible."

—*News of the Weird*, Nov. 28, 1998

THAT'S B-U-R-T, RIGHT?
"Scrawling his way into immortality in the concrete in front of Mann's (formerly Grauman's) Chinese Theatre in Hollywood, Burt Reynolds misspelled his own name."

—*Hollywood Confidential*

LETTER BOMB
NORWALK, Conn.— "The Caldor department store chain apologized this week after 11 million copies of an advertising circular showed two smiling boys playing Scrabble around a board with the word 'rape' spelled out. Caldor said it does not know who did it or how it got past the proofreaders. 'Obviously, it's a mistake,' said Caldor spokeswoman Jennifer Belodeau."

—*The Progressive*, February 1999

FORGET ABOUT THAT RAISE
LONDON— "A trader cost his employers an estimated $16 million when he pressed the wrong key on his computer during training, launching the largest single trade in German futures."

"*The Daily Telegraph* did not name the trader of the firm, but described him as a junior trader working out of London for a German finance house."

"Apparently, while training on what he thought was software simulating financial transactions, he posted an offering of 130,000 German bond futures contracts, worth $19 billion. But he had pressed the wrong button, entering the system for actual dealing."

—*Medford Mail Tribune*, Nov. 20, 1998

AND EYES LIKE BONZO?
"During a high-level meeting with Arab leaders, Reagan off-handedly remarked to the Lebanese foreign minister, 'You know, your nose looks just like Danny Thomas's.'"

—*Hollywood Confidential*

LET ME WRITE SIGN— I GOOD SPEAK ENGLISH

When signs in a foreign country are in English, any combination of words is possible. Here are some real-life examples.

At a Tokyo bar: "Special cocktails for the ladies with nuts."

At a Budapest zoo: "Please do not feed the animals. If you have any suitable food, give it to the guard on duty."

At a Budapest hotel: "All rooms not denounced by twelve o'clock will be paid for twicely."

In a Hong Kong supermarket: "For your convenience, we recommend courteous, efficient self-service."

At a Norwegian cocktail lounge: "Ladies are requested not to have children in the bar."

In a tailor shop in Rhodes: "Order your summer suit. Because is big rush we will execute customers in strict order."

A laundry in Rome: "Ladies, leave your clothes here and spend the afternoon having a good time."

In a Czech tourist agency: "Take one of our horse-driven city tours—we guarantee no miscarriages."

On a Viennese restaurant menu: "Fried milk, children sandwiches, roast cattle and boiled sheep."

In a Swiss mountain inn: "Special today—no ice cream."

A doctor's office in Rome: "Specialist in women and other diseases."

In a Moscow hotel room: "If this is your first visit to the USSR, you are welcome to it."

At a Vienna hotel: "In case of fire, do your utmost to alarm the hotel porter."

At a Hong Kong dentist: "Teeth extracted by the latest Methodists."

At a Swedish furrier: "Fur coats made for ladies from their own skin."

Ketchup was once sold as a medicine.

"IT'S NOT A WORD...
IT'S A SENTENCE"

A page by people who know the true meaning of "wedded bliss."

Bigamy is having one husband too many. Monogamy is the same."

—Erica Jong

"Marriage is the triumph of imagination over intelligence. Second marriage is the triumph of hope over experience."

—Anonymous

"Marriage is really tough because you have to deal with feelings and lawyers."

—Richard Pryor

"Marriage is a three-ring circus: engagement ring, wedding ring, and suffer-ring."

—Anonymous

"A man in love is incomplete until he has married. Then he's finished."

—Zsa Zsa Gabor

"Love is blind, but marriage restores the sight."

—Georg Lichtenberg

"Politics doesn't make strange bedfellows—marriage does."

—Groucho Marx

"Before marriage, a man yearns for the woman he loves. After marriage, the 'Y' becomes silent."

—Anonymous

"The poor wish to be rich, the rich wish to be happy, the single wish to be married, and the married wish to be dead."

—Ann Landers

"Marriage teaches you loyalty, forbearance, self-restraint, meekness, and a great many other things you wouldn't need if you had stayed single."

—Jimmy Townsend

"Love is an ideal thing, marriage a real thing; a confusion of the real with the ideal never goes unpunished."

—Johann von Goethe

"It's a bit dangerous out there, and I guess men have to choose between marriage and death. I guess they figure that with marriage at least they get meals. But then they get married and find out we don't cook anymore."

—Rita Rudner

The navel divides the body of a newborn baby into two equal parts.

HAPPY LITTLE VEGEMITES

Ahh, Vegemite! It starts the day for millions of Aussies around the country. It goes with cheese. It is a dubious colour (what else is that colour?), kinda gooey and looks suspiciously like axle grease. The rest of the world can't stand it! And any Aussie traveller worth their salt will have a jar (or a tube) of it tucked into their backpack for a little slice of home wherever they roam.

Did you know that Vegemite:

- has been around since 1922
- was invented by a chemist called Cyril
- is made from brewer's yeast
- is one of the world's best-known sources of Vitamin B
- was named via a competition
- was called Parwill for a while
- isn't Australian owned (it is owned by Kraft USA)
- gained official endorsement from the British Medical Association
- went to war with Australian soldiers in 1939 and demand was so high that the folks back home had to miss out
- was the first product to be electronically scanned in an Australian supermarket

and…that Australians eat 22 millions jars a year!

WHERE DID IT COME FROM?

In 1918, World War I had rather selfishly been causing the delay of importing popular yeast extracts into Australia. A young entrepreneur by the name of Fred Walker saw this as an opening into the Aussie market and enlisted the help of a brilliant young chemist, Dr Cyril Callister, to play around with some yeast extract. After many hit-and-misses, Dr Cyril developed a spread. Well, Fred was so excited about young Dr Cyril's discovery, that he ran a national competition in order to find a name for his new baby. The winning entry was Vegemite! The winner went home with 50 pounds but, alas, his or her name was never recorded, nor

The only tree from which we eat the flower is the fig.

any explanation on how or why they chose that name.

Unfortunately Aussies weren't yet happy little Vegemites and no one was buying this wonderful new product. It was decided that perhaps a name change might improve sales and the name Parwill was adopted. Why Aussies would embrace that name over Vegemite one can only guess, but sanity was soon restored and the name Parwill was dropped.

Meanwhile, back in the lab, Dr Cyril also was working on a cheese that wouldn't go off too quickly. He found a patent that was registered by one James Kraft, a Canadian who lived in Chicago. In 1929, Fred went to American to talk to James Kraft and the Kraft Walker Cheese Company (later to become the juggernaut of all things cheesy) was born.

Prior to World War II, Vegemite was officially recognised by the British Medical Association as a Vitamin B-rich nutritionally balanced food, which allowed GPs to be able to recommend Vegemite to their patients (as in "Got the sniffles, hey? Well, just take one teaspoon of Vegemite three times a day and you'll be as right as rain by next week!") No wonder most Poms now hate the stuff!

In 1996, Vegemite came in a tube! No longer were we happy to see our beloved spread encased in its familiar glass jar with the big red and gold logo, we now wanted to take it around the world with us! So Vegemite is now available in a cute plastic tube for us to spread on our bagels, croissants, or foccacia for that little taste of home no matter how far flung we are!

VEGEMITE GOES AUSSIE

In 1996, eccentric entrepreneur and Aussie crusader Dick Smith decided to launch his own line of Australian-owned, Australian-made products. Vegemite was the first target and he was going to call it OzEmite. Unfortunately, others got whiff of this and Dick was unable to buy supplies of brewer's yeast. But keep watching! It's hard to hold our Dick down! He is now planning to take on the match market and bring out Aussie competition to Redhead matches. Naturally enough his matches are to be called Dickheads! Can't you see the advertising campaign; "You'll be a Dickhead not to buy them!"

If the average male never shaved, his beard would be 13 feet long on the day he died.

FLUBBED HEADLINES

These are 100% honest-to-goodness headlines.
Can you figure out what they were trying to say?

British Left Waffles on Falkland Islands

Shot Off Woman's Leg Helps Nicklaus to 66

Plane Too Close to Ground, Crash Probe Told

Juvenile Court To Try Shooting Defendant

Stolen Painting Found by Tree

BOMB HIT BY LIBRARY

After Detour to California Shuttle Returns to Earth

Boy Declared Dead, Revives as Family Protests

Dead Coyote Found in Bronx Launches Search for Its Mate

CHILDBIRTH IS BIG STEP TO PARENTHOOD

42 Percent of All Murdered Women Are Killed by the Same Man

National Hunting Group Targeting Women

Fire Officials Grilled Over Kerosene Heaters

POLICE CAN'T STOP GAMBLING

Ability to Swim May Save Children from Drowning

LOW WAGES SAID KEY TO POVERTY

Youth Hit by Car Riding Bicycle

Hostage-Taker Kills Self; Police Shoot Each Other

TESTICLE CARGO SEIZED

Check With Doctors Before Getting Sick

Police Kill Youth in Effort to Stop His Suicide Attempt

INTERN GETS TASTE OF GOVERNMENT

Convicted S&L Chief Donated to University

Study: Dead Patients Usually Not Saved

PARKING LOT FLOODS WHEN MAN BURSTS

U.S. Ships Head to Somalia

U.S. Advice: Keep Drinking Water from Sewage

SUICIDES ASKED TO RECONSIDER

Cold Wave Linked to Temperatures

Gators to Face Seminoles With Peters Out

New Autos to Hit 5 Million

Experts tell us that the human body has about 60,000 miles of blood vessels.

KELLOGG'S—IT'S AUSTRALIAN FOR BREAKFAST!

Cornflakes. Nutri-Grain. Rice bubbles. Fruit Loops. Coco-Pops. They're Australian institutions. Yet legend has it that the famous cereals were first invented to deter people from getting too, well, frisky in the mornings! Another bowl anyone?

A HEALTHY START TO THE DAY
Kellogg's cereals were invented by a stern-looking American gentleman by the name of William Keith (WK) Kellogg and his brother, Dr John Harvey Kellogg. They were sick of all the fatty, starchy breakfasts available at the time and wanted to make something nutritious instead. Then, in 1894, a freak laboratory accident occurred when the pair was trying to create a more easily digestible form of bread. Apparently the bread dough was left too long and dried out, so the pair decided to flake it to see what happened and voila! Cornflakes!

Unofficially, our beloved cornflakes were invented to stop people from having sex in the morning! Yes, apparently the Kellogg brothers were both staunch Seventh-Day Adventists and rampant anti-sex campaigners. They thought they could create a nutritious breakfast cereal to deter naughty couples from their early morning romp. They were wrong…

TASTY FACTS TO CHEW OVER
- 96% of Kellogg's cereals are made in Australia, by Australians, using all-Australian raw products
- Kellogg's is actually based in Battle Creek, Michigan, in the US. Ahem…
- Meanwhile, in the U.K., a study showed that people trusted Kellogg's more than they trusted their police force or even Parliament!
- Kellogg's cereals are available in 16 countries worldwide

- In 1979, Kellogg's became the first food company to print nutritional information on its products
- Kellogg's is the most successful breakfast cereal maker in the world
- Kellogg's have projected annual global sales of over $17 billion (US $9 billion)

COMMUNITY TIES

- WK Kellogg was the pioneer of the six-hour working day and, as a result, his workers got more involved with their children's schools, finished their housework on time, made more elaborate meals at home, met outside the factory more frequently for picnics and BBQ's, and played sport more often. Smart guy!
- Kellogg's supports Netball Australia, Surf Life Saving Australia, Kids' Help Line and collaborates with the Australian Institute of Sport
- The US Kellogg Foundation supports youth services and volunteer work in both the US and in South Africa
- And let's not forget the WK Kellogg Biological Station, the WK Kellogg Eye Centre, the WK Kellogg Collection of Rural Development Resource Services, and last, but not least, the WK Kellogg Arabian Horse Library!

STEPPING ON TOES

Not surprisingly, even multimillion dollar juggernauts have their detractors.

- In April 2000, Kellogg's took petrol mogul Exxon Mobil to court over Exxon's "Whimsical Tiger" cartoon being too much like Kellogg's Tony the Tiger. They're grrr-r-eat…!
- Later in 2000, one of Kellogg's companies, Morningstar Farms, had to recall all its veggie corn dogs because they were found with a genetically modified corn, Starlink, which is approved for livestock but not humans! The plant was forced to temporarily shut down.

CLASSIC (B)AD CAMPAIGNS

*Companies are always trying to come up with new ways to make
their products look attractive. These efforts are notable for
achieving the opposite result.*

CASHING IN YOUR CHIPS
Brilliant Marketing Idea: In 1998 the Bangkok subsidiary
of the American ad agency Leo Burnett came up with a
novel way to sell Thailand's "X" brand potato chips: show that
they're so much fun, even "the sourest man in history" can't help
turning into a fun guy.
Oops: The historical figure they used was Adolf Hitler. In the
commercial, Hitler eats some chips, then strips off his Nazi uniform and dances merrily as a Nazi swastika morphs into the
brand's "X" logo. The ad generated so many complaints—especially from the Israeli Embassy in Bangkok—that they had to pull it
and issue apologies. "The campaign was never intended to cause
ill feelings," an agency spokesperson told reporters.

MYSTERY OF THE EAST
Brilliant Marketing Idea: In England, Smirnoff Vodka's ad agency
created a campaign using the slogan "I thought the Kama Sutra
was an Indian restaurant...until I discovered Smirnoff."
Oops: They were forced to cancel it, a company spokesperson
admitted, "when we conducted a survey and discovered that 60%
of people did think it was an Indian restaurant."

HIGH FLYER
Brilliant Marketing Idea: In 1967 Pacific Airlines, a commuter
airline on the West Coast, hired award-winning adman/comedian
Stan Freberg to design an unorthodox new campaign. As Bruce
Nash and Allan Zullo write in The Misfortune 500, Freberg "suggested PAL poke fun at the one thing airlines never mention—
fear of flying."
Oops: Pacific Airlines, at Freberg's direction, placed full-paged ads
in newspapers that read:

> Hey there! You with the sweat in your palms. It's
> about time an airline faced up to something: Most
> people are scared witless of flying. Deep down inside,
> every time that big plane lifts off that runway, you
> wonder if this is it, right? You want to know some-
> thing, fella? So does the pilot deep down inside.

Freberg also arranged for flight attendants to hand out survival kits containing rabbits' feet and the book *The Power of Positive Thinking*, and instructed that when the plane touched down on the runway, flight attendants were supposed to exclaim, "We made it! How about that!" The airline went under two months after the campaign started.

AH-NOLD GO BOOM!

Brilliant Marketing Idea: In 1993, Arnold Schwarzenegger was America's #1 box-office attraction. Columbia Pictures decided to promote his latest movie, *The Last Action Hero*, with a 23-metre [75-foot] tall balloon of Schwarzenegger's character in New York's Times Square. Instead of holding a gun, like he does in the movie, Arnold had a fistful of dynamite in his hand. "We thought a gun was too violent an image," a Columbia spokesperson explained.

Oops: After months of planning, Columbia Pictures finally launched the balloon. Unfortunately, it was just days after the terrorist bombing of the World Trade Center. The studio tried replacing the dynamite with a police badge, but ended up just taking the balloon down. The Last Action Hero was one of the biggest flops of the decade.

LOVELY RING, MRS....UH...

Brilliant Marketing Idea: Executives in the jewellery department of Neiman-Marcus, an upscale department store, thought it would be good business to send a personal note of thanks to each of their biggest customers.

Oops: According to *The Business Disaster Book of Days*: "Most of the notes were addressed to the men, the people who had paid for the expensive baubles. But most of the envelopes were opened by women. Unfortunately for Neiman-Marcus, many of these women—wives of the purchasers, mostly—had not been the recipients of the costly purchases."

Best-selling posthumous hit of all-time: "(Just Like) Starting Over," by John Lennon.

"SHE'LL ALWAYS BE DAD TO ME!"

What would you do if your gender prevented you from pursuing the career of your choice? Many women faced this problem in the past. For a rare few the solution was, "If you can't beat 'em, join 'em." They literally lived their lives as men.

DR. JAMES BARRY, *British army surgeon and pioneer of sanitary reforms in medicine in the 19th century*
Background: Barry entered Edinburgh University's medical school in 1808 when he was just 15 (only men were admitted to medical school then). He rose to become one of the most skilled doctors in England. As Carl Posey writes in *Hoaxes and Deceptions*, the "tiny, beardless doctor" was no shrinking violet:

> Far from keeping a low profile, the medic courted attention, picked quarrels, fought a duel, flirted outrageously with the ladies, and once horsewhipped a colonel in public. Adored by patients, but despised by colleagues, Barry was finally forced into early retirement in 1859.

Surprise! Shortly after Barry died in 1865, at the age of 73, acquaintances discovered why, despite his having spent 57 years in the army, no one had ever seen him naked: he was a woman.

Note: Apparently, not everyone had been fooled. "Many people seem to have known her secret all along," Posey writes, "and simply—perhaps because of Barry's powerful patrons—declined to mention it."

CHARLIE PARKHURST, *one of the toughest stagecoach drivers of the Old West*
Background: Parkhurst worked for the California Stage Company at the height of the Gold Rush in the 1850s. He was 174 cm [5'7"] tall, had broad shoulders, gambled, and chewed tobacco. "Once," Carl Sifakis writes in *Hoaxes and Scams*, "this legendary master of the whip raced a team across an unstable bridge, reaching the other side just before it collapsed. Another time, stopped by high-

waymen, Charlie shot the leader and escaped with passengers and goods intact."

Parkhurst, who claimed to be an orphan, never grew any facial hair, something that friends attributed to a "fetish" for shaving every day. Unlike his rowdy friends, he also avoided prostitutes, and preferred to sleep apart from other men. Other than that, for all appearances he was one of the guys.

Surprise! In the late 1860s, an illness forced Parkhurst into retirement, and on December 31, 1879, he died alone in his cabin near Watsonville, California. A doctor called in to investigate the death found not only that he had died of cancer, but also that he was a woman who had given birth at some point in her life. Who was this mystery woman? Nobody knows—that was one secret she did manage to take to the grave.

BILLY TIPTON, *jazz musician and leader of the Tipton Trio*
Background: Tipton was a popular jazz musician in Washington from the 1930s to the late 1980s. He married three times and his last marriage, to Kitty Oakes, lasted 19 years. He had three children, all adopted, a fact he attributed to an "injury" that he claimed made "normal" sexual relations impossible. Early in his jazz career his baby face and high-pitched voice caused some listeners to joke that he was too feminine to be a man. But that was about as close as anyone came to suspecting the truth.

Surprise! After years of refusing to see a doctor despite his failing health, Tipton died in 1989 of a bleeding ulcer at his mobile home in Spokane, Washington. He was 74. The paramedics who responded to the call quickly discovered that Tipton was a female, something that apparently only Kitty Oakes had known.

It turns out that at the age of 18, Tipton had borrowed her brother's name and began dressing as a man so she could work as a jazz musician. In those days, most women in jazz were "girl singers," whose careers were short and of limited range.

Tipton's children were shocked. "I'm just lost," her son Jon Clark told reporters after learning his father was a woman. "The guy at the funeral home showed me a little yellow piece of paper where it was marked 'female' under sex. I said, 'What?' and he said it was true. Even so, she'll always be Dad to me."

VEGETABLE TRIVIA

*Did you eat your vegetables today? BRI member Jeff Cheek, a
former CIA man (no kidding) loves to write about food.
He sent us this potpourri of vegetable facts.*

MAIZE. The most versatile of all food plants, it can be
eaten at every stage of development. You can find it in
more than 3,000 grocery items. In fact, according to *The
Great Food Almanac*, "the average American eats the equivalent of
three pounds of maize each day in the form of meat, poultry, and
dairy products."

GARLIC. One of the first foods ever cultivated. First written reference: 5,000 years ago, in Sanskrit. At banquets, ancient Greeks
served each guest a bowl of parsley, believing it would mask "garlic
breath." A vestige of this custom survives. Many restaurants still
drop a sprig of parsley on every plate.

LETTUCE. The name comes from the Latin lactuca (milk)
because of the white liquid that oozes from broken stalks. The
Romans prized it so highly that any slave caught eating lettuce
was given 30 lashes.

EGGPLANT. Originated in China, where it was grown as a decoration. The Chinese called eggplants "mad apples," believing they
caused insanity. It was accepted as a food only after it was brought
to the Mediterranean.

LEEKS. These members of the onion family originated in Egypt,
then spread to Rome. (Emperor Nero drank a quart of leek soup
every day, thinking it improved his singing voice.) The Romans
introduced the leek to Wales and it became the Welsh national
symbol in 640, when Saxons invaded from England. With no uniforms, it was hard to tell friend from foe in the battle, so each
Welsh soldier pinned a leek on his cap to identify himself. They
won, and every March 1, St. David's Day, the Welsh pin a leek to
their hats or lapels to commemorate the victory.

RADISHES. Since they're ready to harvest after only 42 days, the
Greeks named them Raphanos, meaning "easy to grow." The
Romans changed this to Radix, meaning "root."

IT WASN'T 2000 FOR EVERYONE

*Would the new millennium mean the end of the world?…
the beginning of the New Age?…We all had an opinion, but for
much of the world the question was irrelevant—because,
according to their calendars, it wasn't a new millennium…*

…It was 5760
Who Says? The Hebrew (Jewish) calendar. Their year 2000 occurred in 1760 B.C.
Origin: It's a lunar calendar that dates to 3760 B.C—according to Jewish tradition, the date the world began.

…It was 4698
Who Says? The Chinese calendar. Their year 2000 occurred in 698 B.C.
Origin: A lunar calendar dating from 2600 B.C., when the Emperor Huang Ti introduced the first cycle of the zodiac. It begins at the second new moon after the winter solstice.

…It was 1921
Who Says? The Reformed Indian Calendar. Their year 2000 will arrive in 2079 A.D.
Origin: India gained independence from England in 1947. In 1957, it officially adopted this calendar, based on the beginning of the Saka Era (a Hindu time cycle).

…It was 1421
Who Says? The Muslim Calendar. Their 2000 will arrive in 2579 A.D.
Origin: A lunar calendar that dates back to 622 A.D., the year Muhammad and his followers migrated from Mecca to Medina to escape persecution.

…It was 1378
Who Says? The Persian calendar. Their year 2000 arrives in 2622 A.D.
Origin: This solar calendar was created by the poet and mathematician Omar Khayyám. Iranians and many Central Asians celebrate their new year every spring equinox.

…It was 2543
Who Says? The Theraveda Buddhist calendar. Their year 2000 occurred in 1457 A.D.
Origin: Dates from 544 B.C., the commonly accepted date of Buddha's death (he was 80). Theraveda Buddhists celebrate the new year in mid-April.

About 8,000 Americans are injured by musical instruments each year.

FROM FLEMING TOWN TO FLEMINGTON

*From humble beginnings to international event,
myths and magic surround the fabled Melbourne Cup—
the race that stops a nation.*

NATIONAL FOCUS
The Melbourne Cup has been labelled, "the race that stops a nation." And that's no exaggeration. Even Aussies who are hazy about when and why we celebrate Australia Day, for example, can tell you without hesitation that the Melbourne Cup is run on the first Tuesday in November.

Why this horserace has become such a national event is a mystery. Some say it only became so during the depression of the 1930's. In those bleak years when unemployment was rife and poverty widespread, Australians turned to horseracing for diversion and an occasional win with the illegal SP bookmakers who flourished in those pre-TAB (online betting for sporting events) times.

RACE ORIGINS
The first race meeting in Melbourne was in 1838 at Badman's Hill, now the site of busy Spencer Street Railway Station. In 1840 the races moved to Fleming Town, some 6 kms away, on land owned by sheep and cattle farmer, Robert Fleming. Despite dire predictions that the new site was too far from the city centre and was destined for failure, Flemington Racecourse flourished as a venue. The first Melbourne Cup was run there in 1861.

The Cup began inauspiciously. Australians were mourning the recent deaths of explorers Burke and Wills—the first European explorers to cross Australia from coast to coast—whose expedition had ended in tragedy. There were only 4,000 racegoers at Flemington that day to watch the running of the first Melbourne Cup.

STARS OF TRACK AND SCREEN

The race began badly when a horse called Twilight started early and ran the entire course before being captured. And there was more drama when two horses fell during the running of the race. That first Melbourne Cup was won by Archer.

One of the most commonly held myths about the Melbourne Cup is that Archer had walked from Nowra, NSW, to Melbourne to compete in the Cup, a distance of 850kms (560 miles). Perhaps the horse really did accomplish this feat, perhaps not. The truth of the story has been challenged more than once. The following year, Archer won the Cup for the second time. The rumour persisted that the horse had again walked from Nowra to Melbourne, but this time the claim was met with widespread scepticism.

In 1863, Archer's owners and trainer were dismayed when the nomination for his third attempt at the Melbourne Cup arrived late and the champion was refused entry to the race. There was disappointment, even indignation in racing circles. Owners and trainers demonstrated solidarity with Archer's owners by withdrawing their horses. That year, only seven runners lined up for the big race. It remains the smallest field ever to have run in a Melbourne Cup. Archer's story lives on in a movie called *Archer's Adventure*. Hollywood also immortalized another Melbourne Cup winner, the legendary Phar Lap.

In 1930, Phar Lap won the Cup watched by a crowd of 72,358 spectators. A lot of battling punters cheered Phar Lap home. He was the closest thing there was to a "safe bet," having won 37 of his 51 races. "The Red Terror," as Phar Lap was popularly known, is the only horse ever to have been favourite for the Melbourne Cup three years in a row.

Phar Lap's last big win was the Agua Caliente Cup in Mexico. Soon after, he was taken to the United States where he became sick and died. When news of Phar Lap's death reached Australia, he was mourned by fans across the nation.

Phar Lap was brought home to Australia and his noble hide, a miracle of the taxidermist's art, has been the most popular exhibit at the Victoria Museum since 1933.

In medieval Japan, dentists extracted teeth with their hands.

The Melbourne Cup has always attracted horses from across the Tasman. New Zealand champions have long been major placegetters in the big race. Australia is Phar Lap's home only by adoption. "The Red Terror" was born and bred in New Zealand.

These days it's not only New Zealanders who challenge the supremacy of Australian bloodstock. The speed and ease of air travel enable horses to be transported here from all parts of the world to take part in our favourite horserace.

THE RACE THAT STOPS A NATION

At Flemington, on the first Tuesday in November this year, the magic of the Melbourne Cup will happen all over again. The punters will comprise an egalitarian mix. T-shirts and stubbies will walk side by side with top hats and tails and the car parks will bristle with boot parties.

Beyond the course, Aussies from Bondi to Broome will down tools and follow the race on television sets and radios in every conceivable setting from clubs and pubs to shopping malls and even classrooms.

Aussie kids are recruited early into the mysteries of the racetrack. Most schools allow students to watch telecasts of the running of the cup and the Victoria Racing Club invites membership in their Phar Lap Kids' Club. This is open to kids under 15 and offers a variety of race-based interests and activities. All they need to join is a parent's permission. With such incentives, the future of the big race seems assured.

*See "My Body Lies Over the Ocean" on page 150
to find out what happened to Phar Lap's heart.*

* * *

SMILE WHEN YOU SAY THAT

"One of Oscar Hammerstein's rarer finds was 'Sober Sue,' whom he introduced to audiences at New York's Victoria theatre in 1908. During intermissions, Sue would appear on stage and Hammerstein would offer $1,000 to anyone who could make her laugh. There were lots of takers, but no one succeeded. What they didn't know: she couldn't laugh—her facial muscles were paralyzed."

(Felton & Fowler's Best, Worst, and Most Unusual)

THE ORIGIN OF BASKETBALL, PART I

Unlike baseball and football, which trace their roots to games that have been played for centuries, basketball was invented by one man—a Canadian named James Naismith—in a couple of days in 1891. It is the only major sport considered native to the USA. Here's its history.

SOMETHING NEW

Today the YMCA is synonymous with sports, but that hasn't always been the case. In the mid-1880s, it was primarily a missionary group. "In fact," Ted Vincent writes in *The Rise and Fall of American Sport*, "the Young Men's Christian Association condemned almost all sports, along with dancing, card playing, and vaudeville shows, on the grounds that these activities were 'distinctly worldly in their associations, and unspiritual in their influence,' and therefore 'utterly inconsistent with our professions as disciples of Christ."

GOOD SPORT

Then, at the YMCA's national convention in 1889, 24-year-old Dr. Luther Gulick started a revolution when he suggested that "good bodies and good morals" might actually go together. He insisted that keeping physically fit could make someone a better person, rather than inevitably leading them down the path of sin—and he proposed that the YMCA use organized athletics to reach out to youngsters who might otherwise not be interested in the Y's traditional emphasis on religion.

His proposal met with heavy opposition from conservatives, who argued that a "Christian gymnasium teacher" was a contradiction in terms. But when Gulick's idea was put to a vote, he won. Gulick was put in charge of a brand-new athletics teaching program at the YMCA School for Christian Workers in Springfield, Massachusetts.

CHANGING TIMES

Gulick's ideas were actually part of a larger social movement. For decades, America had been making the transition from a largely rural, farm-based society to an industrialized economy, in which much of the population lived and worked in cities. Americans who had once laboured in fields from sunup to sundown were now spending much of their working lives cooped up inside a factory, or behind a desk or sales counter.

Middle-class Americans in particular reacted to the growing bureaucracy and confinement of their work lives, and to the remarkable crowding of their cities, by rushing to the outdoors, on foot and on bicycles," Elliot Gorn writes in *A Brief History of American Sports*. "Hiking, bird-watching, camping, rock-climbing, or simply walking in the new national parks—participation in all of these activities soared in the years around the turn of the century.

MASS APPEAL

Middle-class Americans who embraced physical activity as the answer to their own yearnings also began to see it as an answer to some of society's ills. The repeal of child labour laws and high levels of immigration meant that the tenement districts in America's major cities were full of immigrant youths who had little or nothing to do. Leaders of the "recreation movement," like Dr. Gulick, felt that building public playgrounds and bringing organized play programs into the slums would help the kids stay out of trouble and make it easier for them to assimilate into American life.

Reformers thought of themselves as being on an exciting new mission, Americanizing children by helping them to have fun," Gorn says. "Playground reformers sought to clean up American streets, confine play to designated recreational spaces, and use their professional expertise to teach 'respectable' athletics." In an era in which public playgrounds were virtually unheard of, the facilities and athletic programs that organizations like the YMCA were beginning to offer often provided the only positive outlet for urban kids' energies.

BACK TO SCHOOL

As Gulick set up his program to train YMCA physical education instructors, he also decided to require men training to be "general secretaries" (the official title for men who ran local YMCA chapters) to take phys ed classes.

These students were older and more conservative than other students. They hadn't been sold on Gulick's newfangled sports ideas and, left to their own devices, would avoid physical education classes entirely. Gulick feared that if he didn't bring these future YMCA leaders around to his point of view while they were in Springfield, they wouldn't implement his programs when they got back home—and his efforts would be fruitless.

COLD SHOULDER

Working with the general secretaries was a snap at first: in the early fall they just went outside and played football or soccer. But when the weather turned cold and they were forced indoors, things got difficult. The best recreation Gulick could come up with was a schedule of military drills—followed by German, French, and Swedish gymnastics. Day after day, the routine was the same, and the students became thoroughly bored.

THE INCORRIGIBLES

Within weeks, the class was in open rebellion, and two successive physical education instructors resigned rather than put up with their abuse. They told Gulick that he might as well give up on "The Incorrigibles," as the class had become known.

Gulick wasn't ready to quit yet. For weeks, an instructor named James Naismith had been arguing that The Incorrigibles weren't to blame for the situation. "The trouble is not with the men," he said, "but with the system we are using. The kind of work for this class should be of a recreative nature, something that would appeal to their play instincts." At one faculty meeting, he even proposed inventing a new indoor game. So when Gulick put Naismith in charge of the class, he commented pointedly: "Now would be a good time for you to work on that new game that you said could be invented."

For Part II, turn to page 107.

Queen termites can lay an egg every second, or 86,000 eggs a day.

IT'S A WEIRD, WEIRD WORLD

Proof that truth really is stranger than fiction.

A STRANGE BE-LEAF
"A Swiss woman has left over a half-million dollars to a houseplant. The millionairess, from Geneva, once described her newly rich jade plant as her 'best and only friend.' She is believed to have conversed with the plant for the last five years."

—The Edge, April 19, 1999

LOOK AT THOSE MELONS!
"Britain's biggest supermarket chain has asked growers to supply smaller melons after research showed women shoppers subconsciously compared them to the size of their breasts.

"The Daily Telegraph said buyers working for Tesco were told by researchers that a current preference for smaller busts was the reason why traditional big, fleshy melons were remaining unsold.

"'We were surprised,' said a Tesco spokesman. 'But it's certainly produced results. Since we introduced smaller melons two months ago we have sold more than a million.'"

—Reuters, May 3, 1999

A SILLY SUPERSTITION?
"Gerald Steindam, 24, of Miami, Florida, vowed never to fly Eastern Airlines' flight 401 (New York–Miami) after luckily missing a flight 401 in 1972 that went down in the Everglades.

"In 1980 he overcame his superstitious fear and took the flight. The plane was hijacked to Cuba."

—Encyclopedia Brown's Book of Strange Facts

A REAL CONDOM-NATION
"Police in Sri Lanka recently arrested a man after finding a condom in his wallet. 'Why would anyone want to carry a condom in his wallet, unless of course he was up to some mischief,' a police officer was quoted as saying. The man was released after questioning."

—San Francisco Chronicle, 1993

Proper English: Technically speaking, a female "dude" is known as a "dudine."

Q & A:
ASK THE EXPERTS

*Everyone's got a question or two they'd like answered—basic stuff,
like "Why is the sky blue?" Here are a few of those questions,
with answers from books by some top trivia experts.*

KNUCKLE UNDER
Q: *Why do our knuckles crack?*
A: "The bones in our fingers are separated by small pads of
cartilage, and in between are small pockets of a thick liquid.
When you bend your fingers, the bones pull away from the pads of
cartilage and a vacuum forms. As the bending continues…the
vacuum bubble bursts, making the cracking sound you hear. The
process is very similar to what happens when you pull a rubber
suction cup off a smooth surface." (From *Ever Wonder Why?*, by
Douglas B. Smith)

SEEING THINGS
Q: *What are those little squiggles you see floating on your eyes when
you look at the sky?*
A: "They're called 'floaters.' To some people they look like spots;
to others, like tiny threads. They're not on your eyes, though;
they're in your eyes. That's why blinking doesn't make them go
away. Floaters are all that's left of the hyaloid artery. The hyaloid
artery carried blood to your eye and helped it grow…when you
were still inside your mother's womb."
"When your eyes were finished growing, the hyaloid artery withered and broke into pieces. But since these pieces were sealed up
inside your eye, they had no place to go. You'll see them floating
around the rest of your life." (From *Know It All!*, by Ed Zotti)

STOP, POP AND ROLL
Q: *How does quicksand work?*
A: "Not by pulling you down. Quicksand is nearly always found
above a spring, which creates a supersaturated condition that
makes the sand frictionless and unable to support weight. In
addition, quicksand is airless, which creates suction as you strug-

---

If you visit, bring sunblock: Neptune's summer is 40 years long.

gle to get free. The most effective way to escape quicksand is to position yourself on top of it and 'roll' out." (From *The Book of Answers*, by Barbara Berliner)

LONG-DISTANCE RUNAROUND

Q: Why does the alphabet on a phone start on the #2 button rather than on the #1?
A: Back when dial phones were used, a pulse or clicking sound was made whenever you dialled. The pulses corresponded to the number dialled, so "when you dialled the number 1, it sent out one click...2, sent two clicks, and so on. Sometimes a random clicking caused equipment to think someone was dialling a number beginning with 1, when they actually weren't. Thus a rule was made: No phone number can start with 1. This rule is still observed, though solely for the sake of tradition." (From *Why Things Are, Volume II: The Big Picture*, by Joel Achenbach)

I CAN SEE CLEARLY NOW

Q: How does an X-ray photograph your bones but not your flesh?
A: "An X-ray camera fires electrons at a plate covered with silver halide crystals, which are sensitive to light. Your leg is put in the way of the penetrating stream of particles. When an electron reaches the plate unimpeded, it turns a halide crystal black. The crystals that receive no electrons fall away when the plate is developed and leave that area white under the light. X-ray particles are so highly energized that most of them pass right through flesh. Bones, on the other hand, are very densely packed and contain large amounts of calcium. They stop the X-rays by absorbing them—the crack in your tibia shows up black on the plate because that's where bone isn't." (From *How Do They Do That?*, by Caroline Sutton)

* * *

SLIPPERY WHEN WET

Ice isn't slippery. What makes people and things slip on ice is water. A thin layer of ice melts when pressure is applied to it and it is this wet layer on top of the ice that is slippery.

Sloths even sneeze slowly. And they give birth upside down. Slowly.

WEIRD THEME RESTAURANTS

For a while, it looked as though restaurants modelled after the Hard Rock Cafe were going to sweep the world. Guess which of the following is Uncle John's personal favourite.

THE ROADKILL CAFE, Greenville, Maine
Theme: Animals squashed on the highway
Details: The menu features only "critters that don't move fast enough" to get out of traffic. Sample items: "The Chicken That Didn't Make It Across the Road," and "Bye Bye Bambi Burgers." It's actually just a little black humour, but the staff gets into the act: "A cook named Freddy is fond of yelling 'down boy, down boy' as he pounds on chicken breasts before grilling them. When he's done, he might throw handfuls of feathers out the door."

THE OUTHOUSE, Winnipeg, Manitoba
Theme: Bathrooms
Details: The entire restaurant was decorated to look like a public restroom— "toilet bowls alternate with tables in the main dining room. And their logo, a toilet seat, was on all the menus." Shortly after the Grand Opening in the mid-1970s, health officials shut it down. The reason: "Not enough working bathrooms."

ALCATRAZ BC, Tokyo
Theme: Maximum-security prison
Details: "Diners are handcuffed, eat in cells, and must beg permission from the guards to be allowed out to visit the restroom."

CRASH CAFE, Baltimore
Theme: Disasters and human carnage (just what we like to contemplate over dinner)
Details: The smoking fuselage of what appears to be a crashed DC3 juts from the exterior of the flagship restaurant. "The roof is askew, windows are cracked and the outer wall is shattered in spots. In the drive, a car looks as if it has just smashed into a fire hydrant, which is spewing water." Inside, diners are "entertained"

---

by film clips of train wrecks and collapsing bridges and buildings. "Some may say that it teeters on the verge of unacceptable," says founder Patrick Turner, "but that is precisely its strength. Crash Cafe seduces us to look closer, to indulge our undeniable fascination with the destructive, erotic nature of crashing."

DIVE!, Los Angeles and Las Vegas
Theme: Submarines
Details: "A submarine-shaped restaurant that specialized in gourmet submarine sandwiches." Partners included Hollywood moguls Steven Spielberg and Jeffrey Katzenberg. It had "millions of dollars in special effects," including "computer-controlled flashing light, steam blasts, deep-sea scenes on video screens, and a surging water wall to recreate the experience of 'an actual submarine dive.'" Singer Thomas Dolby provided interactive sound effects that were just a little too real: "Apparently, the virtual aquatic experience was so convincing that it prompted an upsurge in customers visiting the toilet. The L.A. restaurant closed in 1999.

HOUSE OF MAO, Singapore
Theme: Chairman Mao Tse-tung—who ruled China from 1950 until his death in 1976—as a pop icon
Details: "Scores of Mao pictures, poems and sculptures peer down from the walls. The staff wear uniforms similar to those of China's People's Liberation Army (though waitresses are miniskirted)." "Chairman Mao was one of the most feared individuals in the world," the founder says, "but when you come to the restaurant, you see the human side of him, swimming, playing poker." On the menu: Mao burgers, Mao pizza, Mao fajitas, and Mao pasta. "Mao would probably turn in his grave," one Singapore journalist wrote following the restaurant's grand opening.

*   *   *   *

Truth or Urban Legend?
On an American one-dollar bill, there's supposedly an owl in the upper left-hand corner of the "1" encased in the "shield" and a spider hidden in the front upper right-hand corner.

STRANGE LAWSUITS

*These days, it seems that people will sue each other over
practically anything. Here are a few real-life examples
of unusual legal battles.*

THE PLAINTIFF: A Chinese restaurant in Stansted,
England
THE DEFENDANT: Kevin Clifford, a customer
THE LAWSUIT: In 1996 Clifford walked into the restaurant
and ordered a large meal. While he was waiting for it, he
explained later, the smells from the kitchen made him so hungry
that he lost control. He began ripping the leaves off potted plants,
eating them. "By the time his order was ready," according to one
report, "he had eaten the leaves off every plant in the place." The
restaurant owner sued him for the cost of the plants.
THE VERDICT: Guilty. Clifford's unusual salad cost him $700.

THE PLAINTIFF: Donald Drusky
THE DEFENDANT: "God, the sovereign ruler of the universe"
THE LAWSUIT: In 1999 the 63-year-old Drusky filed suit
against God for "taking no corrective action" against an ex-
employer who'd fired him 30 years before. His demands: God must
grant him guitar-playing skills and resurrect either his pet pigeon
or his mother.
THE VERDICT: Drusky claimed that since God didn't show up
in court, he won by default. The judge declared the suit "frivolous."

THE PLAINTIFF: Nellie Mitchell, a 98-year-old Arkansas
woman
THE DEFENDANT: Globe International, publishers of the
supermarket tabloid *The Sun*
THE LAWSUIT: In 1990 *The Sun* ran a "report" about a 101-
year-old newspaper carrier in Australia "who'd quit her route
because she'd become pregnant by a millionaire customer." They
picked a photo of Mitchell to illustrate it. Why? They assumed she
was dead. She wasn't, and sued for invasion of privacy.

THE VERDICT: The jury awarded her $1.5 million (later reduced to $850,000). A judge compared her experience to being "dragged slowly through a pile of untreated sewage."

THE PLAINTIFF: Dave Feuerstein
THE DEFENDANT: Tesco supermarkets, an English chain
THE LAWSUIT: Enthusiastic about Tesco's low prices during a special promotion, Feuerstein kept going back to buy more. In three days, he redeemed over 300 coupons—then claimed he'd hurt his back carrying all the cheap merchandise, and sued. "Offers like this are too good to refuse," he told a reporter. "Tesco should have been more considerate and made it impossible to do what I did. If Tesco hadn't had this offer, I wouldn't have hurt my back."
THE VERDICT: Unknown.

THE PLAINTIFF: Kenneth Bruckner of Gering, Nebraska
THE DEFENDANT: Presbyterian/St. Luke's Medical Center in Denver
THE LAWSUIT: In the spring of 1993, Bruckner sued the hospital, claiming the "highly toxic" cleanser they used to disinfect toilet seats had caused him "permanent burns, neurological injuries, and urologic and sexual dysfunction." Said Bruckner's attorney: "What's the world coming to if it's not safe to sit on the toilet and read the paper?"
THE VERDICT: Unknown—but you know how we'd rule.

THE PLAINTIFFS: Two college students
THE DEFENDANT: Pace University, Long Island, New York
THE LAWSUIT: The students took an introductory computer-programming course at Pace. One day the teacher required them, as homework, to calculate the cost of an aluminum atom. The answer is $6.22054463335 \times 10^{-26}$—less than a trillionth of a penny. Outraged that such a high level of work was required in an introductory course, the pair sued.
THE VERDICT: Believe it or not, the judge found their instructor guilty of "educational malpractice."

NO GOOD DEED GOES UNPUNISHED

Some Good Samaritans get thanks and recognition.
Others get their cars stolen.
Life isn't fair.

LATE FEE

"In 1994, New York City's Metropolitan Transit Authority docked Michael Durant, a 31-year-old bus driver, a day's pay for being twelve minutes late for work. His excuse: He had stopped to pull a man out of a burning car on the highway.

—*Esquire,* **January 1995**

THANKS, YOU ##*!#@!

"New York Jets quarterback Boomer Esiason...was driving home after a 28–24 loss to the Miami Dolphins when he had to stop his car because of an accident....He got out and asked a woman in the car in front of him whether she was all right. Her window was broken and she was crying. Esiason recalls: 'She looked at me and said, 'Boomer?' I said, 'Yes.' She said, 'You guys really (stink). How'd you lose that game today?'"

—*San Francisco Chronicle,* **December 7, 1995**

ALL WET

"In 1981 Peter Stankiewicz of Rockville, Maryland stopped his car and dove into the Potomac River to rescue a driver whose lumber truck had crashed through a bridge railing and plunged 21 metres [60 feet] into the icy water. After hauling the driver to shore, Stankiewicz was informed that his car had been towed to the pound because it was blocking traffic."

—*Encyclopedia Brown's Book of Strange Facts*

THAT'S WHAT YOU GET

"When Lorne Murdock saw a delivery truck collide with a car in L.A., he pulled over his own car and rushed out to calm the bleeding motorist until help arrived. For his trouble, somebody stole

---

Less is more: 95% of the creatures on Earth are smaller than a chicken egg.

Murdock's 1980 AMC Spirit."

"'It's incredible, you try and save someone's life, do the right thing, help somebody out, and this happens,' said the 29-year-old Murdock."

"'That's what you get for being a Good Samaritan,' said officer Kirk Hunter."

—*Santa Rosa Press-Democrat*, May 2, 1993

METER-FEEDING GRANNY

"Sylvia Slayton was just trying to spare a stranger a ticket in Cincinnati, when she plunked a dime and a nickel into two expired parking meters. Instead she got handcuffed and arrested, and Thursday was convicted of a misdemeanor for interfering with an officer trying to ticket overdue cars.

"'I tried to do what I thought was the right thing,' the 63-year-old grandmother of 10 said. She faces as many as 90 days in jail and a $750 fine when she is sentenced later this month."

—*Burlington, Vermont Free Press*, February 7, 1997

REWARD FOR VALOR

"In 1982 Timothy George, a part-time busboy at a family restaurant in Vallejo, California, chased and captured a mugger who had robbed a customer in the men's room. Timothy was promptly fired for 'leaving work' and 'fighting'."

—*Encyclopedia Brown's Book of Strange Facts*

GULL OF MY DREAMS

"In June 1994, Don Weston found a young seagull squawking on the ground in his driveway in Gloucester, England, and put the bird on top of his garage to keep it safe from cats. A few hours later it flew off. Mr. Weston thought he'd done a good deed, but every June and July for the last three years he has been pursued by a vengeful seagull—the very one, he believes, whose life he saved."

"'Its evil squawking is so distinctive,' he said. 'It sounds like a banshee wailing. I've had nightmares about it.' The bird pecks his head, bombs him with droppings...and stalks him through the city by air. 'At the sight of me, it goes crazy,' said Weston."

—*The Fortean Times*

The first open-heart surgery was performed in 1893.

THE YOWIE

Yanks have Bigfoot, Scots have Nessie, and we've got our own special entry in the field of "cryptozoology"— the science of creatures that are too quick to be caught and examined!

WHAT IS A YOWIE?

A Yowie is a large hairy ape that stands eight feet tall and is covered in brown hair. It has a broad face, massive jaw and large eyes that glow red or yellow at night. They have broad shoulders, no neck and strong muscular legs and broad feet with between three and five toes on each foot. They walk upright but a little bent over with arms hanging low. Reports put them at around 300 kilograms! (Does all this sound familiar? I know a couple of footy players that would match this description!)

IS THE YOWIE A HOAX?

How can it be? Sightings have been going on for many thousands of years and in fact, are going on right now! When white man first settled in this country in the late 1700's, aborigines told them in great detail about an ape-man beast that lived in the bush. At first the settler's thought this was just a tale to scare them away but it wasn't long before they witnessed for themselves the legendary creature. In 1790, the first official reported sighting of a Yowie by a white man was released in the local papers in a small country town we now call Sydney. During the 1800's numerous reports followed, with sightings throughout NSW and the rest of the country. Remember, this was before every home had televisions and phones, yet all the reports described the same beast.

The name "Yowie" comes from the aboriginal name "Yowri" which was used to describe the beast. They tend to live in remote mountainous regions although every state in Australia has had sightings.

WHAT DO THEY EAT?

Yowies aren't fussy eaters. They will eat whatever is available. (Sounds like those football players again!) They have been known to steal chickens and other domestic and farm animals. (Lock up your cat if you live near the bush!) They have been seen eating fruit and raiding vegetable gardens. They have even been seen going through people's garbage bins and rubbish tips. They are tidy animals—they help clean up Australia by eating road kill.

WHAT ARE THEIR HABITS?

It is believed that Yowies are solitary creatures because they are normally sighted alone. They are creatures of habit and often stay in the same area for years but can wander vast distances searching for food. They tend to live in remote mountainous regions but they have been seen living in all types of different environments. They are nocturnal creatures spending the daytime sleeping somewhere secure and roaming the bush at night. A lone person walking through the bush at night is looking for trouble!

WHY ARE NO BODIES FOUND?

The Yowie, like other large primates, goes to the most remote locations in the bush to die in peace. After they die, predators pick away at their flesh, leaving only a pile of bones. How many times have you stumbled across a pile of bones and couldn't recognise what animal they have come from? Have a closer look next time. It is not surprising that no bodies are ever found— how many dead koalas have you seen in the bush? None!

WHY HAVE NO PHOTOS OF YOWIES BEEN TAKEN?

The Yowie is a shy, nocturnal creature that roams remote areas of the bush at night. Cameras don't work at night and by the time you manage to get your flash out, the Yowie has long gone. The Yowie keeps himself hidden during the day and if somehow he is seen, he is off before the human can get the camera out! Remember, a Yowie is smarter than your average human!

* * * *

"All women become like their mothers. That is their tragedy.
No man does. That's his."
—*Oscar Wilde*

Poll results: 57% of women would rather go on a shopping spree than have sex.

UNCLE JOHN'S "STALL OF FAME"

You'd be amazed at the number of newspaper articles BRI members send in about the creative ways people get involved with bathrooms, toilets, toilet paper, etc. So we're creating Uncle John's "Stall of Fame."

Honorary: Will Simmons, a freshman at Duke University
Notable Achievement: Turning toilet paper into a political issue
True Story: In his first year at Duke, Simmons discovered that the toilets in his dorm were outfitted with single-ply toilet paper. Outraged, he decided to run for a seat in the student government. His single campaign platform: a promise that students would get two-ply paper in dorm bathrooms.
Simmons won, of course—students know what's important. After the election, university housing officials pledged to cooperate.

Honorary: Donna Summer, pop singer
Notable Achievement: Writing a Top 10 song in the bathroom
True Story: At a posh hotel, Summer was washing her hands in the ladies' room. She mused to herself that the washroom attendant there had to work awfully hard for her money. It suddenly hit Summer that she had a song title. So she rushed into a stall and wrote lyrics for it. "She Works Hard for the Money" was an international hit that went to #3 on the Billboard charts.

Honorary: Jacob Feinzilberg, a San Jose, California, inventor
Notable Achievement: Inventing the ultimate port-a-potty
True Story: In 1993 Feinzilberg came up with the Inflate-a-Potty, a toilet so portable it can actually fit in a purse. It can be inflated in seconds and is used with an ordinary eight-gallon kitchen bag as a disposable liner. He came up with the idea for it at a picnic when his young daughter suddenly "heard nature's call and found no place to answer it."

Honorarys: Philip Middleton and Richard Wooton of Chantilly, Virginia
Notable Achievement: Creating a "commode for dogs"
True Story: According to a 1993 news report, it's called the Walk-Me-Not. The dog walks up stairs at the side of the bathroom toilet, steps onto a platform over the toilet bowl, and squats down to use.

Honoraries: Chiu Chiu-kuei and Lee Wong-tsong, a Taiwanese couple
Notable Achievement: Creating a public bathroom nice enough for a wedding—and then getting married in it
True Story: In the mid-1990s, Chiu Chiu-kuei designed, and her fiancé Lee Wong-tsong built, a bathroom for a public park in the city of Taichung. According to news reports: "The couple said the lavatory, complete with elabourate decoration, had cost about $1 million to build." Chiu explained: "Since the bathroom is the creation of me and my husband it is very meaningful to us and therefore we decided to have our ceremony in here." Not explained: Why seven other couples joined them, making it the largest group wedding ever performed in a lavatory.

Honorary: Bryan J. Patrie, a Stanford graduate student
Notable Achievement: Inventing the Watercolour Intelligent Nightlight, which informs bleary-eyed midnight bathroom-goers whether the toilet seat is up or down—without turning on a blinding light.
True Story: Patrie introduced the device in the early 1990s. He explained: "When you get within two metres [five feet] of the dark commode, it will sense your motion. It looks to see if the room is dark. Then it looks upward by sending out an infrared beam. If it gets a reflection, it knows the seat is up. If it is, the red light comes on."

* * *

…And some vital "Stall-of-Fame" info: According to the Philadelphia Inquirer Toilet Paper Report, women's #1 bathroom complaint is men leaving the toilet seat up. Men's #1 complaint is having to wait to get into the bathroom.

MR. TOAD'S WILD RIDE, PART I

The Wind in the Willows is one of the best-loved books in the English language, and a milestone in children's literature. But it took some very unusual circumstances to get it written and published. And then it took the intervention of the president of the United States to make it a success. Here's the story.

BACKGROUND
By the 1890s, Kenneth Grahame was already a celebrated author. His two books, *The Golden Age* and *Dream Days*—tales of childhood written for adults—had established him as an authority on children's literature. Editors were constantly asking him to review new books and to edit collections of poems and stories.

But Grahame didn't want to write for a living. He was solidly middle-class, and the English middle-class ideal at the time was to be a "gentleman author"—someone who wrote part-time, for love, not money. In his professional life, Grahame was a successful banker—in 1898 he landed the prestigious job of Secretary of the Bank of England.

Wedded Miss
In 1899 Grahame married Elspeth Thompson. It was an unmitigated disaster. Elspeth wound up writing despondent letters and poems to her friends; Grahame developed a severe case of writer's block. He became so distracted that, less than a decade later, he was asked to retire from the bank.

The only good thing to come from the marriage was their son, Alastair. But he had problems, too—he was born "blind in one eye and squinting out of the other." His parents called him Mouse.

MAN OF LETTERS
Writing was difficult for Grahame, but he could still tell stories. Every evening he invented one for Mouse, letting the little boy choose the subject.

One night, Mouse asked his father to make up something

about a rat, a mole, and a giraffe. (The giraffe was soon replaced with Toad—a loose caricature of Alastair). The trio's ongoing experiences became such a favourite that in 1907, when Mouse was supposed to leave on a vacation with his governess, he refused to go—he didn't want to miss his father's bedtime stories.

Grahame promised to write down a new adventure every day and send it to his son—luckily, he kept his word. According to Elspeth, the child's governess was so impressed by the unusual stories that she saved the 15 letters and brought them back to her. These later became the basis for *The Wind in the Willows*.

A SAMPLE LETTER
[Ed. note: Toad was sent to prison for stealing a newfangled motorcar (it was 1907, remember) but escaped dressed as a washerwoman. Now, as he nears home, he looks up and sees the same car he stole headed toward him, and assumes it's pursuing him.]

> 16 Durham Villas
> Campden Hill, W.
> 7th August, 1907
> Dear Mouse:
>
> When the Toad saw that his enemies were close upon him…he sank down in a shabby miserable heap in the road, murmuring to himself…"It's all over now! Prison again! Dry bread and water again!…O what a fool I have been! What did I want to go strutting around the country for, singing conceited songs?…O unhappy toad! O miserable animal! And his head sank down in the dust.
>
> The terrible motor-car drew nearer and nearer…Then it stopped. Some gentlemen got out. They walked round the trembling heap of misery lying in the road, & one of them said— "O dear! Here is a poor washerwoman who has fainted in the road…Let us lift her into the motor-car and take her to the nearest village.
>
> …When the Toad heard them talk that way, & knew he was not recognized, his courage began to revive, & he opened one of his eyes. Then one of the gentlemen said: "See, she is feeling better already!

The fresh air is doing her good! How do you feel now, washerwoman?"

The toad answered in a feeble voice, "Thank you kindly, Sir, I'm feeling rather better. I think if I might sit on the front seat, beside the chauffeur, where I could get more air, I should soon be quite right again."

"That's a very sensible woman," said the gentleman. So they helped him into the front seat....The Toad began to sit up & look about & presently he said to the chauffeur, "Please Mr. Chauffeur, I wish you would let me try to drive the car for a little; it looks so easy; I'm sure I could do it quite well!"

The chauffeur laughed, heartily. But one of the gentlemen said, "Bravo, washerwoman! I like your spirit! Let her try. She won't do any harm."

So the chauffeur gave up his seat to the toad, & he took the steering wheel in his hands, and set the car going, & off they went, very slowly and carefully at first, for the toad was prudent. The gentlemen clapped their hands & cried, "Bravo, washerwoman! How well she does it! Fancy a washerwoman driving a motor-car! Bravo!"

Then the Toad went a little faster. The gentlemen applauded....The Toad began to lose his head. He went faster and faster still. The gentlemen called out warningly, "Be careful, washerwoman!" Then the Toad lost his head entirely. He stood up in his seat and shouted "Ho, ho! Who are you calling washerwoman! I am the Toad! The famous Mr. Toad! The motor-car driver, the toad who always escapes, who baffles his enemies, who dodges policemen, who breaks out of prison, the always victorious, the triumphant Toad!..."

Grahame had already written much of the story, but he had no intention of turning it into a commercial work. Nothing could have been further from his mind.

For Part II of Mr. Toad's Wild Ride, *turn to page 205.*

Fred Astaire's dancing shoes were size 8 1/2.

THE NOSE KNOWS

Smell is an amazing and complex function carried out in a tiny
chamber, half the size of an egg, situated just behind our nose.
With it, we are able to smell thousands of different odours.

THE SCIENCE OF SMELL
How do we smell things? The mystery is still unfolding,
but it starts with "odour molecules." Scientists tell us the
air is filled with them. They enter your nasal cavity every time you
breathe, 23,000 times a day.
• Just behind your nose, these molecules are absorbed by mucous-
covered tissue.
• This tissue is covered with "receptor" cells. (Some scientists say
you have millions of them.) Each one is mounted on a microscop-
ic hair.
• The receptor cells stick out and wave in the air currents we
inhale. Forty of them must detect odour molecules before a smell
is registered.
• When a new smell is detected, the tiny olfactory bulb, located
just above the nasal cavity, flashes data directly to the most
ancient and mysterious part of your brain—the limbic system—
which "handles feelings, lust, instincts, and invention." The limbic system reacts immediately, without intervention of reason or
language, and may provoke powerful emotions, images, or nostal-
gia.

THE DARK AGES OF SMELLING
A keen sense of smell is now accepted as part of the good life—
coffees, wines, cheeses, and gourmet foods would all be lost on us
if we lacked our immense range of smell. However, this faculty
wasn't always appreciated.
• The ancient philosopher Plato looked down on smell as a lowly
instinct that might lead to gluttony and lust, while vision and
hearing opened one to geometry and music and were therefore
"closer to the soul."
• During the 18th and 19th centuries, it was commonly believed
that many diseases were caused by smells. Odours from corpses,
faeces, urine, swamps, and Earth fissures were called "miasmas"

and were thought to have the power to kill you. To ward off these smells, people carried and inhaled "antimephitics," such as garlic, amber, sulphur, and incense. When exposed to miasmic odours, people did not swallow their saliva, but spit it out. The Viennese physician Semmelweis was ostracized by colleagues when he declared that washing one's hands, not breathing antimephitics, would stop most disease from spreading.

• According to some sources, the stethoscope was invented not to hear the heartbeat better, but to give doctors some distance from a patient's bodily odours.

TASTE AND SMELL

• We taste only four things: sweet, sour, salt and bitter. It's the smells that make things really taste. For example, wine's smell, not its taste, is what makes it delicious. With a head cold, drinking wine is an entirely different experience.

• Scientists have categorized smells into seven groups: minty like peppermint, floral like roses, ethereal like pears, musky like—well—musk, resinous like camphor, foul like rotten eggs, and acrid like vinegar.

• Talking with your mouth full expels taste molecules and diminishes the taste of food.

SMELL FACTS

• Women have a keener sense of smell than men.

• By simply smelling a piece of clothing, most people can tell if it was worn by a woman or man.

• Each of us has an odour that is, like our fingerprints, unique. One result, researchers say: Much of the thrill of kissing comes from smelling the unique odours of another's face.

• Smells stimulate learning. Students given olfactory stimulation along with a word list retain much more information and remember it longer.

• Many smells are heavier than air and can be smelled only at ground level.

• We smell best if we take several short sniffs, rather than one long one.

AUSTRALIA'S BIG THINGS

Australians have always had a fascination with BIG THINGS. No other country in the world would have such tasteful tourist attractions as the Big Banana, the Big Prawn, and the Big Pavlova. What does this say about us? Here are some of the best you should put on your "Must Visit" list.

THE BIG BULL

Located at Wauchope, NSW, just inland from Port Macquarie, this massive structure is big, tacky, ugly, and utterly pointless. As with many big things, you can go in it, through it and over it, although why you would want to will always remain a mystery!

THE BIG BOTTLE

Located at Mangrove Mountain, NSW, 80 km south of the Hunter Valley (where at least it would have made some sense), this enormous wine bottle appears out of place in its rugged bushland setting. What is it doing there? This question is often asked of BIG THINGS but seems especially relevant here.

THE BIG ORANGE

This once former glory has seen better days. Neglected, forlorn, dented, and damaged, it now lies wedged between two posts next to a petrol station, but persistent BIG THINGS spotters can track it down on the New England Highway, near Tenterfield, NSW.

THE BIG POTATO

Truly one of the tackiest of all BIG THINGS, this eyesore is devoid of any outstanding or notable features. It does, unfortunately, resemble a giant lump of excrement, hence its more common nickname, "The Big Turd." If this appeals, it can be found at Robertson, NSW.

THE BIG COW

This magnificent creature stares across the road at its competition, the Big Pineapple. Because the two vie for tourists' attention, they are deadly enemies, and rumours abound on what goes on after dark. There has been talk that the cow sabotages the pineapple juice on sale, and for this reason you are advised to take care when visiting.

Goldfish have a memory span of three seconds.

JUST PLANE WEIRD

If you bought this book in an airport, you might want to skip reading this chapter until your flight is over and you're safely back on the ground.

NOTHING TO SNOOZE AT

In May 1995, the pilot of Delta Airlines Flight 198, approaching Palm Beach international Airport, USA, was unable to make contact with the control tower. The pilot landed the plane without any assistance, then alerted the Federal Aviation Administration. According to news reports, "Palm Beach sheriffs deputies entered the control tower and found the lone air traffic controller shoeless and apparently just waking up." The deputies also found a pistol, ammunition, and a gun-cleaning kit nearby (it's against federal law to have a gun in a control tower), and speculate he was cleaning the gun and fell asleep. FAA officials launched an investigation. "Meanwhile," the Associated Press reported, he "remains on the job."

UNLUCKY BREAK

In June 1999, a plane approaching Benbecula Airport in Western Scotland was forced to circle for half an hour while the air traffic controller stopped working to eat lunch. According to wire service reports, "Officials at the airport said there was just one controller at Benbecula, and she had to take a break at the time she did because national air traffic rules forbid any controller from working more than two hours without one....There was an uproar in the terminal building as families watched the plane from Glasgow linger in a holding pattern, 'tantalizingly within view.'"

UNLUCKIER BREAK

In 1999 the air traffic controller in Bournemouth Airport in southern England stepped away from his post for a few minutes to get some coffee—but was gone a lot longer than he'd planned. Greg Fanos, 39, fell down a flight of stairs and broke his ankle. "Crawling back to the tower was only two or three yards," Fanos says, "but it took forever." By the time he made it back to his desk and called an ambulance, several planes, unable to reach the tower on the radio, had gone into a holding pattern over the airport. Two other planes landed safely without assistance.

Siberia contains more than 25% of the world's forests.

CLOSE ENCOUNTER

In April 1998, an air traffic supervisor at New York's LaGuardia Airport spilled some coffee in the control tower. One of the controllers turned from his position to help clean it up, and the momentary distraction caused what may be the closest near-miss in U.S. aviation history. A landing U.S. Airways plane came within 6 metres [20 feet] of colliding with an Air Canada plane that was taking off from an intersecting runway. According to news reports, "experts were unable to immediately cite another incident in which two airborne passenger jets came so close without colliding." When the National Transportation Safety Board investigated the incident and began taking statements from people in the control tower, "neither the supervisor nor the controller mentioned the spilled coffee in their statements."

RATS!

In August 1999, a woman on an Air New Zealand flight from Los Angeles to Auckland felt something on her leg. She lifted her blanket and saw a rat sitting on her knee. The rat had been spotted earlier, but according to an airline spokesperson, "attempts by the crew to catch it failed." According to wire service reports, "Quarantine officials met the plane when it landed in Auckland and conducted a search of the plane including passengers' hand baggage. The rat wasn't found, so the plane was quarantined and fumigated."

SUFFICIENT GROUNDS

In 1999 guards manning security checkpoint at more than 300 U.S. airports began ordering travellers carrying cups of coffee to sip their coffee to prove it really was coffee. "That's policy," says security spokesman Jeff Sledge. "It's so we'd be able to make sure that what's supposed to be in the cup is in the cup—not a weapon of some sort." The policy was reportedly put into place following an FAA test in which an FAA employee made it past security with a "simulated device in a coffee cup." But the FAA denies that it's behind the "clearing of liquids," or "sip test." "It's not an FAA requirement at all," a spokesperson told the Wall Street Journal. If the airlines are doing it, she said, "they're doing it on their own."

No wonder they're gone: In ancient Egypt, pillows were made of stones.

HIS NAME IS MY NAME, TOO!

Remember the tune that goes, "John Jacob Jingleheimer Smith, his name is my name too…"? If you do, you probably won't be able to get it out of your head for the rest of the day. Sorry. Anyway, we've come across some stories about people with the same names as other folks (and one Supreme Being). Here they are.

NOT THE DICTTATTOR

"Adolf Hittler is alive and well. But probably not the guy you're thinking about. Unlike the Nazi leader, this gentleman spells his last name with two Ts, disdains fascism, and never aspired to take over the world. He's a 61-year-old retired school bus driver from Landeck, Austria, and he doesn't like to be teased. 'My whole life this has been a problem,' he says. 'Just try checking into a hotel with my name….But it is in part my choice. I decided not to change my name. I thought it would be an insult to my parents.'"

"Hittler's problem is rare. Only about 2% of German men before World War II were named Adolf, and during his reign, Hitler forbade Germans to name children after him."

—*The Wolf Files,* October 1, 1998

GOD AMONG MEN

"A man who legally changed his name to Ubiquitous Perpetuity God began serving a nine-month sentence for indecent exposure in Marin County, California on Wednesday. God, 68, has been convicted 18 times for similar offenses since 1968. His latest arrest came in October, when he exposed himself to a woman waiting in line at a coffee shop. He did it so that women 'could have some type of awareness of God,' according to police reports….God will be released to a residential mental health facility, if one agrees to admit him."

—*Ashland, Oregon, Daily Tidings,* 1996

FRANK STATEMENT

"Say hello to Frank J. Manibusan and his brother, Frank, both of

Alameda, California. And their brother, Frank. And their other brother, Frank. And his brother, Frank, and one other brother: Frank. Then, of course, there are children: Frank, Frank, Frank, Frank, Frank, and Frank. Frankly speaking, there are 12 Franks in all, at the moment—13 if you count the patriarch, 58-year-old Francisco. …The sons and grandsons all have middle initials: J., J., J., J., J., J., J., J., J., J., J., and J.

"Of course, the advantages definitely outweigh the detriments, they explain. Can't do jury duty? Not to worry. Which Frank are the authorities going to chastise? And if one brother is out of cash, who cares? He need only tear out a cheque from the wallet of one of his siblings. 'We don't leave no cheques lying around,' explained Frank Joe, No. 2 son, while his brothers and father nodded in agreement."

—*San Jose Mercury News*

A FAN AMONG FANS

"A fanatical British pop fan has changed his name to include the titles of his favourite group's records. And for good measure, Anthony Hicks, 23, added the names of the original line-up of the group, Level 42.

"Hicks this week signed legal papers changing his name to: 'Ant Level Forty Two The Pursuit Of Accidents The Early Tapes Standing In The Light True Colors A Physical Presence World Machine Running In The Family Platinum Edition Staring At The Sun Level Best Guaranteed The Remixes Forever Now Influences Changes Mark King Mike Landup Phil Gould Boon Gould Wally Badarou Lindup-Badarou'.

"'If they release any album or single, I will alter my name to have the new title incorporated into it,' Hicks told reporters."

—*Reuters*, July 30, 1994

SPLIT DECISION

"When Denise Mason of Glasgow, Scotland, gave birth to a son six weeks ago, picking a name created a stir. Clark Kearny, the child's father and a big fan of the Glasgow Rangers soccer team, wanted to name the boy after his favourite Ranger but couldn't make a decision. So, he didn't. The lad is named Cairo Lionel Sergio Lorenzo Colin Giovanni Barry Ian Jorge Gabriel Stephane Rod Mason Kearney—after 11 Rangers."

—*USA Today*, February 3, 1999

A spider's blood is transparent.

THE SHAPE OF THE EARTH

What shape is Earth? You'd say round, right? But scientists would hem and haw about it—and then answer "oblate spheroid."
Read on…

YOU ARE HERE
In the age of space travel, we all know the world is "round." But ancient civilizations had no way to measure the size or shape of the Earth. So they came up with their own imaginative explanations. For example:

• In the Cherokee nation, people believed that mud rose from under the waters and formed an island with four corners—the Earth. The sun went underneath the island at night, and rose again the next day.
• Ancient Babylonians thought the Earth was inside a hollow mountain, floating on a sea. Everything—the sun, moon, sky, stars, water—was inside this mountain.
• Ancient Egyptians believed the whole Earth was part of their god, Keb. The stars were the jewels of a goddess in the sky and their god of air held her aloft.
• Ancient Hindus thought the Earth was in an upside-down bowl, being carried by elephants. The elephants stood on the back of a turtle that was standing on top of a snake. What the snake stood on, they hadn't quite worked out.
• Polynesian creation stories set the Earth in a basket with a lid. A hole cut in the top by a god lets in light. The woven grass at night lets light peek through in the form of stars.

THE GREEKS KNEW
Many people believe that Columbus was the first to realize that the world is round. Actually, the round-earth concept has been with us since ancient Greece.

The very early Greeks thought Earth was a flat disc floating on water. But in about 540 B.C., the renowned mathematician

---

Mmm-mmm good: In the Middle Ages, chicken soup was considered an aphrodisiac.

Pythagoras proposed the theory that the world was a sphere. The concept had many supporters, including Aristotle.

ALL'S WELL

In about 250 B.C., Eratosthenes, librarian at the Library of Alexandria, even came up with a calculation of the Earth's spherical size.

He'd heard that in midsummer in the town of Syene, Egypt, the noonday sun shone directly into a deep well. He measured and discovered that in Alexandria, 787 kilometres north, the angle of the sun was about 7.2 degrees on the same date. With these measurements, he computed the circumference of the Earth. Amazingly enough, considering how he came up with the numbers and how little he had to prove them, Eratosthenes's estimates were very close.

Another scholar, Posidonius (135–51 B.C.), did something similar over a century later, using the bright star Canopus. He measured the angles of the star from the horizon in two locations to get a fairly accurate estimate of the Earth's circumference.

IN FOURTEEN HUNDRED AND NINETY-TWO...

Fifteen hundred years later, Christopher Columbus came along, trying to make his now-famous voyage to Asia by going west. The decision of whether to fund his trip came down to analyzing the accumulation of estimates that had been gathered over the centuries.

Based on Eratosthenes' numbers, King Ferdinand believed that Columbus's fleet could never make it all the way to Asia: it was simply too far. He didn't see any reason to supply ships and crews only to have them die halfway from their goal.

Columbus used a ploy common in modern-day politics, marketing, and engineering: If the numbers don't support your conclusion, find some numbers that do. He found another estimate by Ptolemy dating from about 150 A.D. It was completely erroneous, but estimated that the Earth was about half its true size—so Queen Isabella agreed to support the voyage.

Luckily for Columbus, America got in his way, or he never would've reached India or anywhere else. Crossing both the Atlantic and the Pacific combined would've been an impossible feat with the ships and supplies he had.

FLAT AND FAT
It wasn't until 1958 that the Vanguard I satellite took the first photographs of earth from space and scientists were able to determine the planet's exact shape. The photographs proved the world is round—right?

Well, not exactly. Scientists reported that the Earth is an oblate spheroid—i.e., it's not quite round.

Since the Earth spins, it gets a slight bulge near the equator. Near yes, but not (as you might suspect) exactly on the equator. Because of this bulge, the Earth is flattened very slightly on either end. Its circumference at the equator is 39,843 km [24,902 miles], and the circumference around the poles is 43 km [27 miles] less than that: 39,800 km [24,875 miles]. Not a big deal, really—if the world were the size of a basketball, it would be more perfectly round than a real basketball is. But still, after guessing for so long, scientists can't resist the opportunity to get it exactly right.

* * * *

THE WORLD IS PEAR-SHAPED
Ironically, toward the end of his life, Columbus came to believe the Earth was shaped like a pear. He developed this theory during his third voyage to the New World: When he was sailing west near the equator, he noticed that the North Star made a wider circle around the Pole than it did when he was sailing in more temperate latitudes.

From this he deduced that he had been sailing gradually uphill and therefore closer to the sun, which explained why the weather was getting warmer. "I have come to the conclusion," he wrote in a letter to Queen Isabella, "...that the Earth is not round, but of the form of a pear....Where the stalk grows being the highest and nearest the sky."

Columbus believed that if he sailed far enough, he would eventually reach the Garden of Eden, which was located in the pear's stalk. (*Ripley's Believe It or Not!*)

THE EARTH IS FLAT!

For centuries, scientists have been able to prove that the Earth is round, but that hasn't stopped people from developing their own unique—and entertaining—theories about its shape.

THE EARTH IS FLAT

Who Says So: The International Flat Earth Research Society

What They Believe: The world is a big flat disc, with the North Pole at the center. What is mistakenly believed to be the South Pole is actually a 46-metre [150-foot] high mass of ice that forms a big square around the Earth-disc (the way an album cover makes a square around a record). People who think they're sailing around the world are actually sailing in a circle on the surface of the disc. Flat-Earthers believe the Bible must be interpreted literally. Passages like Revelation 7:1 and 20:8, which refer to "the four corners of the earth," are all the proof they need.

History: In 1849 an English "itinerant lecturer" named Samuel Birley Rowbotham resurrected the flat-Earth theory (which had been widely discredited by the eighth century). The flat-Earth movement grew sporadically over the next 70 years, finally peaking in the 1920s when Wilbur Glen Voliva organized a flat-Earth religious community with several thousand followers in Zion, Illinois. Voliva owned one of the country's first 100,000-watt radio stations, and used it to preach the flat-Earth gospel to folks in the American Midwest. Today the movement lives on in Charles Johnson's Flat Earth Society, which published *Flat Earth News*—until Johnson's house burned down in 1995, incinerating the 3,500-person mailing list. No word on what he's doing now.

THE EARTH IS HOLLOW

Who Said So: Captain John Cleves Symmes, a hero of the War of 1812.

What He Believed: The Earth has four layers, like a big onion. Each is a "warm and rich land, stocked with vegetables and animals, if not men...." What we perceive as the surface of the Earth is actually the fifth and outer layer. And the North and South poles aren't just poles, they're also holes leading to the four interior worlds.

Half of all forest fires are started by lightning.

History: In 1823 Symmes managed to get a bill introduced in the U.S. Congress to finance a steamship voyage to the "North Hole" and to the inner worlds beyond. When the bill received only 25 votes, Johnson talked President Adams's secretaries of the Navy and the Treasury into outfitting three ships for a voyage to the middle of the earth. But before it got underway, Andrew Jackson became president and scuttled the trip. Symmes died in 1829, unfulfilled, but his theory remained popular with unconventional thinkers until 1909, when Robert Peary set foot on the North Pole (or at least came close)—and found no hole.

Even after 1909, the hollow-Earth theory had its admirers—including Adolf Hitler. Today, a few diehard hollow-Earthers believe that Hitler survived World War II, escaped to an interior world under the South Pole, and may still be hiding there, mingling with "a race of advanced hollow-Earth beings who are responsible for the UFO sightings throughout history."

THE EARTH IS SHAPED LIKE THE INSIDE OF AN EGG
Who Said So: Cyrus Reed Teed, in the late 1860s.
What He Believed: Instead of living on the outside of a solid round ball, we're on the inside surface of a hollow one. The rest of the universe—sun, stars, etc—is where the yolk would be.
Background: For years, Teed grappled with the notion of an infinite universe...but just couldn't accept it. Then one night in 1869, he had a dream in which a beautiful woman explained everything:

> The entire cosmos...is like an egg. We live on the inner surface of the shell, and inside the hollow are the sun, moon, stars, planets, and comets. What is outside? Absolutely nothing! The inside is all there is. You can't see across it because the atmosphere is too dense. The shell is 100 miles thick...

The woman in Teed's dream also said he would be the new Messiah, and he took it to heart. In the 1890s, he bought land outside Fort Meyers, Florida, and founded a community called The New Jerusalem that he preached would one day be the capital of the world. He expected 8 million residents, but only got 200. In 1908 Teed died from injuries suffered during a run-in with the local marshal; his dwindling community held on until the late 1940s, when the last of his followers disbanded following a property dispute.

THE WHO?

Ever wonder how rock bands get their names? So did we.
After some digging around, we found these "origin" stories.

THE GIN BLOSSOMS. A gin blossom is slang for the capillaries in your nose and face that burst because of excessive drinking.

PROCUL HARUM. Named after a friend's cat. It's Latin for "Beyond All Things."

THE BOOMTOWN RATS. Named after a gang in Woody Guthrie's autobiography, *Bound for Glory.*

GENERATION X. Named after a book that singer Billy Idol found in his mother's bookcase. It was a mid-1960s sociological essay by Charles Hamblett and Jane Deverson that featured interviews with U.K. teenagers in competing gangs called the Mods and Rockers.

10,000 MANIACS. Came from the cult horror film *2,000 Maniacs.* One of the band members misunderstood the film's name.

FOO FIGHTERS. World War II fighter pilot slang for UFOs.

RAGE AGAINST THE MACHINE. Name refers to a (hoped-for) reaction of ordinary people against corporations, governments and other invasive institutions that control our society.

HOT TUNA. Originally Hot S**t. The band's record label made them change the second word to Tuna.

DIRE STRAITS. Suggested by a friend who was concerned about the state of the band's finances.

MOTHERS OF INVENTION. Frank Zappa's group was originally just The Mothers. But their record company was concerned it would be interpreted as an Oedipal reference and insisted they change it. The band chose the name from the old saying "necessity is the mother of invention."

The earliest form of electric shock treatment involved the use of electric eels.

PEARL JAM. Singer Eddie Vedder suggested the name in honour of his Aunt Pearl's homemade jam, supposedly a natural aphrodisiac containing peyote. "Pearl Jam" is also slang for semen.

BEASTIE BOYS. Beastie supposedly stands for Boys Entering Anarchistic States Towards Inner Excellence.

SQUIRREL NUT ZIPPERS. From a brand of old-time peanut-flavored candy containing caramel and nuts.

BLIND MELON. According to bassist Brad Smith, the name was slang for unemployed hippies in his Mississippi town. Also sounds suspiciously like an anagram of blues singer Blind Lemon.

BLUE ÖYSTER CULT. An anagram of "Cully Stout Beer." It was chosen by a band member one night as he was mindlessly doodling while at a bar with the band's manager.

DEVO. An abbreviation of de-evolution, something that the members of the group believe is happening to the human race.

REM. An acronym for rapid eye movement. REM sleep is the state of sleep in which dreams occur.

MATCHBOX 20. Took its name from the combination of a softball jersey bearing the number 20 and a patch that read "matchbox." The name is meaningless. "The two parts aren't even related," singer Rob Thomas has said.

311. The police code for indecent exposure in California.

ZZ TOP. Said to be have been inspired by a poster of Texas bluesman Z. Z. Hill, and rolling-paper brands "Zig Zag" and "Top."

COUNTING CROWS. A reference to an old British poem that said life is as meaningless as counting crows.

L7. Fifties slang for someone who is "square," or uncool.

THE WHO. According to legend, the group, first called The High Numbers, was looking for a new name. Every time someone came up with an idea, they jokingly asked, "The who?" Finally, a friend said "Why not just call yourselves 'The Who'?"

The first e-mail was sent over the Internet in 1972.

THE LAST LAUGH: EPITAPHS

*Some unusual epitaphs and tombstone rhymes,
sent in by our crew of wandering
BRI tombstone-ologists.*

**Botany cemetery,
Sydney, NSW**
*When William
Jackson was killed by a drunken
David Hennesy riding his horse into a
group of pedestrians, his family made
sure the circumstances were not
forgotten.*
Sacred to the memory of
William Jackson
Who was carelessly rode over
And killed returning
from the races
May 21 1831
Aged 21 years
O Hennesy you did kill
And would not pay my doctor's bill
Your drunkenness
has caused my fall
But you must come
when GOD doth call

**MAN'S BEST FRIEND
Bendigo, Victoria**
Mr W. Webb
Erected in grateful remembrance of
my faithful dog Fido, who died on
March 28, 1904. A patient partner
during ten years of life's journey,
who has eaten the same bread with
me and was to me a friend. The
more I know of men, the more I
admire dogs.

**In St David's Park,
Hobart, Tasmania:**
Stranger take heed as you pass by;
As you are now so once was I,
As I am now so you will be
Prepare yourself to follow me.

In New York:
Harry Edsel Smith
Born 1903-Died 1942
Looked up the
elevator shaft
To see
If the car was on the way down.
It was.

In Massachusetts:
Matthew Mudd
Here lies Matthew Mudd,
Death did him no hurt;
When alive he was only Mudd,
But now he's only dirt.

In England:
Sir John Strange
Here lies an honest lawyer,
And that is Strange.

In Scotland:
Stranger, tread this ground
with gravity:
Dentist Brown is filling
His last cavity.

In Antarctica, sunsets can be green.

In England:
My wife is dead
And here she lies:
Nobody laughs
And nobody cries:
Where she is gone to
And how she fares
Nobody knows
And nobody cares.

In New York:
He angled in the
babbling brook
With all his angler's skill.
He lied about the fish he took
And here he's lying still.

In Ireland:
Tears cannot
Restore her:
Therefore I weep.

In England:
Beneath this stone
Lie Humphrey and Joan,
Who rest together in peace,
Living indeed,
They disagreed,
But now all quarrels cease.

In Belgrave:
John Racket
Here lies John Racket
In his wooden jacket:
Kept neither horses nor mules
Lived a hog
Died a dog
And left all his money to fools.

In Massachusetts:
Here lies Ann Mann.
She lived an old maid
But died an old Mann.

In England:
Mrs Nott
Nott born, Nott dead
...Here lies a woman
Who was,
And who was Nott.

In England:
Dr. I. Lettsom
When people's ill, they comes to I,
I physics, bleeds, and sweats'em;
Sometimes they live,
sometimes they die;
What's that to I?
I. Lettsom.

* * * *

Smile When You Say That

"One of Oscar Hammerstein's rarer finds was 'Sober Sue,' whom he introduced to audiences at New York's Victoria theatre in 1908. During intermissions, Sue would appear on stage and Hammerstein would offer $1,000 to anyone who could make her laugh. There were lots of takers, but no one succeeded. What they didn't know: she couldn't laugh—her facial muscles were paralyzed."
(Felton & Fowler's Best, Worst, and Most Unusual)

Nothing's new: Ancient Rome had rent-a-chariot businesses.

TRICK SHOTS:
FAMOUS FAKED PHOTOS

*If there's a lesson to be learned from these historic phonies, it's that
people believe what they want to believe. In the face of overwhelming logic—or even solid contrary evidence—people have clung to
the notion that the real truth was revealed in these photographs.*

FAIRY TALE
Famous Photo: English fairies
Trick Shot: In 1917 Sir Arthur Conan Doyle, "an ardent
believer in the occult," announced that, just as he'd always
believed, sprites, gnomes, and other types of fairies really did exist.
His proof: photographs of fairies taken by 16-year-old Elsie Wright
and her 10-year-old cousin Frances Griffiths. "The pictures
showed the girls by a wooded stream, with winged sprites and
gnomes who danced and pranced and tooted on pipes," Michael
Farquhar writes in the *Washington Post.* "Several of the photography
experts who examined the pictures declared them free of
superimposition or retouching," and the photos, backed by Conan
Doyle's testament to their authenticity, launched a national fairy
craze.
The Real Picture: "In 1983, the girls, by then old women, admitted that they had posed with paper cutouts supported by hatpins."

SECOND TIME AROUND
Famous Photo: American troops raising the flag on Iwo Jima
Trick Shot: The bloody battle of Iwo Jima (an island 1040 km
[650 miles] from Tokyo) took place on February 23, 1945. The
Japanese were nearly wiped out, and the Americans lost over one-third of their troops. When the U.S. Marines finally took Iwo
Jima's highest point, Mt. Suribachi, they raised an American flag
at the summit. AP photographer Joe Rosenthal was on hand to
catch it on film; his dramatic picture is one of the most famous
images of the 20th century. It won the Pulitzer Prize, was commemorated with a postage stamp, and was the inspiration for the
Marines Memorial in Arlington National Cemetery.
The Real Picture: Rosenthal's photograph was so good that *Life*

magazine editor Daniel Longwell wondered if it was too good. He asked a *Life* correspondent on Iwo Jima to investigate. Stephen Bates writes in *If No News, Send Rumors:*

> The correspondent reported, that as Longwell suspected, the photo had been staged. The marines had raised a small flag for a photographer from *Leatherneck*, the Marine Corps magazine. Rosenthal had arrived four hours later. At his request, the marines had reenacted the event with a larger flag.

Longwell refused to use a staged photograph in *Life*, but other publications did run it, and it caught on with the public. "The country believed in that picture," Longwell recounted later, "and I just had to pipe down."

UN-LOCH-ING THE TRUTH

Famous Photo: Loch Ness monster

Trick Shot: On April 19, 1934, Robert Wilson and a companion were walking along the shore of Loch Ness when the friend suddenly shouted, "My God, it's the monster!" Wilson grabbed his camera and snapped a quick photograph of what appears to be "a sea beast with a humpback and a long neck"—the legendary Loch Ness monster, an elusive creature with sightings dating as far back as 565 A.D. The Daily Mail ran the photograph, and news of the find spread round the world. Based largely on the strength of Wilson's photograph, it remains one of the most widely believed monster legends to this day. Nearly one million tourists visit Loch Ness each year, hoping to spot "Nessie" and pumping $37 million into the local economy while they're there.

The Real Picture: In 1995 a friend of Wilson's named Christian Spurling made a deathbed confession that the photograph was a hoax and the "monster" was actually "a toy submarine fitted with a fake sea-serpent head" that Spurling had made himself. "Wilson," the Associated Press reported in 1995, "was part of a hoax hatched by his friend Marmaduke Wetherell, a film maker and self-styled big game hunter hired by London's *Daily Mail* newspaper in 1933 to look for Nessie."

Note: Hard-core believers are unimpressed by the revelation. "Eyewitness accounts still suggest that there is something powerful in the loch," says Adrian Shine, founder of a group called The Loch Ness Project.

WEIRD TOYS

Looking for a gift for a special young friend or relative? Want to surprise them with something out of the ordinary? Well, if you don't mind being thrown out of the house, you might want to pick up one of these 100% real (we guarantee it) playthings.

The Tamahonam. Sold in Hong Kong, the Tamahonam is a Tamagotchi toy with Mob connections. Instead of feeding Tamahonam like you would other virtual pets, you "care" for Tamahonam by plying him with cigarettes and booze; instead of playing with him, you give him a knife "to let him wage turf battles."

Feral Cheryl. "A doll that has unshaved legs, dreadlocks, tattoos, pubic hair, and pierced nipples." Made in Australia.

The Grossinator. Made by SRM, the company that brought you the Insultinator. "A minicomputer with a sound chip and programmable buttons with phrases you can mix and match." This one says things like, "I'm going to make a horrible, gross fart" and "How about a foul, smelly barf?"

Brian Jones Pool Toy. "An inflatable, life-size pool toy of Brian Jones, deceased member of the Rolling Stones, that floats face-down in the water, simulating the guitarist's death by drowning in his pool."

Gooey Looey. Exciting action! "Children use their fingers to relieve Louie's congested proboscis before the top of his head flies off."

Savage Mondo Blitzers. "A line of 48 characters named Bad Fart, Snot Shot, Projectile Vomit, Puke Shooters, Loaded Diaper, Eye Pus, and the like."

Letter Bomb. The manufacturer urges kids to "have fun and become a terrorist." Looks like an airmail envelope— "kids write the target's name on it, clap on it heavily, and then give it to the victim within seven seconds so it 'explodes' in his hand." Sold in the Philippines.

HOW WE GOT
THE DOLLAR

Ever wondered why we—as well as the Yanks—call our money the "dollar?"
At the BRI, we've been trying to find a good explanation for years. Finally,
courtesy of BRI member Erin Keenan, we got the answer.
We wrote up the dollar's arrival in Australia ourselves, though.

BACKGROUND
In 1519 Stephan Schlick, a Czech nobleman, discovered a
rich vein of silver on his estate in the Joachimsthal Valley.
He began minting his own coins, which were accepted as *groschen*,
the official currency of the Holy Roman Empire, in 1520.
Schlick's coins were first referred to as *Joachimsthalergroschen*, after
the valley in which they originated. But that was too hard to pro-
nounce; people began shortening it. The coins became known as
thalergroschen—and eventually *talers* or *thalers*.

What Goes Around...
Schlick and his neighbours produced millions of thalers. By 1600
there were 12 million of the coins (an enormous amount for the
time) circulating around Europe. One result was that the thaler—
which started out as the equivalent of three German marks—lost
its specific value. It was considered local currency wherever it was
used, and its value changed from region to region.

After a while, the term *thaler* didn't even refer to Schlick's
money anymore. It became generic—synonymous with "any large
silver coin." Eventually, many cultures came up with their own
version of the word. In Italy, for example, a large silver coin
became known as a "*tallero;*" in Holland, it was a "*daalder;*"
Denmark and Sweden had "*dalers;*" in Hawaii, silver coins were
"*dalas;*" Ethiopians exchanged "*talari;*" and in English-speaking
countries, a silver coin was called a "*dollar.*"

COMING TO AMERICA
The term *dollar* was particularly popular in Scotland. As Jack
Weatherford writes in *The History of Money:*

The average cat has 24 whiskers—12 on each side of its nose.

The Scots used the name dollar to distinguish their currency, and thereby their country and themselves, more clearly from their domineering English neighbours to the south [who used *pounds, shillings, pence,* etc]. Thus from very early usage, the word 'dollar' carried with it a certain anti-English or antiauthoritarian bias that many Scottish settlers took with them to their new homes in the Americas and other British colonies. The emigration of Scots accounts for much of the subsequent popularity of the word "dollar" in British colonies around the world.

THE AUSTRALIAN WAY

Until 1966 Australia followed the British system of currency and used pounds, shillings, and pence. However that all changed on 14 February 1966, when decimal currency was introduced. For all of those old enough, I bet you can still sing the song that was used to introduce this funny new money.

"In come the dollars and in come the cents,
Out goes the pounds, the shillings and the pence..."

It was certainly catchy!

The dollar was the unit of currency consisting of 100 cents. Seven notes were introduced in 1, 2, 5, 10, 20, 50 and 100-dollar bills. The $1 and $2 notes were eventually replaced with coins. Six coins were introduced in 1, 2, 5, 10, 20 and 50 cent denominations. The 1 and 2 cent coins were eventually removed from circulation and new $1 and $2 coins introduced.

Close your eyes and try and remember what is featured on each coin. Not the Queen, wise guy—she is on the reverse side of all our coins. What's on the other side? The 5-cent coin has an echidna, the 10-cent coin a male lyrebird, the 20-cent coin a platypus, the 50-cent coin the coat of arms of the Commonwealth of Australia, the $1 coin portrays five leaping kangaroos and the $2 coin has a bust of an aborigine against the background of the Southern Cross.

The 5-cent, 10-cent, 20-cent and 50-cent coins are made from cupro-nickel while the other coins are made of aluminium-bronze. The $1 coin has milling around the edge to help the visually impaired as it is a similar size to the 20-cent coin. A $5 and $10 coin made out of sterling silver and a $200 coin made out of 22 carat gold have been minted but are not generally circulated, although they are legal tender.

Did you know that Australia was the first nation to introduce plastic notes? The first was introduced in 1988 and it's true—they do survive the washing machine! All notes now have a clear window, which can be embossed to stop counterfeiting. This replaces the metallic thread and watermark that was used on the old paper notes.

* * *

MOTHERS OF INVENTION

Here are two women you may never have heard of, but who may have affected your life.

Mother of Invention: Kate Gleason, a New York architect in the 1920s.
The Invention: Tract housing
Background: After watching engines being put together on a Cadillac assembly line, Gleason decided to try using mass production techniques to build affordable housing for soldiers who'd returned from World War I. Her first development was "Concrest," a 100-unit concrete housing project. Its six-room homes sold for $4,000 each.

Mother of Invention: Ruth Wakefield, owner of the Toll House Inn and restaurant in Whitman, Massachusetts, USA in the 1930s.
The Invention: Chocolate chip cookies
Background: One afternoon Wakefield was baking a batch of "chocolate butter drop" cookies for her restaurant. She decided to smash a semisweet chocolate bar into tiny chunks and dump the pieces into the batter, rather than take the time to melt the bar first. She figured the chunks would melt into the batter in the oven, and the cookies would be indistinguishable from her regular ones. She was wrong—and her customers loved the difference. Today Americans consume more than 68 million kilograms [150 million pounds] of chocolate chip cookies every year.

LET THEM EAT LAMINGTONS

What does Russell Crowe have in common with a big meringue? They both look good covered in whipped cream? Perhaps, but both are famous Australians who were born in New Zealand. Pavlova the ballerina did the dying swan in 1934, but Pavlova the dessert lives on. Forget the Oscar, Russell, your own cake is the key to immortality.

The first Australians lived happily cakeless for 40,000 years, but the first Europeans to arrive in Australia nearly starved after two, until grain was brought from the other side of the world so they could grow some wheat. Then came cows and hens for butter and eggs, then imported sugar. Then came cake. This is the story of cake and the shaping of a modern nation. These are the three great sugar icons of Australia.

THE PAV

Star of backyard BBQs, the celebration dessert of choice for generations, the big puffy meringue inspired by a ballet tutu is always under challenge from flashy imports, but it holds its ground. Should the centre be crisp or squishy? Does the cream go in the middle or on the top? Are strawberries or passionfruit the best topping? Did it make its debut in New Zealand or Australia? The pav is not so much an icon as an international dispute.

The question of origin was settled when Helen Leach of Otago University discovered a New Zealand recipe for a fruit-filled meringue dating from 1926, the year of Anna Pavlova's tour. The first Australian pav sighting was not till 1935, four years after Pavlova's death. Herbert Sachse, chef of the Esplanade Hotel in Perth, is generally credited with creating the Australian pav, although some sources claim it was a chef in Adelaide who saw Pavlova dance and was inspired to create a dessert as light and airy as her dancing. Wherever and however it originated, the pavlova caught on and evolved into the pud we know today—a large meringue tutu with a crunchy outside and marshmallow-gooey centre piled with cream and fruit. Not just any fruit. A New

Zealand pav must have its kiwifruit, but across the Tasman a pav without passionfruit or strawberries is simply un-Australian.

PEACH MELBA

Best (or should we say worst?) remembered as ice-cream and tinned peaches covered in sticky red syrup, Peach Melba has suffered from bad cooks and bad PR. Originally a delicate confection of spun sugar, vanilla ice-cream, raspberry sauce, and peaches served in an ice-carved swan, Peche Melba was created in 1892 by Auguste Escoffier, chef of the Savoy hotel in London, as a tribute to Nellie Melba.

Melba, opera singer, binge eater and Australia's first 'cultural industry', was prima donna of London's Covent Garden from 1889 until her farewell (one of many) 37 years later. Also known for her toast and wafers, Melba patented her own name and invented herself as a brand long before Madonna did. She made a fortune from her voice and even more from her investments.

"It is no use having a perfect voice," she said, "unless you have brains, personality, magnetism, great will-power, health, strength and determination."

But in the end even Melba's formidable talents were not enough. She died from septicaemia following an unsuccessful facelift. The Savoy still serves her namesake dessert but Peach Melba has fallen out of favour with the masses.

LAMINGTONS

Portable, indestructible and a survivor, the lamington is a national treasure. In 1952, Mrs Ruth Baxter of Epping, NSW, wrote to the Sydney Morning Herald, "I object to paying fourpence each for unsold cakes wrapped up in coconut and called lamingtons," but half a century later lamingtons are still found at every supermarket, bakery and fundraising event in the land. The small square cake is a survivor. Like all true Australian heroes, the lamington is unpretentious, dry, and gritty, and at its most appealing when dripping with chocolate icing.

It was named after Charles Wallace Baillie, Baron Lamington, Governor of Queensland from 1896-1902, who also gave his name to a magnificent Queensland national park. Just why a square of stale cake dipped in chocolate and rolled in coconut was named after the Governor is less than clear. Perhaps he was more grateful for his accolades than Queen Victoria, who, on being invited to the opening of Victoria Mews, said, "We have no objection to being a falls, a lake, or even an orstralian state, but we are not a mews."

Would Queen Victoria be a mews if someone were to take a small block of foam rubber, coat it in chocolate sauce and hide it on the lamington plate? Australian cake lore can be tricky. Here are a few other ideas:

The Tim Tam Suck
Bite off opposing corners
Dip one corner of the biscuit in a mug of hot tea or coffee
Suck hard
Hot tea and coffee melts the cream filling and the biscuit becomes a delicious chocolate straw

Vegemite Worms
Take one Vita wheat biscuit
Spread thickly with vegemite
Sandwich second biscuit on top of the first
Squeeze hard
Watch the vegemite worms squish out

The Lamington Dunk
Take one lamington
Dunk in a mug of tea or coffee
Rush soggy cake to mouth before it falls apart
(NB if cake drops into the tea or coffee do not attempt rescue with fingers)

Serving suggestion for the over-18s:
Try dunking lamington in beer

The Mallowpuff Batter
Bash mallowpuff against the forehead to crack chocolate shell
Peel off chocolate piece by piece and eat
Suck exposed marshmallow till blob of jam appears
Lick off jam
Crunch remaining biscuit

On average, 25% of the fish you eat are raised on fish farms.

UNCLE JOHN'S LISTS

For years, the BRI has had a file full of lists. We've never been sure what to do with them—until now.

TITLES OF 4 HOLLYWOOD FILMS RE-DUBBED IN HONG KONG:

1. *Fargo:* "Mysterious Murder in Snowy Cream."
2. *The English Patient:* "Don't Ask Me Who I Am."
3. *Boogie Nights:* "His Powerful Device Makes Him Famous."
4. *Nixon:* "The Big Liar."

4 NAMES FOR THINGS YOU DIDN'T KNOW HAD NAMES

1. Aglet: "The covering on the end of a shoelace."
2. Phosphenes: "The lights you see when you close your eyes hard."
3. Kick or Punt: "The indentation at the bottom of wine bottles."
4. Harp: "The metal hoop that supports a lampshade."

2 PRESIDENTIAL SUPERSTITIONS

1. Franklin Roosevelt (1933–1945) refused to sit at a table set for 13 guests.
2. Woodrow Wilson (1913–1921) Believed 13 was his lucky number. He once ordered a ship to slow down so he would arrive in Europe on the 13th instead of the 12th.

9 BEANS THAT CAUSE THE MOST WIND

1. Soybeans
2. Pink beans
3. Black beans
4. Pinto beans
5. California small white beans
6. Great northern beans
7. Lima beans
8. Garbanzos
9. Blackeyes

—*U.S. Department of Agriculture*

3 MOST INFLUENTIAL PETS OF THE MILLENNIUM

1. Lassie
2. Snoopy
3. Arnold the Pig (from TV's *Green Acres*)

—*The American Pet Product Manufacturers Association*

5 THINGS YOU SHOULDN'T SAY WHEN A COP PULLS YOU OVER

1. "Aren't you the guy from the Village People?"
2. "That's great. The last guy only gave me a warning also."
3. "You're not gonna check the boot, are you?"
4. "Hey, you must've been

doing 100 just to keep up with me."

5. "I thought you had to be in good physical condition to be a cop."

3 REAL EXCUSES USED IN COURT

1. "I was thrown from the car as it left the road. I was later found in a ditch by some stray cows."
2. "The indirect cause of the accident was a little guy in a small car with a big mouth."
3. "To avoid hitting the bumper of the car in front, I struck the pedestrian."

TOP 5 BILLBOARD SONGS ON APRIL 5, 1964

1. "Can't Buy Me Love" (The Beatles)
2. "Twist and Shout" (The Beatles)
3. "She Loves Me" (The Beatles)
4. "I Want to Hold Your Hand" (The Beatles)
5. "Please Please Me" (The Beatles)

3 CELEBRITIES WHO SAY THEY'VE SEEN A UFO:

1. Muhmmad Ali
2. Jimmy Carter
3. William Shatner

7 WEIRD PLACE NAMES

1. Peculiar, Missouri
2. Smut Eye, Alabama
3. Loudville, Massachusetts
4. Disco, Illinois
5. Yeehaw Junction, Florida
6. Slaughter Beach, Delaware
7. Humptulips, Washington

3 MEN KNOWN BY THEIR MIDDLE NAMES

1. James Paul McCartney
2. William Clark Gable
3. Ruiz Fidel Castro

5 MOST-HATED HOUSEHOLD CHORES

1. Washing dishes
2. Bathroom cleaning
3. Ironing
4. Vacuuming
5. Washing Windows

—*Gallup Poll*

4 WORDS NOBODY USES ANYMORE

1. Podge (To walk slowly and heavily.")
2. Roinous ("Mean and nasty.")
3. Battologist ("Someone who pointlessly repeats themselves.")
4. Battologist ("Someone who pointlessly repeats themselves.")

3 MOST PRIZED AUTOGRAPHS

1. Shakespeare (6 are known to exist)
2. Christopher Columbus (8 exist)
3. Julius Caesar (None are known to exist)

JUST THE
FAX, PLEASE

*Here are a few things to think about the next time
you find yourself standing at a fax machine.*

ONE WORLD

Fax machines are so common today that it's easy to forget how rare they once were. In 1977 fax machines cost more than $20,000 each—and transmitted one blurry, hard-to-read page every six minutes.

By 1989, fax machines began changing not just the way the world did business, but perhaps even the course of history. For example:

• When Lithuania seceded from the USSR, the secessionist government bypassed Soviet censors and communicated directly with the outside world using fax machines.

• Pro-democracy demonstrators on China's Tiananmen Square used fax machines to communicate with supporters within the country and around the world.

• When Nelson Mandela, still a political prisoner in South Africa, began negotiating the terms of his release from prison, the end of apartheid, and South Africa's transition to a full democracy, he did it using a fax machine.

The fax machine revolution "makes totalitarianism impossible," says Max Kampelman, the head of Freedom House, a human rights organization. "Totalitarianism requires the total control of information. That isn't possible anymore."

FAX HISTORY

The fax machine isn't a new idea. Believe it or not, the first one—called a *pantelegraph* because it was supposed to transmit messages over telegraph lines—was patented in 1843, 33 years before Alexander Graham Bell patented the telephone. It was created by Alexander Bain, a Scottish clockmaker who envisioned using pendulums at each end of the telegraph to transmit messages, (we won't get into exactly how it worked—it's too confusing). Unfortunately, Bain never figured out how to synchronize the

In India, playing cards are round.

pendulums, and he eventually gave up.

However, in 1864 a Catholic priest named Giovanni Caselli and his partner, Gustav Froment, finally got all the bugs out of Bain's invention. Their version not only worked, it sent messages written on ordinary paper, and could send several of them simultaneously over a single wire.

The duo demonstrated their machine to Emperor Napoleon III of France—and he loved it. Under his direction, the French legislature passed a law establishing the world's first fax service between Paris and Lyons—a distance of more than 200 miles. It was inaugurated on May 16, 1865, and by 1868 it was capable of sending more than 110 telegrams an hour. But it never really had a chance to catch on with the public. The system was disrupted by war and the siege of Paris in 1870, and was never resumed.

PHOTO AGE

Over the next four or five decades, scientists worked at perfecting the technique of sending not only messages, but pictures. In 1902 a German physicist named Arthur Korn figured out how to send photo-quality images using special wires. And in 1913 Edouard Belin invented what he called a "Belinograph" (Belino for short), a portable machine, smaller than a typewriter, that could transmit photographic images over standard telephone lines.

This invention revolutionized news reporting. For the first time in history, a newspaper could send someone to any corner of the globe (or at least any corner that had telephones) and, with the portable Belino machine, get photographic images in a matter of minutes—not weeks or months as had been the case before. Invented just in time for the outbreak of World War I, the Belino had an immediate impact on wartime news coverage. By the early 1920s, it was even possible to send "wirephotos" using radio waves, eliminating the need for telephones.

MODERN FAXES

For the next 50 years, these early machines were used almost exclusively to send news pictures around the world and to transmit weather maps by radio to ships at sea. The system was too expensive and too slow to be of much interest to other types of businesses. Besides, AT&T had a monopoly on telephone service in the United States—and because they didn't manufacture fax machines, they fought to prevent customers from using telephone lines for anything other than voice. However, by the late 1960s, the FCC and the courts abolished most AT&T restrictions, opening the way for big companies like Xerox, IBM and others to create the technology that resulted in the modern fax.

MADE IN JAPAN
• Still, fax machines might never have come into widespread use were it not for the fact that the Japanese language uses thousands of characters (too many to fit on a typewriter keyboard). Typing and telexing is thus much more difficult in Japanese than it is in English.
• Japanese businessmen needed a way to send handwritten communications quickly and accurately over the telephone, so companies like Matsushita, Ricoh, Canon, and NEC spent tens of millions of dollars figuring out how to make fax machines cheaper, faster, and easier to use. They succeeded.
• Sales of fax machines boomed in Japan in the early 1980s, and by the late 1980s the fever had spread to the rest of the world. The steady decline of the price of the machines fueled the boom: by 1983 fax machines that had cost $21,000 in 1977 were selling for $2,600; by 1988 the price slipped under $1,000 for the first time, enabling millions of small business to afford them. By the mid-1990s, the price as low as $130 and most companies—even small ones—couldn't afford not to have a fax machine. Of course, now everyone needs computers and e-mail—but, that's another story.

* * * *

FAX LINGO
Fax Potato: Someone who faxes materials from one floor of a building to another, because they're too lazy to use the lift.

ZORRO

"Out of the night, when the full moon is bright, comes a horseman known as Zorro." Here's the story of how the masked man known as Zorro was created.

PULP FICTION
In 1919 a hack fiction writer name Johnston McCulley published a story called "The Curse of Capistrano" in *All-Story Weekly*, the country's premier serial fiction magazine.

The story was set in Los Angeles during the Spanish Mission period of the late 18th and early 19th centuries. The hero was Don Diego de la Vega, son of a wealthy hacienda owner—a foppish dilettante who detested violence as much as he loved poetry, intellectual pursuits, and finely tailored clothing. By night, however, Don Diego was El Zorro— "the Fox"—a sword-fighting, masked man in black who protected the helpless peasants from the territory's corrupt and greedy land barons.

THE END—AND A NEW BEGINNING
"The Curse of Capistrano" ran for five instalments. In the end, Zorro defeats his enemy and reveals his true identity to the assembled crowd, saying, "It was difficult to fool you all...and now Señor Zorro shall ride no more."

The story was over—or so McCulley thought.

Using pen names, McCulley had written hundreds of stories, featuring such characters as Captain Fly-By-Night, Señor Vulture, Señor Devil-May-Care, and Don Peon. None of these survive today, and the same fate might have befallen El Zorro if actor Douglas Fairbanks hadn't picked up a copy of *All-Story Weekly* while he was on his honeymoon in March 1920.

Fairbanks, the "King of Hollywood," was famous for his action-comedy films. They were hits at the box office, but appealed mostly to men—and in the early 1920s, afternoon matinee audiences were made up mostly of females, who preferred romances. Theatre owners complained that although Fairbanks's films packed the house in the evening, they played to empty theatres during the day.

When he read "The Curse of the Capistrano," Fairbanks

knew he'd found the role that would allow him to combine the athletics for which he was famous with romantic subplots that would bring women into the theatre. He was right.

OPENING NIGHT

The Mark of Zorro, which opened in the Capital Theatre in New York—then the world's largest movie theatre—made more money on opening day than any previous film had. The theatre was so full that the police had to be called after the 9:00 show to disperse the crowds.

The film propelled Fairbanks's career to even greater heights: by the end of 1920, he ranked higher in film popularity polls than his wife, Mary Pickford, and higher even than Charlie Chaplin. But it also made Zorro a star. Over the next 80 years, the masked avenger would make hundreds of appearances on film and TV, becoming one of the best-known and most influential icons of pop culture.

For *The Return of Zorro*, turn to page 168.

* * * *

THE TRUTH ABOUT TAROT CARDS?

Apparently, Tarot cards weren't always used to tell people's fortunes—they originally made up a game called *tarocchi* that was popular with the Italian nobility in the 15th century. *Tarocchi* was played much like bridge or whist, except that there was a fifth suit of cards which trumped all the other suits. The earliest recorded use of tarot cards in fortune telling is in Venice, Italy in 1527, but the fad didn't take off until 1781, when a French scholar proposed that cards in the deck contained the knowledge of the Egyptian hieroglyphic *Book of Thoth*, which he claimed had been saved from the ruins of sacked and burned Egyptian temples centuries earlier.

ZAP! MODERN DEBT COLLECTION

At the beginning of the 20th century, people regarded electricity as a miracle of modern science. Many imagined that by the year 2000, electricity would be used to solve every social problem. Does that seem absurd now? It's food for thought—we may be doing the same thing with contemporary scientific marvels, like computers. Here's an example of what they were thinking at the turn of the last century excerpted from Looking Forward, *a 1903 science-fiction novel by Arthur Bird.*

In 1899, the relations between creditor and debtor were not as cordial as they should be. [But that gradually changed.]

Beginning in 1930, creditors and debtors kept in closer electrical touch with one another. If the sum due was $50 or over and of long standing, the law allowed the creditor to connect his debtor with an electrical battery....If the debt was over three months due, the creditor was allowed to occasionally "touch up" his debtor without having to hunt him up. The creditor always had him "on the string" so to speak.

It was further specified by law that creditors must employ only as many volts as there were dollars due on account in shocking a debtor. These electrical shocks were merely reminders, intended to refresh the memory of the debtor. A man owing $200 was liable to receive two hundred volts until the debt was satisfied.

This plan for the collection of bad debts worked very successfully. In 1999 no debtor could tell when his creditor might touch him up. The shock reminding him of his old debt might come during the night and disturb his pleasant sleep. Perhaps while seated at the family table, or perhaps even while engaged in family worship, an electric shock might come that would raise him three feet [one metre] off the floor.

Such little occurrences were rather embarrassing, especially if the debtor was talking at the time to some lady friend. A man owing $500 was in danger of his life. His creditor was liable to dun him by giving him a shock of five hundred volts. Such sensations, certainly, are not as pleasant as watching a yacht race, with your boat an easy winner.

A curious illustration of the operation of this new condition between creditors and bad debtors came to light in a parish church on the banks of the St. Lawrence. The members of the choir were in their places, while the village school teacher stood near the communion-rail, facing the choir, with his back turned towards the empty pews. He was speaking, when suddenly his red hair stood on end, his whiskers straightened out at right angles, while his eyes looked big as door knobs. He then gave a leap in the air, turned a somersault backwards and cleared ten pews before landing again on his feet. It appears that he owed his landlord an old board bill of $120 and the latter had just given him an electrical dun. The choir was astounded at the professor's performance. The latter excused himself and merely said it was a slight attack of the "grippe."

*   *   *   *

PLANNING TO WATCH
TV TONIGHT?

The TV remote control has become a vital instrument in modern homes. According to a 1994 survey by Magnavox:

• One third of the people interviewed say that TV "wouldn't be as pleasurable" without it.
• 18 percent of women and nine percent of men would rather give up sex for a week than their remote control.
• Some 55 percent lose their remote five times a week and 63 percent spend at least five minutes a day looking for it. (Most frequent places the remote is left: under furniture, 38 percent, kitchen or bathroom, 20 percent and in the fridge, 6 percent.)
• Twice as many men lose the remote as women. And twice as many men as women get to hold the remote.

RANDOM ORIGINS

*Once again, the BRI asks—and answers—the
question: where did this stuff come from?*

GOLD RECORDS

In 1941 RCA Victor released Glenn Miller's "Chattanooga Choo Choo" after he performed it in the movie
Sun Valley Serenade. It was a huge hit: 1.2 million records were
sold in less than three months. So RCA came up with a great publicity gimmick to promote it: They sprayed one of the "master
records" with gold paint and on February 10, 1942, presented it to
Miller during a radio broadcast in honour of his selling a million
copies.

Eventually the Record Industry Association of America
(RIAA) copied the idea and started honouring million-selling
records with an official Gold Record Award.

Nobody knows for sure what the first million-selling record
was. One likely candidate: "Ragging the Baby to Sleep," recorded
by Al Jolson on April 17, 1912. (*Yankee Ingenuity*)

CIRCUS TIGHTS

"Tights are believed to have been introduced in 1828 by Nelson
Hower, a bareback rider in the Buckley and Wicks Show, as the
result of a mishap. The performers wore short jackets, knee
breeches, and stockings, but Hower's costume failed to arrive and
he appeared for the show in his long knit underwear." (*The
People's Almanac*)

KITTY LITTER

In January 1948, in Cassopolis, Michigan, a woman named Kay
Draper ran into trouble: the sandpile she used to fill her cat's litter
box was frozen solid. She tried ashes, but wound up with paw
prints all over the house. Sawdust didn't work, either.

As it happened, her neighbours, the Lowes, sold a product
called Fuller's Earth, a kiln-dried clay that was used to soak up oil
and grease spills in factories. Ed Lowe, their 27-year-old son, had
been looking for a new market for the stuff—he'd tried unsuccessfully to sell it to local farmers as nesting material for chickens. On

the spur of the moment, he convinced Draper that this stuff would make great cat litter. He really had no idea if it would—but it did! He sensed the sales potential, put some Fuller's Earth in paper bags and labelled it "Kitty Litter" with a grease pen. Then he drove around, trying to sell it. (Actually, he gave it away at first to get people to try it.) Once people tried it, they invariably came back for more.

"The success of kitty litter enabled pet owners to keep cats inside their homes with little muss or fuss (let's not discuss smell). As a result, an entire industry consisting of cat foods, toys, grooming products, and the like was launched." (*Useless Information Web site*)

RUGBY

William Webb Ellis was playing soccer at the Rugby School in Warwickshire, England, in 1823. His team was losing so badly that he grabbed the ball (a foul—in soccer, you're not allowed to touch the ball with your hands) and started running for the opposing goal. When he got close he drop-kicked the ball into the goal. The score didn't count, of course, and the captain of Ellis's team was so embarrassed that after apologizing to the officials, he suspended Ellis from the team.

The tale of "that play at Rugby" circulated for years afterward, and in 1839 Arthur Pell, the star forward of the Cambridge soccer team, drew up some rules for a new game—named after the Rugby School—that legalized holding, throwing, and running with the ball. The new sport was also the direct forerunner of American football. (Fenton & Fowler's *Best, Worst and Most Unusual*)

AEROSOL CANS

In 1943 the U.S. Agriculture Department came up with an aerosol bug bomb. It used liquid gas inside steel cans to help WWII soldiers fight malaria-causing insects (malaria was taking a heavy toll on the troops). By 1947, civilians could buy bug bombs, too, but they were heavy "grenadelike" things. Two years later, Robert H. Abplanalp developed a special "seven-part leak-proof" valve that allowed him to use lightweight aluminum instead of heavy steel, creating the modern spray can.

HOW TO MAKE A MONSTER, PART I

Godzilla is one of the most popular movie monsters in film history.
Now here's the story behind Japan's largest export.

NUCLEAR AGE

On March 1, 1954, at the Bikini atoll in the South Pacific, the United States tested the world's first hydrogen bomb. It was 1,000 times more powerful than the A-bombs that had been dropped on Hiroshima nine years earlier.

American ships were warned to stay out of the test area—but because the project was top-secret, the U.S. government provided little advance warning to other countries. U.S. officials were certain that the resulting nuclear fallout would land in an empty expanse of the Pacific Ocean and no one would be in jeopardy. Unfortunately, they were wrong. The fallout didn't travel in the direction they expected, and a small Japanese fishing boat named the *Daigo Fukuryo Maru* ("Lucky Dragon") was in the area where the nuclear cloud came to earth. Within hours of the blast, the boat's entire crew became violently ill from radiation poisoning.

On September 23, 1954, after more than six months of agony, a radioman named Aikichi Huboyama died.

The fate of the crew of the *Daigo Fukuryo Maru* made international news. In Japan, headlines like "The Second Atomic Bombing of Mankind" compared the incident to the bombing of Hiroshima and Nagasaki in 1945.

ART IMITATES LIFE

While all of this was going on, Japanese movie producer Tomoyuki Tanaka arrived in Indonesia to oversee a film called *Beyond the Glory*. It was scheduled to be the main release for Japan's Toho Studios the following year but it never got off the ground; the Indonesian government refused to issue work visas to the film's two stars.

Suddenly, Tanaka found himself with time, money, and

The Mayan Empire lasted six times as long as the Roman Empire.

actors—but no film to make. In addition, Toho Studios had a big hole in their release schedule. The producer had to come up with a new movie concept—*fast*.

On his flight back to Tokyo, Tanaka stared out the window at the ocean below, desperately trying to think of something. His mind wandered to the H-Bomb tests in the South Pacific and the crew of the *Daigo Fukuryo Maru*—and then it hit him: He would combine an American-style monster movie with a serious message about the threat of radiation and nuclear weapons tests.

PROJECT G

Commercially, it made sense. For obvious reasons, the Japanese public was very concerned about nuclear testing. And in theatres, monster movies were hot. The 1933 classic, *King Kong*, had been re-released in 1952 and made more than $3 million in international ticket sales—four times what it had earned the first time around. *Time* magazine even named the giant ape "Monster of the Year." Its huge success inspired a "monster-on-the-loose" film craze.

One of the first to cash in on the fad was *The Beast from 20,000 Fathoms*, which featured a dinosaur attacking New York City after nuclear tests awakened it from a million-year sleep. The film cost $400,000 to make and was a critical flop—but with $5 million in box office receipts, it was one of the top-grossing movies of the year.

Tanaka got approval from his studio to do a Japanese version. He hired a prominent Japanese science fiction writer to write a knock-off screenplay tentatively titled *Big Monster from 200,000 Miles Beneath the Sea*, but he still wasn't sure what kind of monster to use, or what to call it. So to start out, the film was referred to simply as "Project G" (for Giant).

A PAIR OF EXPERTS

Meanwhile, he began assembling a crew. For director, Tanaka picked Ishiro Honda, a documentary filmmaker who had been Akira Kurosawa's assistant on *The Seven Samurai* (considered the best Japanese film ever made by most critics). Like many of the Toho Studios crew, Honda was a veteran of the Imperial Army. He had visited Hiroshima several months after the atomic bomb was dropped. "When I returned from the war and passed through

Hiroshima," he told an interviewer years later, "there was a heavy atmosphere—a fear that the Earth was already coming to an end. That became my basis. Believe it or not, we naively hoped that Godzilla's death in the film was going to coincide with the end of nuclear testing."

Special effects were handled by Eiji Tsuburaya. During the war, he had made unusual propaganda films for the Imperial Army—he recreated battles in miniature, so Japanese movie audiences could follow the progress of the war. His work was so skillful that when the American occupation forces got hold of his reenactment of the bombing of Pearl Harbour, they were convinced they were watching actual combat footage. Since childhood, Eiji had dreamed of making monster movies with his miniature sets. Now he would have his opportunity.

FAT CHANCE

As it turned out, finding a name for the monster was easy. "At the time there was a big—I mean huge—fellow working in Toho's publicity department," director Ishiro Honda recalled. "Employees would argue, that guy is as big as a gorilla.' 'No, he's almost as big as a *kujira* (whale).' Over time, the two mixed and he was nicknamed Gojira' (pronounced GO-dzee-la). So when we were stuck for a name, Tanaka said, 'Hey, you know that guy over in publicity…?'"

The name *Gojira* would turn out to be a great choice, but in the beginning it was very confusing. "Very few people, even the cast, knew what Gojira would be," says actor Yoshio Tsuchiya. "Since the name was derived from *kujira* [whale] and gorilla, I imagined some kind of giant aquatic gorilla."

GETTING STARTED

Since the scenes using human actors were filmed separately from the special-effects monster footage, Honda didn't have to wait for Tanaka to work out the monster details before beginning to film.

And he didn't: "Honda would direct me to act surprised that Gojira was coming," recalled actor Yu Fujiki, who played a sailor in the film. "But since I didn't know what Gojira would look like, it was kind of weird. So I asked Honda what Gojira would be like, and he said, 'I don't know, but anyway, the monster is coming!'"

For Part II of *How to Make a Monster*, turn to page 146.

At least 8,000 human-made objects are orbiting the Earth.

DUMB CROOKS

With crooks like these, we hardly need cops.
Here's proof that crime doesn't pay.

GIVE ME ALL YOUR COUPONS

OSWEGO, New York— "His name may be Jesse James, but that's where any similarity ends. Jesse Clyde James IV was arrested last week after he used his shopper's bonus card to get a discount...just before allegedly robbing a grocery store.

"Police said James asked a market clerk if three pies would be cheaper if he used his card, police said. The clerk scanned the card. Then James and two accomplices pulled out a pellet gun and demanded money, police said. They made off with $600. James was arrested soon after."

—Medford, Oregon, *Mail Tribune*, June 8, 1999

MUG SHOT

"There are dumb criminals, and then there's the fellow who was found guilty of stealing Matthew Holden's car in London. In the glove compartment, the thief found a camera, which his girlfriend used to photograph him posing with the car in front of his own house. The vehicle was later recovered—with the camera and film still inside. Holden had it developed and brought the prints to the cops on the case...who recognized the crook, and arrested him."

—*Christian Science Monitor*, July 26, 1999

CAUGHT WITH HIS PANTS DOWN

"Knife-wielding James Boulder was caught in September 1993 when his [pants] fell down as he fled from a store in New Jersey that he'd just robbed. He then tripped over a fire hydrant and knocked himself out."

—The *Fortean Times* Book *Inept Crime*

DUMB AND UNLUCKY

CARDIFF, Wales— "Mark Cason, 29, decided to rob a local post office. He purchased gloves and a mask but forgot to put them on....

"Mark took more than $15,000 worth of British pounds, but his arms were so full he could not open the post office door to leave. So he asked two children to hold the door for him. They did, and jotted down his car licence number as he pulled into traffic.

"Mark promptly got stuck in a traffic jam, so he ran to a train station, where he caught a train to a nearby town. He checked into a hotel using a fake name and said to the clerk, 'If the police ask for me, I'm not here.' He asked if he could put 'a large amount of money' in the hotel safe.

"When police arrived, Mark told them his occupation was 'armed robber.' He was sentenced to five years in prison."

—*The Portland Oregonian*

NO ANCHOVIES, PLEASE
"Christopher Kennedy, 36, and Johnny Poston, 26, allegedly ordered a couple of pizzas using their real names, phone number and home address. When the delivery man had trouble finding their house, he called and arranged to meet the two men nearby.

"The delivery person got out carrying the pizzas and they put a gun to his face,' Lt. Julius Lee said. 'So the delivery person threw the pizzas at them, got back in his car and drove off.' He called the police, who had no problem finding the correct house. The pair was charged with armed robbery."

—*Dumb Crooks Web site*

HOW 'BOUT A BREAKFAST BURRITO?
YPSILANTI, Michigan— "The Ann Arbor News reported that a man failed to rob a Burger King because the clerk told him he couldn't open the cash register without a food order. So the man ordered onion rings, but the clerk informed him that they weren't available for breakfast. The frustrated robber left."

—*A Treasury of Police Humour*

RIGHTEOUSLY INDIGNANT
"A robbery suspect in a Los Angeles police lineup apparently just couldn't control himself. When detectives asked each man in the lineup to repeat the words, 'Give me all your money or I'll shoot,' the man shouted *'That's not what I said!'*"

—*The Edge*, April 12, 1999

VIDEO TREASURES

Ever found yourself at a video store staring at thousands of films you've never heard of, wondering which ones are worth watching? It happens to us all the time—so we decided to offer a few recommendations.

CHAN IS MISSING (1982) *Comedy (B&W)*
Review: "Two cab drivers try to find the man who stole their life savings. Wry, low-budget comedy filmed in San Francisco's Chinatown was an art-house smash. The first full-length American film produced exclusively by an Asian-American crew." *(VideoHound's Golden Movie Retriever) Director:* Wayne Wang.

THE YEAR OF LIVING DANGEROUSLY (1983) *Drama*
Review: "Indonesia, 1965: In the middle of revolutionary fervor, a wet-behind-the-ears reporter and a member of the British Embassy find steamy romance. This politically charged, mega-atmospheric winner has the romance and intrigue of a modern *Casablanca*." *(Seen That, Now What?) Stars:* Sigourney Weaver, Mel Gibson, Linda Hunt (won an Oscar for the role). *Director:* Peter Weir.

THE BIG SLEEP (1946) *Mystery*
Review: "One of the most stylish and satisfying film noir mysteries of the '40s. Lauren Bacall is at her sexiest and Humphrey Bogart is at his peak. The plot is exquisitely intricate, so don't blink— and DON'T MISS THIS MOVIE. The atmosphere and dialogue are impeccable." *(Mark Satern's Illustrated Guide to Video's Best)*

EUROPA, EUROPA (1991) *French-German/Drama*
Review: "Based on the death-defying autobiography of Solomon Perel, this stunning film traces the author's real-life adventures during World War II. A Jewish teenager accepted into the Nazi Youth Party, Perel sees the war from all sides in this ironic, spine-tingling story." *(Video Movie Guide) Director:* Agnieszka Holland

CHASING AMY (1997) *Romantic Comedy*
Review: "Winning, original comedy-drama about a comic book artist who lives with his dour work partner—until he meets an attractive up-and-coming female artist with a dynamic personality. He's seriously smitten—and stays that way even after learning that

An ergasiophobe is someone who's afraid of work.

she's gay. Writer-director Kevin Smith hits all the right notes in this honest and appealing film, which refuses to take the easy way out (just like his lead character) right to the end." (Leonard Maltin's 1998 *Movie and Video Guide*) Stars: Ben Affleck, Joey Lauren Adams.

THE MAN WHO SHOT LIBERTY VALANCE (1962) *Western*
Review: "One of the greatest of director John Ford's westerns, a moving, bitter meditation of immortality and survival. Jimmy Stewart is cast as an idealistic lawyer who becomes famous for killing a notorious badman, played by Lee Marvin. John Wayne incarnates his own with subtle melancholy." *(Movies on TV)*

TAMPOPO (1986) *Japanese/Social comedy*
Review: "The tale of a Japanese widow who perfects the art of making noodles under the instruction of an urban cowboy truck driver is cleverly interspersed with amusing vignettes about food and social pretension. Funny, enjoyable, and you'll find yourself craving a bowl of hot ramen." *(Seen That, Now What?) Director:* Juzo Itami.

THE EMERALD FOREST (1985) *Adventure*
Review: "Captivating adventure about a young boy who is kidnapped by a primitive tribe of Amazons while his family is travelling through the Brazilian jungle. Boothe is the father who searches 10 years for him. An engrossing look at tribal life in the vanishing jungle. Beautifully photographed and based upon a true story." *(VideoHound's Golden Movie Retriever) Director:* John Boorman.

A GREAT WALL (1986) *Comedy*
Review: "A warm comedy about the clash of cultures that results when a Chinese-American family returns to its homeland. It is the first American movie to be made in the People's Republic of China. As such, it gives some fascinating insights into Chinese culture and often does so in a marvellously entertaining way." *(Video Movie Guide) Director/Star:* Peter Wang.

THE NASTY GIRL (1990) *German/Drama*
Review: "A teenage girl innocently decides to write about 'My Town in the Third Reich'…and her research reveals the truth behind the good citizens' official story. Based on a true story." *(Seen That, Now What?) Director:* Michael Verhoeven.

"SPEAK FOR YOURSELF, JOHN!"

Ever let someone speak for you? Sometimes it works, sometimes it doesn't. The other day Uncle John was in the—uh—reading room with nothing but a book of poetry. He opened it to Longfellow's "The Courtship of Myles Standish," and emerged wondering out loud how often "that sort of thing" happened. We took the hint and began looking for examples. Here's what we found.

MARRIAGE PROPOSAL

Who Said It: John Alden
Speaking For: Myles Standish

What Happened: As military leader of the pilgrims, Capt. Myles Standish was fearless. With ladies, however, he was the opposite. Standish was so afraid of expressing his love to Priscilla Mullens that he asked his young friend Alden to do it for him. The only problem: Alden was also in love with Mullens. Nonetheless, he went off to proclaim Standish's love to the woman, keeping his own a secret.

As it happened, Mullens harboured her own secret feelings for Alden. When Alden delivered Standish's proposal instead, legend has it she replied, "Why don't you speak for yourself, John?" Note: Mullens married Alden. Standish supposedly went into the woods for a few days and sulked. He eventually got over it.

HISTORIC SPEECH

Who Said It: Norman Shelley
Speaking For: Winston Churchill

What Happened: A week after the demoralizing defeat of British and French troops by Germany at Dunkirk in 1940, Prime Minister Winston Churchill made one of the most stirring radio addresses in history. Speaking to the English public, he declared, in no uncertain terms, that the British would not fold.
We shall fight on the beaches, we shall fight on the landing grounds, we shall fight in the fields and in the streets, we shall fight in the hills; we shall never surrender.

48% of men think balding has a negative effect on business and social relationships.

Historians say that this specific speech provided the morale boost that helped England summon the strength to continue the war effort—and ultimately win.

But Churchill didn't make the speech. He was "too busy to appear on the radio," so he asked Shelley to fill in—an actor who had perfected the Churchillian delivery to such a degree that few people could pick which voice was Shelley's and which was Churchill's.

PRESIDENTIAL QUOTE
Who Said It: Larry Speakes
Speaking For: President Ronald Reagan
What Happened: In 1985 President Reagan and Soviet premier Mikhail Gorbachev met for a summit in Reykjavik, Iceland. Afterward, Speakes told the press that Reagan had declared to the Russian: "There is much that divides us, but I believe the world breathes easier because we are talking together."

In truth, Reagan hadn't said it—or anything Speakes considered worth quoting that day. So the press secretary made it up. No one at the White House objected at the time. But when Speakes later admitted it in his 1988 book *Speaking Out,* all hell broke loose. The press was "outraged," and Reagan (who had to have at least implicitly condoned it at the time) strongly condemned the quotes as "fiction." Speakes paid for it: he was pressured to resign his job as senior public relations officer at Merrill Lynch, which had hired him after he left the White House. Speakes later apologized publicly for his "mistake."

PHILOSOPHICAL RAMBLINGS
Who Said It: Yoda
Speaking For: Obi-Wan-Kenobi (Alec Guinness)
What Happened: On the set of *The Empire Strikes Back,* Alec Guinness had an easy way of avoiding dialogue he didn't feel comfortable saying. Yoda was in nearly all of his scenes, so "if he didn't want to deliver one of his philosophical speeches," Dale Pollock writes in *Skywalking,* "he'd say to the director, 'Why doesn't the little green thing do this one?'" And Lucas would accommodate him.

The average American dog will cost its owner $14,600 over its lifetime.

CLASSIC HOAXES

The BRI library has a whole section of books on hoaxes and frauds. We've noticed that there are a few dozen hoaxes that appear in almost every book that set the standard for all hoaxers to come. Here are two of our favourites.

THE MANHATTAN ISLAND HOAX

Background: In 1824 a well-known retired carpenter and charismatic speaker named Lozier stood on a soapbox in Manhattan's busy Centre Market and announced to the crowd that because of all the buildings recently constructed, the southern tip of Manhattan Island had become too heavy and was in danger of sinking. The solution, he said, was to saw the island off at the northern end, tow it out to sea, turn it 180 degrees around, and reattach it.

Lozier claimed, that sawing Manhattan Island in half would be one of the biggest public works projects New York had ever seen, and that Mayor Stephen Allen had put him in charge of the project.

The idea sounded preposterous to most of Lozier's listeners; but then again, so had the Erie Canal, and that wonder of the world was nearly finished, wasn't it? Besides, if it wasn't true, why would he publicly declare that the mayor had authorized him to handle the project?

What Happened: Lozier began signing up hundreds of labourers for the task, offering triple wages to anyone willing to saw underwater. He directed blacksmiths and carpenters to begin designing the 30-metre [100-foot] saws and 76-metre [250-foot] oars needed to saw the island and row it out to sea. He also arranged for the construction of barracks and a mess halls for his labourers, and the delivery of 500 cattle, 500 pigs, and 3,000 chickens, so his workers would have plenty to eat.

After two months of planning, the date arrived for construction to begin. Scores of labourers, carpenters, blacksmiths, butchers, and animals—as well as a marching band and hundreds of onlookers—arrived at Spring Street and Bowery to see the historic project get underway. About the only people who didn't show up were Lozier and his accomplices, who'd suddenly left town "on

---

When it was introduced in 1848, the modern golf ball was called a "gutta-percha" ball.

account of their health."

They were actually holed up in Brooklyn, and although there was talk of having them arrested, Alexander Klein writes in *Grand Deception*, "no one seemed willing to make a complaint to the authorities or admit that he had been duped, and Lozier went scot-free."

THE WILD ANIMAL HOAX

Background: On November 9, 1874, subscribers to the *New York Herald* opened their morning papers to read an eyewitness account of the "escape" the night before of every wild animal from the Central Park Zoo. According to the *Herald* article, 49 people had been killed by the rampaging beasts, 200 more had been injured, and a Who's Who of New York notables, including future president Chester A. Arthur, were hunting the animals up and down Broadway and Fifth Avenue. At least a dozen of the animals were still at large, the story reported, the mayor had declared a "state of siege," and "all citizens, except members of the National Guard, are enjoined to keep within their houses or residences until the wild animals at large are captured and killed."

What Happened: "Much of the life of the city came to an abrupt halt," Carl Sifakis writes in *Hoaxes and Scams*, "and few ventured out, most cowering behind furniture that barricaded home doors and windows." Even James Gordon Bennett, owner of the *New York Herald*, collapsed in bed upon reading his own newspaper's story, and stayed there for the rest of the day. The *Herald's* war correspondent, George Hosmer, showed up in the newsroom with two large Navy revolvers shouting, "Well, here I am."

What Bennett, Hosmer, and tens of thousands of other *Herald* subscribers failed to do that morning was read the story to the very end—where, in the last paragraph, managing editor Thomas Connery revealed that the story was "a huge hoax, a wild romance, or what ever epithet of utter untrustworthiness our readers may care to apply to it." Connery's motive for publishing the story: to "direct attention to the zoo's shortcomings," so that such escapes might never happen in the future. (So far, they haven't.)

More hoaxes on page 210.

The average car in Japan is driven 4,400 miles a year. In the U.S., it's 9,500 miles a year.

A BRIEF HISTORY OF BUGS BUNNY

Who's your favourite cartoon character? Ear's ours.

IMPRESSIVE STATS
Bugs Bunny is the world's most popular rabbit:
• Since 1939, he has starred in more than 175 films.
• He's been nominated for three Oscars, and won one—in 1958, for "Knighty Knight, Bugs" (with Yosemite Sam).
• Every year from 1945 to 1961, he was voted "top animated character" by movie theatre owners (when they still showed cartoons in theatres).
• In 1985 he became only the 2nd cartoon character to be given a star on the Hollywood Walk of Fame (Mickey Mouse was the first).
• For almost 30 years, starting in 1960, he had one of the top-rated shows on Saturday-morning TV.
• In 1976, when researchers polled Americans on their favourite characters, real and imaginary, Bugs came in second—behind Abraham Lincoln.

THE INSPIRATIONS
Bugs was born in the 1930s, but cartoon historians say his ancestry goes further back. A few direct descendents:
• Zomo. You may not have heard of this African folk-rabbit, but he's world-famous. Joe Adamson writes in *Bugs Bunny: Fifty Years and Only One Grey Hare:*

> Like jazz and rock 'n' roll, Bugs has at least some of his roots in black culture. Zomo is the trickster rabbit from Central and Eastern Africa who gained audience sympathy by being smaller than his oppressors and turning the tables on them through cleverness—thousands of years before Eastman invented film. A con artist, a masquerader, ruthless and suave, in control of the situation. Specialized in impersonating women.

• Br'er Rabbit. Slaves brought Zomo to America and in the New World, he became Br'er Rabbit, whose stories were retold by Joel

Chandler Harris in *Tales of Uncle Remus* (1880). Typical plot: Br'er Fox catches Br'er Rabbit, who begs not to be thrown in the briar-patch (which is exactly where he wants to go). Br'er Fox falls for it, tosses him in, and the rabbit laughs all the way home. Occasionally, you'll see Bugs pull the same trick.

Closer to home, a few comedic geniuses helped mould Bugs:
• Charlie Chaplin. "It was Chaplin who established that 'gestures and actions expressing attitude' give a screen character life," Adamson writes. The Looney Tunes directors, all fans of Chaplin, even stole many of his gags. For example:

> The abrupt and shocking kiss Charlie plants [on] someone who's getting too close for comfort in *The Floorwalker* went on to become one of Bugs' favourite ways to upset his adversaries. [And] the walking broomstick in *Bewitched Bunny* does Chaplin's trademark turn, with one foot in the air, at every corner.

There are literally dozens of other Chaplin rip-offs. Bugs also lifted bits from silent comedians Harold Lloyd and Buster Keaton.
• Groucho Marx. "Bugs uses his carrot as a prop, just as Groucho used his cigar," points out Stefan Kanfer in *Serious Business*. "Eventually Bugs even stole Marx's response to an insult: 'Of course you know, this means war!'"

TIMELINE

1937: Warner Bros. animation director Tex Avery makes "Porky's Duck Hunt." Porky Pig hunted a screwball duck named Daffy—"who didn't get scared and run away when somebody pointed a gun at him, but leapt and hopped all over the place like a maniac." "When it hit the theatres," recalls another director, "it was like an explosion."

1938: Warner Bros. director Ben "Bugs" Hardaway remakes the cartoon with a rabbit instead of a duck, as "Porky's Hare Hunt." Says one of Bugs's creators: "That rabbit was just Daffy Duck in a rabbit suit."

1939: Bugs Hardaway decides to remake "Porky's Hare Hunt" with a new rabbit (as "Hare-um Scare-um"). Cartoonist Charlie Thorson comes up with a grey and white rabbit with large buck teeth. He labels his sketches "Bugs' Bunny."

1940: Director Tex Avery becomes the real father of Bugs Bunny

---

General Dwight Eisenhower owned a pair of pajamas with five stars on the lapels.

with "A Wild Hare." Bugs is changed from a Daffyesque lunatic to a streetsmart wiseass. "We decided he was going to be a smart-aleck rabbit, but casual about it," Avery recalled. "His opening line was 'What's up, Doc?' It floored 'em!…Here's a guy with a gun in his face!…They expected the rabbit to scream, or anything but make a casual remark….It got such a laugh that we said, 'Let's use that every chance we get.' It became a series of 'What's Up, Docs?' That set his entire character. He was always in command, in the face of all types of dangers."

• Bugs also gets his voice in "A Wild Hare." Mel Blanc, who did most Looney Tunes voices, had been having a hard time finding one for the rabbit—until Bugs Hardaway showed him the latest sketch for "A Wild Hare." Blanc wrote:

> He'd obviously had some work done. His posture had improved, he'd shed some weight, and his protruding front teeth weren't as pronounced. The most significant change, however, was in his facial expression. No longer just goofy, he was a sly looking rascal.

"A tough little stinker, ain't he?" Hardaway commented—and the light went on in Blanc's brain.

> A tough little stinker….In my mind I heard a Brooklyn accent…. To anyone living west of the Hudson River at that time, Brooklynites were associated with con artists and crooks….Consequently, the new, improved Bugs Bunny wouldn't say jerk, he'd say joik.

• The rabbit is now so popular that he needs a name. According to some sources, he is about to be dubbed "Happy Rabbit." Tex Avery wants "Jack E. Rabbit." But when Thorson's year-old drawing labeled "Bugs' Bunny" is turned up, producer Leon Schlessinger chooses that. Avery hates it. "That's sissy," he complains. "Mine's a rabbit. A tall, lanky, mean rabbit. He isn't a fuzzy little bunny!" But the name sticks.

1941: Bugs Bunny becomes competitive. Four extremely talented directors—Avery, Friz Freleng, Bob Clampett, and Chuck Jones—try to top each other with new gags and aspects of Bugs's personality. It's the key to the character's success—he's constantly growing. "As each director added new levels to this character," Adamson explains, "it was picked up by the others and became a part of the mix."

1943: Animator Robert McKimson (later a director himself), working for Bob Clampett, refines Bugs's features into what they are today. "We made him cuter, brought his head and cheeks out a little more and gave him just a little nose," McKimson says. He looks more "elfin" and less "ratlike" now.

1945: During World War II, Bugs has become a "sort of national mascot." Critic Richard Schickel writes: "In the war years, when he flourished most gloriously, Bugs Bunny embodied the cocky humour of a nation that had survived its economic crisis [in surprisingly good shape], and was facing a terrible war with grace, gallantry, humour and solidarity that was equally surprising." By the end of the war, Bugs isn't just a cartoon character, but an American icon.

BUGS FACTS

Saved by a Hare. The inspiration for the original rabbit came from Walt Disney. In 1935 Disney put out a cartoon featuring a character called Max Hare. Hardaway's rabbit looks suspiciously like Max.

Trademarks. Where did Bugs's carrot-crunching and "What's up, Doc?" come from? No one's sure, but experts have suggested they might have been inspired by a couple of popular films:

• In Frank Capra's 1934 Oscar-winning comedy, *It Happened One Night*, Clark Gable nervously munches on carrots.

• In the classic 1939 screwball comedy *My Man Godfrey*, William Powell uses the line "What's up, Duke?" repeatedly.

On the other hand, Tex Avery had a habit of calling everyone Doc—so he may have inspired the phrase. (Mel Blanc also claims in his autobiography that he ad-libbed the line, but he seems to take credit for everything—so we don't believe him.)

Tough Act. Blanc, Bugs's voice, says that recording the "What's up, Doc?" line turned out to be the most physically challenging part of doing the voice:

> "What's up, Doc?" was incomplete without the sound
> of the rabbit nibbling on the carrot, which presented
> problems. First of all, I don't especially like carrots, at
> least not raw. [Ed note: In another BR, we erroneously
> reported that he was allergic to carrots. Oops.] And
> second, I found it impossible to chew, swallow, and be
> ready to say my next line. We tried substituting other

vegetables, including apples and celery, but with unsatisfactory results. The solution was to stop recording so that I could spit out the carrot into the wastebasket and then proceed with the script. In the course of a recording session I usually went through enough carrots to fill several wastebaskets. Bugs Bunny did for carrots what Popeye the Sailor did for spinach. How many…children were coerced into eating their carrots by mothers cooing… "but Bugs Bunny eats his carrots." If only they had known.

Eat Your Veggies. Actually, there were pressures to switch from carrots. "The Utah Celery Company of Salt Lake City offered to keep all the studio's staffers well supplied with their product if Bugs would only switch from carrots to celery," Adamson reports. "[And] later, the Broccoli Institute of America strongly urged The Bunny to sample their product once in a while….Mel Blanc would have been happy to switch…but carrots were Bugs's trademark."

Surprise Hit. To his creators, Bugs Bunny was just another character that would probably run in a few cartoons and fade unnoticed into obscurity. "We didn't feel that we had anything," Avery recounted years later, "until we got it on the screen and it got a few laughs. After we ran it and previewed it and so forth, Warners liked it, the exhibitors liked it, and so of course [the producer] ran down and said, 'Boy, give us as many of those as you can!' Which we did."

Bugs Bunny became so popular with the public that he got laughs even when he didn't deserve them. "He could do no wrong," remembers dialogue writer Michael Maltese. "We had quite a few lousy Bugs Bunnies. We'd say, 'Well we haven't got time. Let's do it.' And we'd do it, and the audience would laugh. They loved that rabbit."

* * * *

LOONEY TRIVIA

• The name "Looney Tunes" is a takeoff on Walt Disney's popular 1930s cartoon series, "Silly Symphonies."

• The real name of the Looney Tunes theme song is "The Merry-Go-Round Broke Down." It's a pop tune from the 1930s.

• The first Looney Tune, "Sinking in the Bathtub," appeared in 1930. It featured a character called Bosko.

LIFE AFTER DEATH

What do Sherlock Holmes, Davy Crockett, and Superman have in common? They were all popular characters whose creators killed them off—and then had to bring them back from the dead.

S HERLOCK HOLMES
Born: 1887 — Died: 1893 — Resurrected: 1903

Background: Sherlock Holmes first appeared in 1887 but didn't become famous until 1891, when "A Scandal in Bohemia" was published in London's *Strand* magazine. Overnight, Holmes and his creator, Arthur Conan Doyle, became national celebrities.

Over the next two years, Doyle turned out an average of one new story per month. But the more popular Holmes became, the less Doyle liked him. Doyle considered his historical novels to be his real work and felt that Holmes kept people from appreciating them. By 1893, Doyle loathed the detective.

Untimely Death: In 1893, at the end of *Strand's* 24th Holmes story, Doyle placed Holmes on top of Switzerland's Reichenbach Falls, grappling with his arch-enemy, Professor Moriarty. Then he had both characters plunge to their deaths.

The author gleefully wrote to his mother: "The gentleman vanishes, never to return!" But others weren't so happy. Twenty thousand *Strand* readers (an enormous number for the time) cancelled their subscriptions; businessmen in London wore black bands to mourn Holmes's death; Doyle was inundated with letters. But he was unmoved, and snapped: "Holmes is at the bottom of Reichenbach Falls, and there he stays."

Resurrection: What could change Doyle's mind? Money. In 1903 *McClure's* (a U.S. magazine) offered him the astronomical sum of $5,000 dollars per story if he would resurrect the character—and *Strand* offered more than half that for the British publication rights. Doyle decided to "accept as much money as slightly deranged editors were willing to pay." Soon after, excited readers learned that Holmes hadn't died after all; he had merely gone into hiding.

The publisher couldn't print copies of the new Holmes stories fast enough. People waited in huge lines and mobbed bookstalls to get them. Doyle continued writing about Sherlock Holmes until 1927, then retired the detective for good.

DAVY CROCKETT
Born: December 15, 1954 — Died: February 23, 1955
Resurrected: November 16, 1955

Background: Walt Disney's first TV program, *Disneyland*, debuted in October 1954. A few months later, it featured TV's first miniseries—a three-part adventure about a real-life Tennessee politician and frontiersman named Davy Crockett (see page 169 for more about him). The Disney version was mostly fiction, but America took it to heart. One critic recalls, "Disney's Crockett instantly became the most popular hero television had ever seen. Just about every boy in the country owned a coonskin cap like Davy's." Coonskin caps sold so quickly that raccoons actually became hard to find—forcing hat makers to use foxes and rabbits instead. All Crockett items—colouring books, play sets, bubblegum cards, etc.—sold like wildfire. It was TV's first huge, merchandising fad, and it was making Disney a fortune.

Untimely Death: There was just one problem—when the three episodes had been filmed months earlier, no one at Disney had a clue the public would respond so enthusiastically. So they followed Crockett's standard biography, and killed him off at the end of the third episode (while defending the Alamo). Uncle Walt couldn't believe the blunder. "We had one of the biggest hits in television history," he moaned, "and there we were with a dead hero."

Resurrection: "This was the first time that a major hero had died in a television series," writes Jeff Rovin in The Great TV Heroes, "and many youngsters went into mourning for the noble warrior.

More important, however, is the way in which television and the profit incentive were able to conquer death! Disney was not so foolish as to let a financial giant stay long expired."

The company went to work on new episodes, which they set before the Alamo. But it took too long to produce them. "We tried to come back with two more called *The Legend of Davy Crockett*," Walt Disney told a reporter, "but by that time the fever

Insect rule of thumb: Drunk ants always fall over on their right side.

had run its course." The King of the Wild Frontier returned on November 16, 1955, in *Davy Crockett's Keelboat Race* and December 14, 1955, in *Davy Crockett and the River Pirates*.

"Those two never did catch on the way the original three did," Disney sighed. After that, Crockett stayed dead.

SUPERMAN
Born: 1938 — Died: November 18, 1992 — Resurrected: 1993

Background: DC Comics' Superman was the nation's first superhero. He was introduced in 1938, took the nation by storm, and over the next three decades, became the most successful comic book character in history.

Untimely Death: By the 1990s, comics had changed. They featured complex heroes who were tormented by angst and who killed their foes in vengeful bloodbaths. Comic fans delighted in "the smart-aleck snarl of Wolverine," and "the devilish depravity of Spawn." But Superman never killed his enemies; he preferred to turn them over to the proper authorities. Fans found his patriotism and politeness—boring. Superman's comic sales "plummeted faster than a speeding bullet," so DC Comics made plans to kill him.

The impending death was nationwide news. Social commentators lamented a society that could no longer find interest in a "decent" hero. Comic stores played up the hype, flying flags with the Superman "S" dripping blood, displaying Superman art, and having the "Death" issue delivered in hearses. Sales of Superman skyrocketed, but after a few issues that explored the world without Superman, DC stopped publishing the title.

Resurrection: But not for long. It turned out that Superman's death was a publicity stunt. Only four months later, the Superhero was back in a new form. It turned out his dead body had been taken to a space-age "regeneration centre," which brought him back to life. Buyers of the "Death" issue who thought they were getting a collector's item were outraged, and loyal fans resented DC's toying with them. But the publicity did increase sales, at least temporarily—leading DC's executive editor Mike Carlin to happily proclaim death "good for Superman."

The islands of Antigua and Barbuda issued Elle Macpherson postage stamps in 1999.

UNFINISHED MASTERPIECES

Uncle John was chatting by e-mail with BRI stalwart Jack Mingo, and this topic came up. "How many are there, do you think?" Uncle John asked—and Mingo sent back a list that was so long, he probably still hasn't finished it. Here are our favourites—so far.

THE UNFINISHED SYMPHONY. Composed by Franz Schubert, this is perhaps the most famous unfinished modern masterpiece. Ironically, no one is sure if it really is unfinished.

Background: Schubert grew up in early 19th-century Vienna. He was a prodigy who could dash off brilliant songs on the back of envelopes, but his genius was unrecognized. He was never able to attract the patronage that would have enabled him to concentrate exclusively on music—so he never heard many of his own works performed by a full orchestra (or even by professional musicians). He died of venereal disease in 1828, at age 31.

Unfinished Masterpiece: By 1865 Schubert was recognized as a master. A group of his ardent fans (The Schubert Society) heard a rumour that an old lawyer acquaintance of Schubert's had a copy of a lost symphony—and it turned out to be true. The piece was Schubert's *Eighth Symphony*, written in 1822. He had submitted it to an orchestra called the *Gesellschaft der Musikfreunde*, asking them to perform it. When it was rejected, he sent it to the lawyer—who held onto it for over 40 years. At the fans' request, he dug out the symphony— "but it was soon clear that the two last movements were missing. Only the first three bars of the third movement were found." What makes this particularly frustrating for music-lovers is that the symphony is generally considered Schubert's best work.

Update: The Schubert Society begged the lawyer to find the rest, but he insisted he'd only received two movements. True? Maybe. There are three theories:

1. Schubert wrote the first two movements as a sampler to see if any orchestrsa would be interested, then never bothered finishing.

The Tour de France bicycle race is 2,300 miles long.

2. The last movement was incorporated into one of Schubert's later works.

3. The second half had to have been lost. Potential proof: The last page of the second movement was not blank— three bars of the third movement were at the bottom of the page, "strongly implying that it continued…somewhere," explains one Schubert expert. "Since then, a sketchbook apparently containing 250 bars of the third movement has been discovered. Fans hope that the rest of the papers are in an attic somewhere, waiting to be found."

KUBLA KHAN. By Samuel Taylor Coleridge. One of the best-known poems in the English language, notorious as an unfinished piece because of the explanation Coleridge gave for not completing it.

Background: Coleridge was sedated with opium and recovering from an illness one summer day in 1797 when he nodded off reading a book called *Purchas's Pilgrimage*. The last sentence he read before falling asleep was "Here the Khan Kubla commanded a palace to be built, and a stately garden thereunto. And thus ten miles of fertile ground were enclosed with a wall."

Coleridge said that he slept deeply for about three hours, during which he dreamed a complete 200- to 300-line poem about Khan.

Unfinished Masterpiece: When he awoke, Coleridge immediately started putting the words on paper. He had written the first 40 lines or so when a knock came at the door. But instead of sending his visitor away (some accounts say it was a salesman)—or refusing to answer the door altogether—Coleridge chatted for over an hour.

On his return to his room, Coleridge wrote, he found, to his "surprise and mortification, that though [I] still retained some vague and dim recollection of the general purport of the vision, with the exception of some eight or ten scattered lines and images, all the rest had passed away!" He managed to put a total of 54 lines to paper, but that was it—the rest of his 300-line poem was lost forever.

Update: Today scholars question whether Coleridge was being honest about his unfinished work. It's possible he simply wasn't sure what to write next, and never got around to working it out.

SPECIAL UNDERWEAR

*At the BRI, we don't believe in keeping underwear innovations
under cover. Here are three to take us into the future.*

SAFETY FIRST

"A Vermont inventor has figured out a way to prevent
senior citizens from breaking bones when they take a spill:
underwear air bags. Carl Clark, who also devised the first air bags
for Lockheed Martin in the 1960s, says his emergency underwear
has a sensor that automatically inflates two cushions around the
wearer's hips when it detects the person starting to fall."

—*Los Angeles Times*

LARGER THAN LIFE

"A Tokyo man made international news recently when his inflatable underpants accidentally went off in the subway. He had
invented the special underwear to allay his phobia of drowning.
The good news is, they worked, inflating to 30 times their normal
size. They had to be stabbed with a pencil to stop them from
crushing other passengers."

—*The Edge*

THE ARMAGEDDON BRA

Nostradamus' prophecies are popular in Japan; millions there
believed his prophecy that a terrible calamity would strike in July
1999—a war that would kill a third of the world's population. One
company decided to take advantage of this, as the *Times of London*
reported:

"Now the lingerie firm, Triumph International Japan, is
cashing in on the nation's doomsday boom with a hi-tech
'Armageddon Bra' that alerts its wearer to incoming missiles."

"Presented at a fashion show yesterday, the 'Armageddon Bra'
includes a sensor on the shoulder strap, and a control box to warn
of objects falling from the skies."

"Ideally the Armageddon Bra should be worn without outer
garments to work efficiently."

—*The Times of London*

When it was invented in India, badminton was known as poona.

MY BODY LIES OVER THE OCEAN

This section was inspired by an article in Harper's *about the fact that Albert Einstein's brain was removed when he died. We at the BRI wondered if other famous people "lost" a body part or two when they died. We did a little research—and were surprised by what we found.*

GALILEO'S MIDDLE FINGER

Where It's Located: Museum of the History of Science, Florence, Italy

How It Got There: In 1737, when Galileo's body was being moved from a storage closet to its final resting place in a mausoleum in the church of Santa Croce, a nobleman named Anton Francesco Gori cut off three fingers from Galileo's right hand for a souvenir. The middle finger was eventually acquired by the Museum of the History of Science; the other two surviving fingers "are in a private collection."

NAPOLEON'S "NOBLE ORGAN"

Where It's Located: Columbia University's College of Physicians and Surgeons

How It Got There: In 1828 Abbé Ange Paul Vignali, the priest who administered last rites to Napoléon in 1821, was murdered. Among the many Napoleonic souvenirs found in Abbé Vignali's personal effects was the most personal effect of all—a tiny, "unpleasant looking piece of desiccated tissue" alleged to be Napoleon's private part—which was supposedly removed from the deposed emperor's corpse following his autopsy.

The artifact remained in the Vignali family until 1916, when it was sold to a London dealer of rare books. In 1924 it was sold to Dr. Abraham Rosenbach, who placed the withered item "inside a glass casket, in a tasteful case of blue morocco leather and velvet bearing Napoleon's crest," where it was displayed to friends, family, and just about anyone else who asked to see it. "Few so intimate portions of a man's anatomy," Rosenbach's biographer writes, "have ever been displayed to so many."

On average, the Statue of Liberty's fingernails weigh 100 lbs. apiece.

In November 1944, the "shriveled short arm,"—which by now was said to look like "a maltreated strip of buckskin shoelace, or a shriveled eel"—was sold to a Philadelphia autograph dealer named Bruce Gimelson. He tried to auction it at Christie's, but withdrew it when it "failed to attract a $40,000 minimum bid." Seven years later, he sold it to a urologist named John K. Lattimer for a mere $3,000. Dr. Lattimer owns it to this day, and it's only one of the many odd but historically significant items in his collection. As Harvey Rachlin reports in *Lucy's Bones, Sacred Stones, and Einstein's Brain*, Dr. Lattimer also owns "Hermann Goering's suicide capsule container, a lock of Hitler's hair, and the nooses used to hang two of the conspirators for the murder of President Lincoln, Mary Surratt and Lewis Powell."

EINSTEIN'S BRAIN
Where It's Located: Lawrence, Kansas
How it Got There: When Einstein died in April 1955, he left a request that his friend and colleague Dr. Harry Zimmerman examine his brain. So Dr. Thomas Harvey, the pathologist who performed the autopsy on Einstein, removed the brain and had it cut into 200 pieces, some of which he gave to Zimmerman. The rest (representing about 75% of Einstein's brain) he took home and stored in formaldehyde-filled jars that he kept under his sink for nearly 40 years—occasionally doling out specimens to brain researchers upon request. (One such researcher keeps his section in his refrigerator, in a jar marked "Big Al's Brain.")
At last report, Harvey, who'd lost his medical licence and was working in a plastics factory, was looking for a research lab or some other institution to take possession of Einstein's brain and preserve it for posterity.

PHAR LAP'S HEART
Where It's Located: National Museum, Canberra
How It Got There: Phar Lap was one of the greatest racehorses of all time. He was born in New Zealand in 1926 and sold for the bargain price of 160 guineas ($336.00). He was sent to Australia and soon became a racing legend by winning 37 out of his 51 starts including the 1930 Melbourne Cup. In 1932, he was shipped over to America to race in the prestigious Caliente Handicap,

America's richest horse race but died in mysterious circumstances on 4 April 1932. When an autopsy was performed on Phar Lap, it was found that the great gelding's heart weighed 14 pounds (6.4 kilograms) compared to the average 9 pounds (4 kilograms). His heart today is housed at the National Museum, Canberra.

OTHER CELEBRITY BODY PARTS
• Walt Whitman's brain. Donated to the Wistar Institute at the University of Pennsylvania, where it "was dropped on the floor by a lab technician and was discarded long ago." The Wistar Institute is no longer accepting new brains.
• Lord Byron's lungs. "Kept in a jar, somewhere in Greece."

More on page 150.

* * *

OOPS!

"British education officials were red-faced Friday after having to scrap 48,000 literacy posters sent to teachers with two glaring spelling mistakes. It shouldn't have happened. The Department of Education failed to notice that 'vocabulary' was misspelled 'voca-bluary' and that pupils were being urged to learn about writing 'though' their own work instead of 'through' it. The posters have been reprinted and sent to schools with letters blaming the blunder on [the proofreaders]."

—*Reuters*

"Wine merchant William Sokolin had paid $300,000 for a 1787 bottle of Châteaux Margaux once owned by Thomas Jefferson. He presented it before a group of 300 wine collectors at Manhattan's Four Seasons restaurant in 1989, hoping that one of them might offer $519,000 for it. Before bidders could get out their checkbooks, he dropped the bottle and broke it."

—*Oops!*, by Smith and Decter

AMAZING LUCK

*Sometimes we're blessed with it, sometimes we're cursed
with it—dumb luck. Here are some examples of people
who've lucked out—for better and for worse.*

CELLULAR MEMORY
"In the Dent de Crolles region in France, shepherd
Christian Raymond, 23, was rescued from a cliff from
which he had been hanging by his fingers. He had called the
emergency rescue operator on his cell phone earlier in the day and
managed to make another call from the cliff by pressing "redial'
with his nose against the phone, which had fallen down the
mountain with him but had landed right beside him."

—*The Edge,* **March 25, 1999**

TRAIN KEPT A-ROLLIN'
"Participants in this tale of survival still can't believe it really
happened. Thrown through the steel roof of his car in a head-on
collision, a Denver man landed 30 metres [a hundred feet] away—
on railroad tracks, directly in the path of a speeding train. Too late
to brake before passing over the body, the engineer stopped as fast
as he could and rushed back to the spot, certain he had killed the
man. What he found was a guy limping, shaken, but very much
alive. His only injury was the broken leg he suffered in the car
collision."

—*Oops*

LUCK BE A LADY
"A mistake on a national Pick 7 ticket was worth $1.6 million to a
bettor who selected the wrong number on Breeders' Cup Day."

"The 51-year-old engineer who bought the winning ticket
said he punched 11 instead of 1 for his selection in the seventh
race."

"'I liked the one and 11 horses in the sixth race, and I liked
the No. 1 in the seventh,' the bettor said. 'But when I punched
out my ticket for the seventh, I hit one and 11—the same
numbers I had in the sixth—by mistake.'"

"The 11 turned out to be Arcangues, the unknown French
horse who won the Classic at odds of 133 to 1. It was the largest

in Breeders' Cup history."

"He had three other tickets with six winners, too, and collected a total of $1,152,317 after taxes."

—*San Francisco Chronicle*, November 11, 1993

BLESS THE TORPEDOES!

"A charmed life. That describes the experience of seaman Roy Dikkers during World War II. Sealed in a compartment when a German torpedo struck his tanker, he was freed by a second torpedo explosion. Racing on deck he found the sea around the floundering vessel ablaze with oil fires. He never had to make the fateful decision whether to stay with the sinking ship or risk the fiery sea. A third torpedo blew him far from the scene, beyond the oil slick. Landing near a floating raft, he crawled aboard and was found by a Norwegian freighter three days later."

—*Oops*

MY FORTUNE FOR A KISS

"Hauled before a Melbourne court in 1907 for hugging and kissing spinster Hazel Moore when she entered his shop, young Michael O'Connor defended himself by claiming it had been a lovely spring day and he was in high spirits. O'Connor had to serve a few months for breach of peace. So imagine his amazement ten years later when an attorney representing Miss Moore's estate gave him her bequest of 20,000 pounds! She left the fortune in memory of the only kiss she had received from a man in her adult life."

—*Oops*

AMAZING LOTTERY WINNERS

• "Randy Halvorson was one of 14 employees to share a $3.4 million jackpot in 1988. The Iowa resident then won $7.2 million with his brother in 1990."

• "In Wisconsin, Donald Smith of Amherst has won the state's SuperCash game three times: On May 25, 1993, June 17, 1994, and July 30, 1995. He won $250,000 each time. The odds of winning the SuperCash game just once are nearly one in a million."

• "Joseph P. Crowley won $3 million in the Ohio lottery in 1987. Six years later, he retired to Boca Raton, Florida, and played the Florida Lotto on Christmas Day of 1993. He won $20 million."

—*The Good Luck Book*

ANIMAL MYTHS

Here are a few examples of things that some people believe about animals—but just aren't true.

Myth: Bats are blind.
Fact: Bats aren't blind. But they evolved as nocturnal hunters, and can see better in half-light than in daylight.

Myth: Monkeys remove fleas in each other's fur during grooming.
Fact: Monkeys don't have fleas. They're removing dead skin—which they eat.

Myth: Male seahorses can become pregnant and give birth.
Fact: What actually happens is this: The female seahorse expels eggs into the male's brood pouch, where they are fertilized. And while the male does carry the gestating embryos until they are born 10 days later, he doesn't feed them through a placenta or similar organ (as had previously been thought). Instead, the embryos feed off of nourishment in the egg itself—food provided by the female. Basically, the male acts as an incubator.

Myth: Porcupines can shoot their quills when provoked.
Fact: A frightened porcupine tends to run from danger. If a hunter catches it, though, a porcupine will tighten its skin to make the quills stand up—ready to lodge in anything that touches them.

Myth: Whales spout water.
Fact: Whales actually exhale air through their blowholes. This creates a mist or fog that looks like a water spout.

Myth: Moths eat clothes.
Fact: Not exactly. Moths lay their eggs on your clothes, which eventually develop into larvae. It's the larvae that eat tiny parts of your clothes; adult moths do not eat cloth.

Myth: Bumblebee flight violates the laws of aerodynamics.
Fact: Nothing that flies violates the laws of aerodynamics.

THE ORIGIN OF BASKETBALL, PART II

*Here's more on how the game of basketball
was invented. Part I starts on page 24.*

Part I starts on page 24.

PROMISES, PROMISES

As James Naismith admitted years later in his memoirs, the new game he had in mind was an indoor version of an existing sport, like baseball or rugby. And when Dr. Gulick put him in charge of The Incorrigibles' physical education classes, he set out to find one he could adapt.

Naismith spent two weeks experimenting with different games, but something always seemed to get lost in the translation: Indoor soccer, for example, was fun—but too many windows were broken. And rugby turned out to be too dangerous on the gymnasium's hardwood floors. Other sports were safer—but they were so boring, The Incorrigibles refused to play them.

Outdoor games were meant to be played outdoors, Naismith concluded, and that was that.

BACK TO THE DRAWING BOARD

Time was running out. With only 24 hours left till his deadline for reporting to the faculty on the success of his efforts, Naismith decided to try a different approach: he would analyze a number of different games systematically, and figure out what made them challenging and fun. Then he would incorporate many of those elements into a new game that would be, as he put it, "interesting, easy to learn, and easy to play in the winter and by artificial light."

Do Unto Others

Naismith's new game would also have to walk a political tightrope: it had to be physically challenging enough to sustain the interest of The Incorrigibles, but not so rough or violent that it would offend conservatives within the YMCA movement. They had opposed getting involved with sports in the first place—and Naismith didn't want to give them any excuse to declare the experiment a failure.

HE GOT GAME

Amazingly, Naismith then sat down and, step-by-step, invented one of the most popular games in sports history.

Step 1. He figured that since nearly all popular sports have balls, his game should have one, too. But should it be small or large? Small balls like baseballs and lacrosse balls required bats, sticks, and racquets. Naismith was afraid players might use them to hit each other. He chose a big ball.

Step 2. Naismith felt that running with a ball would invariably lead to tackling the person carrying it—and tackling was too violent for the YMCA (not to mention too dangerous on a wood floor). So in the new game, the person who had the ball wouldn't be allowed to run with it; they wouldn't even be allowed to move. Instead, the player with the ball would have to stand in one place and pass it to the other players. That was the key to the game. "I can still recall how I snapped my fingers and shouted, 'I've got it!'" Naismith recalled years later.

Step 3. And what about the shape of the ball? It would either have to be round or shaped like a rugby ball (the predecessor of the football). Rugby balls were easier to carry under the arm, but that would encourage tackling. Round balls were easier to throw, which made them perfect for a passing game. Naismith decided to use a soccer ball.

Step 4. Naismith figured that there should be a goal at each end of the gymnasium—but what kind of goal? A huge one, like a soccer goal, would make scoring too easy—so the goal would have to be smaller. But a tiny goal would be easy to block—and blocking the goal would lead to pushing and shoving. So he decided to put the goal high over people's heads, where it would be impossible to block.

Step 5. This led to another consideration: if the goal was vertical, like the goalposts in football, players would throw the ball at it as hard and as fast as they could—which would be dangerous indoors. It would also reward force over skill, which was the antithesis of what Naismith wanted.

Naismith suddenly remembered a game he'd played as a child, called Duck on the Rock. The object was to knock a "duck" off of a rock by throwing stones at it. The best players always threw their rocks in an arc rather than directly at the duck, so that if they missed, they wouldn't have to run as far to retrieve the rock.

That inspired Naismith to use a horizontal goal, parallel to the ground. That way, players wouldn't be able to score just by throwing the ball as hard as they could: they'd have to throw it in an arc to get it in.

SERENDIPITY STRIKES

Naismith figured a wooden box nailed to the balcony that ran around the gym would work pretty well as a goal, and asked the janitor if he had any boxes lying around.

"No," the janitor told him, "but I have two old peach baskets down in the store room, if they will do you any good." "Thus," Robert Peterson writes in *Cages to Jump Shots*, "did the game miss being called box ball."

Naismith nailed one peach basket to the balcony at one end of the gym, and one at the other end. The balcony of the YMCA in Springfield just happened to be 3 metres [10 feet] off the floor—which is why, today, a regulation basket is 3 metres [10 feet] high.

THE FIRST GAME

Naismith typed up a list of 13 rules and posted them on the gym's bulletin board. The following morning, he read The Incorrigibles the rules; then he divided the 18-man class into two teams of 9 and taught them to play the game.

He promised to change any rules that didn't work out. "It was the start of the first basketball game," he recounted in his memoirs years later, "and the finish of the trouble with that class."

Basketball still had a long way to go. Turn to page 161 for the last part of our story.

* * * *

"Women want mediocre men, and men are working hard to be as mediocre as possible."

—*Margaret Mead*

What's the common name for the animal anobium pertinax? Bookworm.

HOW EN-LIGHTNING

Zap! BRI member Kurt Stark requested these facts about lightning.

Every second, there are 100 to 125 flashes of lightning somewhere on Earth.

A lightning bolt can be anywhere between 61 metres [200 feet] and 32 km [20 miles] long, but the average length, cloud-to-ground, is 3.2 to 16 km [2 to 10 miles].

Lightning speeds toward the Earth at an average of 200,000 miles per hour.

The average flash of lightning contains 125 million volts of electricity—enough to light a 100-watt bulb for more than three months.

The chances of being hit by lightning in your lifetime are about 1 in 600,000. Still, anywhere from 500 to 1000 people are struck by lightning every year in the U.S.

The temperature of a lightning stroke can reach 50,000°F—hotter than the sun's surface.

Lightning bolts actually flicker—a flash is a series of strokes that follow the exact same path as the first one. The record number of strokes ever recorded in a single flash is 47.

When you see a lightning flash, count the seconds until you hear the bang of thunder. Divide by five—sound travels about 1.6 km [one mile] every five seconds—and this will give you an approximation of the storm's distance from you.

About one-quarter of all lightning strikes occur in open fields; 30% happen in July; 22% in August.

You can get struck by lightning while you're on the phone. It happens to about 2.5% of all lightning-strike victims.

Trees are lightning bolts' favourite targets—lightning is the largest cause of forest fires in the western U.S.

Estimated diameter of a lightning channel: 1.5 to 2.5 centimetres [0.5 to 1 inch].

A charge of 100 million to 1 billion volts of electricity needs to be generated in a cloud to start a cloud-to-ground lightning strike.

For the last decade, an average of 20 million cloud-to-ground flashes have been counted over the continental U.S. each year.

How do you know when you're playing with an Italian deck of cards? No queens.

WE AIN'T LION: THE MODERN ZOO IS BORN

It wasn't that long ago that seeing an elephant at the London Zoo was about as shocking to the average person as meeting a Martian would be today. Here's the story of how zoos got their start.

OLD-TIME MENAGERIES

People have "collected" exotic animals for more than 5,000 years. Priests in ancient Egypt raised lions, tigers, and other sacred animals in and around temples, and as early as 1100 B.C., China's Zhou Dynasty established what was called the "Garden of Intelligence," a 900-acre preserve filled with deer, antelope, birds, fish, and other animals that were studied as well as hunted.

Exotic animals were also popular in ancient Rome, where they were collected by wealthy families and used in gladiator games. Sometimes the lions, tigers, bulls, bears, and other creatures fought each other to a bloody death for public amusement; other times they were pitted against Christians, heretics, or condemned criminals (or, if none were available, ordinary criminals). Sometimes the Romans even filled their coliseums with water, so gladiators in boats could hunt water animals like hippos and crocodiles.

These games were so popular—and killed so many animals—that by the time they finally came to an end in the 6th century A.D., numerous species in the Roman empire, including the elephants of North Africa, the hippopotami of Nubia, the lions of Mesopotamia, and the tigers of Hycrania, had all been driven to extinction.

THE DARK AGES

When Rome fell in the 5th century A.D., interest in animals declined, and it wasn't until the 13th century that nobles and other wealthy Europeans began collecting animals on a large scale again. They even exchanged them like trading cards.

King Frederick II of Sicily was a typical collector of the era: his menagerie included hyenas, elephants, camels, lions, monkeys, cheetahs, and a giraffe—and when he got tired of the giraffe, he traded it to the sultan of Egypt for a polar bear.

THE LONDON ZOO

In 1235 King Henry III of England moved his grandfather's animal collection to the Tower of London. The collection included camels, lions, leopards, and lynx—and King Louis IX of France contributed an elephant—the first one ever seen in Great Britain. The animals were put on display for the royal family and its guests, but were also occasionally pitted against one another—tigers vs. lions, bears vs. dogs—to entertain royal visitors. However, the novelty eventually wore off, and the animals became neglected.

Then, in 1445, Margaret of Anjou, wife of Henry VI, received a lion as a wedding gift—which inspired her to have the entire Royal Menagerie—what was left of it—restored. But when the royal family moved out of the Tower in the early 1700s, they left their animals behind. That created a problem: if the royal family wasn't going to support the menagerie, who was? Finally, someone came up with the idea of opening the collection to the public, and charging them admission. Price: three half-pence, or if you preferred, a dog or cat to feed to the lions.

CHANGING TIMES

As the British Empire expanded to the far corners of the globe in the early 1800s, interest in exotic animals grew beyond mere curiosity. In 1826 an explorer named Sir Stamford Raffles founded the London Zoological Society, which took its name from the ancient Greek word *zoion*, which means "living being."

Two years later, the Society moved the royal family's animal collection from the Tower of London to a new site in Regent's Park. It was a big hit with members of the royal family, many of whom contributed animals.

But unlike the Tower of London, the Zoological Park was closed to the public—the animals were "objects of scientific research," Raffles explained, "not of vulgar admiration." Only members of the Zoological society and their guests were allowed to visit. (A written voucher would allow a non-member to enter, and these became very common and were even traded in pubs.)

The public was officially excluded from the "zoo," as it had become known, until 1846, by which time the novelty had worn off and attendance had fallen dramatically. So the Zoological Society opened its doors to anyone with a penny, and hundreds of thousands of new visitors streamed into the park. "For the city dweller," Linda Koebler writes in *Zoo*, "[it] provided a place of greenery that was a relief from the ugly, dirty cities of this period."

The term "zoo" entered mainstream culture a year after the London Zoological Garden opened to the public, thanks to the popularity of one particular song: "Walking in the Zoo is an Okay Thing to Do."

ZOOS IN EUROPE

In the early 1800s, having a public zoo became a status symbol for any European city that considered itself modern and sophisticated. If they still had royal collections of animals available, they quickly converted them to zoological parks. If they didn't, they created new zoos. Zoos in Dublin, Berlin, Frankfurt, Antwerp, and Rotterdam were among the best known.

Le Zoo

In France, however, the development of public zoos was slowed by the Revolution of 1789. Common people saw private collections of captive animals as a way for the rich to flaunt their wealth. According to one account, when a mob of revolutionaries arrived at the Ménagerie du Parc to free the animals, "The crowd wanted the animals set free so that others could catch them and eat them, outraged that these animals grew fat while the people starved. But once the zoo director explained that some of the creatures would eat the crowd rather than vice versa, the du Parc revolutionaries decided to liberate only the more edible captives."

Cat got your tongue? Did someone call you a cheetah?
Don't monkey around, turn to page 213
for more wild facts about zoos.

ODD JOBS

Looking for an exciting new job? Here's a list of the most unusual-sounding occupations we could find.

Killer Bee Hunter. Your mission: Track down Africanized "killer" bees, which are migrating north from Central America, and destroy them before they can take up residence in North America.

Chicken Shooter. Fire dead chickens out of a cannon at aircraft to see what kind of damage occurs.

Mother Repairer. It's not what you think. It actually entails repairing metal phonograph record "mothers" (the master from which records are pressed) by removing dirt and nickel particles from the grooves.

Anthem Man. A unique profession: King Alfonso of Spain was tone deaf so he employed one man whose job was to alert him when the Spanish national anthem was playing (so he would know when to salute).

Worm Collector. Get ready to crawl through grass at night with a flashlight, to catch the best worms for fishing. Tip: Grab them in the middle to avoid bruising.

Weed Farmer. If you like gardening, here's a change of pace: grow weeds then sell them to chemical companies for herbicide research.

Pig Manure Sniffer. Workers try to recognize chemical markers in manure so researchers can determine which foods make pig manure so foul smelling. Women only, because estrogen increases sensitivity to smell.

Sewage Diver. Put on a diving suit and plunge into a sewage-containment vat.

Animal Chauffeur. We've only heard of one—a guy named Stephen May. His "limousine" is equipped with, among other things: a blanketed floor, 20-cm. [8-inch] colour television, stereo speakers, and silk flowers.

Flush Tester. A gold star from Uncle John to the gallant professionals who test toilet-bowl standards by trying to flush rags down various toilets.

Armpit Sniffer. Enough said.

Why was the shark model in *Jaws* called Bruce? Steven Spielberg named it after his lawyer.

AUSTRALIAN QUOTES

Friends as a rule are a mistake.
Marcus Clarke

He looks like he was weaned on a pickle.
Bill Hayden commenting on Malcolm Fraser

Australia is a lucky country run mainly by second-rate people who share its luck.
Donald Horne

One of the men saw an animal something less than a grey-hound; it was a mouse colour, very slender made and swift of foot.
Captain James Cook on first sighting a kangaroo

Every now and then a shark eats an Australian or two. But every day Australians eat enormous numbers of sharks. The trade balance is very much in our favour.
Cyril Pearl

I can't really say I am batting badly. I'm not batting long enough to be batting badly.
Greg Chappell, 1982

It's like swimming in sewerage.
Charles, Prince of Wales, on swimming at St Kilda beach, Melbourne 1970

Bowl faster, bowl faster. When you play test cricket you don't give the Englishmen an inch. Play it tough, all the way. Grind them into the dust.
Sir Donald Bradman

Seriously friends, Melbourne is unique. It's the only place on earth where the visitor can close his eyes and wonder if there really is life before death.
Barry Humphries

The game of cricket existed long before I was born. It will be played centuries after my demise. During my career I was privileged to give the public my interpretation of its character in the same way that a pianist might interpret the works of Beethoven.
Sir Donald Bradman

From what I have seen of the Natives of New Holland they may appear to some to be the most wretched people upon Earth, but in reality they are far more happier than we Europeans; being wholly unacquainted not only with the superfluous but the necessary conveniences so much sought after in Europe. They are happy in not knowing the use of them. They live in tranquillity ...the Earth and sea of their

own accord furnishes them with all things necessary for life; they live in a warm and fine climate and enjoy a very wholesome Air.
Captain James Cook on sighting Aborigines

That man was too mean to hang himself.
Bill Wannan

I was looking for an American symbol. A Coca-Cola bottle or a Mickey Mouse would have been ridiculous, doing anything with the American flag would have been insulting, and Cadillac hubcaps were just too uncomfortable.
Lizzy Gardiner (who wore a dress of American Express gold cards to the 1995 Academy Awards)

Distrust the men who make bargains. They are a disgrace to humanity. No man ever saw a dog swap a bone with another dog.
Marcus Clarke

This nation (Australia) was built on a cup of tea, a Bex, and a good lie-down.
Phillip Adams

Keep your brain right and the rest of you will sort of drag along behind you.
Paul Keating

I believe I have the greatest amount of talent at the present time…This is unquestionably the opinion of my colleagues, and this is not an issue on which I feel disposed to differ from them.
Gough Whitlam

I am the Placido Domingo of politics.
Paul Keating

Friendship, if you know how to work it, is better than a cousin in parliament.
Marcus Clarke

As I see it, the little that is subtle in the Australian character comes from the masculine principle in its women, the feminine in its men.
Patrick White

You can call me bourgeois, but not decadent.
Gough Whitlam

Aussie Rules remains in its condition of benign stagnation.
Max Harris

No man has the right to inflict the torture of bad wine upon fellow creatures.
Marcus Clarke

I have heard rumours about an impending union, but considering the parents it is likely to be barren.

Gough Whitlam

When I am in office I always keep members of Parliament talking. If they stopped they might start thinking.

Robert Menzies

If this government cannot get the adjustment...and a sensible economic policy, then Australia is basically done for...We will end up being a third-rate economy...a banana republic.

Paul Keating

The people have got to be told that if they want to express their views to the State Government, and have those views reflected in legislation, then the proper thing for them to do is to move to some state where this sort of garbage is tolerated.

Fred Dagg

Advertising men and politicians are dangerous if they are separated. Together they are diabolical.

Phillip Adams

Nothing the west has done to the tribes of the world exceeds the wickedness we have done to our own.

Les Murray

And all lying mysteriously within the Australian underdark, that peculiar, lost weary aloofness of Australia. There was the vast town of Sydney. And it didn't seem to be real, it seemed to be sprinkled on the surface of a darkness into which it never penetrated.

DH Lawrence

It was a symptom of Britain's post-war condition that anyone given power before his hair turned white was called a whizz-kid.

Clive James

Funny how a country shaped people to its ideas more than they shaped the country.

Kylie Tennant

Flexibility in pursuit of the nation's interests must never be allowed to degenerate into expediency.

Malcolm Fraser

"We hang the petty thieves, but appoint the great ones to public office." —Aesop

AESOP: FACT OR FABLE?

Chances are, you've heard of Aesop's fables—people have been repeating them for thousands of years. But did you know there was a real person named Aesop?

BACKGROUND
If you were asked to name the most influential writers in Western history, you might include Aristotle, or Shakespeare, or even Dr. Spock. But you probably wouldn't think of Aesop.

Yet his works have been around for over 2,000 years, and he's had an impact on everything from ancient Greek philosophy to 20th-century American culture. Adages such as "Don't cry over spilled milk" and expressions like "sour grapes," for example, come directly from his fables.

On the other hand, Aesop wasn't technically a writer. Nothing was written down during his lifetime; it was oral tradition that kept both his legend and his fables alive. Still, scholars are reasonably certain he existed—and that he was a revered storyteller. "The best evidence we have of Aesop's life comes from remarks about him in early ancient sources like Herodotus, Aristotle, Aristophanes and Plato," writes Leo Groarke Wilfrid of Laurier University. In fact, Socrates, considered the greatest philosopher of ancient Greece, "is said to have passed the time awaiting execution by putting Aesop's fables into verse."

A BRIEF BIOGRAPHY
Scholars have established a few facts about Aesop's life:
• He was born a Greek slave in the sixth century B.C.
• He had a natural gift for fables and became famous in ancient Greece because of it. Eventually his "learning and wit" earned him his freedom.
• As a freed man he travelled widely until Croesus, the rich and powerful king of ancient Lydia, invited him to become an ambassador. Aesop accepted and was sent to various republics of Greece,

---

Why don't wolves bark like dogs? One theory: They don't want to.

trying to establish peace "by telling his wise fables."

• Aesop's last diplomatic mission was to Delphi. Croesus gave him gold to distribute to the citizens. However, Aesop was so offended by the Delphians' greed that he just sent the loot back to Croesus. Proving his point, the Delphians became so enraged that they accused Aesop of "impiety"—a major crime—and executed him as a public criminal. According to legend, they pushed him off a cliff.

• Following the execution of Aesop, a myth grew up around the incident. It was said that a series of calamities befell the citizens of Delphi. The disasters got worse and worse until, finally, the people confessed their crime and made reparations. After that, "the blood of Aesop" became a common reference to the fact that evil deeds will not go unpunished.

HOW THE FABLES CAME TO US

After his death, Aesop became a sort of mythical figure (like Mother Goose) to whom fables were automatically attributed, no matter who invented them. For a thousand years after his death, he was more famous than ever. But with the coming of the Dark Ages, he was forgotten.

Then, 600 years later, in the 1300s, a Turkish monk named Planudes assembled a collection of about 150 of Aesop's fables. When Italian scholars of the mid-1400s became interested in antiquity, Planudes' book was one of the first works they translated and printed, along with works by Homer and Aristotle.

Aesop's tales spread from Italy to Germany, where his popularity grew. The "great fathers of the Reformation" used his fables to inveigh against the Catholic Church; Martin Luther himself translated 20 of Aesop's fables and said that next to the Bible, he valued *Aesop's Fables* above all other books.

Finally, in 1610, a Swiss scholar named Isaac Nicholas Nevelet printed a version of Aesop's fables called *Mythologica Aesopica*. It was popular all over Europe and made Aesop a permanent part of Western civilization. "No book," wrote the compiler of a 19th-century collection, "with the exception of the Holy Scriptures, has had a wider circulation than *Aesop's Fables*. They have been translated into the greater number of the languages both of Europe and of the East, and have been read, and will be read, for generations by the inhabitants of all countries."

Experts say: If you're typical, your body contains about four ounces of salt.

AESOP'S FABLES

Aesop's fables (see page 118) have been told and retold for thousands of years. Here are some of our favourites.

THE FOX & THE CRANE

A fox once invited a crane to dinner and served soup in a very shallow dish. He thought it was funny that the crane, with his long beak, couldn't drink any of the soup.

Then he said, "My dear crane, I'm so sorry to see that you're not eating anything. Didn't you like the soup?"

"Oh, everything is just fine," the crane answered. "And now you must do me the honour of paying me a visit."

When the fox came to the crane's house and sat down to dinner, a very tall jar was placed in front of him. It was so tall and narrow that the fox couldn't get his snout into it.

"I'm so glad to be able to return your courtesy," said the crane as he reached his long beak into the jar. "I hope you enjoy your dinner every bit as much as I did mine when I visited you."

Moral: *What goes around, comes around. You get what you deserve.*

THE FIR TREE & THE BRAMBLE

A fir tree boasted to a bramble, "You're useful for nothing at all; while I am used for roofs and houses and all kinds of things." The bramble answered: "You poor creature, if you would only call to mind the axes and saws which are about to cut you down, you would wish you'd grown up a bramble, not a fir tree."

Moral: *Better poverty without care, than riches with a worried life.*

BELLING THE CAT

Long ago, a group of mice had a general council to consider what measures they could take to outwit their common enemy, the cat. Some said this, and some said that; but at last a young mouse got up and said he had a proposal to make, which he thought would meet the case. "You will all agree," said he, "that our chief danger consists in the sly and treacherous manner in which the enemy approaches us. Now, if we could receive some signal of her approach, we could easily escape from her. I venture, therefore, to propose that a small bell be procured, and attached by a ribbon round the neck of the cat. By this means we should always know when she was about, and could easily retire while she was in the neighbourhood."

This proposal met with general applause, until an old mouse got up and said: "That is all very well, but who is to bell the cat?" The mice looked at one another and nobody spoke. Then the old mouse said: "It is easy to propose impossible remedies."

Moral: *Talk is cheap.*

THE BUFFOON & THE COUNTRYMAN

At a country fair there was a Buffoon who made all the people laugh by imitating the cries of various animals. He finished off by squeaking so like a pig that the spectators thought that he had a porker concealed about him. But a Countryman who stood by said: "Call that a pig's squeak! Nothing like it. You give me till tomorrow and I will show you what it's like." The audience laughed, but next day, sure enough, the Countryman appeared on the stage, and putting his head down squealed so hideously that the spectators hissed and threw stones at him to make him stop. "You fools!" he cried, "see what you have been hissing," and held up a little pig whose ear he had been pinching to make him utter the squeals.

Moral: *Men often applaud an imitation and hiss the real thing.*

THE DOG'S REFLECTION

Once there was a dog who was given a fine, meaty bone. With the bone firmly between his teeth, the dog trotted homeward, thinking of what a fine meal he was going to enjoy.

On the way, he had to cross a narrow bridge over a brook. As he looked over the side of the bridge, he caught sight of his own reflection in the water. Thinking it was another dog carrying a bone between his teeth, the foolish animal made up his mind that he would have that bone, too.

He leaned over and snapped at the dog beneath him. As he did, the bone fell into the water and was lost.

Moral: *Be careful that you don't lose what you have by trying to get more.*

AUSTRALIAN PLACE NAMES

Ever wondered what your suburb name means? Or what the name of your town means? Many of our place names are derived from Aboriginal words but their origins and meaning are unknown to most Australians. Here are a few for you to polish up on so you can really impress your friends.

Ballina (NSW) . . . . fighting ground or bleeding wound

Becchal (QLD) . . . . where a man was speared

Benelong (NSW) . . . . . . named after a young aboriginal man who was taken to England to meet the King

Bouradie (NSW) . . . . place to knock out teeth

Bugabada NSW) . . . . stinking maggots

Bunagan (QLD) . . . . old woman high in tree

Bunnacower (VIC) . . . . . place where emus make dust

Codobine (WA) . . . . place where man removes heart from another man

Coogee (NSW) . . . . place of rotting seaweed

Coolibullup (WA) . . . . . . place infested with kangaroo ticks

Coomalwangra (WA) . . . talking possums

Crumbana (QLD) . . . . . . dead man near camp

Curragundi (NT) . . . . place of many spiders

Dewitt (NSW) . . . . plenty of blowflies

Dubbo (NSW) . . . . a cap covering the head

Echuca (VIC) . . . . junction of rivers

Eurabuga (NT) . . . . maggoty emu

Geelong (VIC) . . . . swampy plain

Gerringong (NSW) . . . . . I fear myself

Gundagai (NSW) . . . . . . cut back of knee with tomahawk

Indooroopilly (QLD) . . . . gully of leeches

Jabiru (NT) . . . . a native stork

Kakadu (NT) . . . . named after the local tribe

Kuranda (QLD) . . . . a plant

Kybybolite (SA) . . . . place where ghosts are found

Kurnel (NSW) . . . . wild carrot

Legerup (WA) . . . . place where kangaroos dance

Leura (NSW) . . . . lava

Manly (NSW) . . . . named after the 'manly' aborigines seen here

Munagin (WA) . . . . plenty of snakes near a lake

Murrumbidgee (NSW) . . big water, track goes down from here

Myponga (SA) . . . . divorced wife

Nimbin (NSW) . . . . pointed rock

Onkaparnga River (SA) . mother river, woman's river

Prahran (VIC) . . . . partly surrounded by water

Queanbeyan (NSW) . . . . clear water

Renmark (SA) . . . . red mud

Taronga park (NSW) . . . beautiful view

Toowoomba (QLD) . . . . . swamp, underground water

Tomingley (NS) . . . . piece of bark that looks like a death adder

Turramtalone (QLD) . . . . place where large eel escaped over waterfall

Uluru (NT) . . . . meeting place, family name

Wagga Wagga (NSW) . . . place of many crows

Wilpenapound (SA) . . . . place of bent fingers

Wollongong (NSW) . . . . five islands, hard ground near water, monster comes

Woolloomooloo (NSW) . young kangaroo, whirling round

Woy Woy (NSW) . . . . . . deep water, porpoise

Yarra River (VIC) . . . . . . running water, hiding place

Yeulup (WA) . . . . place where kangaroos lie down in dust

The London Zoo reportedly employs an "entertainment director" for the animals.

"RUMOURS OF MY DEATH…"

While he was visiting England in 1897, Mark Twain received an inquiry from the U.S. about a report that he had died. "Rumours of my death," he cabled back, "are greatly exaggerated." He's not the only celebrity whose death has been erroneously reported. Here are three of our favourite "false death" stories, and their impact.

A PRIZE MISTAKE

Who "Died": Alfred Nobel, Swedish inventor of dynamite, blasting caps, smokeless gunpowder, and hundreds of other explosion-related items

Cause of "Death": Mistaken identity. On April 13, 1888, Nobel awoke in Paris, opened a newspaper, and was astonished to read his own obituary. But it was actually his brother Ludwig who'd died; the newspaper had goofed.

What Happened: As a result of this mistake, Nobel was given a rare gift—a chance to see how he would be remembered—and he didn't like what he saw. As David Zacks writes in *An Underground Education*:

> Alfred was shocked to see himself portrayed as the Merchant of Death, the man responsible for escalating the arms race….[Even though] he had made high-powered explosives much easier to use and was proud of how this power had been unleashed to mine precious minerals and to build roads, railways, and canals.

The obituary painted him as a "bellicose monster" whose discoveries "had boosted the bloody art of war from bullets and bayonets to long-range explosives in less than 24 years."

Determined to change his image and redeem the family name, Nobel hatched a shrewd plan. He used his wealth to create prizes in several areas—including peace. (Sort of like "the Exxon award for environmental safety…(or) the John F. Kennedy award for marital fidelity," Zacks says). It was successful spin control. Today, the Nobel Prizes are the most prestigious in the world—and few of us connect their creator to "the art of killing."

JUST A RUMOUR

Who "Died": American Vice President Thomas Jefferson

Cause of "Death": Dirty politics. America's first really nasty presidential campaign was underway in 1800 when, on June 30, the *Baltimore American* reported that Jefferson (running against incumbent president John Adams) had died suddenly at his Virginia home. The story was confirmed the next day by the *Philadelphia True American*.

What Happened: According to Bruce Felton and Mark Fowler in their book *The Best, Worst and Most Unusual*:

> Reports of the death of the vice president elicited no statements of sympathy, no words of grief from President Adams, vice presidential candidate Charles Cotesworth Pinckney, or any other prominent Federalist politician, which is a measure of the bitterness of the campaign. On the other hand, Jefferson's friends spent July 4 in sombre mourning. News travelled slowly in that era, and reports of Jefferson's death did not reach some outlying areas until the middle of July. And the truth followed about one week behind.

What happened? The *Gazette of the United States* finally explained: "An old Negro slave called Thomas Jefferson, being dead at Monticello, gave rise to the report of the demise of the Vice-President—the slave having borne the name of his master."

But the whole episode "was no innocent misunderstanding," write Felton and Fowler. "The rumours and reports were cleverly calculated to underscore Jefferson's slave-owning status, and the gossip about his affairs with black women. Had the timing been better, it might have influenced the election."

WRITTEN IN THE STARS

Who "Died": John Partridge, best-known English astrologer of the early 1700s and publisher of the annual astrology almanac *Merlinus Liberatus*

Cause of "Death": A practical joke. Satirist Jonathan Swift, author of *Gulliver's Travels*, hated astrologers (he thought astrology was nonsense) but loved April Fools' Day jokes. In 1708 he pulled one on Partridge. Taking the pen name Isaac Bickerstaff and posing as a "true astrologer" who wanted to expose the "gross abuses… nonsense, lies and folly" put out by "false astrologers" like Partridge, Swift published a penny pamphlet of bogus prophesies, titled *Predictions for the Year 1708*. He wrote:

> [My first prediction] relates to Partridge the almanac-maker; I have consulted the star of his nativity by my own rules, and find he will infallibly die upon the 29th of March next, about eleven at night, of a raging fever.

What Happened: On March 30, Swift—using a different pen name this time—published a second pamphlet: *The Accomplishment of the First of Mr. Bickerstaff's Predictions*. It supplied a graphic description of Partridge's supposed final moments, including a scene in which the anguished, repentant astrologer admitted in a deathbed confession that he was a fake. "All pretences of foretelling by astrology are deceits," Partridge supposedly said, "and none but the poor ignorant vulgar give it any credit." As and historian Rowse writes,

> Swift's plan succeeded beyond his wildest expectations. His own penny pamphlet sold in multitudes and pirate publishers were soon offering halfpenny reprints, replies, and imitations….What had begun as a simple practical joke grew into a full-blown fantasy until more people knew of Partridge's death than had ever heard of him alive.

In the next issue of his almanac, Partridge protested that he wasn't really dead, and attacked Bickerstaff as an "impudent, lying fellow." Swift anonymously shot back with another pamphlet: *Vindication of Isaac Bickerstaff*, in which he provided several "proofs" that Partridge really was dead. He even accused Partridge of being an impostor of himself.

Result: People really came to believe that Partridge was dead and that the person claiming to be him—Partridge—was an interloper trying to take over the business. Because of this, sales of Partridge's almanacs plummeted, forcing him out of business. He never found out who was behind the hoax.

OOPS!

*More tales of outrageous blunders to let us know that
someone's screwing up even worse than we are. So
go ahead and feel superior for a few minutes.*

JUST DO IT

TICONDEROGA, New York— "A company is trying to erase an embarrassing mistake it made on pencils bearing an anti-drug message. The pencils carry the slogan: 'Too Cool To Do Drugs.'

"But a sharp-eyed fourth-grader in northern New York noticed when the pencils are sharpened, the message turns into 'Cool To Do Drugs' then simply 'Do Drugs.'

"'We're actually a little embarrassed that we didn't notice that sooner,' spokeswoman Darlene Clair told today's *Press-Republican* of Plattsburgh."

—Associated Press, December 11, 1998

WELL, NEVER MIND THEN

"We shall never know the identity of the man who in 1976 made the most unsuccessful hijack attempt ever. On a flight across America, he rose from his seat, drew a gun and took the stewardess hostage."

"'Take me to Detroit,' he said."

"'We're already going to Detroit,' she replied."

"'Oh…good,' he said, and sat down again."

—Book of Heroic Failures

STAMPS OF APPROVAL

WASHINGTON— "The Grand Canyon has been misplaced by the post office.

"A newly printed batch of 100 million 6-cent international stamps carry a picture of the canyon and, on the bottom of each stamp, the words 'Grand Canyon, Colorado.'

"The Grand Canyon is actually located in the state of Arizona."

—Associated Press, May 17, 1999

BEASTLY MISTAKE

"After Cody Johnston, 22, of Bozeman, Montana, was fined $195 for a traffic violation, a court computer error turned it into a conviction for deviate sexual conduct. That's the way it appeared in a crime report in the *High Country Independent Press*, where Johnston's parents read it. When he told them it wasn't true, his wife and his sister accused him of being in denial and urged him to seek counselling. Even though the *Independent Press* printed a correction, Johnston filed a libel suit against the paper and the court system, noting, 'I've heard every sheep joke you can imagine.'"

—*Weird News*

IF YOU DON'T COUGH, YOU MIGHT GET OFF

CARDIFF, Wales— "When a juror coughed, defendant Alan Rashid had a right to feel sick."

"The cough came just as the jury foreman announced a verdict of 'not guilty' in Rashid's trial on a charge of threatening homicide."

"The cough coincided with 'not,' Judge Michael Gibbon only heard 'guilty' and Rashid was sentenced to two years in prison."

"As the jury left the court Thursday, one inquisitive member of the panel asked an usher why Rashid was going to jail after being found innocent. So the jurors were herded back into court."

"Rashid was brought back to court, the jury confirmed its 'not guilty' verdict and Gibbon told the defendant he was free to go."

"'I am very relieved, as you would imagine,' Rashid said."

—**Associated Press, April 16, 1999**

HAPPINESS IS A WARM GUN

"Madison, Wisconsin, police chief Richard Williams turned on his oven to roast some turkey but forgot that was one of his favourite hiding places for his gun. "Shortly thereafter: boom!" police spokesperson Jeanna Kerr said, adding that Williams was given a one-day, unpaid suspension for violating his department's firearms policy."

—*News of the Weird*, **November 1998**

In an average minute, 20,900 gallons flow from the Amazon River into the sea.

CREME de la CRUD

*Most celebrities are famous because they're good at what
they do—but a rare few are remembered as the
absolute worst. We at the BRI salute them.*

THE CHERRY SISTERS, *world's worst variety act*
Background: In the mid-1890s, Broadway impresario
Oscar Hammerstein promoted a number of spectacular
stage shows, only to see them lose money due to lack of public
interest. So he decided to change gears. "I've been putting on the
best talent and it hasn't gone over," he groused to reporters. "Now
I'm trying the worst." He was referring to the Cherry Sisters.
Career Notes:
The four Cherry Sisters were from Cedar Rapids, Iowa. Tall, thin
Addie, Effie, and Lizzie were the singers in the group; short fat
Jessie "kept time," thumping intermittently on a bass drum.
• The sisters started by touring vaudeville houses in the Midwest
and were so awful—even to small-town audiences starved for
entertainment—that wire screens had to be erected across the
front of the stages where they performed, to protect them from
rotten vegetables and other garbage that audiences routinely
threw at them.
• Hammerstein signed them to a $1,000-a-week contract to play
at his Olympia Theatre. Their debut on November 16, 1896,
marked a turning point in their career: instead of being pelted
with garbage, they were met with a shower of bad reviews. In an
article titled "Four Freaks From Iowa," a *New York Times* reviewer
described the sisters as "genuine products of the barnyard," and
speculated that their performance might be due to poor diet. "It is
sincerely hoped," he wrote, "that nothing like them will ever be
seen again."
• Just as motorists slow down to look at traffic accidents, more
and more people went to see the Cherry Sisters perform. Their
reputation for being the world's worst variety act grew, and soon
they were playing to sold-out crowds. Hammerstein made a small
fortune off the act, and the Cherry Sisters became "the best-
known, if not the best-loved stage performers in America."

FLORENCE FOSTER JENKINS, *world's worst opera singer*
Background: There may have been worse opera singers, but none
who achieved fame for it. "She clucked and squawked, trumpeted
and quavered," said one observer. Another noted that she was
"undaunted by...the composer's intent." And in *The Book of Heroic Failures,* Howard Pyle writes: "No one, before or since, has succeeded in liberating themselves quite so completely from the
shackles of musical notation."

Career Notes:
• Singing opera was Jenkins's lifelong dream. But she was unable
to pursue it until 1909, at age 40, when her father died and left
her a fortune. Since no one in their right mind would finance
Jenkins's recitals, she paid for them herself, and developed an
enthusiastic following.
• "Different audiences reacted in various ways," writes Carl Sifakis
in Great American Eccentrics. "Some roared with laughter until
tears rolled down their cheeks; others sat in utter silence, according her unique voice an attention befitting the world's greatest
singers."
• Critics were at a loss as to how to describe her. Some called her
"The First Lady of the Sliding Scale." When she released a record,
Newsweek commented: "In high notes, Mrs. Jenkins sounds as if
she was afflicted with a low, nagging backache."
• Jenkins's trademark was outrageous costumes. Pyle writes: "One
minute she would appear sporting an immense pair of wings to
render 'Ave Maria.' The next she would emerge [as] a senorita,
with a rose between her teeth and a basket full of flowers." She
often threw roses into the audience—then sent her accompanist
to gather them up so she could throw them out again. Once she
became so excited that she threw the basket, too.
• On October 25, 1944, the beloved 75-year-old diva rented out
Carnegie hall—and performed to a sold-out crowd. "So great was
the demand for tickets," writes Sifakis, "that they were scalped at
the then-outrageous price of $20 apiece. More than 2,000 lovers
of music had to be turned away." La Jenkins took it in stride, as
she had over her 30-year career. "Some may say I couldn't sing,"
she quipped, "but no one can say that I didn't sing." A month
later, she died.

BRI'S WIND HALL OF FAME

It used to be that no one talked about farts—now, it's no big deal. You can't get away from it. Which is fine by us. Here is the very first section honouring people and institutions that have made an art out of passing wind. (By the way—if this is your favourite part of the book, we recommend a tome called Who Cut the Cheese?, *by Jim Dawson.)*

Honorary: Caryn Johnson, a.k.a. Whoopi Goldberg
Notable Achievement: First Hollywood star named after frequent farting
True Story: In her autobiography, Goldberg says she came up with the stage name Whoopi because she "frequently passed gas and sounded like a walking whoopee cushion."

Honorary: Taoism
Notable Achievement: Most interesting philosophy about farts
True Story: A 1996 BBC-TV program about the first Chinese emperor, reported that "Chinese Taoists believe everyone is allotted a certain amount of air at birth which it is important to conserve. Belching and farting are considered to shorten one's life. Taoists therefore carefully control their diet, avoiding foods which lead to flatulence."

Honorary: King Ahmose of Egypt
Notable Achievement: Most effective use of a fart as a political statement
True Story: In 568 B.C., King Apries of Egypt sent a trusted general named Amasis to put down a mutiny among his troops. But when Amasis got there, the troops offered to make him their leader instead—and he accepted.

King Apries couldn't believe it. He sent a respected adviser named Patarbemis to bring Amasis back. Amasis responded to the king's entreaties by raising himself from his saddle and farting. Then he told Patarbemis to "carry that back to Apries." Unfortunately, the king was so enraged by the message that he had

Patarbemis's nose and ears hacked off. Committing such a
barbarous act against such a respectable man was the last straw for
many Egyptians—they turned pro-Amasis. With their support,
Amasis's troops attacked and defeated Apries's army.
Note: Amasis became King Ahmose and reigned for 44 years, from
569 to 525 B.C., which modern historians call one of Egypt's most
prosperous periods.

Honorary: Richard Magpiong, a career criminal
Notable Achievement: The ultimate self-incriminating fart
True Story: In 1995 the residents of a home on Fire Island (near
New York City) were awakened by a noise. They got up and
looked around, but couldn't find anyone. They were about to go
back to bed when, according to the *New York Daily News,* "they
heard the sound of a muffled fart." Magpiong was discovered
hiding in a closet and was held until the police arrived.

Honorary: Edward De Vere, the seventh earl of Oxford and a
courtier in Queen Elizabeth's court
Notable Achievement: Craziest overreaction to a fart
True Story: De Vere accidentally farted while bowing to the
queen. He was so embarrassed that he left England and did not
return for seven years. When he got back, the queen pooh-poohed
the whole affair. "My Lord," she reportedly said, welcoming him
back, "I had forgot the Fart."

Honorary: Spike Jones and His City Slickers
Notable Achievement: Bestselling fart record
True Story: According to *Who Cut the Cheese?:* "During World
War II, Bluebird Records released a disc called 'Der Fuehrer's Face'
by Spike Jones and His City Slickers (an orchestra noted for
parodying pop tunes), only a few months after the U.S. joined the
war. Jones's band, armed with rubber razzers to create flabby
farting noises, [created] a zany gas attack on Adolf Hitler: "And
we'll Heil! [fart!] Heil! [fart!] right in der Fuehrer's face!" It sold a
million and a half copies in the U.S. and Great Britain.

MYTH-CONCEPTIONS

Common knowledge is frequently wrong. Here are a few examples of things that people believe—but that just aren't true.

Myth: The captain of a ship at sea can perform weddings.
Fact: U.S. Navy regulations—and those of the navies of many other nations—actually prohibit ships' commanders from joining couples in marriage.

Myth: Your hair and nails continue to grow after you die.
Fact: They don't. Your tissue recedes from your hair and nails, making them appear longer.

Myth: Bananas spoil faster when you put them in a refrigerator.
Fact: This belief comes from an old ad jingle. The purpose of the jingle was to tell people to keep bananas out of the refrigerator—but only until they had ripened. Once ripened, bananas will last longer in the refrigerator.

Myth: You should never wake a sleepwalker.
Fact: There's no reason not to wake a sleepwalker. This superstition comes from the old belief that a sleepwalker's spirit leaves the body and might not make it back if the person is wakened.

Myth: Any American can make a citizen's arrest.
Fact: According to law enforcement officials, the concept of a citizen's arrest is pure fiction.

Myth: Shaving your hair makes it grow in faster and thicker.
Fact: The rate of your hair's growth is determined by hereditary factors. Shaving will have no effect on the rate of its growth.

Myth: During a flight, you'll sometimes hit an "air pocket."
Fact: What's often called an "air pocket" is actually a downdraft.

Myth: It's darkest just before the dawn.
Fact: Actually, it's darkest at about 2 a.m.

If you weigh 120 pounds on Earth, you'll weigh about 20 pounds on the moon.

MORE FAKED PHOTOS

*A few more historic photographs that people chose to
believe, even though they were pretty obvious phonies.*

FICTIONAL NEWS

Famous Footage: The "California Election Report"

Trick Shot: In 1934 Upton Sinclair, legendary muckraker
and author of *The Jungle*, an exposé of Chicago's meatpacking
industry, ran for governor of California. Sinclair's candidacy
marked one of the best chances a socialist had ever had of winning a statewide office in the U.S. That's when newsreels like the
"California Election Report" appeared. It featured interviews in a
railyard with one hobo after another, each saying that "he rode
the rails to the Golden State just as soon as he heard that the new
governor would be handing out free lunches."

The Real Picture: The newsreels were pure Hollywood, put
together by director Irving Thalberg with the support of Samuel
Goldwyn. Both considered Sinclair "a dangerous red who wanted
to rob the rich to support the poor." The hobos were just actors
(Thalberg and his crew wanted real hobos, but couldn't find any
in the L.A. railroad yard), and the "railyard" was a set on the
MGM back lot. Other newsreels were just as phony.

Development: In the days before television, newsreels were a primary source of news for the public, and this negative coverage—
shown repeatedly in California theatres—helped ensure Sinclair's
defeat.

ON TOP OF THE WORLD

Famous Photos: Frederick Cook at the North Pole

Trick Shots: On September 6, 1909, an exhausted Robert Peary
wired from Labrador, "Stars and Stripes nailed to the Pole—
Peary." Peary, 53, had apparently realized a goal he'd set 23 years
earlier—to be the first person to reach the North Pole. But it
turned out that he was too late: On September 1, explorer Frederick Cook had wired from the Shetland Islands that he'd made it to
the North Pole the year before. Cook's proof: photographs of him
and his Eskimo companions at the Pole. Cook's photographs,
which were published all over the world, marked the completion

of one of the last great exploratory challenges on earth—or did they?

The Real Picture: As it turned out, it was another of Cook's "accomplishments" that got him into trouble. Cook had previously claimed he'd been to the summit of Mount McKinley. "On the day Cook received the keys to New York City for his North Pole trek," write the editors of Reader's Digest in *Strange Stories of America's Past,* "the man who'd supposedly climbed McKinley with him admitted they'd never really been near the 20,320-foot peak." The Explorer's Club investigated and found that the McKinley 'summit' picture had been taken from a 5,300-foot ridge.

Development: The scandal brought Cook's North Pole claims into question but, amazingly, he so charmed the public that many people sided with him over Peary. His spurious North Pole pictures weren't totally discredited until 1918, two years before Peary's death. (Dr. Cook later served four years in Leavenworth prison for promoting stock in a company owning oil he "discovered" in Wyoming.)

WHO'S WHO IN THE REVOLUTION?

Famous Photos: Spanish Loyalists committing atrocities in the Spanish Civil War (1936–1939)

Trick Shot: In 1936, "when the Spanish Civil War broke out, U.S. newspaper baron William Randolph Hearst jumped into the fray. He ran photos showing atrocities—being committed by the pro-democracy Loyalists against Fascist followers of Francisco Franco."

The Real Picture: The Spanish picture was actually Franco's men committing atrocities against the Loyalists.

Development: The controversy helped turn public opinion against the Loyalists and hastened World War II. Without more support from the U.S. and other Allied powers, the Loyalists faltered and the Nazi-supported fascists were able to defeat their enemies—providing momentum for Hitler and Mussolini.

Is it true that the average person speaks only 10 minutes each day?

UNFINISHED MASTERPIECE: LEONARDO'S HORSE

*Here's an unfinished masterpiece from one
of the Renaissance's greatest geniuses.*

THE HORSE STATUE. *Created by Leonardo da Vinci.
Would have been the largest equestrian monument on earth if it
had been built. Leonardo considered it a crowning achievement.*
Background: In the 1480s, the Duke of Sforza commissioned
Leonardo to build a huge statue of a horse to honour his father,
Francesco Sforza. Da Vinci worked on it for nearly 17 years,
studying horses and making a series of models, including a full-
sized clay model that was 7.3 metres [24 feet] tall. Next he made
moulds, into which more than 50 tons of molten bronze would be
poured to create the final horse. Then a war broke out.
Unfinished Masterpiece: On September 10, 1499, before da Vinci
could cast the horse, the French captured Milan. Some soldiers
camped nearby—and a company of them used the clay model for
target practice, riddling it with holes. Afterwards, the model was
totally destroyed by exposure to the weather. When Leonardo died
20 years later, he was "still mourning the loss of his great horse."
Update: In 1977 an American named Charles Dent happened to
pick up a copy of *National Geographic* magazine, which contained
an article on Leonardo and his horse. Dent was an Italian Renaissance buff and decided that completing Leonardo's horse would be
a fitting way to honour the greatest mind of the period. Leonardo
had left no detailed drawings or other notes that indicated what
the final horse was supposed to look like; all that survived were
preliminary sketches. No matter—Dent decided to wing it, and on
September 10, 1999, exactly 500 years to the day that Da Vinci
was forced to abandon his dream, his horse (or at least an approximation) was unveiled in Milan. It was intended, Dent explained,
as a gift "to all the Italian people from the American people." But,
ironically, few Italians attended the unveiling—mostly Americans
showed up (not Dent, though, he'd died a few years earlier).

Bet on it: Horse jockeys are the only U.S. athletes legally allowed to bet on themselves.

DRAT, SHE'S DEAD!

You don't always get a Hollywood ending when you're making a Hollywood film. Sometimes the star dies or becomes incapacitated during filming. It happened in these movies. Here's how they handled it.

SARATOGA (1937), *starring Jean Harlow and Clark Gable*
The Situation: The 26-year-old Harlow, "Hollywood's original platinum blonde," died of kidney failure when the film was only about half complete. MGM wanted to abandon production and scrap what they had, but Harlow's fans protested. So the studio "and a very reluctant Gable" continued filming.
Body Double: Harlow's scenes were filmed with her stand-in, Mary Dees, who was "carefully lit and photographed in long shots, over the shoulder, from behind, looking through binoculars, or under wide-brimmed hats." Ironically, the film, which grossed $3.3 million, was the most successful of Harlow's career—and also the most critically acclaimed (although the *New York Times* complained that in the film, "Harlow was patently not her tempestuous self.")

THE CROW (1994), *starring Brandon Lee—son of martial-arts star Bruce Lee*
The Situation: A horrible accident occurred just three days before filming was to be completed. In the story, Lee's character is shot and killed. In real life, that's what happened to Lee. The tip of one of the blanks loaded in a .44-caliber handgun hit Lee, 27, in the stomach when the gun was fired during a scene. He died shortly after. Police said it was an accident.

Producer Ed Pressman says: "We weren't so sure if we wanted to finish it. But Brandon's mother and his girlfriend, whom he planned to marry just after it was finished, wanted it finished and released. So we finished it."
Body Double: The producers altered some existing footage digitally and made plans to film new footage using stuntmen who would be wearing special face masks made from a plaster cast of Lee's face. But the stuntmen refused to wear the masks, arguing they were in bad taste. 'No one felt good about wearing the masks," says make-up artist Lance Anderson. "The director finally got around that problem by filming long shots instead."

YOU CAN'T CHEAT AN HONEST MAN (1938), *starring W. C. Fields*

The Situation: Fields was one of Hollywood's legendary drunks Most of the time that didn't interfere with his films, but *You Can't Cheat an Honest Man* was different—Fields, who was supposed to both write the film and star in it, was too drunk to do either.

Body Double: Director George Marshall compensated by hiring a writing "assistant" named Everett Freeman for Fields, and by casting other stars like Edgar Bergen and Charlie McCarthy in the film to take up some of Fields's screen time. He also hired a double for Fields and filmed him in long shots. That turned out to be a particularly smart move: one afternoon, in the middle of production, Fields shuffled off the set into his limousine (which had a wet bar in the back) and never returned.

Marshall still didn't have all the footage of Fields that he needed to finish the film—so he improvised. He combined what he had with shots of Fields's double and put Edgar Bergan and Charlie McCarthy onscreen even longer.

Despite its flaws—or more likely because of them—the movie was a hit and to this day is considered a W. C. Fields classic. "All the critics," says Everett Freman, "referred to the movie's daring innovations, its departure from formula, and its innovative use of the camera—especially on the long shots intercutting to the close-ups."

THE THREE STOOGES (1955)

The Situation: Shemp Howard replaced his brother Curly in the Stooges in 1949 and co-starred with them for six years. In 1955, while working on several Stooges films, he had a heart attack and died.

Body Double: Moe and Larry considered appearing as a duo, but Columbia Pictures wouldn't hear of it. They also wouldn't scrap the unfinished Shemp episodes. Instead, they hired Joe Palma as a double. His face was never seen—his back was always to the camera.

The four episodes: *Hot Stuff, Rumpus in the Harem, Scheming Schemers,* and *Commotion on the Ocean.* Check them out sometime.

TO SLEEP—OR NOT TO SLEEP?

*Here are some random facts about sleeping that you may not know.
Complied for us by the BRI's own John Darling, who has never met
Peter Pan and would like us to stop asking if he has, already.
(He probably hasn't had enough sleep.)*

THE NEED FOR SLEEP

Newborn babies sleep about 16 hours a day—adults average half that. Teens, especially girls, are gluttons for sleep (10 hours average), but it's not because they're lazy, as many parents think. Stanford researchers found it was tied to the complex inner labours of puberty. This hunch is underlined by teen girls' need for extra Z's during their periods.

• We sleep best at certain times and if we stray from our required sleep needs, there's no telling what will happen. The nuclear disasters at both Chernobyl and Three Mile Island, as well as the Exxon Valdez wreck and Challenger shuttle explosion, have been linked to lack of sleep or altered sleep cycles among key people at key moments.

• "Jet lag" shifts our sleep cycle, often creating confusion, mental dullness and a desire to sleep at odd times. The Army was disappointed to find that troops flown overseas often require a week to overcome their disorientation. This phenomenon is the bane of passenger jet crews. In one instance, for example, all three members of a jetliner crew fell asleep as they reached the end of their overnight New York-to-Los Angeles flight. While air traffic controllers radioed them frantically, the jet flew 100 miles out over the ocean. Finally, one of the crew woke up and saw the sea in every direction. They had just enough fuel to make it back to the Los Angeles airport.

TO NAP OR NOT TO NAP?

• According to Stanley Coren, in his book *Sleep Thieves,* science has identified the two big peaks in our need for sleep—at 3 a.m. and 3 p.m. The first is dead in the center of our sleep cycle, but the second is smack in the middle of our workday. Shouldn't we

be napping in mid-afternoon? At present, only 38% of us do.
• Who's getting the most sleep? Surveys find:
—In the U.S., Westerners and Southerners sleep longer than Easterners and Midwesterners.
—Women sleep more than men.
—Poor people sleep more than the rich.
—People who work evening or night shifts get far less sleep—about 5.6 hours—than day workers. No matter how hard they try, researchers say, people who sleep out of their normal cycle never fully adjust.

DOES LESS SLEEP = SUCCESS?
• A short sleep cycle is not inherently bad. Some people seek it out and sing its praises. Multi-millionaire magnate Donald Trump boasts of needing only three to four hours a night. Former junk-bond king Michael Millken gets only four to five hours.
• This raises the question: is there a link between sleep and success? Tufts University researcher Ernest Hartmann found that people who sleep less than 5.5 hours tend to be extroverted, ambitious and efficient, while people who sleep more than 9 hours tend to be anxious, insecure, introverted and indecisive. Other researchers think this is nonsense, noting that short-sleepers tend to be fast-paced, Type-A personalities (thus prone to heart disease), while long-sleepers include society's creative, alternate type thinkers and artists.
• Researchers hoped a survey of the CEO's and chairs of the Fortune 500 companies would settle the question of whether "the early bird really does get the worm." Apparently, it does. They found that 46% of the leaders they surveyed slept an hour less than the national average of 7.5 hours. Fifteen percent slept 5–6 hours and 2% slept 4–5 hours.

THE TRICK OF GETTING MORE SLEEP
Most of us, however, aren't looking for ways to sleep less—our focus is on how to get more. Here are some tips from the experts:
• Go to bed about the same time each night.
• Avoid nightcaps, except warm milk.
• Avoid illuminated clocks (they're a reminder you can't sleep).
• Exercise before going to bed.
• A dark and slightly cool bedroom is best (about 18° C).

MORE
STRANGE LAWSUITS

Here are a few more real-life examples of unusual legal battles.

THE PLAINTIFF: Janet R.
THE DEFENDANT: Kay-Bee Toys at Valley View Mall, Roanoke, Virginia
THE LAWSUIT: She claimed that while shopping in the mall in 1996, she was hit by a truck—a toy truck. Apparently a customer, playing with a radio-controlled 4 x 4, bumped Robinson in the ankle. She sued for $100,000, asking compensation for "pain, humiliation, aggravation and disability."
THE VERDICT: Suit dropped by plaintiff.

THE PLAINTIFF: Etta Stephens of Tampa, Florida
THE DEFENDANT: The Barnett Bank
THE LAWSUIT: In 1995 Stephens opened the envelope containing her monthly money market statement—and found the account balance listed as zero, instead of $20,000 as she expected. "Upon seeing this," says one report, "Stephens clutched her bosom and fell to the ground" with a heart attack. Officials of the bank said it was a mistake caused by a "printing error" and apologized. But Stephens still sued them for nearly killing her.
THE VERDICT: Unknown.

THE PLAINTIFF: Katherine Balog, 60-year-old Californian
THE DEFENDANTS: Bill Clinton and the Democratic Party
THE LAWSUIT: In 1992 Balog filed suit "to recover damages for the trauma of Clinton's candidacy." She claimed she was suffering "serious emotional and mental stress" because Clinton, a "Communist sympathizer" and "draft dodger," was about to be elected president.
THE VERDICT: Unknown.

THE PLAINTIFF: Bennie Casson
THE DEFENDANT: PT's Show Club, an Illinois strip joint

THE LAWSUIT: In 1997 a stripper named Busty Heart allegedly approached Casson during her act and "slammed" her 2.2-metre [88-inch] bust (a reported 18 kilograms [40 pounds] per breast) into his head and neck. He sued for "emotional distress" and claimed an old neck injury had been aggravated by the attack.
THE VERDICT: No lawyer would take the case, so the judge had to dismiss it.

THE PLAINTIFF: Debra Lee Benagh, 44, of Denver
THE DEFENDANT: Elitch Gardens, an amusement park
THE LAWSUIT: In 1997, according to Benagh's suit, she rode on the Mind Eraser roller coaster—and actually suffered memory loss. Benagh sued for negligence, contending that the park operators should have known of the ride's hazards.
THE VERDICT: Unknown.

THE PLAINTIFF: Swee Ho, a Chinese merchant in Thailand
THE DEFENDANT: Pu Lin, a rival merchant
THE LAWSUIT: As reported by Gerald Sparrow, once a judge in Bangkok: "Pu Lin had stated sneeringly at a party that Swee Ho's new wife, Li Bua, was merely a decoration to show how rich her husband was. Swee Ho, he said, could no longer 'please the ladies.' Swee Ho sued his rival for slander in the British Consular Court, claiming that Li Bua was his wife in every sense."
THE VERDICT: Swee Ho won—without a word of testimony. Swee Ho's lawyer "simply put the blushing Li Bua in the witness box. She was quite obviously pregnant."

* * * *

IRONIC TWIST
The Ramses brand condom is named after the great Pharaoh Ramses II, who fathered over 160 children.

When medieval Europeans burned witches, the witches' families had to pay for the firewood.

THE ULTIMATE TASTE TEST

According to Dr. Alan Hirsch's Smell & Taste Treatment and Research Foundation, the fruits and vegetables you prefer tell a lot about your personality. Want proof? Take this test that Dr. Hirsch has put together—no cheating!—then let us know if you think we should print more.

1. Which groups of fruits do you prefer?
a) Oranges, Bananas, and Grapes
b) Eggplant, Corn, and Tomatoes
Analysis: If you prefer the first group, this indicates a strong-minded, ambitious, aggressive, dominant individual, who is a natural leader. If you prefer the second group, this indicates an introspective, self-searching person who is sensitive to the needs of others. You tend not to be impulsive in your decision-making processes, but rather weigh all the alternatives in question before making your decision.

2. Of these pairs of fruits, which do you prefer? (Must choose one of each pair.)
a) Applesauce or Fresh Apples
b) Pineapple Chunks or Pineapple Glaze
c) Creamed Corn or Corn on the Cob
Analysis: If at least two of the above are the first choice, then you are a passive, easy-going, agreeable sort, who tries to solve problems without raising a commotion. If at least two of the above are the second choice, you tend to be an aggressive "go-getter" who will not take "No" for an answer. You work hard and play hard.

3. Do you like spicy pickles?
Analysis: If YES, you tend to be pessimistic. If NO, you tend to be optimistic.

4. Do you like:
a) Bananas; **b)** Boiled fish; **c)** Fruit; **d)** Honey;
e) Tapioca; **f)** Celery; **g)** Nuts; **h)** Hot Curry

60% of the country of Leichtenstein's GNP is generated by the sale of false teeth.

Analysis: If five or more is YES you are a natural optimist and view life through rose-coloured glasses. You are a pleasant co-worker and would make a good friend. If five or more is NO, you tend to be pessimistic. Before being involved in social intercourse, you tend to be careful, doubting others' intentions.

5. Which do you prefer?
a) Green Olives or Black Olives
b) Pecans or Almonds
c) Pickles or Cucumbers
Analysis: If two or more are the first choice, you tend to be assertive in your relationships and enthusiastic in all endeavors. Although anxious at times, you are a decisive, resilient person, prone to action. If two or more are the second choice, you tend to take responsibility for your actions. You are self-confident and a natural leader.

6. Which do you prefer?
a) Lemons or Oranges
b) Potatoes or Yams
c) Grapefruit or Tangerines
Analysis: If two or more are the first choice, you tend to be reserved, quiet, and contemplative. You usually are not impulsive. You tend towards introspection. If two or more is the second choice, you tend to be an out-going, gregarious person who enjoys a sound relationship. Many consider you to have a good sense of humour. You would make a good disc jockey, used car salesman, or politician.

* * * *

RANDOM ANIMAL FACT
A female lobster, called a hen or chicken, can lay
as many as 100,000 eggs at one time.
Most end up as "food for
other marine life."

BEEN NOWHERE, DONE NOTHING

BRI member Debbie Thornton sent in this list of real-life bumper stickers. Have you seen the one that says...

SUBURBIA: *Where They Tear Down the Trees and Name Streets After Them*

I Have No Idea What I'm Doing Out of Bed

Been Nowhere, Done Nothing

Support Bacteria: It's the Only Culture Some People Have

I Used to Be Indecisive; Now I'm Not Sure

No Sense Being Pessimistic— It Wouldn't Work Anyway

The More You Complain, the Longer God Lets You Live

Forget About World Peace— Visualize Using Your Turn Signal!

Warning: *Dates in Calendar Are Closer Than They Appear*

Consciousness: That Annoying Time Between Naps

Age Is a Very High Price to Pay for Maturity

I Doubt, Therefore I Might Be

The Older You Get, the Better You Realize You Were

Dyslexics Have More Fnu

Men Are from Earth. Women Are from Earth. Deal With It.

The Gene Pool Could Use a Little Chlorine

So You're a Feminist— Isn't That Cute!

Time Is What Keeps Things from Happening All at Once

Your Kid May Be an Honour Student but You're Still an Idiot

We Have Enough Youth, How About a Fountain of "Smart"?

HOW TO MAKE A MONSTER, PART II

Here's the second instalment of our history of Uncle John's favourite movie monster—Gojira, the original Japanese name for Godzilla. (Part I starts on page 79.)

DESIGNING A MONSTER

It took the model department three tries to come up with the right design for Gojira. The first model had fishlike scales for skin and a line of pointy spikes running down its back. Producer Tomoyuki Tanaka liked the spikes, but thought the head was too big and the scales too "fishy." Next they created a "warty" Gojira with a smaller head and large rounded bumps on the skin. Tanaka didn't like this treatment either, so they came up with "alligator" Gojira, this time with much smaller, linear bumps arranged in rows like bumps on an alligator's back. Alligator Gojira got the nod.

SUITS ME FINE

Now Tanaka had a name and a look for his monster—but what kind of special effects would he use? Stop-motion animation, (e.g. claymation) used tiny, moveable clay models, and was filmed frame by frame. It produced excellent results—King Kong was filmed with stop-motion animation—but was time consuming and expensive. Plus, it limited the amount of detail that could be shown—a big problem, since so much of the script involved the monster knocking down buildings. (It's almost impossible to make a building collapse realistically when filming frame by frame.)

The alternative: use a man in a monster suit. That could be filmed at a larger scale, making higher levels of detail possible. And because the footage would be filmed in "real time" instead of frame by frame, it could be finished in a few weeks instead of several months. The problem with such a low-tech technique was that if the filmmakers weren't careful, the man in the monster suit would end up looking like—a man in a monster suit.

In the end, it was scheduling that decided the issue—a

monster suit was quicker, and Toho studios had only a year to produce the film, so Gojira became a man in a costume.

The special-effects crew built a full-sized Gojira model, which
they used to create plaster moulds for the monster suit. Then they
poured latex rubber into the moulds to make Gojira's skin. The
skin was then attached to a cloth "inner skin," made of cloth
stuffed with polystyrene foam and bamboo to provide the
monster's bulk. The fully assembled suit weighed more than 100
kilograms [220 pounds].

The actor entered the costume via a zipper that ran along the dor-
sal fin; he was (barely) able to see out of the costume through four
tiny holes in Gojira's neck. The monster's head was then mounted
on a brace that rested on the actor's head; an offscreen technician
used a radio-controlled mechanism to open and close the mouth.

SWEATY WORK

Gojira's action sequences were filmed at a high speed so that when
it was slowed down for viewing, the buildings crumbled more realistically. But this meant that the set had to be lit twice as bright as
when filming at normal speed, and the hot lights caused temperatures inside the suit to climb as high as 49° C [120°F], with the
only ventilation provided by the eyeholes in Gojira's neck.

Under these conditions it was nearly impossible to film for
more than a few minutes at a time. Typically, the actor inside the
suit would spend 7 to 10 minutes rehearsing a scene in costume
with the studio lights turned off. Then the lights came on and the
scene was filmed for about 3 minutes, which was all the actor
could take before he risked passing out from heat prostration and
suffocation. Collapsing mid-scene was not unusual, and two actors
who alternated as Gojira sweated so profusely that the crew
drained as much as half a pint of sweat from the suit at the end of
the day.

The on-screen result of filming in such difficult conditions
was a slow, lumbering creature who shuffled and lurched across the
tiny cityscapes—but that was just the look that Tanaka wanted: in
the 1950s, paleontologists incorrectly assumed that most dinosaurs
were huge, slow-witted, slow-moving creatures, and Tanaka's quest
for dinosaur accuracy dovetailed nicely with the limitations
imposed by the heavy suit and hot studio lights.

TINY TOWN
Entire city blocks of downtown Tokyo were reconstructed in elaborate detail for the film. For the scene in which Gojira destroys Tokyo's famous Ginza district, special effects man Eiji Tsuburaya's technicians reproduced a three-square-block section of the district in miniature, complete with interior floors and walls to make sure the buildings would crumble realistically when Gojira smashes them. Tsuburaya also insisted that the tiny automobiles, buses, and trains be hand made from cast iron to ensure that when Gojira stepped on them, the sturdy little vehicles would crush realistically.

MAKING NOISE
Finding a suitable roar for Gojira was one of the trickier aspects of creating the monster. The film's sound-effects team tried numerous actual animal sounds: grunts, growls, roars, and other noises. They played them backward, forward, individually, and in groups, but nothing seemed to work. Then composer Akira Ifukube tried rubbing the strings of a bass violin with the fingers of a resin-coated rubber glove, and reverberating the sound. That did the trick.

OPENING NIGHT
Finally, after 122 days of filming, Gojira premiered in Japan on November 3, 1954. The film had cost a fortune to make—the final tally was 60 million yen (about $65 million in 1999 dollars), about 250 times the average cost of a Japanese film at that time.

But it turned out to be a good investment: Gojira was one of the most popular films of the year and earned a fortune for Toho.

Gojira was also a critical success. "While American monster-on-the-loose films used radiation to get the monster up and running around," David Kalat writes in *A Critical History and Filmography of Toho's Godzilla Series*, "Honda saw his monster as a narrative device to discuss the terror of the nuclear age." Less than a decade after World War II, Japanese critics understood and appreciated the implicit message.

Turn to page 184 for Part III.

MODEL CITIZENS

Some thoughtful commentary from the mouths of "babes."

"I don't have to fake dumb. I am dumb."

—**Jerry Hall**

"I don't wake up for less than $10,000 a day."

—**Linda Evangelista**

"Everywhere I went, my cleavage followed. But I learned I am not my cleavage."

—**Carole Mallory**

"I'm so naive about finances. Once when my mother mentioned an amount and I realized I didn't understand, she had to explain: 'That's like three Mercedes.' Then I understood."

—**Brooke Shields**

"Blah, blah, blah. I'm so tired of talking about myself."

—**Elle Macpherson**

"I don't think I was born beautiful. I just think I was born me."

—**Naomi Campbell**

"I've always been a bit more maturer than what I am."

—**Samantha Fox**

"Everyone should have enough money to get plastic surgery."

—**Beverly Johnson**

"I believe that mink are raised for being turned into fur coats and if we didn't wear fur coats those little animals would never have been born. So is it better not to have been born or to have lived for a year or two to have been turned into a fur coat? I don't know."

—**Barbi Benton**

"People think modelling's mindless, that you just stand there and pose, but it doesn't have to be that way. I like to have a lot of input. I know how to wear a dress, whether it should be shot with me standing up or sitting. And I'm not scared to say what I think."

—**Linda Evangelista**

"I look at modelling as something I'm doing for black people in general."

—**Naomi Campbell**

"I can do anything you want me to do so long as I don't have to speak."

—**Linda Evangelista**

"I wish my butt did not go sideways, but I guess I have to face that."

—**Christie Brinkley**

MY BODY LIES OVER THE OCEAN

*More stories about miscellaneous body parts
removed from famous people after they died.*

EINSTEIN'S EYES

Where They're Located: Bank vault in New Jersey
How They Got There: It turns out Dr. Harvey wasn't the
only sticky-fingered professional at Einstein's autopsy (see p. 102):
at about the same time Harvey was absconding with the brain,
Einstein's ophthalmologist, a doctor named Henry Abrams, was
removing the eyes. He placed them in a jar and locked them away
in a bank vault until 1994, when he reportedly began looking for a
buyer. "When you look into his eyes, you're looking into the beau-
ties and mysteries of the world," he told Britain's Guardian newspaper. "They are clear as crystal; they seem to have such depth."

JOSEPH HAYDN'S SKULL

Where It's Located: In Haydn's marble crypt in Eisenstadt, Austria, after being separated from the rest of the body for more than
145 years
How It Got There: Haydn's patron, the Prince of Esterhazy, saw
to it that Haydn's body was buried intact following the composer's
death in 1809. But some phrenologists (people who "read" skulls)
wanted to see if they could divine the source of the composer's
genius by looking at his skull. So they dug up his body, removed
the head, took it away for study—and then refused to bring it back
unless the Prince of Esterhazy paid them a ransom. The prince
balked at paying the blackmail, so Haydn was reburied, without
his head.

The head eventually ended up in the Musikverein museum in
Vienna, Austria, where it was stolen, eventually resurfacing "in
the home of an Austrian professor, who displayed it on his piano,"
and then returned to the museum in 1895. That year the village of
Eisenstadt began lobbying for the head's return to Haydn's crypt.

They negotiated until 1935, to no avail. Then, at the end of

Medical term for earwax: cerumen.

World War II, they tried again. Negotiations dragged on for nine years, and finally, in 1954, Haydn's head was reunited with the rest of his body.

SANTA CLAUS'S FINGERS
Where They're Located: "Now on display in the city of Antalya, Turkey"
How They Got There: Saint Nicholas, the Catholic bishop believed to be the inspiration for Santa Claus, died in the fourth century A.D. He was buried in his old church, in what is now the Turkish town of Demre, on the Mediterranean coast. But somehow, his remains ended up in a church in the Italian port of Bari (tradition has it Italian merchants from Bari stole them in 1087), and the town of Demre has been trying to get the bones back for 900 years. All they have left is "a finger or two," on display in a nearby city.

"One reason Christians aren't keen to send the bones back," the Wall Street Journal reports, "is because Turkey is now predominantly Muslim. In fact, some believe the 11th-century Christian monks in Myra allowed the Italians to remove the bones in order to save them from the advancing Turkish armies."

Muammer Karabulut, chairman of the Santa Claus Foundation, which seeks the return of the bones, says his group's mostly Muslim membership should not be an issue. After all, he insists, "Santa Claus is [a] universal figure."

STONEWALL JACKSON'S ARM
Where It's Located: The Chancellorville battle site near Fredericksburg, Virginia
How it Got There: On May 2, 1863, as he was returning to camp after engineering an important victory for the Confederacy, the legendary general was accidentally shot by his own troops. Jackson was hit in the right hand and in the left wrist and shoulder, and his left arm had to be amputated above the elbow.

Jackson's chaplain, B. Tucker Lacy, had a brother who owned a house near the hospital, so he took the severed limb to his brother's for burial. Confederate troops buried the arm in a nearby field, complete with a religious ceremony and a marble tombstone. When Jackson died from complications eight days later, he was buried in Lexington, Virginia.

According to Roadside America, "The arm was exhumed in 1929 and reburied in a steel box on a plantation known as Ellwood. Around the field in which it now lays, there is only one gravestone: the one belonging to Jackson's arm."

OTHER CELEBRITY BODY PARTS

• **Thomas Hardy's heart.** "Hardy's heart was to be buried in Stinsford, England, his birthplace, after the rest of his body was cremated in Dorchester. All went according to plan until the great poet's sister's cat snatched the heart off her kitchen table and disappeared into the woods with it."

• **Emanuel Swedenborg's skull.** The famous Swedish philosopher's skull was stolen by a retired sea captain 50 years after Swedenborg's death. It turned up in an antique shop in Wales a century later. When Swedenborg's descendents learned of the skull's existence, they went to Wales and bought it—and then auctioned it off at Sotheby's for $3,200.

• **Buddha's teeth.** Tradition has it that two or three teeth (depending on who you ask) were found in Buddha's cremated remains following his death 2,400 years ago. Today the teeth are in temples in Beijing, China; Sri Lanka; and Taipei, Taiwan.

• **Percy Bysshe Shelley's heart.** When he drowned in 1822, Shelley "was cremated on the beach to which his body had washed. For some reason his heart would not burn and it was taken from the fire and given to his wife, Mary Wollstonecraft Shelley (author of Frankenstein), who carried it with her in a silken shroud everywhere she went for the rest of her life."

• **Chang and Eng Bunker's liver.** The two brothers, born in Thailand in 1811, were attached at the chest. P. T. Barnum made them world-famous (coining the term "Siamese twin"). One or both of their livers was apparently removed upon their death, and now sits in a jar at the Mutter Museum in Philadelphia.

*   *   *   *

Random Fact: On average, cats spend 30% of their waking hours grooming themselves. They purr at 26 cycles per second, about the same frequency as an idling diesel engine.

Squirrels cannot see the color red.

WORD ORIGINS

Ever wonder where words come from?
Here are some interesting stories.

JACKPOT
Meaning: A huge prize
Origin: "The term goes back to draw poker, where stakes are allowed to accumulate until a player is able to 'open the pot' by demonstrating that among the cards he has drawn he has a pair of jacks or better." (From *Dictionary of Word and Phrase Origins, Vol. II,* by William and Mary Morris)

GRENADE
Meaning: A small, hand-thrown missile containing an explosive
Origin: "The word comes from the French pomegrenade, for pomegranate, because the military missile, which dates from the sixteenth century, both is shaped like the fruit and explodes much as the seeds burst out from it." (From *Fighting Words,* by Christine Ammer)

AMMONIA
Meaning: A potent, odourous cleaning fluid
Origin: "Ammonia is so called because it was first made from the dung of the worshippers' camels at the temple of Jupiter Ammon in Egypt." (From *Remarkable Words with Astonishing Origins,* by John Train)

HEATHEN
Meaning: An ungodly person
Origin: "Christianity began as primarily an urban religion; people in rural districts continued to worship older gods. The Latin word for countryman was paganus—whence, of course, pagan; the Germanic tongues had a similar word, something like khaithanaz, 'dwelling in the heath' (wilderness)—whence heathen." (From *Loose Cannons and Red Herrings,* by Robert Claiborne)

On average, adults have 2 gallons of air in the space between their skin and their clothes.

CALCULATE
Meaning: Add, subtract, divide, and/or multiply numbers or money
Origin: "In Rome 2,000 years ago the merchant figured his profit and loss using what he called calculi, or 'little stones' as counters. So the Latin term calculus, 'pebble,' not only gave us calculate but…our word calculus…one of the most complicated forms of modern mathematics." (From *Word Origins*, by Wilfred Funk, Litt. D.)

MUSEUM
Meaning: Building or collection of art, music, scientific tools, or any specific set of objects
Origin: A shrine to the Greek Muses. "Such a shrine was known as a mouseion…When the Museum at Alexandria was destroyed in the fourth century…the word nearly dropped out of use. Three hundred years ago, a scholar rediscovered the word." (From *Thereby Hangs a Tale*, by Charles Earle Funk)

DOPE
Meaning: Drugs
Origin: "This word was originally a Dutch word, doop, meaning a sauce or liquid. Its first association with narcotics came when it was used to describe the viscous glop that results from heating opium. Then, by rapid extension, it came to mean any narcotic." (From *Dictionary of Word and Phrase Origins, Vol. III,* by William and Mary Morris)

RIVAL
Meaning: Competitor
Origin: "A rival is etymologically "someone who uses the same stream as another.' The word comes from Latin *rivalis*, meaning 'of a stream.' People who use or live by the same stream are neighbours and, human nature being as it is, are usually in competition with each other." (From *Dictionary of Word Origins*, by John Ayto)

Q & A:
ASK THE EXPERTS

Here are some more random questions, with answers from trivia experts.

THE COLD, WET TRUTH

Q: Why does your nose run in cold weather?

A: "It is not necessarily because you have a cold. If very cold air is suddenly inhaled, the mucous membranes inside your nostrils first constrict, then rapidly dilate as a reflex reaction. This permits an excess of mucous to form, resulting in a runny nose or the 'sniffles.'" (From *The Handy Weather Answer Book*, by Walter A. Lyons, Ph.D.)

HAPPY TRAILS

Q: Why do jets leave a trail of white behind them?

A: "The white trail that you see is, in fact, a man-made cloud. At low altitudes, the air is able to absorb large quantities of water. But at high altitudes, water has a tendency to come out of the air, which can form a cloud. This only happens, though, if the air contains small particles—such as dust—on which the water can condense. It also helps the process if the air is agitated.

"Now enter the high-flying jet. Its exhaust fills the air with a huge supply of spent fuel particles, and at the same time it shakes or agitates the air...leaving a long, narrow cloud behind it." (From *Ever Wonder Why?*, by Douglas B. Smith)

EURASIA, EURASIA

Q: Why are Asia and Europe considered two continents even though they appear to be one?

A: "The ancient Greeks thought the Eurasian landmass was divided in two by the line of water running from the Aegean Sea to the far shore of the Black Sea.

"By the time they found out otherwise, Europeans were not about to surrender their continental status." (From *Why Things Are*, by Joel Achenbach)

YOU EXPECT ME TO SWALLOW THAT?
Q: How do circus sword swallowers do it?
A: Believe it or not, they really do swallow the sword. The main problem is learning how to relax the throat muscles and stop gagging. This takes weeks of practise—but it can be done.

"The sword doesn't cut the sword swallower's throat because its sides are dull. The point is usually sharp, but that's not a problem as long as the sword swallower doesn't swallow any swords long enough to poke him (or her) in the pit of the stomach." (From *Know It All!*, by Ed Zotti)

METHOD TO THE MADNESS?
Q: How are interstate highways numbered in the U.S.?
A: "Believe it or not, this is one government practice that is organized and logical. All east-west interstate highways are even-numbered and increase from south to north. Thus, east–west Interstate 80 is north of I-10. North–south interstates are odd-numbered and increase from west to east. City bypasses and spurs have triple digits and are numbered odd or even depending on their directional orientation." (From *Thoughts for the Throne*, by Don Voorhees)

YOU GET WHAT YOU PAY FOR
Q: If you dropped a penny from the top of the Empire State Building (or any skyscraper) and it happened to hit someone on the head, would it easily pierce their skull?
A: "Given that the Empire State Building is 381 metres [1,250 feet] tall and ignoring such factors as wind resistance, a penny dropped from the top would hit the ground in approximately 8.8 seconds, having reached a speed of roughly 85 metres [280 feet] per second. This is not particularly fast. A low-powered .22 or .25 caliber bullet, to which a penny is vaguely comparable in terms of mass, typically has a muzzle velocity of 244 to 335 metres [800 to 1,100 feet] per second....

"On top of this we must consider that the penny would probably tumble while falling, and that the Empire State Building...is surrounded by strong updrafts, which would slow descent considerably. Thus, while you might conceivably inflict a fractured skull on some hapless New Yorker, the penny would certainly not 'go through just like that.'" (From *The Straight Dope*, by Cecil Adams)

An exocannibal is a cannibal who eats only enemies. An endocannibal eats only friends.

MONKEY SEE, MONKEY DO

Do television and movies influence our actions?
Of course, but unfortunately, some people take it
to extremes. There's just no cure for stupidity.

MONKEY SEE: In the 1971 film *The Godfather*, Corleone family henchmen intimidate a Hollywood mogul by killing his prize race horse and sticking the horse's head in his bed.

MONKEY DO: In 1997 two New York crooks decided to use a similar method to intimidate a witness scheduled to testify against them at trial: "On the morning the witness was scheduled to testify, they left the head of a slaughtered animal as a death threat. 'We wanted to leave a cow's head because his wife was from India, and they consider cows sacred,' one said. 'But where do you find a cow's head in Brooklyn? So I went to some butcher in Flatbush and found a goat head. I figured it was close enough.'" One crook was sentenced to 4 years in prison; the other got 14 to 42 years.

MONKEY SEE: In the video for Joe Diffie's song "John Deere Green," a boy climbs a water tower and paints a green heart."

MONKEY DO: "This apparently gave some genius in Mississippi the bright idea of scaling his local water tower and painting 'Billy Bo Bob Loves Charlene' in green paint. Perhaps tuckered out from having to write all three of his first names on the water tower, the guy then lost his balance and was seriously injured when he hit the ground." (*Chicago Sun-Times*)

MONKEY SEE: In the 1993 film *The Program*, "drunk college football players lie down in the middle of a busy road to prove their toughness."

MONKEY DO: "A scene in the movie *The Program* will be deleted after one teenager was killed and two others critically injured while apparently imitating the scene, the Walt Disney Co. said Tuesday....Sources indicated it will cost $350,000 to $400,000 to re-edit." (*Daily Variety*)

Al Capone's older brother Vince Capone was a policeman in Nebraska.

MONKEY SEE: In 1997 Taco Bell introduced a new advertising campaign featuring a talking Chihuahua that has since become known as the "Taco Bell Dog."

MONKEY DO: Since then, sales and adoptions of Chihuahuas have gone through the roof. "Before the Taco Bell commercials became popular, no one wanted Chihuahuas," says Marsha Teague of the Portland, Oregon, humane society. "Now people ask specifically for the 'Taco Bell Dog.'" The dogs, priced from $300 to $600, "sell within two days, faster if their colouration resembles the actual TV star. "We can't even keep them in stock," a pet-shop owner says. "Everybody always comes in and imitates the Taco Bell commercial." *(Portland Oregonian)*

On the other hand, it isn't necessarily all bad:

MONKEY SEE: The *Nancy Drew* series is about a strong-willed, independent teenage detective who constantly finds herself in danger, then has to think her way out of it.

MONKEY DO: In the early 1990s, an eleven-year-old Michigan girl was kidnapped and thrown into the trunk of a car. "Instead of panicking," The *Christian Science Monitor* reported, "she asked herself what Nancy Drew would do in such a situation. Then she found a toolbox, pried the trunk open, made a call from a nearby phone booth, and her assailant was arrested."

* * * *

MORE MORE MORE!

• In 1997 an employee at a Bangkok hotel was sent to prison for robbing guests' safe deposit boxes. His method: he rubbed his nose on the buttons, making them oily so he could tell which ones the guests had pushed to open the safe. His inspiration: an episode of the TV show *MacGyver*.

• In 1996, 17-year-old Steve Barone was booked for robbing a gun store. He claimed he did it "only because he was taken over by another personality, which was an amalgam of guys from the movies *Pulp Fiction*, *Reservoir Dogs*, and *Goodfellas*." *(News of the Weird)*

The ancient Greeks played cards. In those days, aces were known as "dogs."

SEEMED LIKE A GOOD IDEA AT THE TIME

*There are many plants and animals in Australia that have been
deliberately introduced. Seemed like a good idea at the time?
It's a good history lesson to examine these introductions
so that the same mistakes are not repeated in the future.*

You have to love the English! In 1859, Thomas Austin
imported 24 rabbits from England and released them on a
property in Victoria to be used for game shooting. They
must have been lousy shots! Today there are over 200 million rabbits in Australia. You can see where the term, "breed like rabbits"
came from!

You just need to look at a cane toad to realise that good looks are
not the only road to fame! Cane toads were imported from Hawaii
in 1935 to protect the sugar cane fields from the cane beetle. But
guess what? It didn't work! Scientists warned the farmers not to
bring the cane toad to Australia but the farmers didn't listen!
Cane toads are highly poisonous and have no natural predators.
They can live for up to 20 years and lay up to 40,000 eggs a year
compared to native frogs that lay 1,000 eggs. Watch out! They
will be visiting your home soon!

The European red fox was introduced near Melbourne in 1845 for
sport. It spread quickly and today is found all over Australia
except the tropical north and Tasmania. In some areas, especially
urban environments, there are an estimated 12 foxes every square
kilometre! Foxes are responsible for the decline of Australian
wildlife and small ground-dwelling native mammals are particularly vulnerable. To date they have wiped out over 50 species of
native animals.

The humble house sparrow was introduced into Australia to
alleviate the pangs of homesickness felt by those people coming
from Europe. It is now regarded as a pest because of its habit of

nesting under roofs. The common starling was introduced to help control insects and farm pests. Guess what? It was an outstanding failure and is itself a pest today.

Even our rivers haven't been immune from introductions! Five species of carp were introduced in the 1800's to enhance the sporting and aesthetic qualities of Australian waterways. They thrived and have greatly reduced stock of native fish. The mosquitofish was introduced to Australia from the Gulf of Mexico drainage system and released in 1925 to help control mosquito larvae. Sounds like a good idea? It would have been except they attack native fish and cause substantial damage to their fins as well as aggressively competing with them for food.

Even our bush hasn't been spared! Lantana was introduced into Australia once again by homesick Poms who craved for a little bit of the old country in this new foreign land. They sell this weed as a houseplant in England! Blackberries were introduced for their berries and as a source of dye. Today both plants are noxious weeds and are chocking our bush.

* * * *

CLASSIC TRIVIA
•Alexander Dumas, author of *The Three Musketeers* and *The Count of Monte Cristo*, always wrote his novels on blue paper, his poetry on yellow paper, and his non-fiction on rose-coloured paper. Always—to do otherwise, he explained, was "unspeakable."
• In one production of the opera Carmen at New York's Metropolitan Opera House, real horses were used to draw a coach carrying Enrico Caruso and co-star Maria Jeritza onstage. The bright lights and large audience so startled one of the horses that he "expressed his stage fright in a highly unsanitary fashion right on center stage."
• In a following scene, Caruso was supposed to stab Jeritza, and she was supposed to fall to the stage. But she refused to die, even when stabbed. So Caruso stabbed her again and shouted, "Die! Fall, will you!"—to which Jeritza screamed back, "I'll die if you find me a clean place."

THE ORIGIN OF BASKETBALL, PART III

We could go on and on about basketball, but we have to leave room for other subjects. So this is the last instalment of our b-ball history—for this edition. (Part I starts on page 24.)

BY ANY OTHER NAME

In 1891, when James Naismith posted the rules to his new game on the YMCA bulletin board, he didn't bother to give it a name. He just called it "A New Game." One of The Incorrigibles suggested calling it "Naismith Ball"—but the phys-ed teacher just laughed.

"I told him that I thought that name would kill any game," Naismith recalled in his memoirs. "Why not call it Basket Ball?" The delighted player spread the word, and it's been basket ball (changed to basketball in 1921) ever since.

SCORE!

The Incorrigibles took to the game right away, and by the end of the week their games were drawing a crowd. Teachers and students from a nearby women's school started showing up on their lunch hour; a few weeks later, they began organizing their own teams.

When The Incorrigibles went home for Christmas a few weeks later, they brought copies of the rules—and their enthusiasm for the game—to YMCA chapters all over the country. In January, a copy of the Springfield school paper, complete with an introduction to basketball (including diagrams and a list of rules), was sent to each of the nearly 200 YMCAs in the U.S. "We present to our readers a new game of ball," the article read, "which seems to have those elements in which it ought to make it popular among the Associations."

In the months that followed, these chapters introduced basketball to high schools and colleges in their communities; YMCA missionaries to other countries began spreading the game all over the world.

"It is doubtful whether a gymnastic game has ever spread so

There is no leading cause of death for people who live past the age of 100.

rapidly over the continent as has 'basket ball,'" Dr. Gulick wrote proudly in October 1892, before the game was even a year old. "It is played from New York to San Francisco and from Maine to Texas by…teams in associations, athletic clubs and schools." But just as soon as the rules for basketball began to spread, people began trying to change them. Sometimes they succeeded—even in the face of opposition from its founders—and sometimes they didn't. Overall, the game proved to be extraordinarily adaptable, a factor that has been instrumental in keeping it popular.

THE INVENTION OF DRIBBLING

One of the first rules to come under attack was the no-running-with-the-ball rule. When he invented the game, Naismith wanted the person with the ball to stand still and throw it to another player—who then had to stop moving and either shoot or pass.

But players quickly found that when they were cornered and couldn't pass, they could escape by either rolling or throwing the ball a few feet, then running to get it themselves. From there it was just a matter of time before they realized that by repeatedly throwing the ball in the air, they could move across the court alone—even though they weren't supposed to be moving at all. "In the early years," Paul Ricatto writes in *Basket-Ball*, "it was not uncommon to see a player running down the floor, juggling the ball a few inches above his hand. This so closely approximated running with the ball (travelling) that a rule was inserted saying that the ball must be batted higher than the player's head."

Down to Earth

Players also discovered that it was easy to move with the ball if they repeatedly bounced, or "dribbled," it with both hands. The idea is believed to have been born on the urban playgrounds of Philadelphia; from there it spread to the University of Pennsylvania and beyond. Eventually it became the preferred method of advancing the ball down the court (beating out juggling the ball over one's head).

Dr. Gulick and other basketball powers were not amused. In 1898 they inserted a rule into the official basketball rulebook outlawing two-handed dribbling. "The object of the [new] rule," Dr. Gulick wrote, "is largely to do away with dribbling….The game must remain for what it was originally intended to be—a passing game. Dribbling has introduced all of the objectionable features that are hurting the game."

Gulick assumed that the issue was dead, since one-handed dribbling was obviously too difficult for anyone to try. But players confounded the doctor. In fact, one-handed dribbling proved so effective that it became the standard.

HOW MANY PLAYERS?

Naismith originally recommended using nine players per team, but said the game could be played with almost any number—depending on the size of the court and how many people wanted to play.

Some teams took this advice to extremes: in the early 1890s, Cornell University played a game with 50 people on each side! So many spectators complained about losing sight of the ball at such games that most university teams began scaling back. Then in 1896, the University of Chicago and the University of Iowa played the first collegiate basketball game with only five players on a team. It worked so well that within a year, nearly every college team in the country used five players.

OUT-OF BOUNDS

In his original list of rules, Naismith wrote that the first player to retrieve a ball after it had gone out-of-bounds got to throw it back into play. But he wasn't sure that rule worked; it seemed to encourage dangerous play: "It was not uncommon," Naismith wrote in his memoirs, "to see a player who was anxious to secure the ball make a football dive for it, regardless of whether he went into the apparatus that was stored around the gym or into the spectators in the bleachers."

The rule ended for good one day while Naismith was supervising a game in Springfield. As occasionally happened, the ball ended up in the balcony that circled the gym. Normally, the teams would race up the stairs to get to the ball first. But on this day, while one team scrambled upstairs, the other showed it had been practising in secret. They used an acrobatic manoeuvre, boosting one player up onto the shoulders of another until they were high enough to jump over the railing onto the balcony. Naismith immediately changed the rule to what it is today (the last team to touch the ball before it goes out-of-bounds loses it).

Speechless: When William Shakespeare moved into his new home, he named it New Home.

NOTHING BUT NET

The wooden peach baskets broke easily when players threw balls at them, and within a year the YMCA replaced them with sturdier wire mesh rubbish bins. But these were a problem, too: every time someone scored, the action had to stop until the referee climbed a ladder and retrieved the ball by hand. (Apparently, nobody thought of removing the bottoms of the baskets.)

Over the next few years, the rubbish bins were replaced by specially made baskets with trapdoors that opened when the refer-ee pulled a string—and then by bare metal hoops, which let the ball drop to the ground by itself.

But the bare hoops went a little too far. When nobody was standing near the basket, it was difficult to tell whether the ball really had gone in. So the YMCA suspended a rope net under the hoop to catch the ball. Believe it or not, these nets were closed at the bottom—the ball was pushed out with a stick. It wasn't until 1912 that they finally cut off the bottom. From then on, the "swish" made it obvious whether the ball had gone in or not.

THE ORIGIN OF BACKBOARDS

It's hard to imagine shooting a basketball without a backboard. But the backboard wasn't created to help players score—it was created to keep fans out.

In gyms like the one at Springfield, the only place for fans to sit was in the balcony. It became common for them to gather near the basket during the game. From there, Robert Peterson writes,

> "It was easy for a fervid spectator to reach over the rail and guide the shots of his favourites into the basket or deflect those of his opponents. So for 1895–96, the rules called for a 4-by-6-foot [1.2-by-1.8 metre] wire or wood screen behind the basket to keep fans from interfering. Wire screens were soon dented by repeated rebounds, giving the home team an advantage because the players knew…their own back-board. So wood gradually supplanted the wire mesh boards."

ON THE MAP

From Dr. Gulick's point of view, basketball was an unqualified success. It had helped encourage interest in sports and physical fitness, increased attendance at YMCA chapters all over the country, and raised the profile of the YMCA in the communities it served. "One of the best solutions to the difficulty of maintaining the interest of the members has been the judicious introduction of the play element into the work," the journal *Physical Fitness* reported in the summer of 1894, "and in this line nothing has been so peculiarly and generally satisfactory as Basket Ball." Thanks in large part to the success of basket ball, Dr. Gulick's anti-sports critics were silenced and the YMCA became synonymous with sports and physical fitness.

WAR GAME

For all its successes, basketball was still just a game and might never have become a national pastime if it hadn't been for some bad publicity the U.S. Army generated for itself.

In 1916 Gen. John J. Pershing led the "Punitive Expedition" into Mexico in an unsuccessful attempt to capture Pancho Villa. "The newspapers had made much of the drinking and prostitution that had served to entertain an army with time on its hands," Elliott J. Gorn and Warren Goldstein write in *A Brief History of American Sports*, and when the U.S. entered World War I in 1917, it was determined that such embarrassing publicity would not be generated again.

"For the first time in American history," Gorn and Goldstein write, "sports were formally linked to military preparedness....As American troops were deployed overseas in 1917, they were accompanied everywhere by 12,000 YMCA workers who brought sports along with them"—including basketball. More than a million U.S. troops fought in World War I, and tens of thousands of them learned to play basketball while they were in Europe. By the time the war was over, basketball had become an inextricable part of American life.

* * * *

OOPS

"In 1994, an Emergency Medical Service crew in New York rushed an abandoned bag of spaghetti to the hospital after they mistook it for a foetus."

—*Esquire,* **January 1995**

How did black sheep get such a bad rap? Their wool is harder to dye than that of white sheep.

THE RIDDLER

What's white, and black, and read in the middle? This page of riddles. Here are some BRI favourites.

1. What unusual natural phenomenon is capable of speaking in any language?

2. A barrel of water weighs 9 kilgrams [20 pounds]. What do you have to add to it to make it weigh 5 kilograms [12 pounds]?

3. Before Mount Everest was discovered, what was the highest mountain on Earth?

4. What word starts with an "e," ends with an "e," and usually contains one letter?

5. Forward I am heavy, but backward I am not. What am I?

6. He has married many women, but has never been married. Who is he?

7. How many bricks does it take to complete a building made of brick?

8. How many of each animal did Moses take on the ark?

9. How many times can you subtract the number 5 from 25?

10. If you have it, you want to share it. If you share it, you don't have it. What is it?

11. In Okmulgee, Oklahoma, you cannot take a picture of a man with a wooden leg. Why not?

12. The more you have of it, the less you see. What is it?

13. The more you take, the more you leave behind. What are they?

14. The one who makes it, sells it. The one who buys it, never uses it. The one who uses it, never knows that he's using it. What is it?

15. What can go up a chimney down but can't go down a chimney up?

16. What crime is punishable if attempted, but is not punishable if committed?

17. What happened in the middle of the 20th century that will not happen again for 4,000 years?

18. What is the centre of gravity?

19. What question can you never honestly answer "yes" to?

20. You can't keep this until you have given it.

Answers are on page 462.

How can you tell when a panda is roaring? It sounds like it has indigestion.

SPECIAL UNDERWEAR

More important underwear innovations to keep abreast of.

SIX-DAY UNDERWEAR

"The Honda Motor Company's bi-annual inventiveness contest for employees has unearthed some unique innovations, but none to match 6-day underwear, the 1987 winner. According to the story in the Wall St. Journal, the underwear has three leg holes, which enables it to last for six days without washing. The wearer rotates it 120 degrees on each of the first three days, then turns it out and repeats the process."

—Forgotten Fads and Fabulous Flops

THE ALARM BRA

LONDON— "A newly developed techno-bra—the latest in personal alarm systems—is the brainchild of Royal College of Art design student Kursty Groves. Targeted at young urban women, the bra uses miniature electronics and conductive fabric to monitor the wearer's heart rate. If it detects a sudden change in pulse—one that indicates panic—it radios a distress call to police and identifies the bra's location. And since the electronics are contained in jell-like cushions inside each cup, the bra enhances the wearer's figure. 'You can also have some lift and support if you like,' Groves says."

—Wire Service Report, 1999

SWEAT PANTS

Want to give off a manly, territorial odour without having to sweat for it? Japanese scientists have a new product—sweat-laced underpants.

Apparel and cosmetics maker Kanebo Ltd. says millions of tiny capsules in the fabric contain a synthesized pheromone found in the sweat of a man's underarms. Friction breaks the capsules, releasing the pheromone; an added musk scent intensifies the effect.

"Unfortunately, the power is fleeting—Kanebo estimates the pheromones are completely dissipated after ten washings."

—Parade Magazine, 1998

When you're looking at someone you love, your pupils dilate.

THE RETURN OF ZORRO

Here's the second part of our history of
"The Fox." (Part I is on page 73.)

THE MARK OF ZORRO
When Johnston McCulley created Zorro—the first "super-hero" with a secret identity—in 1919, he didn't have any idea what mark he would leave on pop culture. "Zorro not only became a vehicle for stars such as Fairbanks," Sandra Curtis writes in *Zorro Unmasked*, "the character also directly inspired numerous dual-identity imitators, including the Phantom, the Lone Ranger, the Green Hornet, and Superman."

He was especially important to Batman. Creator Bob Kane saw *The Mark of Zorro* when he was 13, and credits Fairbanks with providing the inspiration for the Caped Crusader:

> [Zorro] was the most swashbuckling, derring-do, super hero I've ever, ever seen in my life, and he left a lasting impression on me.
>
> And of course later, when I created the Batman, it gave me the dual identity, because Zorro had the dual identity. During the day, he played a foppish count, Don Diego…a bored playboy, and at night became Zorro. He wore a mask and he strapped his trusty sword around his waist. He came out of a cave… which I made into a bat cave, and he rode a black horse called Tornado, and later on I had the Batmobile. So Zorro was a major influence on my creation of Batman.

THE NEXT ACTION HERO

McCulley went on to write a total of 64 Zorro short stories, many of which were the basis for the 10 feature films, 5 film serials, several TV series, and more than a dozen foreign films that have appeared over 70 years. Tyrone Power played Zorro in the 1940 remake of The Mark of Zorro, and nine years later Clayton Moore played the masked man—before going on to find fame as the Lone

Ranger. In 1998 *The Mask of Zorro*, starring Antonio Banderas as the young protégé of the original, grossed over $90 million.

THE TWO MOST UNUSUAL ZORRO FILMS:

• *Zorro's Black Whip* (1944). The only female Zorro. "Linda Stirling dons a black outfit and becomes the Black Whip, riding in the hoofprints of her crusading brother [Zorro], who was killed for his just beliefs." (Video Movie Guide)

• *Zorro, The Gay Blade* (1981). "Tongue-in-cheek sword play with George Hamilton portraying the swashbuckling crusader and his long-lost gay brother, Bunny Wigglesworth." (*Videohound's Golden Movie Retriever*)

ZORRO ON TV

The most popular post-World War II Zorro was Guy Williams, who played "The Fox" on the Walt Disney TV series from 1957 to 1959.

Disney bought the rights to Zorro in 1953, but spent so much money building Disneyland (which opened in 1954) that he didn't launch the Zorro series until 1957. Disney had been looking for an unknown actor to play the part of Zorro, and found his man in Williams—whose father and uncle were experienced swordsmen. Williams himself had studied fencing since the age of seven.

The Crockett Syndrome

A few years before (see page 96), Disney's "Davy Crockett" had created TV's first merchandising boom—every kid in America wanted a coonskin cap. Disney was caught off-guard and wasn't able to fill the demand. This time, he vowed not to make the same mistake. At the same time Zorro went on the air, the country was flooded with Zorro lunch boxes, puzzles, watches, pyjamas, trading cards, Pet dispensers, and even sword sets—complete with a mask and chalk-tipped plastic sword, with which kids could mark "Z's" all over the house.

Disney had a hit on his hands, but cancelled the show after only two seasons when he couldn't agree with ABC on a price for it. Guy Williams was stunned by the decision, but went on to play Professor John Robinson on TV's "Lost in Space." (Special note to Zorro fans: We don't know what happened to Sgt. Garcia—but we're trying to find out.)

THE GREAT AUSSIE INSULT

Australians have a great tradition of hurling out insults.
Whether it be a politician or an everyday bloke, we are
not known for being backward in coming forward.
Here are just a few examples:

(Original spelling and punctuation retained)
"I would like to know who put that article that reminds me of a poodle dog half clipped in the lion fashion, called Brook E Smith, Superintendent of Police. He knows as much about commanding police as Captain Standish [the Victorian Police Commissioner] does about mustering mosquitoes and boiling them down for their fat on the back blocks of the Lachlan."

—**Ned Kelly**

(Original spelling and punctuation retained)
"I have been wronged and my mother and four men lagged innocent and is my brothers and sisters and my mother not to be pitied also who has no alternative only to put up with the brutal and cowardly conduct of a parcel of big ugly fat-necked wombat headed big bellied magpie legged narrow hipped splay-footed sons of Irish bailiffs or english landlords which is better known as officers of Justice or Victorian Police who some calls honest gentlemen but I would know what business an honest man would have in the Police as it is an old saying it takes a rogue to catch a rogue and a man that knows nothing about roguery would never enter the force."

—**Ned Kelly**

"No Government has ever promoted education as I have. After listening to you, I can understand what vast amounts will still have to be spent."

—*Sir Robert Menzies to an*
interjector at a university gathering

Hot chocolate: In Japan, you can buy cocoa flavored with 2% chili pepper sauce.

"He has more hide than a team of elephants."

> —*Paul Keating*
> *referring to*
> *John Howard*

Heckler at an election meeting: "Wotcha gunna do about 'ousing?"
Sir Robert Menzies: "Put an 'h' in front of it."

*   *   *   *   *

GREAT AUSTRALIAN ONE-LINERS

She is a sandwich short of a picnic.

She is three bricks short of a load.

May all your chooks turn into emus and kick your dunny over.

He's sharper than a sewer rat.

He's as flash as a rat with a gold tooth.

If at first you don't succeed, skydiving is not for you!

Money can't buy happiness but it sure makes misery easier to live with.

She'd talk ten feet under wet cement.

If your brains were gunpowder they wouldn't blow off your hat!

Don't you love nature despite what it did to you?

I wish you were a headache, then I could take an aspirin and you'd go away.

His father was an electrician and he was his first shock.

His mother should have thrown him away and kept the stork.

IN MY EXPERT OPINION...

Think the experts and authorities have all the answers?
Well, they do—but often the wrong ones.

"Animals, which move, have limbs and muscles; the Earth has no limbs and muscles, hence it does not move."

—*Scipio Chiaramonti, Professor of Mathematics,*
University of Pisa, 1633

"Nature intended women to be slaves. They are our property. What a mad idea to demand equality for women! Women are nothing but machines for producing children."

—*Napoleon Bonaparte*

"I must confess that my imagination refuses to see any sort of submarine doing anything except suffocating its crew and floundering at sea."

—*H. G. Wells, 1902*

"You ain't goin' nowhere, son. You ought to go back to drivin' a truck."

—*Jim Denny, Manager*
of the Grand Ole Opry,
to Elvis Presley, 1954

"If excessive smoking actually plays a role in the production of lung cancer, it seems to be a minor one."

—*The National Cancer Institute, 1954*

The horse is here to stay, but the automobile is only a novelty—a fad."

—*Marshall Ferdinand Foch,*
French military strategist, 1911

"With over 50 foreign cars already on sale here, the Japanese auto industry isn't likely to carve out a big slice of the U.S. market for itself."

—*Business Week, 1968*

"We don't believe Jackie Robinson, coloured college star signed by the Dodgers for one of their farm teams, will ever play in the big leagues."

—*Jimmy Powers, New York Daily News*
Sports Columnist, 1945

During the summer months in Reykjavik, Iceland, the sun is visible 24 hours a day.

READ ALL ABOUT IT!

Two good reasons not to believe everything you read in the newspapers.

THE STORY: In the early 1920s, the *Toronto Mail and Empire* reported that two scientists named Dr. Schmierkase and Dr. Butterbrod had discovered "what appeared to be the fossil of the whale that had swallowed Jonah." The whale had a muscle that functioned like a trapdoor, giving access to its stomach.

The next day, evangelists all over Toronto read the story from the pulpit, citing it as confirmation that the Biblical story of Jonah and the whale was true—.and the day after that, a rival newspaper ran a story reporting on the evangelists' speech.

THE TRUTH: Three days after the original story ran, the *Toronto Mail and Empire* ran a second story exposing the first one as a hoax, the work of a journalist named Charles Langdon Clarke.

Clarke liked to spend his free time cooking up news items based on Biblical stories, and then attributing them to fictional newspapers like the *Babylon Gazette* or the *Jerusalem Times* for added credibility. Anyone who spoke German would have had an inkling that the story was a joke—Dr. Schmierkase and Dr. Butterbrod translates as Dr. Cheese and Dr. Butter Bread.

THE STORY: In January 1927 the *Chicago Journal* reported that a "killer hawk" had been seen preying on pigeons in the downtown area. The next day other Chicago papers ran the story on their front pages, and continued doing so for five consecutive days, igniting considerable public hysteria in the process: A prominent banker offered a reward for capture of the hawk dead or alive; a local gun club sent shooters downtown to stalk the bird, with help of local Boy Scouts troops who joined in the hunt.

THE TRUTH: A week after the Journal ran the hawk story, it announced the start of a newspaper serial called "The Pigeon and the Hawk." The other papers, realizing they'd been tricked into publicizing a rival paper's promotion on their front pages for an entire week, never printed another word about the killer hawk.

I BET YOU DIDN'T KNOW!

*So you think you're a bit of an expert on Australiana, huh?
Well, I bet you didn't know some of these facts!*

People

In Australia there is:
- one birth every 2 minutes and 8 seconds
- one death every 3 minutes and 52 seconds
- a gain of one international migrant every 5 minutes and 50 seconds leading to...
- an overall population increase of one person every 2 minutes and 37 seconds

In our culturally diverse country:
- 3.9 million people have been born overseas
- 3.8 million have one or both parents born overseas
- 2.6 million people speak a language other than English at home
- there are 92 different religious denominations in Australia
- 282 different languages are spoken (including 170 Aboriginal and Torres Strait Islander languages)

Do you know how many people live in each state?

New South Wales	6,411,700
Victoria	4,712,200
Queensland	3,512,400
South Australia	1,493,100
Western Australia	1,861,000
Tasmania	470,300
Northern Territory	192,900
Australian Capital Territory	310,200
TOTAL	18,963800

(Figures based on June 1999 numbers)

The world's first golf rule book was published in Scotland in 1754.

- 85% of Australians live in a city.
- Australia has only 0.3% of the world's population.
- The total distance travelled by vehicles in Australia during the last year was 181 billion km. The average distance for each car was 14,800 km.

Animals
- There are over 200 species of blowflies in Australia and it costs more than $150 million a year in trying to control them.
- There were no hoofed animals in Australia until Europeans arrived in 1779.
- About 90% of our native animals are found nowhere else in the world.
- Since European settlement, seven species of bird and 19 species of mammal have become extinct.
- Animals that have since been introduced and are disastrous to our ecology are the rabbit, cane toad, camel, water buffalo and, believe it or not, the dingo, which was originally from Asia and brought to Australia by Aborigines.
- Only 24 rabbits were released in Australia in 1859 and today there are over 200 million.
- Dingoes don't like water and can't bark.
- Kangaroo is an Aboriginal word meaning, "don't understand." When asked by Europeans what that strange hopping creature was an Aboriginal man answered, "kangaroo" meaning, "I don't understand." The Europeans thought that was its name and it stuck.
- Eleven of the world's top 15 most poisonous snakes live in Australia.
- The Crown of Thorn starfish is killing the Great Barrier Reef as we speak by eating it.
- The most popular cat name in Australia is Puss.
- The most popular gold fish name in Australia is Jaws.
- The funnel web is the world's second deadliest spider. The number one winner is the banana spider found in Central and South America.

History

- Australia is smaller, drier and flatter than any other inhabited continent in the world.
- Aborigines arrived in Australia 60,000 years ago.
- During European settlement, approximately 160,000 convicts were sent to Australia.
- Australia only began to receive convicts after Britain lost its colonies in America.
- You could be shipped to Australia for something as simple as stealing a loaf of bread.
- During the gold rush in 1850, hardly any miners made it rich. It was the shopkeepers and merchants who really struck gold.

Places and things

- The Great Barrier reef is 2,000 km long.
- Over 90% of Australia is dry, flat, and arid.
- Ayers Rock (Uluru) is the biggest rock in the world.
- The highest temperature ever recorded in Australia was 53°C, recorded in 1889 in Cloncurry, Queensland.
- The coldest temperature ever recorded in Australia was -23°C, recorded in 1994 in Charlotte Pass, NSW.
- The Sydney Opera House took 14 years to build and cost $102 million.
- Australia has the longest railway line in the world, the Indian Pacific, which includes a stretch of perfectly straight railway line that runs for 478 km.

* * *

TEN INTERNATIONAL WORDS FOR WIND
1. Afrikaans—maagwind 2. Israeli—nuhfeechah
3. Japanese—he 4. Cantonese/Chinese—fang
5. German—furz 6. Bantu—lu-suzi
7. Hindu—pud 8. Polish—pierdzenic
9. Italian—peto 10. Russian—perdun

Tigers can be taught to use litter boxes. *Big* litter boxes.

THE DEVIL'S DICTIONARY

Ambrose Bierce was one of the most famous newspaper columnists of the late 1880s—known as "the wickedest man in San Francisco" at a time when S.F. was a pretty rough-and-tumble town. Although not as popular as Mark Twain, his wit was just as satirical and biting. Case in point: The Devil's Dictionary, a caustic set of definitions for otherwise harmless words, written in instalments for his column, then compiled in a book. Your library probably has a copy; if you like dark humour, it's great bathroom reading. Here's a sample of what you'll find in it.

Abstainer, n. A weak person who yields to the temptation of denying himself a pleasure.

Alone, adj. In bad company.

Bequeath, v.t. To generously give to another that which can no longer be denied to somebody.

Consult, v.t. To seek another's approval of a course already decided on.

Depraved, p.p. The moral condition of a gentleman who holds the opposite opinion.

Divorce, n. A resumption of diplomatic relations and rectification of boundaries.

Faith, n. Belief without evidence in what is told by one who speaks without knowledge, of things without parallel.

Fault, n. One of my offenses, as distinguished from one of yours, the latter being crimes.

Forbidden, p.p. Invested with a new and irresistible charm.

Governor, n. An aspirant to the United States Senate.

Heaven, n. A place where the wicked cease from troubling you with talk of their personal affairs, and the good listen with attention while you expound your own.

Homesick, adj. Dead broke abroad.

Hypocrite, n. One who, professing virtues that he does not respect, secures the advantage of seeming to be what he despises.

Impiety, n. Your irreverence toward my deity.

Impunity, n. Wealth.

Intimacy, n. A relation into which fools are providentially drawn for their mutual destruction.

Survey result: 35% of people watching TV yell at it.

Jealous, adj. Unduly concerned about the preservation of that which can be lost only if not worth keeping.

Lawyer, n. One skilled in circumvention of the law.

Lecturer, n. One with his hand in your pocket, his tongue in your ear, and faith in your patience.

Marriage, n. The state or condition of a community consisting of a master, a mistress and two slaves, making in all, two.

Mythology, n. The body of a primitive people's beliefs concerning its origin, early history, heroes, dieties and so forth, as distinguished from the true accounts which it invents later.

Novel, n. A short story padded.

Once, adj. Enough.

Optimism, n. The doctrine, or belief, that everything is beautiful, including what is ugly, everything good, especially the bad, and everything right that is wrong.

Pantheism, n. The doctrine that everything is God, in contradistinction to the doctrine that God is everything.

Patience, n. A minor form of despair, disguised as a virtue.

Piety, n. Reverence for the Supreme Being, based upon His supposed resemblance to man.

Politician, n. An eel in the fundamental mud upon which the superstructure of organized society is reared.

Pray, v. To ask that the laws of the universe be annulled in behalf of a single petitioner, confessedly unworthy.

Rack, n. An argumentative implement formerly much used in persuading devotees of a false faith to embrace the living truth.

Reporter, n. A writer who guesses his way to the truth and dispels it with a tempest of words.

Road, n. A strip of land along which one may pass from where it is too tiresome to be to where it is futile to go.

Selfish, adj. Devoid of consideration for the selfishness of others.

Senate, n. A body of elderly gentlemen charged with high duties and misdemeanors.

Trial, n. A formal inquiry designed to prove and put upon record the blameless characters of judges, advocates and jurors.

Twice, adv. Once too often.

Year, n. A period of three hundred and sixty-five disappointments.

Zeal, n. A certain nervous disorder afflicting the young and inexperienced. A passion that goeth before a sprawl.

Going down: Bottle-nosed whales can dive 3,000 feet in two minutes.

VEGETABLE NAMES

More vegetable facts from BRI member Jeff Cheek.

CABBAGE

Originated in Asia and introduced to Europe by Alexander the Great, about 325 B.C. The name comes from the Latin *caput*, meaning "head." It's high in vitamin C, but contains sulphurous compounds that, when cooked, give off odours similar to rotten eggs or ammonia.

SCALLIONS

These tiny green onions owe their name to the biblical city of Ashkelon. When the Romans conquered the city, they called the tiny onions *caepa Ascolonia* or "onions of Ashkelon," This became "scallions."

JERUSALEM ARTICHOKES

These sweet, starchy roots did not grow in Jerusalem and they are not artichokes. Native Americans used them as bread. The mix-up came when a Spanish explorer thought they were some kind of sunflower. *Girasol* (turn to the sun) is "sunflower" in Spanish. An American heard it as "Jerusalem." No one knows why he also added "artichoke."

BROCCOLI

The word comes from the Latin *bracchium*, or "branch." It was developed about 2,500 years ago on the island of Cyprus and was a popular dish at ancient Roman banquets. (The Roman emperor Tiberius, who ruled from 14 to 37 A.D., once publicly scolded his son for eating all the broiled broccoli at a state banquet.) It was popularized in the U.S. by Italian immigrants.

KIWI FRUIT

Originally from China, they were imported to New Zealand in the early 1900s and renamed "Chinese Gooseberry." They finally made it to the U.S. in 1962, and a Los Angeles distributor named Frieda Caplan named it after the New Zealand national bird, the kiwi. It took 18 years before the American public started buying it.

CANTALOUPE

A type of muskmelon brought to Italy from Armenia in the first century A.D., and grown in the town of Cantalupo, which is where it gets its name.

STRANGE ANIMAL LAWSUITS

*In the Middle Ages, it was not unusual for animals to be
put on trial as if they could understand human laws.
These lawsuits were serious affairs.*

THE PLAINTIFFS: Vineyard growers in St.-Julien, France
THE DEFENDANTS: Weevils
THE LAWSUIT: In 1545 angry growers testified to a
judge that the weevils were eating and destroying their crops.
According to one source: "Legal indictments were drawn, and the
insects were actually defended in court."
THE VERDICT: Since the weevils were obviously eating the
crops, they were found guilty. In 1546 a proclamation was issued
by the judge demanding that the weevils desist—and amazingly,
they did. The farmers weren't bothered by weevils again until
1587. Once more, the insects were put on trial; however, the out-
come is unknown.

THE PLAINTIFFS: The people of Mayenne, France
THE DEFENDANT: Mosquitoes
THE LAWSUIT: In the 1200s, a swarm of mosquitoes were
indicted as a public nuisance by the people of the town. When the
bugs failed to answer the summons, the court appointed a lawyer
to act on their behalf.
THE VERDICT: The lawyer did such a good job pleading their
case that the court took pity. The judge banished them, but gave
them a patch of real estate outside town where they would be
allowed to swarm in peace "forever."

THE PLAINTIFF: The city of Basel, Switzerland
THE DEFENDANT: A rooster
THE LAWSUIT: In 1474 the rooster was accused of being (or
helping) a sorcerer. The reason, according to the prosecutor: it
had laid eggs—and as everyone knows, an egg laid by a rooster is
prized by sorcerers. On top of that, it was shown "that Satan
employed witches to hatch such eggs, from which proceeded

In the 19th century, India imported ice harvested from ponds in the United States.

winged serpents most dangerous to mankind."

The rooster's lawyer admitted it had laid an egg, but contended that "no injury to man or beast had resulted." And besides, laying an egg is an involuntary act, he said, so the law shouldn't punish it.

THE VERDICT: The judge refused to allow the lawyer's argument and declared the rooster guilty of sorcery. Both the unfortunate fowl and the egg it had allegedly laid were burned at the stake.

THE PLAINTIFFS: Barley growers in Autun, France
THE DEFENDANTS: Rats
THE LAWSUIT: In 1510 the rodents were charged with burglary, having eaten and destroyed the barley crop. A young lawyer named Bartholomew de Chassenée was appointed to defend them. When the rats failed to appear in court, Chassenée successfully argued that since the case involved all the rats of the diocese (the area under jurisdiction of one bishop), all of them should be summoned. When the rats failed to appear again, Chassenée argued that it was because they were scared by "evilly disposed cats which were in constant watch along the highways." Since, by law, the rats were entitled to protection to and from court, the plaintiffs "should be required to post a bond" that would be forfeited if the cats attacked the rats on their way to court.
THE VERDICT: Unknown, but the publicity from the case helped Chassenée to establish a reputation as a sharp lawyer. In fact, many historians now regard him as one of France's greatest lawyers.

THE PLAINTIFF: The Grand Vicar of Valence, France
THE DEFENDANTS: Caterpillars inhabiting his diocese
THE LAWSUIT: In 1584 the Grand Vicar excommunicated the insects for causing destruction to crops, and ordered them to appear before him. When they didn't appear, a lawyer was appointed to defend them.
THE VERDICT: The lawyer argued his case, but lost. The caterpillars were banished from the diocese. "When the caterpillars failed to leave, the trial continued until the short-lived caterpillars died off. The Vicar was then credited with having miraculously exterminated them."

WEIRD DOLL STORIES

*Maybe it's because they look human that dolls seem to inspire
such bizarre behavior in people. Here are a few examples.*

STAR TREK'S MR. SPOCK DOLL

In 1994, England, under the auspices of the European
Union, slapped import quotas on all "nonhuman creature"
dolls manufactured in China. The quota did not apply to human
dolls, which meant that Captain Kirk dolls were allowed into the
country. But the quota did apply to Mr. Spock, since he is a Vulcan and therefore a nonhuman creature (even though Spock's
mother was human). "It seems very strange," said Peter Waterman,
a spokesperson for the British toy industry, "that we should have
customs officials involved in a discussion of whether Mr. Spock is
an alien or a human being."

GROWING UP SKIPPER

Introduced by Mattel in the spring of 1975, Skipper—Barbie's little sister—really did grow up. When you cranked her arm, she
grew 7 millimetres [one quarter inch] taller and sprouted breasts
and an hourglass figure. The doll was attacked by feminists, who
charged that the doll was "a grotesque caricature of the female
body," and "caters to psychotic preoccupation with instant culture
and instant sex object." The doll sold well anyway.

EARRING MAGIC KEN

In 1993 Mattel introduced Earring Magic Ken; a version of Barbie's boyfriend that came with a lavender mesh shirt, a lavender
vest, and an earring. It became an instant camp classic in the gay
community—which interpreted Ken's choice of clothing and jewelry to mean that there was a very good reason why, after more
than 30 years of dating, Barbie and Ken had never gotten married.

Mattel insisted there was no hidden agenda. "The designers
were amazed when all of this surfaced," they claimed. Then they
took the doll off the market.

TALKING BARBIE AND G.I. JOE DOLLS

In 1993 a group calling itself the Barbie Liberation Organization

(BLO) claimed it switched the voice boxes on as many as 300 G.I. Joe and Barbie dolls in France, England, and the U.S. at the peak of the Christmas shopping season, to protest "gender-based stereotyping in children's toys." So when kids opened their G.I. Joes, they said things like, "I love school. Don't you?" and "Let's sing with the band tonight" in a female voice; Barbie said "Dead men tell no lies," in a deep, booming male voice.

TELETUBBIES
In 1998—shortly after televangelist Jerry Falwell attacked Tinky-Winky as a stalking-horse for gay culture—a woman who bought a Teletubby at a New York toy store claimed that when she got the doll home, it shouted obscenities like "bite my butt" and whispered anti-gay remarks. A spokesman for the manufacturer said that the doll, named Po, was actually bilingual—and was saying "Faster, faster!" in Cantonese.

THE CABBAGE PATCH SNACKTIME DOLL
The 1996 Snacktime doll came with a motorized set of gears that powered its lower jaw, allowing it to chew and "eat" plastic carrots and cookies. That, however, was not all it liked to eat—in 1997 the Consumer Produce Safety Commission received more than 100 reports of children getting their fingers and hair stuck in the mechanical mouth, "which would not stop chewing until the battery back was removed." Mattel later admitted that it had not fully tested the product, withdrew the doll from the market, and offered to buy back dolls for $40 apiece. Only about 1,000 of the 500,000 dolls sold were returned.

FURBIES
In 1999, the National Security Agency issued a Furby Alert, warning that the dolls—which come with sophisticated computer chips that allow it to record and mimic human speech—might "overhear secret information and 'start talking classified,'" inadvertently passing secret information along to America's enemies. Accordingly, Furbies were banned from sensitive areas in the Pentagon.

HOW TO MAKE A MONSTER, PART III

*Here's the third installment of the Godzilla
story. (Part I starts on page 79.)*

COMING TO AMERICA

Gojira's box-office success in Japan caught the attention of American movie studios; in 1955 Joseph E. Levine of TransWorld Films bought the film's U.S. rights for $25,000. The spelling of the monster's name was changed to Godzilla, an approximation of how it was pronounced in Japanese (GO-dzee-la); and the title was changed to *Godzilla, King of the Monsters*.

Levine knew that if he released *Godzilla* with Japanese dialogue, it would appeal only to art-house film crowds—and he wouldn't make back his investment. A subtitled film would miss the youth audience entirely, since many kids were too young to read them. So Levine adapted the film for Americans by dubbing it into English.

MADE IN USA

It wasn't the only change Levine made: The plot was revised, scenes were rearranged or removed entirely, and brand-new scenes were filmed to insert an American character into the previously all-Japanese film. The American, played by Raymond Burr (of TV's *Ironsides* and *Perry Mason*), is a newspaper reporter named Steve Martin who happens to be on assignment in Japan when Godzilla goes on the attack.

Burr couldn't appear on screen at the same time as the Japanese actors in the original version of the film, but numerous scenes of Japanese actors talking to one another were re-edited to make it look like they were talking to him.

FROM A TO B

The effect of Levine's changes was to turn what had been a polished, serious film for adults into a monster movie made for drive-in movie theatres and kiddie matinees. But that was precisely what he wanted: In the mid-1950s, the American film industry

---

Bug rule of thumb: Centipedes are carnivores, millipedes are vegetarians.

was in a slump. The advent of television, combined with laws that had forced the major studios to sell off their theatre chains, caused a dramatic drop in movie attendance and movie profits. Major studios became extremely cautious, making fewer A-films than they had in the 1940s.

As a result, several companies sprang up to make cheapo B-movies for drive-ins and faded downtown movie palaces. Then, along came *Gojira*. "Though a big budget, major studio film in Japan," Stuart Galbraith writes in *Monsters are Attacking Tokyo!*, "the Americanized Gojira was released [solely] as an exploitation feature." Because it was intended for the B-movie market, the changes were done on the cheap, which lowered the quality of the American version of the film. The poor dubbing and sophomoric dialogue made it difficult for Western filmgoers, already used to clichéd American monster movies, to take the film seriously. And they didn't.

SON(S) OF GODZILLA

Say what you will about the changes Levine made to the original *Gojira*, he knew his audience. *Godzilla, King of the Monsters*, opened in the U.S. on April 26, 1956, and made more than $2 million at the box office, an astonishing sum for the 1950s. The American version did so well that it was exported back to Japan under the title *Monster King Godzilla* (Raymond Burr's dialogue was dubbed into Japanese), where it added to the profits already made by the original *Gojira*. And Burr's character was so popular with Japanese audiences that reporter characters became a staple of later Godzilla movies in the 1960s and 1970s.

Enthused by the success of the first *Gojira* film, Toho ordered up the first of what would become more than 20 sequels. *Gojira's Counterattack* (the U.S. version was called *Gigantis the Fire Monster)* was released in 1955. Toho made nine non-Gojira monster movies between 1955 and 1962, featuring such monsters such as the Abominable Snowman, and a robot mole named Mogera. But as J. D. Lees writes in *The Official Godzilla Compendium*, the release of *King Kong vs. Godzilla* in 1962 made Godzilla a superstar. "The pairing with the famous ape elevated Godzilla from the swelling ranks of interchangeable atomic monsters of the fifties and placed him among the classic pantheon of cinema creatures."

GODZILLA FLICKS

- **Godzilla Raids Again (1955).** The first cheesy Godzilla sequel, it was brought to America in 1959 as *Gigantis the Fire Monster,* to avoid confusion with the original. Plot: "Yearning for a change of pace, the King of Monsters opts to destroy Osaka instead of Tokyo, but the spiny Angorous is out to dethrone our hero. Citizens flee in terror when the battle royale begins." *Director:* Ishiro Honda (*Videohound's Golden Movie Retriever*)

- **King Kong vs. Godzilla (1963).** Developed from an idea by Willis O'Brien, creator of the original *King Kong's* stop-motion animation. O'Brien's story was about a fight between Kong and "the Ginko," a monster made by Dr. Frankenstein's grandson. But the only studio willing to make the film was Toho—and they insisted on using Godzilla. The Japanese played it as a satire, with the two monsters wrestling in Tokyo (where else?) and on top of Mt. Fuji. King Kong wins. *Director:* Ishiro Honda (*A Critical History of Godzilla*)

- **Godzilla vs. Mothra (1964).** Released as *Godzilla vs. the Thing.* "When the egg of giant monster Mothra is washed ashore by a storm, a greedy entrepreneur is quick to exploit it. Meanwhile, Godzilla reappears and goes on a rampage.... Godzilla, who seems to be really enjoying his reign of destruction, shows more personality than in previous appearances....Excellent in all departments." *Director:* Ishiro Honda (*Cult Flicks and Trash Pics*)

- **Godzilla vs. Monster Zero (1965).** "Novel Godzilla adventure with the big guy and Rodan in outer space. Suspicious denizens of Planet X require the help of Godzilla and Rodan to rid themselves of the menacing Ghidra, whom they refer to as Monster Zero. Will they, in return, help Earth as promised, or is this just one big, fat double cross?" *Director:* Ishiro Honda (*Videohound's Golden Movie Retriever*)

- **Godzilla vs. Sea Monster (1968).** "This exercise in cardboard mayhem stars the saucy saurian as a crusty critter suffering a case of crabs when he's attacked by colossal crustaceans (notably Ebirah, a giant lobster) and does battle with the Red Bamboo bad-guy gang." *Director:* Jun Fukuda (*Creature Features Movie Guide Strikes Again*)

- **Godzilla on Monster Island (1972).** "In this harmless, toy-like movie, Godzilla talks, as he and spiny Angillus battle alien-summoned Ghidrah and new playmate Gigan, who has a buzzsaw in his belly." *Director:* Jun Fukuda *(Leonard Maltin's Movie & Video Guide)*

• **Godzilla vs. the Smog Monster (1972).** "A Japanese industrial city has an ecology woe; its bay of waste and rotting animal life breeds Hedorah, which shoots laser beams from its eyepods and flies at will....To the rescue comes the flat-footed Godzilla to indulge in a duel-of-the-titans." Godzilla flies in this one, and it looks really cheap— "the army consists of about 10 guys." *Director:* Yoshimitsu Banno *(Creature Features Movie Guide Strikes Again)*

• **Godzilla vs. Megalon (1973).** "The 400-foot-tall [122-metre-tall] green lizard is aided by a jet-packed robot in fighting off Megalon (a giant cockroach with Zap Killer Beam), Baragon the stomper, and a race of underground Earthlings, the Seatopians." *Director:* Jun Fukuda *(Creature Features Movie Guide Strikes Again)*

• **Godzilla vs. the Cosmic Monster (1974).** Japanese sci-fi sukiyaki with the King of Monsters battling a cyborg Godzilla controlled by aliens bent on conquest. A huge rodent creature said to embody Asian spirits comes to the real Godzilla's aid when the languid lizard squares off against antagonistic Angorus." *Director:* Jun Fukuda *(Creature Features Movie Guide Strikes Again)*

• **Godzilla: 1985 (1984).** "After 30 years, the Big G recovers from his apparent death...and returns to destroy Tokyo all over again. Disregarding the previous fourteen sequels (most of which were set in "the future" anyway), the plot marches along much like a '70s disaster film." *Director:* Kohji Hashimoto. *(Cult Flicks and Trash Pics)*

• **Godzilla vs. Biollante (1989).** "Genetic scientist Surigama uses cells from Godzilla's body to create hardy new crop strains, while also splicing the cells' DNA to that of his dead daughter, using that of her favourite rose as a catalyst. His experiments result in the gigantic plant/animal monster Biollante, a nightmare of creeping vines, snapping teeth, and corrosive sap." *Director:* Kazuki Ohmori *(Cult Flicks and Trash Pics)*

• **Godzilla (1998).** Charmless big-bucks travesty starring Matthew Broderick. Bad career move.

WORD ORIGINS

Here are some more interesting word origins.

PUNCH
Meaning: A fruity drink
Origin: "From Sanskrit panca or Hindustani panch, which means 'five,' the theory being that there were five ingredients—alcohol, water, lemon, sugar, and spice." (From *The Story Behind the Word*, by Morton S. Freeman)

EAVESDROP
Meaning: Secretly listen to someone else's conversation
Origin: "In Anglo-Saxon England, a house had very wide over-hanging eaves...to allow rain to drip safely away from the house's foundation. So the eavesdrip, later the eavesdrop, provided a place where one could hide to listen clandestinely to conversation within the house." (From *Morris Dictionary of Word and Phrase Origins*, by William and Mary Morris)

CHEAT
Meaning: A dishonest person; the act of deceiving someone for gain
Origin: Comes from escheat—a medieval legal term for "the reversion of property to the state in the absence of legal heirs, and of the state's rights to such confiscation. The officer who looked after the king's escheats was known as the cheater....The dishonest connotations of the word evolved among thieves in the 16th century." (From *Wicked Words*, by Hugh Rawson)

SNOB
Meaning: A snooty person; someone who puts on airs
Origin: "It seems that Oxford freshmen were required to register 'according to rank.' Those not of noble birth added after their names the phrase sine nobilitate which was then abbreviated to 's. nob.,' thus creating...a perfect definition for the commoner who wishes to mingle with the nobles." (From *Dictionary of Word and Phrase Origins, Vol. III*, by William and Mary Morris)

You can buy horseradish ice cream in Tokyo.

ZANY
Meaning: Crazy
Origin: "Dates back to the commedia dell'arte in Italy of the 16th century. The zanni (as it was spelled in Italian) was a buffoon who mimicked one of the characters, usually the clown. The English changed its spelling to zany and used it to refer to any simpleton or bumbling fool." (From *Dictionary of Word and Phrase Origins, Vol. II*, by William and Mary Morris)

AMBITION
Meaning: Single-minded drive toward achieving a goal
Origin: Ambitio is the Latin term for "running around." The term originally referred to the way politicians in ancient Rome ran around "in search of voters to persuade or buy." (From *Loose Cannons and Red Herrings*, by Robert Claiborne)

ALCOHOL
Meaning: An intoxicating beverage
Origin: "The word comes from Arabic al-kuhul, a powder used as a cosmetic. Borrowed into English, alcohol came to mean any distilled substance. Alcohol of wine was thus the 'quintessence of wine'...by the middle of the 18th century alcohol was being used on its own." (From *Dictionary of Word Origins*, by John Ayto)

DIAPER
Meaning: A cloth used to capture a baby's waste
Origin: "From Greek diaspros, meaning 'pure white'....Originally, a fabric woven of silk, sewn with gold threads, and used for ecclesiastical robes." (From *Thereby Hangs a Tale*, by Charles Earle Funk)

DOODLE
Meaning: Aimless, absent-minded scribbles on scraps of paper
Origin: The word doodle comes from the German word dudeln, meaning 'to play the bagpipe.' The notion seems to be that a person who spends his time playing bagpipes would be guilty of other frivolous time-wasting activities." (From *Dictionary of Word and Phrase Origins, Vol. III*, by William and Mary Morris)

PLAYMATE IQ TEST

*In 1997, two Playboy "Playmates of the Year"—Julie Cialini
(1995) and Stacy Sanches (1996)—showed up on Howard
Stern's radio show. Because playmates are role models for young
girls everywhere, Stern asked a few questions to test the gals'
grasp of current affairs. Here's the text of the quiz.*

Q: Who is the President of Russia?
Julie: "Gorbachev."
Stacy: "Gretzky."
(*CORRECT ANSWER:* Boris Yeltsin.)

Q: What is the centre of our solar system?
Julie: "The equator."
Stacy: "The moon."
(*CORRECT ANSWER:* The sun.)

Q: Define the NAACP.
Julie: "Something, something, something, for Certified Pianists."
Stacy: "It's some kind of police organization."
(*CORRECT ANSWER:* National Association for the Advancement of Coloured People.)

Q: Who invented the light-bulb?
Julie: "I know Edison invented the telephone, but I can't remember the lightbulb guy."
Stacy: "I don't know."
(*CORRECT ANSWER:* Thomas Edison. Alexander Graham Bell was the telephone guy.)

Q: Who's the Speaker of the House?
Julie: "Gore or something-or-other."
Stacy: "Bill Clinton."
(*CORRECT ANSWER* [in 1997]: Newt Gingrich.)

Q: Define the meaning of the letters CIA.
Julie: "I don't know."
Stacy: "Certified Investigation Association."
(*CORRECT ANSWER:* Central Intelligence Agency.)

To give the playmates better odds, Stern tried a few "industry-related" questions.

Q: What do the initials "DK" stand for?
A: Both playmates knew it was fashion designer Donna Karan.

Q: What car company has a model known as "911"?
A: Both knew it was Porsche.

Q: Whose face is on the $100 bill?
A: Both knew it was Ben Franklin.

In 1912 the Archbishop of Paris declared dancing the tango a sin.

A STRAIGHT FACE

Ever wonder what the Big Guys of poker know that you don't? They swear it's all in keeping a straight face, and watching the table for the players who don't. Here are a few pointers from the experts.

IT'S ALL IN THE GAME

There are well over 400 great professional poker players in the world today. So if poker is truly a game of "chance," then how can so many people be consistently good at winning? It's not the card itself, say the experts, as much as the flip of the card that gives away the game to people who know what to look for. Players, particularly weaker players, give away "tells," or unconscious reflexes during the game that the tried and true poker player can use to get the edge.

One of the poker greats, the self-proclaimed "Mad Poker Genius" Mike Caro, has made a living from poker and a killing from studying the psychology of the game. On his web site, Mike Caro's World, he talks at length about the various "tells" to watch for in others, and how to avoid them yourself.

#1: WEAK AND STRONG
The first rule of thumb in gauging your fellow players is the "Strong When Weak" guideline.
• In general, players who have lousy hands subconsciously act more aggressively; players with strong hands act indifferent and passively. Why? "Because," Caro says, "deception is fundamental to poker—otherwise we'd play with our hands fully exposed."
• When a player looks down and has a lousy hand, he doesn't want to give away his emotions because then he's lost the game up front. So unconsciously, he usually acts the opposite of the way he is feeling. An experienced player knows this and watches for the cues. An even better player will play off these psychological indicators.

TELL ME TRUE
"Tells" are far more prevalent in weak and mediocre players than in the pros. But watch out—really good players are good actors, and a top-of-the-line poker player knows how to fake a "tell" to

---

Face value of a *Titanic* boarding pass auctioned in 1999: $8. It sold for $100,000.

throw off his opponents. The situation can become so complex that it's next to impossible to tell whether a gulp (for example) was a sign of fear—or simply a great acting job. Here, according to Caro, are some of the universal poker tells to watch for.

The Heavy Heart: A sad sigh during the bet usually means a player has a good hand. Be somewhat cautious and don't call unless your hand is very good too.

Shifty Eyes: A glance away from the table once the hand has been dealt. This usually indicates a player who's holding a good hand and wants to hide his excitement.

Stare Down: A direct stare into another player's eyes after the cards have been dealt or during a bet is usually a sign of a weak hand. Staring into anyone's eyes is considered somewhat aggressive and can therefore be read that a player is bluffing.

Pokerclack: Pokerclack is a soft clucking noise that sounds morose or shameful. It's a term coined by Caro, and he describes it as the noise you'd make after saying something like, "I'm feeling terrible today. My old dog Shep ran into the street and got run over."

Flair: An extra flamboyance at the toss of a poker chip during a bet is almost always a sign that a player is trying to hide a bad hand. He's bluffing.

The Jitters: Shaky hands during a bet suggests excitement, nervousness, tension in the player. Even skilled players often mistake this sign and think the shaky player is bluffing and scared he's going to lose. That's almost never the case, however, according to Caro. Players who are bluffing tend to be rock-steady, not jittery. It's the player who's got a monstrously good hand who sometimes can't contain his excitement.

The Big Chill: When a player goes quiet after betting, you can almost guarantee he's got a lousy hand and he's bluffing.

The Babbling Brook: When a talkative player begins babbling somewhat incoherently or absentmindedly during or after a bet, he's usually got a lousy hand. His hand disrupted his normal conversation and he didn't want to go silent for fear he'd give himself away. But this cowboy's almost surely bluffing.

Chip Fondling: The hands have been dealt and the guy on your right is fingering his poker chips. Read it as a sign that he's raring to place his bet; he's got a great hand.

The Stiff: If you see a player suddenly go rigid and hold his breath following a bet, take it as a sign of bluffing. Call him.

TATTLING & TELLING

It's betting time around your Friday night poker table and your buddy flips his chip in the air with flair and a wink. With all of this newfound knowledge, you know you've just spotted a bluff. What should you do when you notice a "tell"? Mike Caro says: "Don't let your pride destroy the profit you could make from tells. Never announce that, 'I knew you were bluffing,' if you successfully call and win with a weak hand. Say, instead, 'I don't know why I called. I almost didn't, but at the last second I decided to test you one time. I guess I got lucky.' That kind of talk will encourage an opponent to try again."

* * * *

THE NAME GAME

There are hundreds—maybe thousands—of poker variations, and some of them sound downright funny when said out loud. A few of our favourite goofy-sounding poker games:

Change the Nappy	Cowpie Poker
Dirty Schultz	Five Card Stud with a Bug
Making Babies	There Can Only Be Juan
Three Legged Race	Rubbish Bin
Howdy Doody	Want It? Want It? Got It!
Grocery Store Dots	The Good, the Bad, and the Ugly
Linoleum	Mexican Sweat
Navy Nurse	Pass the Rubbish
Screwy Louie	

ON THE MARK

Quotes from America's great humourist, Mark Twain.

"Eloquence is the essential thing in a speech, not information."

"Good breeding consists in concealing how much we think of ourselves and how little we think of the other person."

"There is no sadder sight than a young pessimist."

"If you pick up a starving dog and make him prosperous, he will not bite you. It is the principal difference between a dog and a man."

"Irreverence is the champion of liberty and its one sure defense."

"Let us endeavor so to live, that when we die, even the undertaker will be sorry.

"Noise proves nothing. Often a hen who has merely laid an egg cackles as if she has laid an asteroid."

"All you need in this life is ignorance and confidence, and then Success is sure."

"Against the assault of laughter, nothing can stand."

"Whenever you find you are on the side of the majority, it is time to pause and reflect."

"You can't depend on your eyes if your imagination is out of focus."

"Golf is a good walk spoiled."

"Let us be thankful for fools. But for them the rest of us could not succeed."

"Everything has its limit—iron ore cannot be educated into gold."

"It is easier to stay out than to get out."

"It is noble to teach oneself, but still nobler to teach others—and less trouble."

"I find that the further I go back, the better things were, whether they happened or not."

"Do the thing you fear most and the death of fear is certain."

The blood vessels of a blue whale are so wide that an adult trout could swim through them.

ON BROADWAY

*Many Broadway hits started out with "no legs," but through the
perseverance, pluck, and luck, of people who believed in them,
managed to get on their feet and become runaway hits.*

SOUTH PACIFIC (1949)

When he first read James Michener's *Tales of the South Pacific*
in the late 1940s, director Joshua Logan knew it would make
a great Broadway show. He told producer Leland Hayward, and
Hayward agreed—but warned Logan not to mention it to anyone
until they owned the rights. Too late: At a party, Logan tipped his
cards to Richard Rodgers—who, with partner Oscar Hammerstein,
immediately purchased a controlling 51% interest and went on to
write the music and lyrics. (Logan wound up co-producing it with
them.)

They cast Mary Martin, fresh from *Annie Get Your Gun,* and
famed opera singer Ezio Pinza in the lead roles. Martin was afraid
she'd be dwarfed by the Pinza's voice, so the composers avoided
duets. Martin had just cut her hair short and, realizing it would
dry in three minutes, suggested the song "I'm Gonna Wash That
Man Right Out of My Hair," which became a classic.

The play is considered one of the earliest entertainment vehicles promoting racial tolerance in its portrayal of love between a
Naval officer and a Polynesian woman. *South Pacific* won Tonys in
all the acting categories, captured a Pulitzer Prize, and was the
top-grossing film of 1958.

LIFE WITH FATHER (1939)

The idea for this play comes from a series of autobiographical *New
Yorker* articles about growing up in a Victorian household in New
York City, written by Clarence Day.

At first, producer Oscar Serlin wanted to adapt it for a movie
starring W. C. Fields, but the author's widow was horrified at the
thought of the bulbous-nosed comedian playing the title role.

Serlin switched his sights to Broadway, but investors were
hohum about such tame fare on the eve of WWII. Serlin brought
in two writers, Howard Lindsay and Russel Crouse, who so loved
the concept that they worked without payment for two years

Farthest distance a pumpkin has been hurled without the use of explosives: **3,718 feet.**

developing scenes for the play. When all major actors rejected the title role, writer Lindsay took it himself. And when the company didn't have enough funds to open in a Maine summer stock production, Lindsay and his wife, Dorothy Stickney ("Mother") mortgaged their home to get it going.

On the eve of the Broadway opening, Lindsay said to Crouse, "We've got a nice little comedy here. We might even get six months out of it." It turned out to be the longest-running of all non-musical shows in Broadway history to date (3,224 performances over eight years). In fact, it so engaged audiences that it was made into a movie in 1947 and a TV series that ran from 1953 to 1955.

THE WIZ (1975)
Producer Ken Harper got the idea of retelling *The Wizard of Oz* using African-American characters, and got 20th Century Fox to invest $650,000. But after disappointing tryouts in Baltimore, he was advised to close it. The director, Gilbert Moses, quit, so Harper replaced him with actor (and costume designer) Geoffrey Holder, who made big changes in cast and concept.

At its Broadway opening, the mostly white critics were disappointed because it "didn't measure up to the original movie." Closing notices were posted that night. But Harper got Fox to mount a huge advertising campaign—TV ads targeting African-Americans. Word of mouth praised the dazzling choreography, staging, and costuming. "The Wiz" stayed open and went on to win seven Tonys, including Best Musical, and was made into a movie in 1978.

THE ODD COUPLE (1965)
"The idea came to me when I was at a party in California," playwright Neil Simon told the *Manchester Guardian*. "There were 24 people there; and do you know that every one of them was a divorcee? The men were either on their second marriage or recently divorced, and the women were in the process of getting divorced. All the men shared apartments because they had to be able to keep up their alimony payments and this was the cheapest method of living....I thought it was a good idea for a play"—and a movie—and a TV show—and a revival of the play—and a sequel to the movie...

YOU'RE MY INSPIRATION

*It's always fascinating to find out who, or
what, inspired cultural milestones like these.*

STAR WARS. According to *Leonard Maltin's Movie Guide*, the 1958 Japanese film that was "acknowledged by George Lucas as a primary inspiration for Star Wars" is *Hidden Fortress*, directed by Akira Kurosawa. The comedy-adventure "deals with the adventures of a strong-willed princess—à la Carrie Fisher, in the space fantasy—and her wise, sword-wielding protector—Toshiro Mifune, in the role adapted for Alec Guinness," says *Video Guide*. The two other main characters, a pair of bumbling farmers, are said to have been models for C-3PO and R2-D2.

THE "MAN WITH NO NAME." The character in *A Fistful of Dollars* (1964), who made Clint Eastwood a movie star, was also inspired by Kurosawa. "It is almost a scene-for-scene remake of Akira Kurosawa's Yojimbo, the tale of a lone samurai (played by Toshiro Mifune) who comes to a town torn by two rival gangs of fighters. He plays them against each other...and in the end finishes off pretty much the whole town and leaves with all the money. Replace a samurai with a gunslinger and replace the Japanese village with a small Western town, and you have *A Fistful of Dollars*." (Real Video)

JAMES T. WEST. Robert Conrad, the original star of TV's "Wild, Wild West," fashioned James West's movements after a favourite actor—Toshiro Mifune.

DOLLY PARTON. Her famous "look" was inspired by a woman in her hometown. (No, not Toshiro Mifune.) Parton says: "There was this tramp [floozy] that lived in our town, I better not say her name, 'cause she's probably got kids and grandkids now. But back then, she wore these bright-coloured clothes and she had this peroxide yellow hair—yellow, not blonde—and she used to walk up and down the streets of our hometown and they always said, 'Oh she's just trash, she's just a whore.' But I thought she was beautiful."

IT'S A WEIRD, WEIRD WORLD

More proof that truth really is stranger than fiction.

YO QUIERO CASA SANCHEZ!

"A Mexican restaurant in San Francisco offered a lifetime of free lunches to anyone willing to get a tattoo of its logo, Jimmy the Corn Man, a sombrero-wearing mariachi boy riding a blazing corncob. Amazingly, 38 people have braved the needle for a permanent coupon at Casa Sanchez so far. 'I think people have gotten much stupider tattoos for much stupider reasons,' says tattoo artist Barnaby Williams, who created 30 of the 'body coupons.'"

—*USA Today,* **April 13, 1999**

TERRORIST VOGUE

"Carlos the Jackal was one of the world's most notorious and elusive terrorists, accused of 83 deaths worldwide and more than a dozen other charges stemming from a 20-year killing spree.

"After two decades of evading the law, he was arrested in a Sudanese hospital while undergoing liposuction and a tummy tuck."

—*San Francisco Chronicle*

NOSING AROUND

"Ruth Clarke, 23, of London, England, underwent surgery to correct a lifelong breathing problem in 1981. She was presented with a tiddlywink, which doctors had removed from her nose.

"Clarke vaguely recalled losing the disk as a tot, but she didn't dream it was right under her nose all the time."

—*Encyclopedia Brown's Book of Strange Facts*

THE POSTMAN RINGS MORE THAN TWICE

"From 1974 to 1976, a young man in Taiwan wrote 700 love letters to his girlfriend, trying to talk her into marriage. He succeeded—she married the mailman who delivered the letters to her."

—*Weird News and Strange Stories*

Iron Age magazine once called Theodore Roosevelt "a drunk." He sued, and won 6¢.

ZZZZ-Z-Z-Z-Z-Z

According to experts we've been chatting with, horses, deer and giraffes sleep an average of only 3 hours a day—while cats get a whopping 15 hours. Humans fall between them, with an average of 7.5 hours. What happens during those 7 (or so) hours while you're sleeping? That will probably always be a big mystery, but we have more answers now than we did just half a century ago.

THE MYSTERY OF SLEEP

It wasn't until 1954 that science made a big breakthrough and recognized that REM (rapid eye movement) during sleep was caused by dreaming. Since then, the science of sleep has expanded rapidly, with over 100 distinct sleeping disorders now classified and many doctors devoting their careers exclusively to sleep problems.

Into the Waves

Scientists now recognize four stages of sleep:

Stage 1) After your muscles relax, your brain produces smaller waves of 9-12 cycles per second. You think normal, everyday thoughts. Pulse and breathing are regular.

Stage 2) Brain waves get larger with sudden bursts. Your eyes go "off" and wouldn't register anything if they were opened. Eyes may roll slowly back and forth.

Stage 3) Brain waves get slower and bigger, about five times larger than in stage 1.

Stage 4) Profound unconsciousness, with the biggest, slowest brainwaves. It takes over an hour to reach this stage.

Most people only go to stage 4 once or twice, then come back to lighter sleep (generally stage 1), and experience REM (dream-state).

THE REM EXPERIENCE

Once you're in REM:

- The muscles of your middle ear begin vibrating (science doesn't know why).
- Brain waves resemble a waking state, but you're dreaming.

In the 1500s, England's Queen Elizabeth I outlawed wife beating after 10 p.m.

- Muscles are relaxed, but may twitch or move.
- Pulse and breathing speed up. But we breathe less oxygen and use fewer calories than in other stages of sleep.
- Blood flow and brain temperature accelerate.
- Eyes dart all over the place, "seeing" what we're dreaming.

The first REM episode averages 10 minutes; then episodes recur on a 90 to 100-minute cycle, with the deeper sleep stages (3 or 4) getting shorter in between. During REM, our bodily processes are not operated by the larger, evolved parts of our brain, but by the brain stem—the "ancient brain" we had millions of years ago when we were arboreal (living in trees) mammals.

REM FACTS

We can dream without REM, but scientists have established that these dreams are simple and uneventful. REM dreaming, on the other hand, is the more exciting, dramatic kind. We do REM dreaming about two hours a night. In a lifetime, this adds up to 5 or 6 years of REM dreaming.

You may think that because your body seems to go offline, your mind does too. Not so. Your brain spends the night integrating the info and experiences you've gained during the day, and most of this happens during REM sleep. Labouratory tests showed that if mice learned complex tasks and then were deprived of their REM time, they forgot what they learned. In tests on University of Ottawa students, researchers noticed that the faster students learned things, the more REM time they required. Slower learners needed less REM time.

- Life stresses and changes also increase the need for REM. Using a group of divorcing women in their early 30s as subjects, psychoanalyst Rosalind Cartwright conducted a study that demonstrated they needed more REM time to assimilate their big changes.

- Among people over 65, those who are mentally sharper experience REM more frequently.

- Most people don't reach REM until about an hour and a half after going to sleep; people with depression, however, get to REM in about half this time. They also experience it more intensely.

- REM occupies approximately 22% of sleeping time. Pleasant dreams.

AUSSIES VS. AMERICANS:
A WORD QUIZ

*People in both countries speak English, but we don't necessarily use
the same words. For example Americans call rubbish "trash."
See if you can match the American words to their
Australian counterparts.*

AMERICAN
a) diaper
b) gas
c) thong
d) eraser
e) a stack
f) ice box
g) cantaloupe
h) cookies
i) gridiron
j) diner
k) french fries
l) the John
m) squash
n) sandal
o) guy
p) loafer
q) bathing suit
r) zoned out

s) drug store
t) go away
u) sunny side up
v) good
w) poor quality
x) naked
y) throw up
z) rubber

* * * * *

AUSSIE
1) football
2) bloke
3) chemist
4) condom
5) bonzer
6) chunder
7) fried egg

8) starkers
9) bugger off
10) lost the plot
11) thong
12) sand shoe
13) shonky
14) nappy
15) g-string
16) cafe
17) rubber
18) pancakes
19) esky
20) petrol
21) biscuits
22) rockmelon
23) dunny
24) pumpkin
25) chips
26) cozzie

Answers

1i, 2o, 3s, 4z, 5v, 6y, 7a, 8x, 9t, 10r, 11n, 12p, 13w, 14a, 15c, 16j,
17d, 18e, 19f, 20b, 21h, 22g, 23l, 24m, 25k, 26q

In France, it's considered good taste to spread your crackers with pig brain paté.

LOST IN TRANSLATION

*Have you ever thought you were communicating brilliantly, only to find
out that others thought you were a lunatic? That's an especially easy
mistake to make when you're speaking a foreign language or dealing
with a foreign culture. A few examples:*

PRODUCT CONFUSION

• **Gerber Baby Food:** Gerber used the same packaging
strategy in Africa that it used in America—a picture of the
Gerber baby on the label. They apparently didn't realize that since
many Africans don't read, it's standard practice to put pictures of
the contents on jar labels. As you might guess, the product didn't
go over well.

• **The Dairy Association:** Taking their "Got Milk?" campaign to
Mexico, they translated their slogan into Spanish. Unfortunately,
it came out as "Are you lactating?"

• **Johnson Wax:** When Johnson introduced their furniture
cleaner Pledge into the Netherlands, they didn't know that, in
Dutch, Pledge means "piss."

MEDIA TRANSLATIONS

• In the late 1970s, the TV sitcom "Laverne and Shirley" was
shown in Bangkok, Thailand—where women did not act like the
show's main characters. Each program was preceded by a
disclaimer saying: "The two women depicted in the following
episode are from an insane asylum."

• According to one source, audiences in Lebanon were going to
see *Titanic* because the title in Arabic slang translates as *Let's Have
Sex.*

MIXED-UP MENUS

These items are from real menus. Bon appétit.

• Horse-rubbish sauce (Rome)
• Torture soup (Djerba)
• Crab Meat Shaag and Botty Kebab (New York)
• Terminal soup (Istanbul)
• Farte aux Fraises (Turkey)
• Frozen soap with Peccadilloes (Madrid)
• Stewed abalone with 3 things and lucky duck (Bangkok)

Sheep snore.

SCREWED-UP SIGNS
• When English/Spanish signs were first posted at Sky Harbour International Airport in Phoenix, Arizona, they were full of mistakes. One sign, meant to remind arriving travellers to declare fruits, vegetables, and meats, read *"Violadores Seran Finados,"* which translates as "Violators Will Be Deceased."

DIPLOMATIC SNAFUS
• A French ambassador, M. Cambon, once thanked a Chicago mayor for a tour of the city. "Thank you," he said. "But I am sorry so to cockroach on your time." The mayor replied, "But you don't mean 'cockroach,' Mr. Cambon; it is 'encroach' you mean." "Oh, is it?" Cambon asked. "I see, a difference in gender."
• An Englishwoman at a French diplomatic party asked a Frenchman for a light. What he heard instead was, "Are you a dung-hill?"

CAMPING INSTRUCTIONS
These regulations were posted at a campground in Italy:
• Cars must enter or go away from the camp with motors out.
• THEN IS STRICTLY FORBIDDEN TO:
a) Reserve box parking, spaces with chairs, fences, rape or other means
b) Dainage of the plants and equipman
c) Dig simples around tents
d) Set to go into the camp, not authorized from the direction
• The above listed rules are inappellable. All of the camping personnel are authorized to send away anyone who does follow them.

IT'S JUST A TITLE, AFTER ALL
You have to wonder what Chinese movie audiences think they're going to see when U.S. films are shown in China as (for example):

> *Kindergarten Cop: Devil King of Children*
> *Indecent Proposal: Peach-Coloured Transaction*
> *The Shawshank Redemption: Excitement 1995*

GO, GO GOETHE

He's reluctant to admit it, but Uncle John does read things besides
The History of Parking Meters *and* Famous Movie Monsters.
He even has a favourite philosopher—Johann Wolfgang von Goethe.

"What is the best government? That which teaches us to govern ourselves."

"Legislators and revolutionaries who promise liberty and equality at the same time are either utopian dreamers or charlatans."

"Only law can give us freedom."

"If a man stops to ponder over his physical or moral condition, he generally discovers that he is ill."

"Preoccupation with immortality is for the upper classes, particularly ladies with nothing to do. An able man, who has a regular job and must toil and produce day by day, leaves the future world to itself, and is active and useful in this one."

"Never tell people how you are: they don't want to know."

"If youth is a fault, one soon gets rid of it."

"Fools and wise men are equally harmless. It is the half-fools and the half-wise who are dangerous."

"A clever man commits no minor blunders."

"Know thyself? If I knew myself, I'd run away."

"Whatever you can do, or dream you can, begin it. Boldness has genius, power and magic in it."

"Only the artist sees spirits. But after he has told of their appearing to him, everybody sees them."

"You can't understand something if you don't possess it."

"Nothing shows a man's character more than what he laughs at."

"Viewed from the summit of reason, all life looks like a malignant disease and the world like a madhouse."

Food for thought: The French eat an average of 200 million frogs each year.

MR. TOAD'S WILD RIDE, PART II

Here's the second part of the story of Kenneth Grahame's classic, The Wind in the Willows—*which has been adapted by everyone from A.A. Milne, who wrote the play* Toad of Toad Hall *in 1930, to Walt Disney, who animated it in 1949. (Part I starts on page 40.)*

SMEDLEY'S WILES

Magazines and publishers regularly begged Kenneth Grahame for articles—or perhaps a sequel to *The Golden Age* or *Dream Days*. But Grahame had become a notorious recluse; even getting an interview with him was nearly impossible.

In 1907 an American magazine called Everybody's put Constance Smedley on the job. The editors told Smedley to get Grahame to write something—anything. She was clever, and wrote to the author saying she was a relative of Governess Smedley—a fictional character in *The Golden Age* and *Dream Days*—who wanted to visit. Grahame was delighted. The two became good friends—but he still wouldn't write for her. Grahame said writing "was like physical torture," and "he hated it."

Smedley visited often. One evening, she overheard Grahame telling Mouse his bedtime story and, as one biographer put it, "moved in for the kill." She insisted that Grahame already had a story—he just needed to write it down. He even had much of the material for the book in the letters he'd written to Mouse. To his own surprise, Grahame agreed, and began expanding the letters into a book—the first professional writing he'd done in nine years.

He finished *The Wind in the Reeds* (as he called it) by Christmas 1907, "and packed it up and sent it to the eager Constance Smedley, who dispatched it to her editors, waiting excitedly in New York."

FALSE START

The New Yorkers were stunned. Grahame's other books had been about children—not wild animals. To Smedley's mortification, they turned the book down flat. The manuscript was sent back to Grahame, who gave it to his agent. But the agent couldn't find anyone in England who was willing to publish it, either.

The problem seemed to be that adults didn't understand *The Wind in the Willows* (now changed from "Reeds" to avoid confusion with an upcoming book by W.B. Yeats). It was a new genre—a novel-length animal fantasy that was not an allegory and had no human protagonist. "*The Wind in the Willows* had no clear generic predecessor," explains a Grahame biographer. "[It] shifted the identification of the reader to the animals themselves…and the first adults to read the work simply couldn't adapt to the change."

When Grahame finally did get his book published, he discovered that critics couldn't relate to his story, either. Some criticized it as a poorly thought-out allegory ("Grown up readers will find it monstrous and elusive"); others assumed that since it expressed such an "intimate sympathy with Nature," it was meant to be natural history. One newspaper commented that *The Wind in the Willows*—a book featuring a toad driving a car—would "win no credence from the very best authorities on biology." Even the Times of London wrote irrelevantly: "As a contribution to natural history the work is negligible."

One result of the confusion was that the book sold poorly.

Another: Grahame couldn't find an American publisher.

THE PRESIDENT STEPS IN

This is where President Teddy Roosevelt figures in the story. Roosevelt was a big fan of Grahame's work. Years earlier, he had met millionaire book collector Austin Purves and learned that Purves knew Grahame. He sent Purves back to England with a request for autographed copies of *The Golden Age* and *Dream Days*.

Grahame, of course, complied, and Roosevelt wrote back, saying "No one you could have sent those books to would have appreciated them more than Mrs. Roosevelt and I." He invited Grahame to stay at the White House if he visited Washington, but Grahame never did.

When *The Wind in the Willows* was published in England, Grahame sent Roosevelt an autographed copy. But Roosevelt chose not to read it. He had recently written an article denouncing stories that confused animals with human beings, and after seeing the reviews of *Willows*, feared it would ruin his love of Grahame's other books.

However, Roosevelt's wife found the book at the White House and started reading it aloud to their children. Roosevelt overheard her and became fascinated with the story. He later wrote to Grahame:

> For some time I could not accept the mole, the water-rat and the badger....But after a while Mrs Roosevelt and two of the boys, Kermit and Ted, all quite independently, got hold of *The Wind in the Willows* and took such a delight in it that I began to feel that I might have to revise my judgement. Then Mrs Roosevelt read it aloud to the younger children, and I listened now and then....I have since read the book three times, and now all the characters are my dearest friends.

The Roosevelt children sent their copies of the book to England to be autographed by Grahame. Meanwhile, Grahame's agent was still trying to find an American publisher. He had just sent the manuscript to Scribner's—who informed him that they were not interested—when a note arrived at the publisher from President Roosevelt. It said: "*The Wind in the Willows* is such a beautiful thing, Scribner must publish it."

"With an apologetic cough, Scribner did." And never regretted it. The book sold slowly at first, but caught on and went through many printings. Its success in the U.S. made it a hit in England, too.

By 1908 Grahame (no longer with the bank) was living comfortably off the royalties from his books. *Willows* changed popular tastes and paved the way for the genre of animal fantasies, which includes everything from Mickey Mouse to Charlotte's Web.

NOTE: The story doesn't have a particularly happy ending, however. Like Peter, who inspired Peter Pan (see page 450), Mouse committed suicide. One day while he was at college, he went for a walk and never came back. He had been hit by a train. Officials called it an accident, but the wounds showed he had been lying on the tracks when the train came.

AESOP'S FABLES

Aesop's fables (see page 118) have been told and retold for thousands of years. Here are a few more we've picked to pass on.

THE FOX & THE GRAPES

A fox was walking along the road, when he spied some delicious-looking grapes growing on a high trellis. "My, they look good!" he said. He jumped up, but couldn't reach them. He tried again and again, but to no avail. Finally he looked angrily at the grapes and said, "Hmmm, who wants the old grapes? They're probably sour anyway."

Moral: It's easy to despise what you can't have.

THE SICK LION

A lion, unable from old age and infirmities to provide himself with food by force, resolved to do so by trickery. He returned to his den, and lying down there, pretended to be sick, taking care that his sickness should be publicly known. The beasts expressed their sorrow, and came one by one to his den, where the Lion devoured them. After many of the beasts had thus disappeared, a Fox, presenting himself to the Lion, stood on the outside of the cave, at a respectful distance, and asked him how he was. "I am very middling," replied the Lion, "but why are you standing out there? Please come in and talk with me." "No, thank you," said the Fox. "I notice that there are many footprints entering your cave, but I see no trace of any returning."

Moral: The wise person learns from the misfortunes of others.

THE FOOLISH TRAVELLERS

A man and his son were walking along the road to market with their donkey. As they walked, they met a couple. "Did you ever see anything so silly?" the man said to his wife. "Two men walking when they have a donkey with them. What's a donkey for, after all, if not to carry a man?"

Hearing this, the man put his son on the back of the donkey and they went on their way. Soon they met two countrymen. "Did you ever see such a terrible thing?" one cried. "The strong young man rides while his poor father must walk." So the boy dismounted and the father got on instead.

They hadn't gone very far when they met two women. "Look at that heartless father!" exclaimed one of them, "His poor little son must walk while he rides." At that, the man said to his son, "Come up here with me. We'll both ride." They both rode for a while until they reached a group of men. "Aren't you ashamed?" they called out. "Overloading a poor little donkey like that." So the man and his son both climbed off the donkey.

They thought and thought. They couldn't walk along with the donkey, or ride it one at a time, or ride it both together. Then they had an idea. They got a tree and cut it into a long pole. Then they tied the donkey's feet to it, raised the pole to their shoulders, and went on their way, carrying the donkey.

As they crossed a bridge, the donkey—who didn't like being tied up—kicked one of his feet loose, causing the father and son to stumble. The donkey fell into the water. Because its feet were tied, it drowned.

Moral: If you try to please everyone, you'll end up pleasing no one.

THE ASS & THE FOX

An ass put on a Lion's skin, and roamed around the forest amusing himself by scaring all the foolish animals he met. Finally, he met a Fox, and tried to scare him, too—but as soon as the Fox heard the ass's voice, he said, "Well, I might have been frightened…if I hadn't heard your bray."

Moral: Clothes may disguise a fool, but his words give him away.

THE THIRSTY PIGEON

A pigeon, overcome by thirst, saw a glass of water painted on a sign. Not realizing it was only a picture, she quickly flew towards it and crashed into the sign. Her wings broken, she fell to the ground—and was captured by a bystander.

Moral: Zeal should not outrun discretion.

THE SERPENT & FILE

A serpent wandered into a carpenter's shop. As he glided over the floor he felt his skin pricked by a file lying there. In a rage he turned and attacked, trying to sink his fangs into the file; but he could do no harm to heavy iron and soon had to give over his wrath.

Moral: It is useless attacking the insensible.

MORE CLASSIC HOAXES

Here are a few more of our favourite frauds.

THE PSALMANAZAR HOAX

The Set-Up: In 1703 a "converted heathen from Formosa" [now Taiwan] named George Psalmanazar was introduced to the Bishop of London by a local cleric (actually, his confederate). "In eighteenth-century London," as Laura Foreman writes in *Hoaxes and Deceptions*, "a Formosan was as great a sensation as a Martian would be today," and Psalmanazar became the toast of English society.

People were fascinated with his stories. They were shocked to learn, for example, that before he joined the Anglican faith, he was a cannibal—and that snakes, snake blood, and raw meat, including the flesh of executed criminals, were delicacies in Formosa. Divorce customs were similarly barbaric: If a Formosan man grew tired of his wife, "he had only to accuse her of adultery, and he then was entitled to cut off her head and eat her." Psalmanazar taught himself to eat raw meat, and whenever he dined with upper-class hosts, would insist on it.

The Bishop of London sent the "reformed savage" to Oxford University to study and to lecture on Formosan language and history. While he was there, the Anglican Church commissioned him to translate the Bible into Formosan (a language he promptly invented). The following year, Psalmanazar wrote his extremely popular *Historical and Geographical Description of Formosa*, complete with comprehensive descriptions of Formosan art, culture, diet, dress, and language. Among his disclosures: Formosan religion demanded that the hearts of 18,000 Formosan boys under the age of nine were sacrificed to the gods every year, "a population-depleting practice offset by the sparing of eldest sons, and polygamy."

Why It Worked: No one in England had ever been to Formosa, and Psalmanazar was so inventive that when a doubting missionary who really had spent 18 years in China challenged him publicly, Psalmanazar made him look foolish. Plus, the English of the time were incredibly gullible about other cultures. When, for example, they asked why he didn't he look Oriental, Psalmanazar explained that the ruling class spent all their time in underground houses—it was only the workers whose skin turned "yellow." The public bought it.

Perhaps the real reason Psalmanazar was so successful was religious chauvinism. He roundly criticized Catholic missionary work in Asia and embraced the Anglican Church—confirming as an outsider what many English felt was true anyway. And in 1700, it was considered a real feather in the English church's cap to have converted a cannibal when Catholics couldn't.

What Happened: Psalmanazar's graphic descriptions of life in Formosa were at odds with everyone else's, and skeptics kept attacking until he was finally exposed as a fraud by Dr. Edmund Halley (of comet fame) in 1706. Halley quizzed Psalmanazar on just how much sunlight those underground houses got—and Psalmanazar got this, as well as other phenomena, wrong. He finally admitted having made everything up—including the "language" he spoke— and confessed to being a Frenchman. But he never revealed his true identity—it remains a mystery to this day.

THE BARON OF ARIZONA

The Set-Up: In 1883 a man named James Addison Reavis filed legal papers claiming ownership of more than 17,000 square miles of territory in what is now Arizona and New Mexico.

This wasn't as far-fetched as it might sound: when the U.S. government purchased the Arizona Territory from Mexico in 1848, it agreed to honour all Spanish land grants, and according to Reavis, the land had been presented to Don Miguel de Peralta de la Cordoba in 1748 by the King of Spain. Reavis said he'd bought the land and title from the family that had inherited it, and now he was staking his claim.

If Reavis's claim was true, the thousands of people living and working in Arizona were there illegally—and could be forced to leave. At the time, there were thousands of land grants being processed and verified by the United States. Reavis's was just the biggest (and most outrageous). Government experts pronounced it real.

Makes sense: The Phoenicians invented the world's first phonetic alphabet, in 2,000 B.C.

"The claim brought panic to the territory," writes one historian, "and an outpouring of riches to the new baron." Railroads, mines, and other businesses began paying him for the right to use his land. Over the next decade, he collected more than $10 million.

Why It Worked: Reavis was an extremely talented forger who had spent years laying the groundwork for his fraud. In particular, he had travelled to Spain where, after getting access to historic documents, he had skillfully altered them to create a record of the (nonexistent) Peralta family and their land grant. Then he produced impeccable copies of the grant itself.

What Happened: There are different accounts of how the hoax was eventually discovered. According to one source, a newspaper publisher noticed that the typestyle on one of the documents was too recent to be authentic, and that the watermark on the paper was from a Wisconsin paper mill that had not even been built when the document was supposedly drafted.

Another says that technology did Reavis in. When he planned his scheme, Reavis knew nothing of scientific innovations that would make it possible for investigators to test the age of paper and ink. By 1893, suspicious officials were able to have the tests done—and they revealed that the 135-year-old documents "were written in the wrong kind of ink on 10-year-old parchment." Reavis was sentenced to six years in prison for his crime, and died penniless in 1908.

* * * *

THAT'S ART!

• How slow a painter was Paul Cézanne? So slow that when he painted a bowl of fruit, it wasn't uncommon for the fruit to begin to rot before he finished painting. So he used waxed fruit for models.

• In the 19th century a 26-year-old painter named Richard Dadd went insane, killed his father, and was confined to an asylum. The asylum let him continue his painting—and his insanity actually improved his painting ability: "Oberon and Titania," one of the works he painted at the asylum, is considered one of the greatest paintings of the Victorian era.

THE MODERN ZOO, PART II

Every year more than 120 million people visit zoos, aquariums, oceanariums, and wildlife parks in the United States and Canada—a greater attendance than that of football, baseball, and hockey games combined! The story of the origin of the modern zoo is on page 111.

STATUS SYMBOL

In the late 1850s, Philadelphian Dr. William Camac visited the London Zoo. Inspired by what he saw, he founded the Philadelphia Zoological Society. His goal: To build a world-class zoological garden and the first scientific zoo in America.

By the late 1850s, major cities all over Europe either had zoos or were in the process of establishing them. They were status symbols: The citizens of Madrid, Hamburg, and Dublin, for example, regarded zoos as a means of communicating to the rest of world that their cities were to be taken as seriously as London or Paris. Dr. Camac wanted the same thing for Philadelphia: "When we see cities such as Amsterdam, Frankfurt, and Dublin—cities not so large as Philadelphia—supporting first-class zoological gardens," he wrote, "we see no reason why Philadelphia, with all its taste, wealth, enterprise, and advantages, should not in time possess one of the finest institutions in the world."

SIDESHOW

The United States lagged far behind Europe in the development of zoos. Westward expansion brought pioneers in contact with animals they had never seen before—and many animals were captured and brought back to cities to be exhibited to curious crowds. But as late as the 1870s, most animal viewing was limited to spectacles like a bear chained up in the corner tavern, or travelling carnivals put on by sea captains to show off exotic animals captured overseas.

EARLY AMERICAN ZOOS
New York

By 1861 New York City had a menagerie in Central Park, but this jumble was little more than a dumping ground for private collections and carnivals, including a black bear, two cows, deer, monkeys, raccoons, foxes, opossums, ducks, swans, eagles, pelicans, and parrots. No rational thought was put into the collection; the keepers just accepted whatever animals people gave them.

Still, the menagerie was a popular attraction. "By the late 1800s," Linda Koebner writes in *Zoo*, "it was a center of entertainment both for wealthy Fifth Avenue strollers and for the poor who were looking for a break from their daily working lives. Newly arrived immigrants lived in dark, crowded tenements on the Lower East Side of New York. A trip up to the green of Central Park to see the menagerie was well worth the walk or the nickel fare on the trolley."

Chicago
The menagerie in Chicago's Lincoln Park wasn't much better than the one in Central Park. It got its start when the Central Park menagerie presented them with a gift of two swans. This prompted similar "gifts," and by 1873 the park had 27 mammals and 48 birds.

GENUINE ARTICLE
While these zoos were popular attractions, neither Central Park nor Lincoln Park knew anything about animals or bothered to hire anyone who did; care and feeding of the creatures was left to the parks department, whose main concern was picking up garbage and raking leaves.

As Dr. Camac proposed it, the Philadelphia Zoological Garden would be something completely different: a well-funded, intelligently planned collection of animals housed in permanent facilities and run by a professional, full-time staff. The public would be admitted into the zoo, but it would also serve a more serious purpose: scientists at the University of Pennsylvania, the Academy of Sciences, and other organizations would be able to study and observe the animals up close.

Planning for the facility began in March of 1859, but the outbreak of the Civil War interfered with construction, so it was not completed until 1873.

Camel rule of thumb: One-hump camels run faster than two-humped camels.

THE TOILET ERA

When it opened to the public on July 1, 1874, the Philadelphia Zoo was a state-of-the-art facility, complete with a monkey house, bird house, prairie dog village, and sea lion pool. But the early zookeepers had a lot to learn about caring for animals. Hunters and trappers who captured the animals knew next to nothing about how the animals lived in the wild or what they ate, and thousands died before they could be delivered to the zoo. The zookeepers didn't know much more, and animals that made it to the zoo didn't live much longer.

Because animal behavior was so poorly understood, animals that lived in social or family groups in the wild were often acquired one at a time and lived alone in bare cages—no attempt was made to simulate their natural environment. Animals frequently had nowhere to hide, and climbing animals like monkeys and wildcats had nowhere to go to get off the floor. The emphasis in cage design was on preventing disease by making them easy to clean: enclosures were usually made of concrete and tile and looked so much like bathrooms, Koebner writes, that "this manner of keeping the animals gave rise to the term 'the toilet era.'"

Visitors to the zoos were similarly shortchanged: displays did little to educate the public other than give the name of the animal and the feeding schedule. Scientific aspects of the zoo were played down; the garden's staffers themselves were poorly informed and so could do little to shed light on any of the exhibits.

Where the public was concerned, the emphasis was on entertainment. Elephants paraded, bears danced, and chimpanzees wore clothes and ate with silverware at dinner tables, part of the zoology garden's attempt to show how "humanlike" they were.

A NEW ERA

Things began to improve at the turn of the century, thanks in large part to a German circus trainer named Carl Hagenbeck, considered the "father of modern zoos." For years Hagenbeck had made his living catching and training exotic animals for zoos. In 1907 he expanded his business by opening his own zoo, which he named the Hagenbeck Tierpark.

As an animal catcher, Hagenbeck had seen animals in the

Coldest towns on earth: Verkyoyanks and Oymyakon, Siberia, with temps as low as –95° F.

wild and was determined that the animals in his zoo would never live in cages that looked like restrooms. "I wished to exhibit them not as captives, confined to narrow spaces and looked at between bars, but as free to wander from place to place within as large limits as possible."

Hagenbeck put his experience as an animal trainer to work, testing the animals to see how high and how far they could jump, and then dug moats so deep and wide that the animals would not try to escape. He also tried to give the exhibits an authentic appearance so that the animals would be as comfortable as possible.

Optical Illusion

Hagenbeck also arranged the exhibits to give them as natural an appearance as possible; it even seemed as if predators and their prey were part of the same exhibit. The lion exhibit was located just in front of the zebra, antelope, and ostriches (safely separated by a moat that was concealed behind bushes and landscape.) All of the animals appeared to be together, just as they would be in their natural habitat in Africa. As a result, Koebner writes, "the public could see the interrelationship of animals, begin to picture what the African landscape looked like and learn about predators, prey and habitats."

The advantages of Hagenbeck's reforms were obvious, and most zoos began adopting his ideas to improve their exhibits. Still, his enclosures had drawbacks: They were expensive, took up more space than cages, and increased the distance between animals and the viewing public from 5 feet to as much as 75 feet. And some zoo directors felt they were too revolutionary. Dr. William Hornaday of the Bronx Zoo, for example, criticized the new enclosures as "a half-baked German fad." But Hornaday was in the minority. Zookeepers from all over the world began making pilgrimages to the Hagenbeck Tierpark to learn as much as they could.

CHANGING TIMES

Hagenbeck's reforms were part of a broader zoological trend: all over the world, zoos were beginning to take better care of their animals. In the old days, the supply of animals in the wild seemed inexhaustible—if an animal in a zoo died, they could just send a hunter into the jungle to get another one. Life was cheap, and animals were expendable.

By the early 1900s, zoos were already beginning to look different. Many animals had been driven to extinction or close to it. And foreign governments—realizing how valuable the surviving animals were—started charging zoos for the privilege of hunting in their territories. As the supply of animals went down and the cost of obtaining them went up, zoos became more interested in preserving and extending the lives of the animals they had.

But the practical aspects of running and maintaining a zoo didn't change as fast as the philosophy. "Even with increased difficulties in capture and export, it would still be many decades before capture in the wild slowed significantly," Koebner writes in *Zoo*. Until about the early 1960s, zoos still obtained the majority of their animals from well-funded expeditions into the wild, which amounted to little more than raids upon wildlife areas in Africa and Asia. Barbaric practices, such as killing a mother elephant or hippopotamus in order to capture its child, were still commonplace and widely accepted.

ZOOS TODAY

In the 1960s and 1970s, however, zoos began to make substantive shifts toward conservation—not just of the animals in the zoo, but also those still in the wild. And instead of competing against one another, they began working together to accomplish these goals. This is critical in the case of endangered species that are extinct, or practically so, in the wild—and survive only in zoos today. In cases where only a few dozen animals survive and their numbers are scattered among several zoos, the only way to bring the species back from extinction is to manage the animals as one population.

"Today's zoos have a very specific message to preach," writes Allen Nyhuis in *The Zoo Book*. "By introducing the public to the world's enormous variety of animals and their native habitats, they hope that people will better appreciate the animals and want to help preserve them."

* * * *

Since 1984, America's zoos have spent more than
$1 billion on upgrading and improvements.

HOT STUFF!

*In 1991 America turned a culinary corner—that's the first
year they spent more money on salsa than on tomato sauce.
If you love "hot" food, this chapter is for you.*

BLAME IT ON COLUMBUS
When Christopher Columbus arrived in the New World,
he thought he'd landed in India. So he called the people
he met there "Indians."

That wasn't the only mistake he made: When his hosts served
a spicy food containing hot chillies, he assumed the chillies were
related to piper nigrum, the plant that produces black pepper.

They're actually part of the Solanaceae, or nightshade, family
and are more closely related to potatoes, tomatoes, and eggplants.
But chillies have been known as chilli "peppers" ever since.

MADE IN BOLIVIA

All varieties of chilli peppers descended from prehistoric wild
chilli plants that originated somewhere near present-day Bolivia.
Scientists believe that most animals avoided the painfully hot
plants, but birds ate them—apparently because they can't taste
chillies —and spread the seeds all over Central and South America. Humans began eating the wild peppers as early as 7000 B.C.,
and had domesticated them by 2500 B.C.

South American and Latin American peoples, including the
Aztecs, revered the peppers. They were used for everything from
treating upper-respiratory disorders to ritualistic morning bever-
ages. Montezuma, the last Aztec emperor, drank a concoction of
chocolate and hot chillies for breakfast. The Incas took their reverence a step further: Agar-Uchu, or "Brother Chilli Pepper" in
English, is one of the four brothers of the Incan creation myth.

Chillies remained exclusive to the New World until Columbus brought some to Europe. From there they spread via trade
routes to every remaining corner of the globe, and within a century they were firmly established in the cuisines of India, China, and
Africa.

Today an estimated 75% of the world's population eats
chillies on a daily basis. Mexico tops the list—Mexicans consume,
on average, one chilli per person, every day.

CHILLI SCIENCE
What Makes Them Hot?
• All chillies contain a powerful alkaloid called capsaicin (cap-SAY-a-sin), which gives chillies their heat—and which isn't found in any other plants. It's so potent that humans can detect it even when it's diluted to one part per million.
• The "capsaicinoids," as they're also known, are produced in the plant by the placenta—the part just below the stem of the chilli. That's also where the seeds and the "ribs" grow. On average, these parts are 16 times hotter than the rest of the plant, so it stands to reason that one way to cool down a chilli (if that's what you want) is to remove the placenta.
• How hot is capsaicin? It's so strong that it's the main ingredient in a product designed to drive grizzly bears away. It's also the "pepper" in pepper spray, which has replaced tear gas spray in more than 1,200 police departments around the U.S. According to *Smithsonian* magazine, when sprayed in the face, "it causes eyes to slam shut and creates a spasm in the respiratory system—an unpleasant experience that lasts 30 to 45 minutes."

What Makes Them So Good?
• When you eat chillies, capsaicin irritates the pain receptor cells in your mouth.
• Some scientists believe the receptors then release something known as "substance P," which rushes to "alert" the brain to the pain. In response, the brain produces chemicals called endorphins that kill the pain and elicit feelings of well-being. Does hot, spicy food taste less hot to you after a couple of bites? Chilli enthusiasts say this is the endorphins at work.
• In fact, some experts theorize that it's the addictive nature of endorphins, not the taste of the chillies themselves, that makes the spice so popular.

Cooling Down
• Do you reach for ice water when you eat a hot pepper? It's not a great idea—it not only won't cool your mouth down, it will probably make things worse by spreading the capsaicin around. Beer might work (experts aren't sure), but the best way to put out the fire is to drink cold milk—or eat any dairy product (e.g., frozen yoghurt) with lactic acid. They contain casein, which acts like a

detergent to help wash away the capsaicin. Other recommended foods: sugar, salt, tortillas, brandy Alexander, hunks of bread, and corn.

THE SCOVILLE SCALE

In 1912 Wilbur Scoville, a pharmacologist with the Parke Davis pharmaceutical company, needed to test the potency of some chillies he was mixing into a muscle salve. He mixed pure ground chillies into sugar-water and had a panel of tasters drink the water, in increasingly diluted concentrations, until the liquid was so diluted that it no longer burned their mouths.

Next, Scoville assigned a number to each chilli based on how much it needed to be diluted before the tasters tasted no heat. The "Scoville scale," as it's still known, measures potency in multiples of 100. Here's how some popular chillies are ranked:

Bell and sweet peppers: . . . . . . 0–100 Scoville Units

New Mexican peppers: 500–1000

Española peppers: 1,000–1,500

Ancho & pasilla peppers: 1,000–2,000

Cascabel & cherry peppers: 1,000–2,500

Jalapeno & mirasol peppers: 2,500–5,000

Serrano peppers: 5,000–15,000

De Arbol peppers: 15,000–30,000

Cayenne & Tabasco: 30,000–50,000

Chiltepin peppers: 50,000–100,000

Scotch bonnet & Thai peppers: . . 100,000–350,000

Habanero peppers: . . . . 200,000 to 300,000

Red savina habanero peppers (the hottest
    chillies ever recorded): . . . . . as much as 577,000

Pure capsaicin: 16,000,000

Today the potency of chillies is measured very precisely by machines that calculate the exact amount of capsaicin in each chilli. But the scale that is used is still named the Scoville scale in Wilbur Scoville's honour.

HEALTH NOTES
Can eating chillies make you sick? Epidemiologists from Yale University and the Mexico National Institute of Public Health concluded that chilli peppers may cause stomach cancer. However, peppers also contain quercetin, a chemical shown to reduce cancer risk in lab animals, so who knows?

Other maladies to watch out for if you're a hardcore chilli eater:
- **Salsa sniffles.** "Sweating and rhinitis (runny nose) caused by eating hot peppers."
- **Hunan hand.** "The skin irritation that comes from chopping chillies."
- **Jaloprocitis.** "The burn jalapeños leave as they exit the body.

On the other hand, according to a book called *The Healing Powers of Chili:*
- A 1986 experiment at Oxford University in England found that eating chillies may assist in burning calories.
- The popular muscle salve Heet is made mostly of capsaicin.
- Chilies are low in fat, high in fibre, and loaded with beta carotene and vitamin C. One half cup of chopped chilli peppers offers more than twice the vitamin C of an orange.
- Capsaicin is a natural antibiotic, slowing down bacteria's growth.
- A few more ailments that have been treated with capsaicin: indigestion, acne, alcoholism, arthritis, bronchitis, cramps, haemorrhoids, herpes, low blood pressure, shingles, wounds.

MORE CHILLI FACTS
- Chilli is the Nahuatl, or Aztec, word for the plant.
- According to most accounts, chilli peppers were introduced into what is now the United States by Capitan General Juan de Oñante, who also founded Santa Fe in 1598.

UNCLE JOHN'S "STALL OF FAME"

More of Uncle John's bathroom heroes.

Honorary: Glen Dorenbush, formerly of San Francisco
Notable Achievement: Being flushed down the toilets of his favourite bars after he died
True Story: According to news reports, "When Dorenbush died in the summer of 1996, his cronies ended up with eight pounds [nearly four kilograms] of his ashes and an interesting predicament. The amiable eccentric left no will when he checked out, but had made it clear to those who knew him best what he wanted done with his remains: He wanted most of his ashes flushed down the toilets of his favourite bars."

The dilemma: "It's technically illegal in California to sprinkle cremated remains down the can, not to mention bad for the plumbing." His friends finally decided to "scatter some ashes on a beach in Puerto Vallarta where he loved to vacation and some more in the ocean off Stinson Cafe on Hyde Street. The rest, it was decided, would go down the latrines at several undisclosed locations."

Honorary: An unnamed homeowner in Fayetteville, Arkansas
Notable Achievement: Creative bathroom-based entrepreneurship
True Story: In 1995 the man bought Jimmy Johnson's former house and had a great idea while rennovating his bathroom. He took out an ad in a local paper, offering "a great for football fans": For only $250, they could own (and sit on) the toilet once used by the ex–Dallas Cowboys coach.

Honorary: Richard List of Berkeley, California
Notable Achievement: Creating a museum (and philosophical statement) featuring painted toilets
True Story: "New York has the MOMA," writes a San Francisco reporter, "Paris has the Louvre. Berkeley has the New Sense Museum, where art is strictly in the eyes of the beholder. The

New Sense (say it fast) consists of a vacant, weed-strewn lot studded with weird objects, most notably a flotilla of commodes painted fluorescent pink, orange and green."

According to Richard List, the museum's guiding force, "People say, 'I don't get the message.' Well, that's the point. Life is a mystery."

Honorary: St. Louis circuit judge Edward Peek
Notable Achievement: Presiding over the first murder trial ever instigated by an argument about toilet paper
True Story: There's nothing funny about this, of course, but it's too weird to leave out. In the late 1980s, a 36-year-old man admitted to the judge that he had shot and killed his younger brother. The reason: He was angry that his brother had "used too much of a new eight-roll package of toilet paper." The man was convicted of second-degree murder.

Honorary: Barney Smith of San Antonio, Texas
Notable Achievement: Created the Toilet Seat Museum in his garage
True Story: Smith, a plumber, asked his customers if he could keep the old toilet seat every time he installed a new one. "Then," says the Houston Post, "he would decorate each seat with something special, things like keepsakes from a vacation or mementos from a historic moment….Smith has decorated and dedicated about 400 toilet-seat lids, artistically altering the functional commode covers to become hanging history. And he has generously hung them for the world to see."

Honorary: Nelson Camus of Hacienda Heights, California
Notable Achievement: Inventing the world's first urine-powered battery
True Story: The "Argentine-born electrical engineer," says John Kohut in *Dumb, Dumber, Dumbest*, "announced that his battery generates more power than standard acid-reaction batteries and is cheaper. His partner, Ed Aguayo, said 10 urine-powered batteries, each about half the size of a normal car battery, could power a normal house." No word on when the battery will become available.

Bagpipes were invented in Iran and brought to Scotland by the Romans.

IT'S A WEIRD, WEIRD WORLD

More proof that truth really is stranger than fiction.

PERFORMING UNDER PRESSURE
"On September 12, the Great Hurricane of 1938 devastated the New England states [of America]. That morning a man in West Hampton Beach received a barometer in the mail. The needle was stuck on 'hurricane.' Disgusted, and thinking it was defective, he marched back to the Post Office and mailed the instrument back to the store from which he had purchased it. When he returned, his home was gone."

—*Our Fascinating Earth*

DID HE CROAK?
"Doctors in a Mexican hospital were in the midst of open-heart surgery when a frog fell out of an overhead lamp and landed on the patient."

—*The Fortean Times*

ROCK YOUR WORLD
"For years, maps have shown that northern Germany's highest mountain, the Brocken, was 3,747 feet [1,139 metres] tall. But recently, more precise measurements revealed that the peak is only 3,741 feet [1,137 metres] tall. To avoid correcting the world's maps, a construction company trucked 19 tons of granite to the summit, stacking the rocks in a 6-foot [1.8-metre] pile."

—*Portland Oregonian,* **February 28, 1998**

NEXT COMES A *STRAITJACKET*
"Despite 18 years working at a Florida fishing camp, Freddie Padgett was so terrified of water that he wore a life jacket to bed on stormy nights. Friends made fun of him, until a twister sucked him out of his RV while he was sleeping and dropped him into Lake Harney over a mile away. He suffered broken ribs and other injuries, but authorities say the life jacket probably saved his life."

—*The Skeptic*

Hardest substance in your body: the enamel in your teeth.

WORD ORIGINS

Here are some more interesting word origins.

AMBULANCE
Meaning: A specialized vehicle for transporting the injured to a hospital
Origin: "The name comes from an invention of Napoleon Bonaparte's, l'hôpital ambulant (walking hospital), a litter fitted with bandages and other first-aid equipment that served as a field hospital for wounded soldiers. In time, the litters became elabourate and mechanized, yielding first to horse-drawn wagons, eventually to motorized ambulances." (From *Fighting Words*, by Christine Ammer)

TABOO
Meaning: A behavior or activity that is prohibited
Origin: "Originally a Tongan word, tabu, meaning 'marked as holy.' The first taboos were prohibitions against the use or even the mention of certain things because of religious belief that to do so would invoke the wrath of the gods. The word gradually was extended in use to cover all sorts of prohibitions or bans based upon social convention." (From *Dictionary of Word and Phrase Origins*, Vol. III, by William and Mary Morris)

BUMPKIN
Meaning: A loutish countryman
Origin: "From the Dutch boomkin, small tree—hence, a countryman thought to possess the tree's intelligence." (From *Loose Cannons and Red Herrings*, by Robert Claiborne)

SENATE
Meaning: A representative body in a republic or democracy
Origin: "Literally, 'a gathering of old men.' Like most cultures, ancient Roman society respected age. In the days before the Roman Empire, tribes would gather. The representatives from these clans were usually elders, whose experience led to wiser, more thoughtful deliberation. When the empire flourished, the tradition of the council of elders continued. To this day there are age requirements for our Senate." (From *Where in the Word?*, by David Muschell)

UNCLE JOHN'S TOP 10 AMAZING COINCIDENCES

*We're constantly finding stories about amazing coincidences,
so in this BR, Uncle John listed his 10 favourites. Send
us yours, and next edition, we'll do a readers' Top 10.*

10. WHAT GOES AROUND...
"In 1965, at age four, Roger Lausier was saved from drowning off a
beach at Salem, Mass., by a woman named Alice Blaise. Nine
years later, in 1974, on the same beach, Roger paddled his raft
into the water and pulled a drowning man from the water. The
man was Alice Blaise's husband."

—*The Book of Lists*

9. NUMBER NINE, NUMBER NINE...
BELOIT, Wisconsin— "Nicholas Stephen Wadle was born at 9:09
a.m. on the ninth day of the ninth month of 1999. But the string
of coincidences doesn't end there. He weighed 9 pounds, 9
ounces.

"A spokeswoman for Beloit Memorial Hospitals said the
mother 'couldn't believe it,' but 'the most surprised were the professionals involved....As the nines started to stack up, they were
going crazy.'

"The baby was due Sept. 15, but complications with the
births of Mrs. Wadles's two older children led her doctor to schedule a cesarean section for Thursday, to be safe. The delivery was
set for 8:00 a.m. but there was an emergency, which allowed the
9:09 birth."

—Appleton, Wisconsin, *Post Crescent,* September 10, 1999
(Contributed by Julie Roeming)

8. ARE YOU MY DADDY?
"Wilf Hewitt, 86, a widower from Southport, wanted to look
through a list of registered voters in the library, and asked the
woman who had the list if she was going to be long. Vivien
Fletoridis replied that she was looking for a man named Hewitt.

In her entire life, Queen Berengaria of England never once visited England.

She was his daughter, whom he had not seen for 46 years. Wilf had had a wartime love affair with Vivien's mother, who had died in 1983. Their daughter was adopted in 1941 and went to Australia with her foster parents. In July 1987 she traced her two brothers and sister through an agency, and then set out to find her father."

—*The Fortean Times*

7. REINCARNATED SURVIVOR
"On three separate occasions—in 1664, 1785, and 1860—there were shipwrecks where only one person survived the accident. Each time that one person's name was Hugh Williams."

—*The Book of Useless Information*

6. I DO, I THINK
"A woman in Kissimmee, Florida, should have no trouble remembering her new husband's name. But, following a bizarre chain of coincidences surrounding the couple's wedding, she might have trouble remembering what he looks like.

"Ronald Legendre married his girlfriend, Hope, in August 1995. The best man—who wasn't related to the groom in any way—was also named Ronald Legendre. And the ceremony was performed by someone who wasn't connected to either man: Judge Ronald Legendre."

—*Knuckleheads in the News*

5. SECRET-AGENT KID
"James Bond, 15, a pupil at Argoed High School, North Wales, and a candidate for examinations in 1990, was given the examination number 007 by a computer quirk."

—*The World's Most Incredible Stories*

4. HER NAME IS MY NAME, TOO
"A computer mix-up that gave two American women the same social security number was responsible for highlighting a further series of incredible coincidences. Patricia Kern of Colorado and Patricia di Biasi of Oregon were brought together by the blunder.

"The women discovered they had both been born Patricia Ann Campbell with fathers called Robert. They were born on the same date, too: March 13, 1941. Both Patricias married military men in 1959, within eleven days of one another, and had children aged nineteen and twenty-one. They also shared an interest in painting with oils, had studied cosmetics and worked as bookkeepers."

—One in a Million

3. AND HER NAME IS MY NAME, TOO
"Mother of two, Michelle Samways, was caught up in a spot of trouble—with mother of two Michelle Samways. The two women moved into numbers 5 and 6 Longstone Close, Portland, England, in Oct. 1994 and hardly a day goes by without a mix-up of some kind. They discovered that they share the same name only when they entered a raffle at a toddlers' group. The two Michelles, aged 26 and 27, were both named after the 1965 Beatles song. They are the same height and build, [and have] similar hair colour."

—The Fortean Times

2. BABIES KEEP FALLING ON MY HEAD
"Joseph Figlock was passing an apartment block in Detroit in 1975 when he was knocked unconscious. A baby had fallen fourteen stories and landed on him. Both survived. One year later, Figlock was passing the same apartment block—and once again he was hit by a falling child…and survived!"

—One in a Million

And the #1 coincidence is:
1. CIVIL SERVANT
"One of the lesser-known figures of American history is Wilmer McLean, a Virginia farmer who took little interest in politics.
"In 1861, most of the Rebel army marched onto McLean's land. The Union forces attempted to bar their way, and the first full-scale battle of the Civil War (Battle of Bull Run), got underway—right on his farm. Thirteen months later, it happened again. The second battle at Bull Run destroyed McLean's land. McLean had had enough. He packed his wagons and moved two hundred miles away from the war.
"Three years later, in a weird twist of fate, two men confronted each other in Wilmer McLean's parlor. These two men talked and signed a document on McLean's best table; for he had moved to a little village called Appomattox Court House—where Robert E. Lee and Ulysses S. Grant negotiated the end of the Civil War."

—Ripley's Believe It or Not

PUSS IN BOATS

In the days of sailing ships cats went to sea to keep rats and mice down, but Trim became a personal pet and companion to explorer Captain Matthew Flinders.

BIRTH
The timbers creak and the sails flap as the vessel pitches and tosses. We're aboard the British ship *Reliance* sailing eastward across the Indian Ocean from Cape Town to Botany Bay. The winds are howling and the waves are huge. The year is 1799.

Below deck (that's downstairs to anyone not *au fait* with sea speak) a birth is taking place. A birth in a berth, as it were.

A littler of mewing, blind, flat-eared kittens is arriving. But I don't suppose either mother or new arrivals are taking much notice of the noisy, heaving weather. Doubtless Mother cat just purposefully gets on with licking and suckling her kittens, purring.

CATS GALORE
It was nothing unusual of course. Cats and ships went together like sausages and mash. They were a form of rodenticide. Almost all vessels were badly infested with nibbling rats and mice. No doubt this particular mother cat had been born at sea herself and knew no other life.

No, what is unusual about this feline happy event is that it was chronicled. That's how we know about it. It's also why, nearly two hundred years later, it was solemnly commemorated in Sydney.

TRIM AND FLINDERS
One of the kittens was a nice little Tom named Trim. He became a personal pet and companion to Captain Matthew Flinders, British explorer. Together they shared some pretty hair-raising adventures. For five years the Captain and the cat were inseparable friends and, together, they travelled tens of thousands of pretty eventful miles.

Flinders, ably assisted by Trim, was the first bloke to chart much of the Australian coast. Eventually he recorded his doings and deeds in a book called *Voyage to Terra Australis*, which was published in Britain after his death in 1814. The enterprising Captain also invented the Flinders Bar to offset the effects of iron on the compass needle and was the first person to use a barometer to predict wind changes. Clever chaps these early explorers!

Man and cat also saw service together on the *Investigator*. Then, in 1800, Trim and Flinders returned to England, a journey that would have taken many tedious and uncomfortable weeks. There Trim made the acquaintance of Mrs Flinders, the Captain's wife. She would have seen a great deal less of her husband than his cat did, although there are no records of her having minded particularly.

WAR

Between 1802 and 1815 Britain was again at war with France. But a little thing like that didn't stop Captain Flinders and his intrepid feline from sailing back to the Antipodes where they enjoyed (or at least survived) a "friendly" meeting with French ships anchored at Encounter Bay on Australia's south coast. How did the conversation go? "Bon jour. Permettez moi de vous present mon chat, Trim." Perhaps. The presence of a cat has always been a useful icebreaker in sticky situations. Perhaps Trim, had he known it, was doing a bit of international diplomatic work.

By 1803, Trim and Flinders were on the *Porpoise*. It was shipwrecked and together they waited two months for rescuers before setting sail again on the *Cumberland*. Their destination was Britain, where Flinders hoped to find a better ship. Alas, the poor *Cumberland* was no more seaworthy than its predecessor and Flinders was forced to call in at the French (and therefore enemy) island of Mauritius and ask for help.

Oh dear. Luck had finally run out. There was no one to vouch for this Englishman on enemy territory in war time. Moreover the "passport" given to Flinders by the French offering him French hospitality should he ever need it, was in the name of the *Investigator* not the *Cumberland*. One can just imagine the heated exchange and level of misunderstanding between the British sea captain and the French governor.

The results were grim for both man and cat. Flinders was held as a spy in captivity for seven years before his release to retirement in Britain, but Mauritius was the end for poor old Trim. He disappeared in mysterious circumstances. "An untimely death, being devoured by the Catopophagi of that island," surmised his master, sadly.

FLINDERS KEEPS RECORD
We know all this because Flinders kept boredom at bay during his period of detention by writing a journal. The original manuscript is now held at the Maritime Museum at Greenwich, England, but an extract was published in Australia. In his journal Flinders was very affectionate about his good mate, Trim. Flinders hoped that there would one day be a memorial to Trim which would call attention to the cat's "little merriment with delight and his superior intelligence with surprise," and to remind us all that, "Never will his like be ever seen again!"

TRIM'S MEMORIAL
It took nearly two centuries, but the State Library of New South Wales, Sydney, finally got round to fulfilling Flinders's wishes in 1996. There's been a statue of Captain Flinders outside the library in Macquarie Street in Sydney since 1925. In 1996, the explorer was joined by a beautiful life-sized statue of this cat, Trim, cast in bronze by the sculptor John Cornwell. It was the idea of a keen amateur maritime historian, Vaughan Evans, who worked as a volunteer at the library. Trim now stands, nose up and best paw forward, inside the building on a sunny windowsill. So that loyal and much loved puss has found a warm, peaceful, and permanent resting place.

Money for the "Trim Project" was raised by public subscription. Many donors sent gifts in the names of their own cats: Sir Basil, Stripey, Smokey, and Jellicle to name but a few. The feline monument was unveiled on 28 March 1996 by Rear-Admiral David Campbell, AM RAN Naval Command, Sydney, in the presence of 400 admirers and the Naval Reserve Band.

SUPERSTITIONS

Here's where some common superstitions come from.

FINDING A FOUR-LEAF CLOVER

The belief that four-leaf clovers are good luck comes from the Druids, ancient residents of the British Isles. Several times a year, they gathered in oak groves to settle legal disputes and offer sacrifices—then they ended their rituals by hunting for four-leaf clovers. Why? They believed a four-leaf clover enabled its owner to see evil spirits and witches—and therefore avoid them.

THROWING PENNIES INTO A WELL

Ancient people believed spirits living in springs and fountains demanded tribute—usually flesh. Young Mayan girls, for example, were sometimes tossed into the Well of Sacrifice (where they would "marry" the spirits). Today we just toss the spirits a coin or two for luck.

KNOCKING ON WOOD

In the Middle Ages, churchmen insisted that knocking on wood was part of their tradition of prayer, since Christ was crucified on a wooden cross. They were right...but the tradition started several thousands of years earlier, with a different deity. Both Native Americans and ancient Greeks developed the belief (independently) that oak trees were the domain of an important god. By knocking on an oak, they were communicating with him and asking for his forgiveness. The Greeks passed their tradition on to the Romans, and it became part of European lore. The oak's "power" was eventually transferred to all wood.

NAILING A HORSESHOE OVER A DOOR

This "good luck charm" is a combination of two superstitions:

1. In early times, horses were considered magical. Because they can find their way in the dark, for example, people believed they could foresee danger or could guide souls through the underworld so anything connected with a horse was lucky.

2. Horseshoes are made of iron, which was considered protective.

The Norse god of battle wore iron gloves and carried an iron hammer. Romans nailed pieces of iron over their doors, believing it could ward off evil spirits.

In the 10th century, Christians added their own twist to the superstition—the tale of a blacksmith named Dunstan, who later became Archbishop of Canterbury. Dunstan had an unusual customer one day, a man with cloven feet who requested iron shoes. Dunstan pretended not to recognize him and agreed to make the shoes. But he knew who the fellow was—he shackled the Devil to the wall, treating him so brutally that Satan cried for mercy. Dunstan released him only after extracting a promise to never enter a dwelling with a horseshoe on the door.

OPENING AN UMBRELLA INDOORS

One of the few superstitions that isn't ancient or irrelevant. In the 18th century, spring-loaded, metal-spoked umbrellas were new and unpredictable. Opening one indoors was courting disaster—it could fly out of control and damage property—or people. It was a practical impulse to regard it as bad luck.

PULLING ON A WISHBONE

Over 2,000 years ago, the Etruscans (an early Italian civilization) believed that chickens—which squawk before they lay their eggs—could tell the future. The powers extended to part of the chicken's skeleton, too, so when a sacred hen died, the Etruscans put its collarbone in the sun until it dried out. Then people would pick it up, rub it, and make a wish. It became known as the "wishbone." Why this particular bone? Apparently because the V-shape looks a little like a human crotch.

Later, as more people wanted to get in on the wishing, the rubbing turned into a symbolic tug-of-war. Not everyone was going to get their wish; it became a contest to see whom the gods favored.

THE STORK BRINGING BABIES

In Scandinavia, storks—gentle birds with strong family ties— habitually nested on top of people's chimneys. So when Scandinavian parents needed to explain to youngsters how babies arrived, the stork was a handy answer. This traditional tale was spread in the 1800s by Hans Christian Andersen, in his fairy tales.

OOPS!

Everyone's amused by tales of outrageous blunders—probably because it's comforting to know that someone's screwing up even worse than we are. So go ahead and feel superior for a few minutes.

HOT CLUE

PHILADELPHIA— "A former Philadelphia fireman, in Federal Court here trying to overturn his dismissal for long hair, set his head on fire.

"William Michini apparently tried to dramatize that his locks were not a safety threat to his job. 'Hair is self-extinguishing. It doesn't burn,' he boasted. With that he struck a match and held it to his head, which caught fire. 'It must have been the hairspray I used,' said the sheepish firefighter."

—*Remarkabilia,* by John Train

...AND HOW'S YOUR WIFE, CARLY?

"Kathie Lee Gifford inadvertently stumbled into talk-show hell on a recent 'Live with Regis and Kathie Lee.'

"Singer-songwriter James Taylor was one of the guests, and the perky one, just making conversation, asked how his older brother, Alex, was doing. Sweet Baby James replied: 'I wish I could say he was doing well....Alex died about four years ago.'

"The *Washington Post* noted: 'Mortification hung in the air for a few long moments.' Blues singer Alex Taylor died of a heart attack in 1993, at age 46."

—*The Portland Oregonian,* May 1, 1997

WHAT ARE YOU DOING HERE?

"The Aldo Oliveri Stadium was meant to be the perfect memorial for one of Italy's greatest sports heroes: a stadium in Verona, dedicated to the memory of the goalie who led Italy to victory in the 1938 World Cup. Everything went smoothly right up to the weekend before it was due to open, when a small problem was discovered. Aldo Oliveri wasn't dead; he was alive, 86, and by all accounts, in the best of health. Plans are now afoot to open the stadium late, under a different name."

—*The Fortean Times,* 1997

AND WHAT ARE YOU DOING HERE?
"In 1964 Gary Grannai escorted Tricia Nixon to the International Debutante Ball in New York City. Seven years later President Nixon was justifying his prosecution of the Vietnam War, despite the family's loss of a friend: 'Gary was a second lieutenant. He was on patrol duty when it happened. You feel the personal tragedy when it comes into your own home. Yet there is no alternative to the war's going on.' Publication of these remarks was followed by the [embarrassing] reappearance of Gary Grannai, who was very much alive and happily married."

—Oops, **by Richard Smith and Edward Recter**

WELL, IN FRANCE KIDS LIKE IT
"French broadcasting system Canal France International blamed a 'technical glitch' that sent an X-rated film instead of children's programming to Arab countries last Saturday. 'We deeply regret this unacceptable incident, and we share in the high feelings prompted in Saudi Arabia and more widely in the Arab world,' a foreign ministry spokesman said. An investigation is under way."

—USA Today, **July 23, 1997**

SURE IT WAS A MISTAKE
TORONTO— "Proofreaders at Canada's postal service let a royal error slip through in the production of a souvenir stamp book—a reference to 'the Prince of Whales.'

"Much to Canada Post's chagrin, the book was printed with a passage describing a visit by the 'Prince of Whales' to the snowy shores in 1860. He eventually became King Edward VII.

"It was human error and there was no intended slight to the Royal Family or to Prince Charles, said a spokesman. He also said Canada Post will not pull the book from shelves."

—Reuters News Service, **1997**

ALPHABET SOUP
In the 1980s, the Pfeiffer Brewing Company decided to use its successful print ad campaign on the radio. They realized it was a mistake when they heard the announcer say their written slogan aloud: "Pfeiffer's—the beer with the silent P."

REEL QUOTES

Here are some of our favourite lines from the silver screen.

ON DATING
Allen: "What are you doing Saturday night?"
Diana: "Committing suicide."
Allen: "What are you doing Friday night?"

—*Play It Again, Sam*

ON LOVE
Darrow: "You ever been in love, Hornbeck?"
Hornbeck: "Only with the sound of my own voice, thank God."

—*Inherit the Wind*

"Jane, since I've met you, I've noticed things I never knew were there before: birds singing...dew glistening on a newly formed leaf...stoplights..."

—*Lt. Frank Drebin,*
Naked Gun

ON ANATOMY
Nick Charles: "I'm a hero. I was shot twice in the *Tribune*."
Nora Charles: "I read where you were shot five times in the tabloids."
Nick: "It's not true. They didn't come anywhere near my tabloids."

—*The Thin Man*

ON GOLF
"A golf course is nothing but a poolroom moved outdoors."

—*Barry Fitzgerald,*
Going My Way

ON RELIGION
Sonja: "Of course there's a God. We're made in his image."
Boris: "You think I was made in God's image? Take a look at me. Do you think he wears glasses?"
Sonja: "Not with those frames... Boris, we must believe in God."
Boris: "If I could just see a miracle. Just one miracle. If I could see a burning bush, or the seas part, or my Uncle Sasha pick up a check [bill]."

—*Woody Allen's*
Love and Death

ON BEING CLEAR
Ted Striker: "Surely, you can't be serious."
Dr. Rumack: "I am serious. And don't call me Shirley."

—*Airplane!*

Ollie: "You never met my wife, did you?"
Stan: "Yes, I never did."

—*Helpmates*

Even if baboons wanted to, they couldn't play baseball. (They can't throw overhand.)

READ ALL ABOUT IT!

We've all heard the expression "Don't believe everything you read." Here are a few examples of why that's true.

PLAINFIELD TEACHERS COLLEGE WINS AGAIN!
(*New York Herald Tribune* and other papers, 1941)
   The Story: In 1941 the *Tribune*, the *New York Post*, and a number of other New York papers began reporting the scores of a New Jersey football team called the Plainfield Teachers College Flying Figments as it battled teams like Harmony Teachers College and Appalachia Tech for a coveted invitation to the first-ever "Blackboard Bowl."
The Reaction: As the season progressed and the Figments remained undefeated, interest in the small college powerhouse grew, and so did the press coverage. Several papers ran feature articles about Johnny Chung, the team's "stellar Chinese halfback who has accounted for 69 of Plainfield's 117 points" and who "renewed his amazing strength at halftime by wolfing down wild rice."
The Truth: Plainfield, the Flying Figments, and its opponents were all invented by a handful of bored New York stockbrokers who were amazed that real teams from places like Slippery Rock got their scores into big-city newspapers. Each Saturday, the brokers phoned in fake scores, then waited for them to appear in the Sunday papers. The hoax lasted nearly the entire season, until *Time* magazine got wind of it and decided to run a story. In the few days that remained before *Time* hit the newsstands, the brokers sent in one last story announcing that "because of a rash of flunkings in mid-term examinations, Plainfield was calling off its last two scheduled games of the season."

PETRIFIED MAN FOUND IN NEVADA CAVE!
(*Virginia City Territorial Enterprise*, 1862)
The Story: According to the article, a petrified man with a wooden leg was found in a cave in a remote part of Nevada. The man was found in a seated position, with

the right thumb resting against the side of his nose,
the left thumb partially supported the chin, the fore-

finger pressing the inner corner of the left eye and
drawing it partially open; the right eye was closed,
and the fingers of the right hand spread apart.

The article claimed the man had been dead for at least 300 years.
The Reaction: The story spread to other newspapers in Nevada,
from there to the rest of the country, and from there around the
world. The archaeological "find" was even reported in the London
scientific journal *Lancet*.
The Truth: The story was the work of the *Territorial Enterprise's*
local editor, Samuel Clemens (later known by his pen name, Mark
Twain). Clemens figured people would know it was a hoax by the
description of the stone man's hand positions. [Uncle John's note:
Try doing it yourself.] But he was wrong. "I really had no desire to
deceive anybody," he explained later. "I depended on the way the
petrified man was sitting to explain to the public that he was a
swindle….[It was] a delicate, a very delicate satire. But maybe it
was altogether too delicate, for nobody ever perceived the satire
part of it at all."

NOISY GHOST HAUNTS SAN DIEGO BANK
BUILDING! (*The San Diego Metropolitan*, 1987)

The Story: The article claimed that the Great American Bank
Building, one of San Diego's best-known landmarks, was plagued
by mysterious footsteps heard late at night, creepy voices, ghost-
like images materializing out of thin air; just about all of the classic ghost clichés. The article even claimed the ghost or ghosts had
reduced janitorial costs 25% by helping the building's custodians
do the vacuuming. The article included a photo of the ghost, and
quoted a "parapsychologist" calling it "one of the finest examples
of spiritual photography I've ever seen."
The Reaction: The public took the story seriously, and when the
tenants of the Great American Bank Building learned of the
incidents, they began reporting their own sightings—including
power failures, carpeting that had been "mysteriously vacuumed,"
and cleaning equipment that moved from one floor to another;
one electrician even reported seeing his tools float in midair and
ghosts walking in the hallway.
The Truth: The article was the brainchild of Metropolitan
publisher Sean Patrick Reily, who later admitted it had been
inspired by Mark Twain's "petrified man" work.

IN DREAMS...

People have always been fascinated by dreams. Where do they come from? What do they mean? D. H. Lawrence put it perfectly when he said, "I can never decide whether my dreams are the result of my thoughts or my thoughts are the result of my dreams." On occasion, art, music, and even discoveries and inventions have resulted directly from information received in a dream. Here are some examples.

THE SEWING MACHINE

Elias Howe had been trying to invent a practical lock-stitch sewing machine for years, but had been unsuccessful. One night in the 1840s, he had a nightmare in which he was captured by a primitive tribe who were threatening to kill him with their spears. Curiously, all the spears had holes in them at the pointed ends. When Howe woke up, he realized that a needle with a hole at its tip—rather than at the base or middle (which is what he'd been working with)—was the solution to his problem.

DR. JEKYLL AND MR. HYDE

Since childhood, novelist Robert Louis Stevenson had always remembered his dreams and believed that they gave him inspiration for his writing. In 1884, he was in dire need of money and was trying to come up with a book. He had already spent two days racking his brains for a new plot when he had a nightmare about a man with a dual personality. In the dream, "Mr. Hyde" was being pursued for a crime he'd committed; he took a strange powder and changed into someone else as his pursuers watched. Stevenson screamed in his sleep, and his wife woke him. The next morning he began writing *The Strange Case of Dr. Jekyll and Mr. Hyde*.

INSULIN

Frederick Banting, a Canadian doctor, had been doing research into the cause of diabetes, but had not come close to a cure. One night he had a strange dream. When he awoke, he quickly wrote down a few words that he remembered: "Tie up the duct of the pancreas of a dog...wait for the glands to shrivel up...then cut it out, wash it...and filter the precipitation." This new approach to extracting the substance led to the isolation of the hormone now known as insulin, which has saved millions of diabetics' lives. Banting was knighted for his discovery.

Lions are the only cats that live in packs.

LEAD SHOT

James Watt is remembered for inventing the steam engine, but he also came up with the process for making lead shot used in shotguns. This process was revealed to him in a dream. At the time, making the shot was costly and unpredictable—the lead was rolled into sheets by hand, then chopped into bits. Watt had the same dream each night for a week: He was walking along in a heavy rainstorm—but instead of rain, he was being showered with tiny pellets of lead, which he could see rolling around his feet. The dream haunted him; did it mean that molten lead falling through the air would harden into round pellets? He decided to experiment. He melted about a kilogram of lead and tossed it out of the tower of a church that had a water-filled moat at its base. When he removed the lead from the water, he found that it had hardened into tiny globules. To this day, lead shot is made using this process.

THE BENZENE MOLECULE

Friedrich A. Kekule, a Belgian chemistry professor, had been working for some time to solve the structural riddle of the benzene molecule. One night while working late, he fell asleep on a chair and dreamed of atoms dancing before him, forming various patterns and structures. He saw long rows of atoms begin to twist like snakes until one of the snakes seized its own tail and began to whirl in a circle. Kekule woke up "as if by a flash of lightning" and began to work out the meaning of his dream image. His discovery of a closed ring with an atom of carbon and hydrogen at each point of a hexagon revolutionized organic chemistry.

JESUS (*as many people think of Him*)

Warner E. Sallman was an illustrator for religious magazines. In 1924 he needed a picture for a deadline the next day, but was coming up blank. Finally, he went to bed—then suddenly awoke with "a picture of the Christ in my mind's eye just as if it were on my drawing board." He quickly sketched a portrait of Jesus with long brown hair, blue eyes, a neatly trimmed beard, and a beatific look—which has now become the common image of Christ around the world. Since 1940, more than 500 million copies of Sallman's "Head of Christ" have been sold. It has been reproduced billions of times on calendars, lamps, posters, etc.

Worldwide, an estimated 85% of all phone calls are conducted in the English language.

THE CONCRETE CAMEL & THE NEW SOUTH WHALE

Australia's colourful language and sardonic humour have carried us through convict days, settler hardship, war and, not least, the building of the Sydney Opera House.

CRAWLED FROM UNDER A LOG

On 30 January 1957 the *Sydney Morning Herald* screamed the headline, "Dane's Controversial Design wins Opera House Contest." The judges called Joern Utzon's work, "original." One architect described it as "a piece of poetry." Another, in the same article, called it "an insect with a shell on its back, which has crawled out from under a log."

IT'LL NEVER FLY

Joern Utzon said he liked to be "modern and work at the edge of the possible." Like viewing a "Gothic church" the eye would "never get tired... of it." It'll never fly," said onlookers as three giant cranes from France were erected like big birds. They had a point. The highest shell was 70 m high, with a very steep pitch. It took the architect and engineers three years to solve the problem of constructing the "fifth façade" or sails. Over 2,000 precast concrete segments were tensioned by 350 km of steel cables and covered by one million specially glazed Swedish tiles in tile-lid segments, each containing two colours.

CONCRETE CAMEL

Sydney-siders watched through 16 years of construction. Knockers sharpened their knives. The Opera House was a "concrete camel," "copulating turtles," "the hunchback of Bennelong Point," "a pack of French nuns playing football," "a petrified Moby Dick and all his children risen from the sea," "the first building to be built upside down," and "the biggest New South Whale." "It might have been cheaper if they'd built it overseas and sailed it across," they said.

Today this work of genius is internationally recognized as one of the great buildings of the 20th century.

THE SYDNEY OPERA HOUSE'S ARCHITECT

Did you know…?

- He was Danish.

- He was only 38 years old when he designed the Sydney Opera House.

- He had never visited Australia, but studied sea charts of Sydney Harbour to show him elevations. He watched the only available film on Sydney at the Australian Embassy in Copenhagen.

- He realised people would look down onto the structure and said, "One could not have a flat roof filled with ventilation pipes—in fact one must have a fifth façade which is just as important as the other facades…Therefore instead of a square form I have made a sculpture."

- He signed his winning entry drawings with an elongated cartoon of himself—with a pen dipped in his cranium like an ink bottle.

- An Australian women's magazine dubbed him, "the Danish Gary Cooper, only better looking."

- On the wall of his Sydney office he had a poster showing a disassembled telephone with the slogan, "Put them together and dial anywhere." He often said, "when some clever people have been able to produce a number of elements, put them together and talk through the result, then we must be able to solve this much more simple problem even if it seems impossible." (Utzon, *Glass Walls Zodiac*, No. 14)

- One of his favourite books was a centuries old manual on Chinese architecture called *Ying zao fa shi* which influenced his architecture. The plinth for the Opera House was inspired by Mexican Mayan temples and the tiles by Japanese ceramics.

- It took nearly a week to reach Sydney by plane from Copenhagen.

- The surface of each curved roof section would fit a large spherical surface. They are like bits of peel cut out of an orange thus prefabricated sections could be made to speed up construction.

- Joern Utzon is an Australian hero. Some people consider him a "Don Bradman" of architecture.

UNCLE ALBERT SAYS...

Cosmic question: What would Albert Einstein think if he knew we consider his comments great bathroom reading?

"Only two things are infinite, the universe and stupidity—and I'm not sure about the former."

"God is subtle, but He is not malicious."

"'Common sense' is the set of prejudices acquired by age eighteen."

"Nationalism is an infantile disease. It is the measles of mankind."

"I never think of the future. It comes soon enough."

"Try not to become a man of success, but rather, a man of value."

"I experience the greatest degree of pleasure in having contact with works of art. They furnish me with happy feelings of an intensity such as I cannot drive from other realms."

"To punish me for my contempt for authority, Fate made me an authority myself."

"Why is it that nobody understands me, and everybody likes me?"

"A life directed chiefly toward fulfilment of personal desires sooner or later always leads to bitter disappointment."

"My political ideal is that of democracy. Let every man be respected as an individual, and no man idolized."

"Whatever there is of God and goodness in the Universe, it must work itself out and express itself through us. We cannot stand aside and let God do it."

"Science without religion is lame, religion without science is blind."

"I am a deeply religious nonbeliever…This is a somewhat new kind of religion."

"With fame I become more and more stupid, which of course is a very common phenomenon."

If you never trimmed your fingernails, on your 80th birthday they'd be about 13 feet long.

FLUBBED HEADLINES

These are 100% honest-to-goodness headlines.
Can you figure out what they were trying to say?

Kids Make Nutritious Snacks

ENRAGED COW INJURES FARMER WITH AXE

Red Tape Holds Up New Bridge

BILKE-A-THON NETS $1,000 FOR ILL BOY

PANDA MATING FAILS; VETERINARIAN TAKES OVER

School taxpayers revolting

Eye Drops Off Shelf

HELICOPTER POWERED BY HUMAN FLIES

Circumcisions Cut Back

POPE TO BE ARRAIGNED FOR ALLEGEDLY BURGLARIZING CLINIC

City wants Dead to pay for cleanup

MOORPARK RESIDENTS ENJOY A COMMUNAL DUMP

Montana Traded to Kansas City

Area man wins award for nuclear accident

International Scientific Group Elects Bimbo As Its Chairman

Storm delayed by bad weather

LEGISLATORS TAX BRAINS TO CUT DEFICIT

DEAD GUITARIST NOW SLIMMER AND TRIMMER

Study Finds Sex, Pregnancy Link

Include Your Children When Baking Cookies

Trees can break wind

RANGERS TO TEST PEETERS FOR RUST

Cockroach Slain, Husband Badly Hurt

Living Together Linked to Divorce

ECUADOR'S PRESIDENT DECLARES HE'S NOT DEAD

LACK OF BRAINS HINDERS RESEARCH

Two Sisters Reunited After 18 Years At Checkout Counter

Man, Shot Twice in Head, Gets Mad

MISSOURI WOMAN BIG WINNER AT HOG SHOW

Teacher Dies; Board Accepts His Resignation

PANTS MAN TO EXPAND AT THE REAR

THE HISTORY OF ROCK: A QUIZ

How much do you know about the early days of rock 'n' roll?
Here's a test to find out. Answers are on page 463.

1. The song that made Elvis a mega-star was the 1956 smash "(You Ain't Nothin' but a) Hound Dog." How did he come up with it?
a) He used to sing it to his real hound dog, "Buster."
b) He copied it from a Las Vegas lounge act.
c) He overheard a woman singing it in a Memphis bus station.

2. The flip side of "Hound Dog," "Don't Be Cruel," was also a big hit. Elvis not only sang it, but co-wrote it with Otis Blackwell. How did Elvis and Otis wind up working together?
a) They were sitting next to each other on an aeroplane in 1955. To kill time, they started playing a rhyming game that turned into a hit song.
b) Otis was a nephew of Colonel Tom Parker (Elvis's manager) and needed money to get married. Elvis co-wrote the song with him as a "wedding present."
c) They didn't. Elvis just insisted on getting a writing credit (and half the royalties) as his "reward" for singing the song.

3. In the 1950s, Pat Boone was known as a "cover artist"—which meant he copied black artists' new songs and usually outsold them (because white artists' records got more airplay). In 1956, he covered Fats Domino's classic "Ain't That a Shame." How did he try to change it?
a) He tried to take the word "ain't" out and replace it with "isn't" because he thought it would reflect badly on his education.
b) He tried to slow it down. "It sounds too much like jungle music," he explained.
c) He tried to turn the sax solo into a tuba solo because his parents were polka fans.

---

4. The Platters were one of the biggest vocal groups in the early days of rock. Their hits were often new versions of old standards. Their biggest hit was the 1955 version of Jerome Kern's "Smoke Gets in Your Eyes." Kern was dead when the song was released, but his wife…
a) Threatened a lawsuit to stop the record.
b) Helped the group become the first rock artists with their own TV show.
c) Tried to get them to record three songs she'd written.

5. Chuck Berry is one of the fathers of rock 'n' roll. He had more than a dozen hits—but only one of them hit #1 on Billboard's charts. It was…
a) "Johnny B. Goode"
b) "Roll Over Beethoven"
c) "My Ding-a-Ling"

6. Jerry Lee Lewis was one of the wildmen of early rock 'n' roll. His first hit, "Whole Lotta Shakin' Goin' On" (1957), was banned from the radio because…
a) His line, "All you gotta do is stand in one place and wiggle your hips," was considered obscene.
b) It was creating riots. Whenever it played on the radio—even in school—teenagers would jump up and start doing a new dance they called "The Shake."
c) A fundamentalist minister claimed he'd played it backward and heard satanic messages—the first time anyone ever said that.

7. Another crazy man of 1950s rock 'n' roll was Little Richard, who recorded classics like "Tutti Frutti" and "Rip It Up." When he recorded "Long Tall Sally," he had one particular thing in mind. What was it?
a) He sang it as fast as he could, so censors wouldn't be able to distinguish the "dirty" lyrics.
b) He sang it as fast as he could, so Pat Boone wouldn't be able to do a cover version of it.
c) He sang it as fast as he could, because he had to go to the bathroom.

It takes 345 squirts from a cow's udder to get a gallon of milk.

THE TRUTH ABOUT LOVE

If you want to know something important, ask a kid. These quotes about love were submitted by BRI member Alan Reder, who got them from the Internet and e-mailed them to us.

HOW DO TWO PEOPLE WIND UP FALLING IN LOVE?

Andrew, age 6: "One of the people has freckles and so he finds somebody else who has freckles too."

Mae, age 9: "No one is sure why it happens, but I heard it has something to do with how you smell….That's why perfume and deodorant are so popular."

Manuel, age 8: "I think you're supposed to get shot with an arrow or something, but the rest of it isn't supposed to be so painful."

WHAT IS FALLING IN LOVE LIKE?

John, age 9: "Like an avalanche where you have to run for your life."

Glenn, age 7: "If falling in love is anything like learning how to spell, I don't want to do it. It takes too long."

HOW IMPORTANT IS BEAUTY IN LOVE?

Anita, age 8: "If you want to be loved by somebody who isn't already in your family, it doesn't hurt to be beautiful."

Brian, age 7: "It isn't always just how you look. Look at me. I'm handsome like anything and I haven't got anybody to marry me yet."

Christine, age 9: "Beauty is skin deep. But how rich you are can last a long time."

The Earth is turning to desert at a rate of 40 square miles per day.

WHY DO LOVERS HOLD HANDS?

Gavin, age 8: "They want to make sure their rings don't fall off because they paid good money for them."

John, age 9: "They are just practising for when they might have to walk down the aisle someday and do the matchimony thing."

WHAT'S YOUR PERSONAL OPINION ABOUT LOVE?

Jill, age 6: "I'm in favour of love as long as it doesn't happen when *Dinosaurs* is on television."

Floyd, age 9: "Love is foolish…but I still might try it sometime."

Dave, age 8: "Love will find you, even if you are trying to hide from it. I been trying to hide from it since I was five, but the girls keep finding me."

Regina, age 10: "I'm not rushing into being in love. I'm finding the fourth grade hard enough."

WHAT'S A SUREFIRE WAY TO MAKE A PERSON FALL IN LOVE WITH YOU?

Del, age 6: "Tell them that you own a whole bunch of candy stores [lolly shops]."

Camille, age 9: "Shake your hips and hope for the best."

Carey, age 7: "Yesterday I kissed a girl in a private place….We were behind a tree."

REFLECTIONS ON THE NATURE OF LOVE

Greg, age 8: "Love is the most important thing in the world, but baseball is pretty good, too."

* * *

"To love a thing means wanting it to live." —**Confucius**

CURSES!

Even if you're not superstitious, it's hard to resist tales of "cursed" ships, tombs, and so on. Who knows—maybe there's something to them. Here are some of our favourites.

THE CURSE OF JAMES DEAN'S PORSCHE

Curse: Disaster may be ahead for anyone connected with James Dean's "death car." It seems to attack people at random.

Origin: In 1955, Dean smashed his red Porsche into a another car and was killed. The wreckage was bought by George Barris, a friend of Dean's (and the man who customized cars like the Munsters' coffin-mobile for Hollywood). But as one writer put it, "the car proved deadly even after it was dismantled." Barris noticed weird things happening immediately.

Among Its Victims:

• The car slipped while being unloaded from the truck that delivered it to Barris, and broke a mechanic's legs.

• Barris put its engine into a race car. It crashed in the race, killing the driver. A second car in the same race was equipped with the Porsche's drive shaft—it overturned and injured its driver.

• The shell of the Porsche was being used in a Highway Safety display in San Francisco. It fell off its pedestal and broke a teenager's hip. Later, a truck carrying the display to another demonstration was involved in an accident. "The truck driver," says one account, "was thrown out of the cab of the truck and killed when the Porsche shell rolled off the back of the truck and crushed him"

Status: The Porsche finally vanished in 1960, while on a train en route to Los Angeles.

THE PRESIDENTIAL DEATH CYCLE

Curse: Between 1840 and 1960, every U.S. president elected in a year ending in a zero either died in office of natural causes or was assassinated. By contrast: Since 1840, of the 29 presidents who were not elected in the 20-year cycle, only one has died in office and not one has been assassinated.

Origin: The first president to die in office was William Henry

---

Harrison, elected in 1840. In 1960, when John Kennedy was shot, people began to realize the eerie "coincidence" involved.

Victims:
- William Henry Harrison, dead in 1841 after one month in office
- Abraham Lincoln (elected in 1860), fatally shot in 1865
- James Garfield (1880), assassinated in 1881
- William McKinley (re-elected in 1900), fatally shot in 1901
- Warren G. Harding (1920), died in 1923
- Franklin D. Roosevelt (elected for the third time in 1940), died in 1945
- JFK (1960), assassinated in 1963
- Ronald Reagan (1980) was nearly the eighth victim. He was shot and badly wounded by John Hinckley in 1983

Status: Astrologers insist that 1980 was an aberration because "Jupiter and Saturn met in an air sign, Libra." That gave Reagan some kind of exemption. They say we still have to wait to find out if the curse is over.

THE CURSE OF THE INCAN MUMMY

Curse: By disturbing a frozen mummy's remains, authorities brought bad luck to the region where it had been buried.

Origin: Three Andean mummies were discovered by an archaeologist/mountaineer in October 1995. They had been undisturbed in snow at the top of 6,096-metre [20,000-foot] Mount Ampato, in Southern Peru, for at least 500 years. Then an earthquake exposed them. One of the mummies was the remains of a young woman, referred to by local shamans as "Juanita." She had apparently been sacrificed to Incan gods.

Among Its Victims:
- Within a year of the discovery, a Peruvian commercial jet crashed and killed 123 people near the discovery site.
- Thirty-five people were electrocuted when a high-tension cable fell on a crowd celebrating the founding of the city of Arequipa (which is near the discovery site).

Status: Local shamans said these were the acts of the angered "Ice Princess." To break the curse, they gathered in the city of Arequipa in August 1996 and chanted: "Juanita, calm your ire. Do not continue to damn innocent people who have done nothing to you." Apparently it worked—we've heard nothing of it since 1996.

THE BIRTH OF THE MICROWAVE

To a lot of us, microwave ovens are "magical mystery boxes." We're not sure how they work—but after a while we can't live without them. Uncle John swore he'd never use one—until he had children. Now he blesses it every time he hauls out an emergency frozen pizza and manages to feed the kids before they kill each other. If you use a microwave, you might be interested to know more about it.

Chances are, you'll use a microwave oven at least once this week—probably (according to research) for heating up leftovers or defrosting something.

Microwave ovens are so common today that it's easy to forget how rare they once were. As late as 1977, only 10% of U.S. homes had one. By 1995, 85% of households had *at least* one. Today, more people own microwaves than own dishwashers.

MICROWAVE HISTORY

Magnetrons, the tubes that produce microwaves, were invented by British scientists in 1940. They were used in radar systems during World War II—and were instrumental in detecting German planes during the Battle of Britain.

These tubes—which are sort of like TV picture tubes—might still be strictly military hardware if Percy Spencer, an engineer at Raytheon (a U.S. defence contractor), hadn't stepped in front of one in 1946. He had a chocolate bar in his pocket; when he went to eat it a few minutes later, he found that the chocolate had almost completely melted.

That didn't make sense. Spencer himself wasn't hot—how could the chocolate bar be? He suspected the magnetron was responsible. So he tried an experiment: He held a bag of popcorn kernels up to the tube. Seconds later they popped.

The next day Spencer brought eggs and an old tea kettle to work. He cut a hole in the side of the kettle, stuck an egg in it, and placed it next to the magnetron. Just as a colleague looked into the kettle to see what was happening, the egg exploded.

BRINGING MICROWAVES TO MARKET

Spencer shared his discovery with his employers at Raytheon and suggested manufacturing magnetron-powered ovens to sell to the public. Raytheon was interested. They had the capacity to produce 10,000 magnetron tubes a week—but with World War II over, military purchases had been cut back to almost nothing. "What better way to recover lost sales," Ira Flatow writes in *They All Laughed*, "than to put a radar set disguised as a microwave oven in every American home?"

Raytheon agreed to back the project. (According to legend, Spencer had to repeat the egg experiment in front of the board of directors, splattering them with egg, before they okayed it.) The company patented the first "high-frequency dielectric heating apparatus" in 1953. Then they held a contest to find a name for their product. Someone came up with "Radar Range," which was later combined into the single word—*Radarange*.

DEVELOPING THE PRODUCT

Raytheon had a great product idea and a great name, but they didn't have an oven anyone could afford. The 1953 model was 1.7 metres [5 1/2 feet] tall, weighed more than 340 kilograms [750 pounds], and cost $3,000. Over the next 20 years, railroads, ocean liners, and high-end restaurants were virtually the only Radarange customers.

• In 1955, a company called Tappan introduced the first microwave oven targeted to average consumers; it was smaller than the Radarange, but still cost $1,295—more than some cars.

• Then in 1964, a Japanese company perfected a miniaturized magnetron. For the first time, Raytheon could build a microwave oven that fitted on a kitchen countertop. In 1967, they introduced a Radarange that used the new magnetron. It sold for $495. But that was still too expensive for the average American family.

• Finally, in the 1980s, technical improvements made it possible to lower the price and improve the quality enough to make microwave ovens both affordable and practical. By 1988, 10% of all new food products in the United States were microwaveable. Surveys showed that the microwave oven was America's favourite new appliance—and it still is today.

How does a microwave oven work? See page 335 to find out.

Q&A: ASK THE EXPERTS

Everyone's got a question or two they'd like answered.
Here are a few of those questions, with answers from
some top trivia experts.

HOLY COW!

Q: Why are there holes in Swiss cheese?
A: Because of air bubbles. "During one of the stages of preparation, while it is still 'plastic,' the cheese is kneaded and stirred. Inevitably, air bubbles are formed in the cheese as it is twisted and moved about, but the viscous nature of the cheese prevents the air bubbles from rising to the surface and getting out. As the cheese hardens, these air pockets remain, and we see them as the familiar 'holes' when we slice the wheel of cheese." (From *A Book of Curiosities*, compiled by Roberta Kramer)

PHOTO FINISH

Q: Why do eyes come out red in photographs?
A: "The flash from the camera is being reflected on the rear of the eyeball, which is red from all the blood vessels." The solution: "Use a flash at a distance from the camera, or get your subjects to look somewhere else. Another trick is to turn up the lights in the room, making them as bright as possible, which causes the subject's pupil to contract and admit less of the light from the subsequent flash." (From *Why Things Are,* by Joel Aschenbach)

READ OIL ABOUT IT

Q: What do the numbers (like 10W-30) mean for motor oil?
A: "Oil is measured in terms of viscosity, which is a measure of a liquid's ability to flow. There are 10 grades, from 0W to 25W for oils… meant for winter weather use (the W stands for winter), and from 20 to 60 for oils rated to work at 100° C [212°F]. The lower the number, the thinner the oil. Multigrade oils, like 10W-30, were developed to stay thin at low temperatures and still work well at high temperatures. Most experts recommend 5W-30 for very cold weather, 10W-30 for warmer weather." (From *Numbers*, by Andrea Sutcliffe)

HOT STUFF

Q: How can you cool off your mouth after eating hot chillies?
A: "Drink milk," says Dr. Robert Henkin, director of the Taste and Smell Clinic in Washington, D.C. "Casein, the main protein in milk, acts like a detergent, washing away capsaicin, the substance in hot peppers [chillies] responsible for their 'fire.'" (From *Parade* magazine, November 14, 1993)

SOMETHING FISHY

Q: Do fish sleep?
A: Hard to tell if they sleep in the same sense we do. They never look like they're sleeping, because they don't have eyelids. "But they do seem to have regular rest periods....Some fish just stay more or less motionless in the water, while others rest directly on the bottom, even turning over on their side. Some species...dig or burrow into bottom sediment to make a sort of 'bed.' Some fish even...prefer privacy when they rest; their schools disperse at night to rest and then reassemble in the morning." (From *Science Trivia*, by Charles Cazeau)

PICK A BALL OF COTTON

Q: Should you toss out the cotton after opening a bottle of pills?
A: Yep. "The cotton keeps the pills from breaking in transit, but once you open the bottle, it can attract moisture and thus damage the pills or become contaminated." (From *Davies Gazette*, a newsletter from Davies Medical Centre in San Francisco)

SLIPPERY QUESTION

Q: A few years ago, we started seeing foods containing "canola oil." What is it?
A: A variety of rapeseed—which, until recently, was only grown for industrial oils. "Scientists in Canada were able to breed new varieties of rapeseed that were suitable for cooking. They named their creation canola to honour Canada. Canola seed contains 40% to 45% oil, of which 6% is saturated fatty acids. Canola oil contains less fat than any other oil: 50% less than corn oil and olive oil, 60% less than soybean oil." (From *Why Does Popcorn Pop?*, by Don Voorhees)

Oldest vehicle in human history: a floating log. Second oldest: a sled.

STRANGE LAWSUITS

These days, it seems that people will sue each other over practically anything. Here are a few real-life examples of unusual legal battles.

THE PLAINTIFF: Wendy Potasnik, a nine-year-old from Carmel, Indiana

THE DEFENDANT: The Cracker Jack Division of Borden, Inc.

THE LAWSUIT: In 1982, Wendy and her sister Robin each bought a box of Cracker Jacks. Robin got a prize in her box, but Wendy didn't…which made her "really mad."

"They advertise a free toy in each box," she told a reporter. "I feel that since I bought their product because of their claim, they broke a contract with me." So she sued, asking the court to make Borden "pay court costs and furnish a toy."

THE VERDICT: Wendy dropped the suit after Borden apologized and sent her a coupon for a free box of Cracker Jacks…even though the company refused to pay the $19 that Potasnik had spent on court costs.

THE PLAINTIFF: Alan Wald

THE DEFENDANT: The Moonraker Restaurant in Pacifica, California

THE LAWSUIT: In 1993, Wald went to the Moonraker for an all-you-can-eat buffet. He'd already eaten between 40 (Wald's count) and 75 (the restaurant's count) oysters—and was still at it—when the restaurant cut him off. Apparently, other customers were complaining that there were no oysters left. The restaurant offered to refund Wald's $40 to get him to go, but Wald insisted he was within his rights—he hadn't had all he could eat yet. He demanded $400 for "humiliation and embarrassment."

THE VERDICT: Wald was awarded $100 by the judge—but the restaurant was the real winner. "It was great publicity," said the owner. "We're going to get a shovelful of oysters and present them to [Wald] at his table. He can come back anytime."

THE PLAINTIFF: The Swedish government

THE DEFENDANT: Elisabeth Hallin, mother of a five-year-old

In Germany, making the "Shhhh" sound means "hurry up."

boy named Brfxxccxxmnpccccllllmmnprxvclmnckssqlbb11116 (which she pronounces "Albin")

THE LAWSUIT: For five years, the Hallins, who say they believe in the surrealist doctrine of "pataphysics," refused to give their son a name. Then Swedish tax officials informed them it was a legal requirement. They chose Brfxxccxxmnpccccllllmmnprxv-clmnckssqlbb11116—which was immediately rejected by the authorities. The couple insisted that the 'typographically expressionistic" name was merely "an artistic creation," consistent with their pataphysical beliefs.

THE VERDICT: The government disagreed. The Hallins were fined 5000 kronor (about $735) and ordered to come up with a different name.

THE PLAINTIFF: Lorene Bynum
THE DEFENDANTS: St. Mary's Hospital in Little Rock, Arkansas
THE LAWSUIT: In 1992, Bynum visited her husband, a patient at the hospital. She wanted to use the bathroom, but the toilet seat was dirty—and there wasn't enough toilet paper to spread out on it. So she took off her shoes and tried to go to the toilet standing on the toilet seat. Unfortunately the seat was loose. Bynum fell, spraining her lower back. She sued the hospital for negligence.
THE VERDICT: A jury awarded Bynum $13,000. But the Arkansas Supreme Court overturned the verdict. "The injuries resulted from her act of standing on the commode [toilet] seat, which was neither designed nor intended to be used in that way," they explained.

THE PLAINTIFF: Victoria Baldwin
THE DEFENDANT: Synergy, a hair salon in Sydney, Australia
THE LAWSUIT: In July 1996, Baldwin had her hair cut at the salon. The result was so bad, she complained, that it made her "look like Hillary Clinton." She sued for damages, plus reimbursement for money spent on hats to cover her head until the hair grew back.
THE VERDICT: Baldwin won $750, plus $234 for the hats.

THE BIG DIPPER

*What's the one constellation everyone knows? The Big Dipper.
After you read this article you'll be able to sound like a know-it-
all the next time you're star-gazing with someone.*

THE NIGHT SKY
The Big and Little Dippers are probably the best-known
star groups, in the northern hemisphere. They're both
parts of larger star groups, or constellations, named after bears.
The Big Dipper belongs to the constellation Ursa Major, "The
Greater Bear," and the Little Dipper is part of Ursa Minor, "The
Lesser Bear."
• Ursa Major is the most ancient of all the constellations. For
some reason, early civilizations all over the world seem to have
thought of it as a bear. This is remarkable, since Ursa Major
doesn't look anything like a bear. It's even more remarkable when
you consider that most of the ancient world had never seen a bear.

THE NATIVE AMERICAN SKY
In the New World, the Iroquois, who had seen plenty of bears,
called it Okouari, which means—bear. The Algonquin and Black-
foot tribes called it "The Bear and the Hunters." For them, the
three stars in the handle of the Big Dipper were three hunters
going after the bear.
• In a typical Native American story, a party of hunters set out on
a bear hunt. The first hunter carried a bow and arrow. The second
hunter brought along a pot or kettle to cook the bear in. The faint
star Alcor, which you can just see above the middle star of the
Dipper's handle, was the pot. The third hunter carried a bundle of
sticks with which to build a fire to cook the bear.
• The bear hunt lasted from spring until autumn. In the autumn,
the first hunter shot the bear. Blood from the wounded animal
stained the autumn leaves in the forest. The bear died, was
cooked, and was eaten. The skeleton lay on its back in the den
through the winter months. The bear's life, meanwhile, had
entered into another bear, which also lay on its back, deep asleep
for the winter.

• When spring returned, the bear came out of the den and the hunters started to chase her again, and so it went from year to year.

THE GREEK SKY

Greek mythology offers another version of how the Bears got into the sky. Calisto, the beautiful daughter of the King of Arcadia, caught the eye of Zeus, the king of the gods. Zeus took her by surprise, leaving her to become the mother of his child. In time, Calisto gave birth to a son, whom she named Arcas. Hera, queen of the gods, changed Calisto into a bear in a jealous rage.

After a number of years had passed, Arcas was out hunting when he saw a bear. Not knowing the bear was his mother, Arcas raised his spear, ready to kill the animal. Before Arcas could throw his spear, Zeus quickly rescued Calisto by placing her in the skies—where she remains today. Areas also became a constellation, Ursa Minor, next to his mother.

• Some say Zeus swung both bears around by their tails and flung them into the sky, which explains why their tails are so long.

• The Greeks called Ursa Major Arktos, which means "Bear." This is where we get out word Arctic. The Greek poet, Homer, described the Bear as keeping watch from its Arctic den looking out for the hunter Orion. Homer also remarked that in his day, the Bear never sank into the ocean, which meant that it never set. Hera was responsible for this, having persuaded the ocean gods not to allow the two Bears to bathe in their waters.

HIPPOS AND PLOWS

But not everyone has thought of these constellations as bears. The Egyptians saw the seven stars of the Big Dipper as a bull's thigh or a hippopotamus. Because its stars circled around the north pole of the sky without setting, or "dying," below the horizon, this constellation was a symbol of immortality and figured in rebirth rituals at funerals. Ursa Minor was the Jackal of the god Set that participated in rites for the dead taking place in the Egyptian underworld.

In Mesopotamia, Scandinavia, Italy, and Germany, people referred to the Big Dipper as a wagon, chariot, or cart. In England it was "Charles' Wain" (the word wain meant "wagon" and Charles stood for Charles the Great). The Little Dipper was the "Smaller Chariot," or "Little Wain." The four stars that make up the bowl of the dipper are the carriage part of the wain, and the dipper's handle is the part of the wain attached to the horses that pull it.

In some parts of England (and elsewhere), people saw the Big Dipper as "The Plough." The four stars of the dipper's bowl form the blade of the plough, behind which stretches its three-starred handle.

DIPPER DIRECTIONS

At the tip of the handle of the Little Dipper is the most celebrated star in the sky, Polaris, the North Star. While not the brightest star in the heavens, Polaris is certainly the most valuable. It has provided directions to countless travellers. The two stars at the end of the bowl of the Big Dipper, called "The Pointers," point to the North Star.

The Greeks used the Greater Bear and the Phoenicians used the Lesser Bear to find north. American slaves called the Big Dipper "The Drinking Gourd" and followed it northward to freedom. Seen from the spinning Earth, the sky appears to move during the night, carrying all the stars along with it. Only the North Star stands in the same spot at the hub of the dome of the sky. The Greeks called this star Cynosure, a word that has found its way into our language meaning the centre of attraction or interest. Others called the North Star the "Lodestar," most likely referring to the magnetic rock lodestone, used in mariners' compass needles to find north.

* * * * *

"It is easier to accept the message of the stars than the message of the salt desert. The stars speak of man's insignificance in the long eternity of time. The desert speaks of his insignificance right now."

—*Edwin Way Teale*

If you have a compulsive urge to dance, you're a dinomaniac.

GO ASK ALICE

When Charles Lutwidge Dodgson met a four-year-old girl named Alice Liddell in 1856, he wrote in his diary, "I mark this day with a white stone"—which meant it was a particularly wonderful day for him. It turned out to be a pretty good day for children all over the world: Charles Dodgson became famous as Lewis Carroll— and Alice Liddell was the child who inspired him to write Alice in Wonderland.

BACKGROUND
• Charles Lutwidge Dodgson was a deacon and professor of mathematics at Christ Church College in Oxford. He was also a poet and photographer who drew his inspiration from children—especially little girls. In fact, he chose teaching as a career because it left him time to pursue photography and poetry.
• In 1856, the same year Dodgson began teaching at Christ Church, a new dean arrived—Henry George Liddell. He had four children, and Dodgson quickly became friendly with them. He especially enjoyed taking them on outings and photographing the girls. The youngest, 4-year-old Alice, had a special relationship with Reverend Dodgson—perhaps because her favourite expression was "let's pretend."

DOWN THE RABBIT HOLE
On what he recalled as a "golden July afternoon" in 1862, Dodgson took the three Liddell girls boating on the river for a picnic.
• As they rowed lazily downstream, Alice begged Dodgson to tell them a story—so he made one up.
• He called his heroine Alice to please her. Then he "sent her straight down a rabbit-hole to begin," he later explained, "without the least idea what was to happen afterwards."
• Amazingly, he made up most of *Alice in Wonderland* on the spot.

SAVING A TREASURE
Alice liked the story so much that she asked Dodgson to write it down. He agreed. In fact, that night—as a gift for his favourite little girl—he sat up and wrote the whole thing out in longhand, adding his own illustrations. He called it *Alice's Adventures Underground.*

A gozzard is a person who owns geese.

• Dodgson had already decided he needed a pseudonym for the humourous poems and stories he'd been contributing to magazines. (He also wrote academic articles on mathematics, and was afraid people wouldn't take him seriously if they knew he was writing nonsense rhymes.)

• He came up with the name Lewis Carroll by scrambling letters in his first two names, and used it for the first time when he signed *Alice's Adventures Underground* for Alice.

A BOOK IS BORN

Fortunately for us, before Dodgson brought the handwritten manuscript to Alice, he happened to show it to a friend named George MacDonald, who read it to his children. If he hadn't, Alice's adventures might have been nothing more than a personal gift to one little girl. But the entire MacDonald family loved the story so much that they urged Carroll to publish it.

• After giving the original to Alice Liddell as promised, Dodgson decided to take their advice. He revised the story, added to it, then hired John Tenniel, a well-known cartoonist, to illustrate it.

• The book was published in 1865 as *Alice's Adventures in Wonderland*. It became so popular that in 1871 Carroll published the further adventures of Alice, entitled *Through the Looking Glass*.

THE ALICE MYSTERY

Shortly after Dodgson presented Alice with the handwritten story, something happened that ended his relationship with the Liddell family. No one knows what it was. But the abruptness of the split has led to speculation about Carroll's sexuality. Why was he so interested in little girls in the first place?

• In fact, however, there's no evidence that his relationships with children were in any way improper. His biographers interviewed many of the women Carroll entertained as children and they always spoke of him with great respect and fondness. It's more likely, say some biographers, that Carroll broached the subject of marriage to one of the Liddell girls and was rejected.

• At any rate, the lazy days of games and stories were over for Alice and Dodgson. By the time Alice received her copy of the published edition of *Alice's Adventures in Wonderland*, the author was no longer a part of her life.

A warthog has only four warts, all of them on its head.

In 1926, Alice Liddell sold the original manuscript of *Alice's Adventures Underground* to an American book dealer for $25,000. He resold it to a group of Americans. They took it to England and presented it as a gift to the British people in gratitude for their bravery in World War II. It remains there today, in the British Museum.

* * * * *

FAMILIAR FACES

Many of the now-classic characters in Carroll's stories were easily recognisable to the Liddell children. For example:

The White Rabbit: Was modelled after Carroll himself. Like the rabbit, he was very proper, usually dressed in an old-fashioned formal black suit and top hat. He always wore gloves—no matter what the weather—which he frequently misplaced.

The Dodo: Carroll had taken the girls to a museum, where they were fascinated by a stuffed Dodo bird. He incorporated the bird into the story as himself because he stammered and his name came out: as "Do-Do-Dodgson."

The Duck, Lory, and Eaglet: The Duck was Carroll's friend, Robinson Duckworth, who'd accompanied him on many of the outings with the children. The Lory was Lorina Liddell, the Eaglet, Edith Liddell. The three sisters show up again in the Dormouse's story as Elsie (from L.C., Lorina's initials), Lacie (an anagram for Alice), and Tillie (a family nickname for Edith).

The Mock Turtle's Song: "Beautiful Soup" was a parody of one of the children's favourite songs, "Star of Evening," and the way they sang in their childish voices.

The Mad Hatter: Supposedly modelled after an eccentric man named Theophilus Carter, who'd been at Christ Church but became a furniture dealer.

THE WORLD ACCORDING TO ALICE

The Alice books are among the most quotable children's stories ever written. There's a gem on practically every page—and some passages are packed with them. In the 1st and 6th Bathroom Readers we included a few sections of Lewis Carroll's work. Here are some more.

I n that direction," the Cheshire Cat said, waving its right paw round, "lives a Hatter: and in that direction," waving the other paw, "lives a March Hare. Visit either you like: they're both mad."

"But I don't want to go among mad people," Alice remarked.

"Oh, you can't help that," said the Cat: "we're all mad here. I'm mad. You're mad."

"How do you know I'm mad!" said Alice.

"You must be," said the Cat, "or you wouldn't have come here."

* * * * *

"It was much pleasanter at home," thought poor Alice, "when one wasn't always growing larger and smaller, and being ordered about by mice and rabbits. I almost wish I hadn't gone down that rabbit hole and yet it's rather curious, you know, this sort of life! I do wonder what can have happened to me! When I used to read fairy tales, I fancied that kind of thing never happened, and now here I am in the middle of one! There ought to be a book written about me, that there ought! And when I grow up, I'll write one but I'm grown up now," she added in a sorrowful tone, "at least there's no room to grow up any more here."

* * * * *

"Alice took up the fan and gloves, and, as the hall was very hot, she kept fanning herself all the time she went on talking: "Dear, dear! How queer everything is today! And yesterday things went on just as usual. I wonder if I've been changed in the night? Let

---

Still life: Your body uses 300 muscles to balance itself when you're standing still.

me think: was I the same when I got up this morning? I almost think I can remember feeling a little different. But if I'm not the same, the next question is, Who in the world am I? Ah, that's the great puzzle!" And she began thinking over all the children she knew, that were of the same age as herself to see if she could have been changed for any of them.

* * * * *

"Who are you?" said the Caterpillar.

This was not an encouraging opening for a conversation. Alice replied, rather shyly, "I, I hardly know, sir, just at present at least I know who I was when I got up this morning, but I think I must have been changed several times since then."

"What do you mean by that?" said the Caterpillar sternly. "Explain yourself!"

"I can't explain myself, I'm afraid, sir," said Alice, "because I'm not myself, you see."

"I don't see," said the Caterpillar. "I'm afraid I can't put it more clearly," Alice replied very politely, "for I can't understand it myself to begin with; and being so many different sizes in a day is very confusing."

"It isn't," said the Caterpillar.

"Well, perhaps you haven't found it so yet," said Alice; "but when you have to turn into a chrysalis—you will some day, you know—and then after that into a butterfly, I should think you'll feel a little queer, won't you?"

"Not a bit," said the Caterpillar.

"Well, perhaps your feelings may be different," said Alice; "all I know is, it would feel very queer to me."

"You!" said the Caterpillar contemptuously. "Who are you?"

* * * * *

"The two *Alices* are not books for children; they are the only books in which we *become* children."

—*Virginia Woolf*

If you take a plant with you on a long airplane flight, it, too, will suffer from jet lag.

IT'S A MIRACLE!

They say the Lord works in mysterious ways. Do you believe it?
These people obviously do—in fact, they may be the proof.

THE GLASS MENAGERIE

The Sighting: An 11-metre [35-foot] image of the Virgin Mary on the side of a building in Cleanvater, Florida
Revelation: In 1996, workers chopped down a palm tree in front of the Seminole Finance Company building. Not long afterward, a customer noticed a discolouration in the building's tinted windows that resembled the Madonna. The discovery was reported on the afternoon news. By the end of the week, an estimated 100,000 people visited the site—including a Baptist minister who was ejected after he "condemned the crowd for worshipping an image on glass."
Impact: The city set up a "Miracle Management Task Force" to install portable toilets at the site, arrange police patrols, and erect a pedestrian walkway over the adjacent road (Route 19) to stop the faithful from dodging in and out of traffic. "That's the busiest highway in Florida," one policeman told reporters. "You want to know the real miracle? Half a million people have crossed that intersection and nobody's been injured or killed."

STRANGE FRUIT

The Sighting: The words of Allah in a sliced tomato in Huddersfield, England
Revelation: In June 1997, 14-year-old Shasta Aslam sliced a tomato in half for her grandparents' salad and saw what appeared to be the Koranic message "There is no God but Allah" spelled out in Arabic in the veins of one half of the tomato, and the words "Mohammed is the messenger" written in the other half.
"There were some letters missing and it was hard to decipher," her grandmother told reporters, "but the message was clear."
Impact: Hundreds of Muslims from all over the United Kingdom went to view the tomato. "They knock on the door and I take them through to the kitchen and open the fridge door for them to have a look," the grandmother explained. The tomato has since been moved to the freezer.

If you feed beer to a laboratory rat, it will live six times longer than a rat that drinks only water.

NICE BUN

The Sighting: The face of Mother Teresa in a cinnamon bun in Nashville, Tennessee

Revelation: In the autumn of 1996, bakers at the Bongo Java coffee-house were baking cinnamon buns when they noticed one that bore a striking resemblance to Mother Teresa.

Impact: Bongo Java owner Bob Bernstein shellacked the bun and put it in a display case beneath the coffeehouse's cash register. The story was reported in newspapers and on national television. The coffeehouse, now a tourist attraction, set up a Web site and began selling "Immaculate Confection" T-shirts, mugs, cards, and "Mother Teresa's Special Roast" coffee beans. More than 2 million people from 80 different countries have visited the Web site, and many have left messages. "I hate to burst your bubble," one visitor wrote, "but to me, it looks more like Abe Vigoda in a hooded sweatshirt."

When Mother Teresa—who didn't even allow her own order to use her image in fundraising—learned of the bun, her lawyers asked the coffeehouse to remove it from display. "If it were sacrilege, we'd stop," a Bongo spokesman said. "But it's not."

THIRSTY FOR ENLIGHTENMENT

The Sighting: A statue of Lord Ganesh, the elephant-headed Hindu god of wealth and power, drinking milk through its trunk

Revelation: On September 21, 1995, a Hindu in India had a dream that Ganesh, the god of wealth and power, "wanted some milk." So he held an offering of a teaspoonful of milk up to the trunk of his Ganesh statue—and it drank it. As word spread over the next few days, the same phenomenon was observed in Hindu communities in England, Hong Kong, Malaysia, Nepal, the Netherlands and the United States. (Skeptics point to capillary action—the ability of porous stone and metals to absorb liquids—as a likely culprit.)

Impact: According to Indian news reports, "So many Hindus were caught up in the mass hysteria that milk supplies were depleted and shopkeepers raised the price of milk 20 times. The military used bamboo canes to control the worshippers flooding Hindu temples." The phenomenon spread to other religions. "After reading news reports," one man in Kuala Lumpur wrote, "I tried the same thing on Mother Mary and baby Jesus. They drank a whole spoonful."

OLYMPIC MYTHS

Every four years, we're treated to another round of Olympics. Whether you watch them or not, it's impossible to avoid all the hype—which, it turns out, isn't all true. Next time someone refers to "Olympic tradition," read them this.

THE MYTH: Athletes who competed in the ancient Greek Olympics were amateurs.

THE TRUTH: Technically, maybe. But in fact, they were handsomely rewarded for their victories. "Contrary to popular belief," says David Wallechinsky in his *Complete Book of the Olympics*, "the Ancient Greek athletes were not amateurs. Not only were they fully supported throughout their training, but even though the winner received only an olive wreath at the Games, at home he was amply rewarded and could become quite rich." Eventually, top athletes demanded cash and appearance fees—even back then.

THE MYTH: In ancient Greece, the Olympics were so important that everything stopped for them—even wars.

THE TRUTH: No war ever stopped because of the Olympics. But wars didn't interfere with the games because: 1) participants were given night-time safe-conduct passes that allowed them to cross battlefields after a day's fighting was done and 2) the Olympics were part of a religious ceremony, so the four olympic sites—including Delphi and Olympia—were off-limits to fighting.

THE MYTH: To honour ancient tradition and discourage commercialism, organizers of the modern Olympics decided that only amateur athletes could compete.

THE TRUTH: Not even close. It was "amateurs only" strictly to keep the riff-raff out. Baron Coubertin, the man responsible for bringing back the Olympics in 1896, was a French aristocrat who wanted to limit competitors to others of his social class. "He saw the Olympics as a way to reinforce class distinctions rather than overcome them," writes one historian. Since only the rich could afford to spend their time training for the games without outside support, the best way to keep lower classes out was to restrict them to amateurs.

THE MYTH: The torch-lighting ceremony that opens the games originated with the ancient Greeks.
THE TRUTH: It has no ancient precedent—it was invented by the Nazis. The 1936 Olympics took place in Berlin, under Hitler's watchful eye. Carl Diem, who organized the event for the Führer, created the first lighting of the Olympic flame to give the proceedings "an ancient aura." Since then, the ceremony has become part of Olympic tradition—and people just assume it's much older than it really is.

THE MYTH: The five-ring Olympic symbol is from ancient Greece.
THE TRUTH: The Nazis are responsible for that myth, too. According to David Young's book, *The Modern Olympics*, it was spread in a Nazi propaganda film about the Berlin Games.

THE MYTH: Adolf Hitler snubbed U.S. runner Jesse Owens at the 1936 Olympics in Berlin.
THE TRUTH: This is one of the enduring American Olympic myths. Hitler, the story goes, was frustrated in his attempt to prove Aryan superiority when Owens—an African American—took the gold. The furious Führer supposedly refused to acknowledge Owens's victories. But according to Owens himself, it never happened. Hitler didn't congratulate anyone that day because the International Olympic Committee had warned him he had to congratulate "all winners or no winners." He chose to stay mum.

THE MYTH: The Olympic marathon distance was established in ancient times to honour a messenger who ran from Marathon to Athens—about 26 miles—to deliver vital news—then died.
THE TRUTH: The marathon distance—26 miles, 385 yards [42,195 metres]—was established at the 1908 Games in London. It's the distance from Shepherd's Bush Stadium to the Queen's bedroom window.

THE MYTH: Drugs have always been taboo in the Olympics.
THE TRUTH: Drugs weren't outlawed until 1967. In fact, according to the Complete Book of the Olympics, drugs were already in use by the third modern Olympic Games: "The winner of the 1904 marathon, Thomas Hicks, was administered multiple doses of strychnine and brandy during the race."

THE EIFFEL TOWER, PART I

It's hard to believe now, but when the Eiffel Tower was proposed in the late 1800s, a lot of Parisians—and French citizens in general—opposed it. Here's a look at the story behind one of the most recognizable architectural structures on earth.

REVOLUTIONARY THINKING

In 1885, French officials began planning the Great Exposition of 1889, a celebration of the 100th anniversary of the French Revolution. They wanted to build some kind of monument that would be as glorious as France itself.

The Washington Monument, a masonry and marble obelisk, had recently been completed. At 170 metres [557 feet] high, it was the tallest building on earth. The French decided to top it by constructing a 305-metre [1,000-foot] tall tower right in the heart of Paris.

Now all they had to do was find somebody who could design and build it.

OPEN SEASON

On May 2, 1886, the French government announced a design contest: French engineers and architects were invited to "study the possibility of erecting on the Champ de Mars an iron tower with a base 125 metres square and 300 metres high."

Whatever the contestants decided to propose, their designs had to meet two other criteria: 1) the structure had to be self-financing—it had to attract enough ticket-buying visitors to the exposition to pay for its own construction; and 2) it had to be a temporary structure that could be torn down easily at the end of the Exposition.

MERCI...BUT NON, MERCI

More than 100 proposals were submitted by the May 18 deadline. Most were fairly conventional, but some were downright weird. One person proposed building a huge guillotine; another suggested erecting a 305-metre [1,000-foot] tall sprinkler to water all of Paris during droughts; a third suggested putting a huge electric light atop the tower that—with the help of strategically placed parabolic mirrors—would provide the entire city "eight times as much light as is necessary to read a newspaper."

NO CONTEST

The truth was, none of them had a chance. By the time the contest was announced, Alexandre-Gustave Eiffel—a 53-year-old structural engineer already considered France's "master builder in metal" had the job sewn up. (He would later become as *le Magicien du Fer*— "the Iron Magician.")

Weeks earlier, he had met with French minister Edouard Lockroy and presented plans for a wrought iron tower he was ready to build. Eiffel had already commissioned 5,329 mechanical drawings representing the 18,038 different components that would be used. Lockroy was so impressed that he rigged the contest so only Eiffel's design would win.

JOINT VENTURE

In January 1887, Eiffel signed a contract with the French government and the City of Paris. Eiffel & Company, his engineering firm, agreed to contribute $1.3 million of the tower's estimated $1.6 million construction cost. In exchange, Eiffel would receive all revenues generated by the tower during the Exposition—and for 20 years afterward. (The government agreed to leave the tower up after the Exposition.) Afterward, full ownership reverted to the City of Paris. They could tear it down if they wanted.

MONEY MACHINE

Unlike other public monuments, the Eiffel Tower was designed to make money from the very beginning. If you wanted to take the elevator or the stairs to the first storey, you had to pay 2 francs; going all the way to the top cost 5 francs (Sundays were cheaper). That was just the beginning: restaurants, cafes, and shops were planned for the first storey; a post office, telegraph office, bakery, and printing press were planned for the second storey. In all, the tower was designed to accommodate up to 10,416 paying customers at a time.

GROUNDBREAKING

Construction began on January 26, with not a moment to spare. With barely two years left to build the tower in time for the opening of the Exposition, Eiffel would have to build the tower more quickly than any similar structure had been built before. The Washington Monument, just over half the Eiffel Tower's size, had taken 36 years to complete.

PARISIAN PARTY POOPERS

A 305-metre [1,000-foot] tower would dwarf the Parisian skyline and overpower the city's other landmarks, including Notre Dame, the Louvre, and the Arc de Triomphe. When digging started on the foundation, more than 300 prominent Parisians signed a petition protesting the tower. They claimed that Eiffel's "hollow candlestick" would "disfigure and dishonour" the city. But Eiffel and the city ignored the petition, and work continued uninterrupted.

OTHER FEARS

The tower still had its critics. A French mathematics professor predicted that when the structure passed the 228-metre [748-foot] mark, it would inevitably collapse; another "expert" predicted that the tower's lightning rods would kill all the fish in the Seine.

The Paris edition of the New York *Herald* claimed the tower was changing the weather; and the daily newspaper *Le Matin* ran a headline story claiming "The Tower Is Sinking." "If it has really begun to sink," *Le Matin* pontificated, "any further building should stop and sections already built should be demolished as quickly as possible." As the tower's progress continued unabated, however, a sense of awe began to replace the fear.

Part II of the story begins on page 390.

* * * * *

Interesting Sidelight

August Eiffel also designed and built the iron skeleton that holds up the Statue of Liberty.

CANINE QUOTES

A few thoughts about man's best friend.

"You can say any fool thing to a dog, and the dog will give you this look that says, 'My God, you're right! I never would have thought of that!'"

—*Dave Barry*

"They say the dog is man's best friend. I don't believe that. How many friends have you had neutered?"

—*Larry Reeb*

"My dog is half pit bull, half poodle. Not much of a guard dog, but a vicious gossip."

—*Craig Shoemaker*

"Outside a dog, a book is man's best friend. Inside a dog it's too dark to read."

—*Groucho Marx*

"If a dog will not come to you after he has looked you in the face, you should go home and examine your conscience."

—*Woodrow Wilson*

"Dogs laugh, but they laugh with their tails."

—*Max Eastman*

"Acquiring a dog may be the only opportunity a human ever has to choose a relative."

—*Morecai Siegal*

"Every dog should have a man of his own. There is nothing like a well-behaved person around the house to spread the dog's blanket for him, or bring him his supper when he comes home man-tired at night."

—*Corey Ford*

"To his dog, every man is Napoleon; hence the constant popularity of dogs."

—*Aldous Huxley*

"To err is human, to forgive canine."

—*Anonymous*

"Dogs have more love than integrity. They've been true to us, yes, but they haven't been true to themselves."

—*Clarence Day*

"Every dog is entitled to one bite."

—*English proverb*

CONSTIPATION STAKES TO CONSERVATION STAKES

Whilst other countries just use toilets, Australia's fun-loving and entrepreneurial nature makes us inventive in the use of everyman's essential throne. Hoist the loo paper, we are a creative nation.

DEFINITION
Dunny: *toilet*
Essential knowledge, as you will be sitting on one, reading this book. How did Australia get a word in daily use that no other nationality understands? Originally it was "dunnekin," from "danna" (British) meaning excrement, and a Gypsy word "ken" meaning "house" (1869). Like other foreigner-flummoxing words, such as *arvo*, *rellies*, and *barbie*, it was soon shortened.

OLYMPIC ICON
What other nation would bring the backyard dunny to international attention—at no less a place than the opening ceremony of the Sydney 2000 Olympic Games? It was featured right there with the lawn-mower, the mounted stockmen and elite athletes for televisions around the world to record. As a nation we have quirkiness, high spirits, sports-worship, and practicality. The event became "the best Olympics ever." (Juan Antonio Samaranch)

DUNNY DERBIES
Dunny racing is often a festival highlight, topping even thong throwing, cockroach racing, lamington eating, keg lifting, gumboot tossing, dummy spitting and cooee calling competitions in popularity. In Queensland, Winton is the heartland of "Waltzing Matilda" and features a $3.3 million "Waltzing Matilda" museum for visitors. The town's biennial dunny derbies are ferociously contested. Rules are tight—there's no room for error with a winner's prize of $1,200 plus a trophy. Racing entries must be at least 1.8 m high and feature a genuine thunderbox for the jockey. This intrepid rider must not be an ounce under 75 kg (no cheating!)

and wear team-racing colours. Design specifications include two to four wheels, with bars front and back for two pushers and two pullers. Maximum line-up is 20 dunnies. Contestants must register their steed's name, for example "Phartlap." (*Official Rules*)

The main race is three lengths of the football field for heats and final. The Constipation Stakes is two lengths. Obstacles are placed on the grass. The jockey runs from the starting line (Le Mans start) to a seated position in the dunny with trousers down around the ankles. No front door is allowed as "nothing's private." Imagine the crowd roaring like the proverbial "dunny door in a storm" as the sweating teams, in racing colours, shove the ungainly tall structures towards the finishing line. After trophy awards, other festival activities include a dunny door auction where artwork on a door has been known to fetch up to $1,000.

Aussie World, near Caloundra in Queensland, runs its annual Australia Day charity Dunny Race near the famous Ettamogah pub and always attracts a crowd of more than 6,000 people. Media celebrities compete fiercely. If you are thinking of nominating as a jockey, you'll have to weigh in at over 50 kg, and if you're thinking of pushing, you'll have to cope with Heartbreak Hill and the occasional overturned dunny.

SPLIT CISTERN ENGINEERING

Recent tests in Seattle on Aussie dual flush indoor dunnies confirmed a one-third saving on water. So impressed were the authorities that they are offering incentives for residents to convert from their single flush (5.6 litres) to the Aussie version (lighter load option 2.8 litres). Other drier American and Canadian cities are expected to follow suit.

CAUTION

When you wander out to the dunny in the paddock, beware of your fellow dunny dwellers. *Atrodectus hasselti*, the red-back spider, is a notorious dunnyphile. He is probably after all those "dunny budgies" ("flies" in other less linguistically well-developed countries) that whirr and buzz in the Australian heat. Keep the good Aussie salute going.

Murders claimed more American lives during the 20th century than wars did.

AFTER THE FUNERAL

Your grave is supposed to be your final resting place. But that isn't always the case, especially if you're famous. Take a look at what happened to these unfortunate folks.

ABE LINCOLN

Claim to Fame: 16th President of the United States
How He Died: Assassinated by John Wilkes Booth on April 14, 1865

After the Funeral: On April 21, his body was laid to rest in a temporary vault in Springfield, Illinois, while a permanent mausoleum was under construction. The body was moved three more times, then entombed in the National Lincoln Monument on October 15, 1874. But in 1876 a ring of counterfeiters made two attempts to kidnap the body and hold it hostage until an accomplice was freed from prison; the second attempt was nearly successful—it was foiled just as the conspirators were prying open the sarcophagus.

Between 1876 and 1901, Lincoln's body was moved 14 more times—sometimes for security reasons, other times to repair the dilapidated crypt. In 1901 Old Abe was laid to rest a final (so far) time. As his son Robert supervised, the coffin was encased in steel bars and buried under tons of cement. As far as anyone can tell, Abe hasn't been moved since.

FRANCISCO PIZARRO

Claim to Fame: 16th-century Spanish explorer and conquistador of the Incas
How He Died: Stabbed to death by his countrymen in 1541 in a feud over Incan riches

After the Funeral: Pizarro's body was buried behind the cathedral in Lima on the night he died, where it remained for 2 1/2 years. In 1544, his bones were exhumed, placed in a velvet-lined box, and deposited under the main altar of the cathedral.

Pizarro's remains were moved repeatedly over the next 350 years because of earthquakes, repair work on the cathedral, and other reasons. On the 350th anniversary of his death, in 1891, a mummified body authenticated as his was placed in a glass and marble sarcophagus, which was set out for public display.

Then in 1977, some workers repairing a crypt beneath the main altar found two boxes—one lined with velvet and filled with human bones. The other box bore the Spanish inscription, "Here is the skull of the Marquis Don Francisco Pizarro who discovered and won Peru and placed it under the crown of Castile."

Which body was Pizarro's? In 1984, forensics experts from the United States flew to Peru to compare the two sets of remains and determined that the bones in the boxes were those of Pizarro. (The boxes fitted the historical description, and of the two sets of bones, the ones in the boxes were the only ones with stab wounds.)

Aftermath: When Pizarro's bones were positively identified, they were placed in a box in the glass sarcophagus, and the "impostor" mummy (who was never identified) was returned to the crypt underneath the altar.

* * *

FROM THE "WEIRD FUNERAL LAWSUIT" FILES

THE PLAINTIFF: Mrs. Margaret Taylor

THE DEFENDANT: Randle & Sons Funeral Home, St. Louis, Missouri, USA

THE LAWSUIT: The casket for William Taylor's 1997 funeral was closed until after the pastor finished his eulogy. Then it was opened…and people yelled "That's not Willie, you got the wrong man!" Mrs. Taylor called the police to keep the funeral home "from literally burying their mistake," and the body was taken to the morgue. It was identified as Frederick Ware—whose own funeral had passed without anyone noticing he wasn't really there. Taylor's body was finally located, but Mrs. Taylor was enraged. She sued for $2.2 million for emotional distress and "fear of not knowing the whereabouts of her husband's body for more than one week."

THE VERDICT: Unknown.

WILDE ABOUT OSCAR

*Wit and wisdom from Oscar Wilde, one of the most
popular and controversial writers of the 19th century.*

"When people agree with me I always feel that I must be wrong."

"I never put off till tomorrow what I can possibly do the day after."

"I sometimes think that God, in creating man, somewhat overestimated His ability."

"As long as a woman can look ten years younger than her own daughter, she is perfectly happy."

"Women are meant to be loved, not to be understood."

"After a good dinner one can forgive anybody, even one's own relations."

"I like men who have a future, and women with a past."

"Women give to men the very gold of their lives, but they invariably want it back in small change."

"Nowadays people know the price of everything and the value of nothing."

"The Americans are certainly great hero-worshippers, and always take their heroes from the criminal classes."

"No great artist sees things as they really are. If he did he would cease to be an artist."

"In this world there are only two tragedies. One is not getting what one wants and the other is getting it."

"Experience is the name everyone gives to their mistakes."

"A gentleman is one who never hurts anyone's feelings unintentionally."

"The one duty we owe to history is to rewrite it."

"The basis of action is lack of imagination. It is the last resource of those who know not how to dream."

FART FACTS

You won't find trivia like this in any ordinary book.

THE NAME

The word fart comes from the Old English term foertan, to explode. Foertan is also the origin of the word petard, an early type of bomb. Petard, in turn, is the origin of a more obscure term for fart—ped, or pet, which was once used by military men. (In Shakespeare's *Henry IV*, there's a character whose name means fart—Peto.)

WHY DO YOU FART?

Wind has many causes—for example, swallowing air as you eat and lactose intolerance. (Lactose is a sugar molecule in milk, and many people lack the enzyme needed to digest it.) But the most common cause is food that ferments in the gastrointestinal tract.

• A simple explanation: The fats, proteins, and carbohydrates you eat become a "gastric soup" in your stomach. This soup then passes into the small intestine, where much of it is absorbed through the intestinal walls into the bloodstream to feed the body.

• But the small intestine can't absorb everything, especially complex carbohydrates. Some complex carbohydrates—the ones made up of several sugar molecules (beans, some milk products, fibre, etc.) can't be broken down. So they're simply passed along to the colon, where bacteria living in your intestine feed off the fermenting brew. If that sounds revolting, try this: the bacteria then excrete gases into your colon. Farting is how your colon rids itself of the pressure the gas creates.

FRUIT OF THE VINE

So why not just quit eating complex carbohydrates?

• First, complex carbohydrates—which include fruit, vegetables, and whole grains—are crucial for a healthy diet. "Put it this way," explains Jeff Rank, an associate professor of gastroenterology at the University of Minnesota. "Cabbage and beans are bad for gas [wind], but they are good for you."

• Second, they're not the culprits when it comes to the least desirable aspect of farting: smell.

In virtually every language on Earth, the word for "mother" begins with the letter "m."

• Farts are about 99% odourless gases—hydrogen, nitrogen, carbon dioxide, oxygen, and methane (it's the methane that makes farts flammable). So why the odour? Blame it on those millions of bacteria living in your colon. Their waste gases usually contain sulphur molecules—which smell like rotten eggs. This is the remaining 1% that clears rooms in a hurry.

AM I NORMAL?

• Johnson & Johnson, which produces drugs for wind and indigestion, once conducted a survey and found that almost one-third of those interviewed believe they have a flatulence problem.

• However, according to Terry Bolin and Rosemary Stanton, authors of *Wind Breaks: Coming to Terms with Flatulence*, doctors say most flatulence is healthy. What's unhealthy is worrying about it so much.

NOTABLE FARTERS

• Le Petomane, a 19th-century music hall performer, had the singular ability to control his farts. He could play tunes, as well as imitate animal and machinery sounds rectally. Le Petomane's popularity briefly rivalled that of Sarah Bernhardt.

• A computer factory in England, built on the site of a 19th-century chapel, is reportedly inhabited by a farting ghost. Workers think it might be the embarrassed spirit of a girl who farted while singing in church. "On several occasions," said an employee, "there has been a faint girlish voice singing faint hymns, followed by a loud raspberry sound and then a deathly hush."

• Joseph Stalin was afraid of farting in public. He kept glasses and a water pitcher on his desk so that if he felt a wind coming on, he could mask the sound by clinking the glasses while pouring water.

• Martin Luther believed, "on the basis of personal experience, that farts could scare off Satan himself."

* * *

True Story: In 1991, the scientists Simon Brassell, Karen Chin, and Robert Harman published a paper proposing that millions of years' worth of dinosaur farts may have helped make the Earth more hospitable for humans and other mammals. How? The methane gas passed by dinosaurs, they suggested, "may have been a…contributor to global warming."

NOW HEAR THIS!

If you weren't reading right now, you might be listening to a "personal tape player"—like a Walkman. But then when people started banging on the door, asking what you were doing in there, you wouldn't hear them. Maybe they'd panic and think you were dead, like Elvis. They'd run outside and get a bunch of people to help break down the door. Wham! And there you'd be, completely oblivious. They'd get so mad that they'd attack you with the toilet plunger, which would get stuck to the top of your head. You'd have to go to the emergency room—and—well, aren't you glad you're reading Uncle John's Bathroom Reader instead? Since it's not safe to listen to a Walkman, we'll print a story about it instead. It's by Jack Mingo.

THE PRESSMAN

In the mid-1970s, a team of Sony engineers headed by Mitsuro Ida created the Pressman—a portable tape recorder that could fit into a shirt pocket. As Sony expected, it quickly became standard equipment for journalists. But there was one small problem: the Pressman recorded in mono, and radio journalists preferred working in stereo. They requested a stereo version.

Sony's engineers put their best into it, shrinking stereo components, trying to get them into a small, pocket-sized case. They almost made it—but could only fit in the playback parts and two tiny speakers. Since the whole point was to come up with a tape recorder, the attempt was an embarrassing and expensive failure. Still, the quality of the sound was surprisingly good. So Ida kept the prototype around the shop instead of dismantling it. Some of the engineers started playing cassettes on it while they worked.

THE MISSING LINK

One day Masaru Ibuka wandered by. Although he'd co-founded the company with Akio Morita, he was considered too quirky and creative to fit into day-to-day operations. So he was made "honourary chairman"—a title that gave him much respect, little authority, and lots of time to wander the halls of Sony.

Ibuka stopped to watch the Pressman engineers working on their design problem. He heard music coming from the unsuccessful prototype and asked, "Where did you get this great little tape player?" Ida explained that it was a failure because it couldn't record.

Ibuka spent a lot of his time roaming around, so he knew what was going on all over the company. He suddenly remembered another project he'd seen that was being developed on the other side of the building—a set of lightweight portable headphones.

"What if you got rid of the speakers and added the headphones?" he asked Ida. "They'd use less power and increase the quality of the sound. Who knows, maybe we can sell this thing even if you can't record on it." The engineers listened politely and respectfully—while privately thinking the old man had finally lost it. Why make a tape recorder that can't record?

LISTENING WELL

Ibuka took the gadget, with headphones attached, to Morita. He too was skeptical—until he heard the quality of the stereo music. To the shock of the engineering team, Morita gave it a green light. It was dubbed the Walkman, to go along with the Pressman.

The marketing department thought it was a terrible idea. They projected that the company would lose money on every unit sold. Even the name seemed wrong. According to American distributors, "Walkman" sounded "funny" to English ears. So Sony rolled the product out as the "Soundabout" in the U.S. and the "Stowaway" in England. Their 1979 publicity campaign—a low-budget, luke-warm affair aimed at teens—got virtually no results. It seemed as though the Walkman's critics were right.

As it turned out, though, Sony had just targeted the wrong market. Teens had boom boxes—it was adults who wanted the Walkman. The little unit was perfect for listening to Mozart while jogging or the Stones while commuting, and was small enough to fit into a briefcase or the pocket of a business suit. To Sony's surprise, white collar workers discovered the Walkman on their own. It became a sudden, raging success. Sony had prepared an initial run of 60,000 units; when the first wave hit, they sold out instantly.

The world still loves the Walkman and its offspring. By 1997, four million personal cassette players were sold a year.

The saguaro cactus does not grow its first arm until it's at least 75 years old.

HERE COMES THE SUN

Some facts about that big lightbulb in the sky, from astronomer (and BRI member) Richard Moeschl.

It takes 8.3 minutes for the sun's light—travelling at 299,791 kilometers a second—to reach Earth. (At that speed, light can travel around the Earth seven times in one second.)

The sun looks yellow-gold because we're viewing it through the Earth's atmosphere. Judging from its surface temperature, the sun's colour is probably closer to white.

The temperature of the sun at its core is around 40 million degrees C [73 million degrees F]. It takes 50 years for this energy to reach the sun's surface, where we can see it as light.

The English astronomer James Jeans once figured that if you placed a piece of the sun's core the size of the head of a pin on Earth, its heat would kill a person 94 miles away.

The temperature of the sun's photosphere, the part that sends us light, is about 5,500 degrees C [10,000 degrees F].

The sun contains 99.9% of the matter in the solar system.

The sun produces more energy in one second than human beings have produced in all of our history. In less than a week, the sun sends out more energy than we could make by burning all the natural gas, oil, coal, and wood on Earth.

The total energy output of the sun is 1.92 calories per minute per square centimetre, or 3.83 x 1,000,000,000,000,000, 000,000-000,000 watts.

The Earth receives 2 one-billionths of the sun's power.

The surface gravity on the sun is 28 times that of Earth. If you weigh 54 kilograms [120 pounds] on Earth, on the sun you would weigh 1,524 kilograms [3,360 pounds].

The sun rotates once every 26.8 days.

With every passing day, the sun is losing energy—but it still has about 5 billion years of life left in it.

The Apaches referred to horses as "God dogs."

CELEBRITY GOSSIP

*Here's the BRI's cheesy tabloid section—a
bunch of gossip about famous people.*

ALBERT EINSTEIN
• He applied to the Federal Polytechnic Academy in
Zurich, but flunked the entrance exam. When his father
asked his headmaster what profession Albert should adopt, he got
the answer, "It doesn't matter, he'll never amount to anything."
• For many years, Einstein thought of his work in physics as something of a hobby. He regarded himself as a failure because what he
really wanted to do was play concert violin. Einstein was unchar-
acteristically intense when he played his violin, cursing a blue
streak whenever he made a mistake. One evening, while playing
violin duets with Queen Elizabeth, Einstein suddenly stopped in
the middle of the piece and unceremoniously told her she was
playing too loudly.

MUHAMMAD ALI
• For some reason, as a child, he always walked on his tiptoes.
When he got older, he played touch football, but wouldn't play
tackle because he thought it was too rough.
• Because he was afraid to fly, Ali (then going by his original
name, Cassius Clay) almost didn't make it to the 1960 Rome
Olympics, where he won the gold medal that launched his career.

JANIS JOPLIN
• In 1965, when she was on the verge of becoming a blues star,
strung out on heavy drugs, hanging out with Hell's Angels, Joplin
wrote to her parents and asked them to send her one present for
Christmas: "a *Betty Crocker* or *Better Homes and Gardens* cook-
book."
• She once went on a blind date with William Bennett. He was
apparently so traumatized that he eventually became drug czar
under Ronald Reagan, and a conservative "family values" advo-
cate.

GENERAL GEORGE PATTON
• On the way through Europe during World War II with his troops, Patton was continuously in danger from shelling, strafing, and bombing. In the middle of one scorched, scarred, and burning landscape, with the sound of explosions around him, he threw out his arms and looked to the skies as if bathing in a warm spring rain. "Could anything be more magnificent?" he shouted to the soldiers endeavouring to shrink to insignificance. "God, how I love it!"

MICHAEL JACKSON
• Jackson's favourite song? He told a group of reporters that it was "My Favourite Things," performed by Julie Andrews.
• His opinion of other singers: Paul McCartney? Okay writer, not much of an entertainer. "I do better box office than he does." Frank Sinatra? "I don't know what people see in the guy. He's legend, but he isn't much of a singer. He doesn't even have hits anymore." Mick Jagger? "He sings flat. How did he ever get to be a star? I just don't get it. He doesn't sell as many records as I do." Madonna? "She just isn't that good…She can't sing. She's just an OK dancer…She knows how to market herself. That's about it."

FIDEL CASTRO
• For Castro's first revolutionary attack on a military post, he forgot his glasses. As a result, he could barely drive to the post, much less aim his gun accurately.
• Castro fancies himself quite a lady's man. In fact, there are dozens of children in Cuba who claim him as father. His technique? One purported lover, a dancer at the Tropicana Hotel, said he read while making love. A French actress complained that he "smoked his damned cigar." An American woman said he never took his boots off. Other women said he took them to romantic spots and then talked for hours on end about things like agricultural reform.

ALFRED HITCHCOCK
• When he sat on a public toilet and another man entered the room, he'd quickly raise his legs in the stall "so that no one could tell anyone was there."

An adult horse eats 15 pounds of hay and 9 pounds of grain every day.

LUCKY FINDS

In an earlier Bathroom Reader, *we included a section about valuable things people have found. Since then we've found many more stories. Hey—maybe it's not such a rare occurrence. It could happen to you!*

G ARAGE SALE TREASURE
The Find: Two Shaker "gift" paintings
Where They Were Found: Inside a picture frame
The Story: In 1994, a retired couple from New England, USA, bought an old picture frame for a few dollars at a garage sale. When they took the frame apart to restore it, two watercolour drawings—dated 1845 and 1854—fell out.

A few months later, the couple was travelling in Massachusetts and noticed a watercolour on a poster advertising the Hancock Shaker Village Museum. It was similar to the two they'd found. Curious, they did some research and found out the works were called "gift paintings."

It turns out that the Shakers, a New England religious sect of the 1800s, did not allow decorations on their walls; Shaker sisters, however, were permitted to paint "trees, flowers, fruits and birds…to depict the glory of heaven." The paintings were then "gifted" to other sisters and put away as holy relics. And one of the couple's paintings was signed by the most famous of all "gift" artists, Hannah Cohoon.

They called a curator of the Hancock Museum with the news, but he didn't believe them. Only 200 Shaker "gift" paintings still exist—and very few are of the quality they described. Moreover, all known paintings were in museums—none in private hands. Nonetheless, in January 1996, the couple brought the paintings to the museum, where they were examined and declared authentic. A year later, in January 1997, Sotheby's sold them for $473,000.

BIZARRE BITE
The Find: A diamond
Where It Was Found: In a plate of pasta
The Story: In October 1996, Liliana Parodi of Genoa, Italy, went to her favourite restaurant for some pasta. The meal was uneventful—until she bit down on something hard and it wedged

painfully between her teeth. She complained to the management, then left. The next morning, she went to a dentist, who extracted the object—a one-carat, uncut diamond worth about $3,000. Parodi took it to a jeweller and had it set in a ring. How it got into the pasta is still a mystery.

A BEATLE'S LEGACY

The Find: Dozens of sketches by John Lennon
Where They Were Found: In a notebook
The Story: In 1996, a man named John Dunbar—who'd been married to British singer Marianne Faithfull in the 1960s—was going through some old belongings and came across a notebook he hadn't seen in over 25 years. He'd had it with him at a London party in 1967, on a night when he and his friend John Lennon were taking LSD together. But he'd stashed it away and forgotten about it.

During that week in 1967, Lennon had seen an ad in the newspaper offering "an island off Ireland," for about $2,000. At the party, the drugged-out Beatle suddenly decided to buy it. He and Dunbar immediately flew to Dublin, travelled across Ireland in a limousine, and hired a boat to get there. "The island was more like a couple of small hills joined by a gravelly bar with a cottage on it," Durbar recalled. "When we got there, John sat down and started drawing." The pair stayed on the island for a few days. Lennon did buy it, but never lived there. (In fact, he gave it away a few years later, to a stranger who showed up at Apple Records.)

Dunbar kept the notebook as a memento of the trip, and today, experts estimate the drawings at about $165,000. The incredulous Dunbar can always look as it as a belated "thank you"—he was the fellow, it turns out, who introduced Lennon to Yoko Ono.

LOTTERY TICKET

The Find: A wallet with $224.
Where It Was Found: On a street in Adelaide, Australia
The Story: In the 1970s, Joan Campbell found a wallet and tracked down the owner, hoping for a nice reward. She was disappointed—all the man gave her was a 55¢ lottery ticket. Later, she cheered up: the ticket paid $45,000.

In the Middle Ages, you were supposed to throw *eggs* at the bride and groom.

BOND—JAMES BOND

Here's a shaken—not stirred—history of the most popular (and profitable) British secret agent in Hollywood history—and of the former World War II intelligence officer who brought the character to life.

SPY STORY

Even before World War II started, Great Britain knew it would never be able to patrol the entire northern Atlantic and defend all its ships against the German Navy. But the British also knew that if they could learn the locations of Nazi ships and submarines by deciphering coded German radio communications, they'd be able to reroute convoys of food and weapons around German patrols. In 1939 they launched a massive effort, code-named Ultra, to do just that.

The Enigma. The Germans sent coded messages using an encryption machine called the "Enigma." By September 1940 the British had managed to put together a working model of the Enigma using parts captured in several raids on German ships. But the Enigma was so sophisticated that even when the British had one in their possession, they couldn't crack the German codes. They needed a copy of the Nazis' special codebook.

FLEMING—IAN FLEMING

How were they going to get one? The wildest suggestion came from the assistant to the Director of Naval Intelligence, a man named Ian Fleming. On September 12, 1940, Fleming wrote the following memo to his boss:

> Director of Naval Intelligence:
>
> I suggest we obtain the loot [codebook] by the following means:
>
> 1. Obtain from Air Ministry an air-worthy German bomber.
>
> 2. Pick a tough crew of five, including a pilot, wireless telegraph operator and a word-perfect [fluent] German speaker. Dress them in German Air Force uniform, add blood and bandages to suit.
>
> 3. Crash plane in the Channel after making S.O.S. to rescue service in plain language.

Snakes can get malaria.

4. Once abroad the rescue boat, shoot German crew, dump overboard, bring rescue boat back to English port.

In order to increase the chances of capturing a small or large minesweeper, with their richer booty, a crash might be staged in mid-[English] Channel. The Germans would presumably employ one of this type for the longer and more hazardous journey.

OPERATION RUTHLESS

The Director of Naval Intelligence passed the plan along to Prime Minister Winston Churchill, who gave it his personal approval. A German twin-engine Heinkell 111, shot down during a raid over Scotland, was restored to flying condition and a crew was recruited to fly it. "Operation Ruthless" was ready to go. But as David Kahn writes in *Seizing the Enigma*,

> In October, Fleming went to Dover to await his chance. None came. Air reconnaissance found no suitable German ships operating at night, and radio reconnaissance likewise found nothing... The navy awaited favorable circumstances. But they never materialized, and the plan faded away.

Even though Great Britain never did attempt a raid as daring as Fleming proposed, it did manage to capture codebooks from German ships. By 1943 they were cracking Enigma codes regularly; and by May of that year the Battle of the Atlantic was effectively over.

A NOVEL IDEA

After the war Fleming got out of the intelligence business and became an executive with the company that owned the *London Sunday Times*. He never forgot his wartime experiences.

First Person. By 1952 Fleming was in his forties and about to be married for the first time. He was apparently tense at the thought of giving up his bachelorhood, and his future wife suggested he try writing a novel to ease the strain. Fleming had wanted to write a novel for years, so he decided to give it a try. Drawing on his intelligence background, he wrote a spy thriller called *Casino Royale* during his two-month winter vacation in Jamaica.

Picking a Name. The book was filled with murders, torture, and lots of action. It was an autobiographical fantasy, the adventures of a British secret agent named James Bond that Fleming—who spent World War II stuck behind a desk in London—wanted to be, but couldn't.

Fleming thought that giving the agent an unexciting name would play off well against the plot. But what name? As Fleming later recounted, he found it "in one of my Jamaican bibles, *Birds of the West Indies* by James Bond, an ornithological classic. I wanted the simplest, dullest, plainest-sounding name that I could find. James Bond seemed perfect."

ON HIS WAY

Casino Royale was published in England in April 1953, and in the U.S. a year later. The book was a critical success, but sales were disappointing. Luckily for Fleming, he took a two-month vacation in Jamaica every year, and in each of the next several years he wrote a new Bond novel during his vacation, including *Live and Let Die* (1954), *Moonraker* (1955), and *Diamonds are Forever* (1956).

Live and Let Die became a bestseller in England, and Fleming began building a considerable following in the U.K. But in America, sales remained sluggish for the rest of the 1950s.

Thanks, JFK. The Bond bandwagon got rolling in the U.S. beginning in 1961, when *Life* magazine published a list of President John F. Kennedy's favourite books. Among the scholarly tomes was one work of popular fiction—*From Russia, With Love*. "This literally made Bond in America overnight," Raymond Benson writes in *The James Bond Bedside Companion*. "From then on, sales improved almost immediately….It was good public relations for Kennedy as well—it showed that even a President can enjoy a little 'sex, sadism, and snobbery.'"

How did a little-known Scottish actor named Sean Connery land the role of the most famous secret agent in Hollywood history?
The story continues on page 316.

* * * * *

Happy Anniversary! The first push-button phones were installed Nov. 18, 1963. They were put into service between Carnegie and Greensburg, Pennsylvania.

How can you tell when a porpoise is searching for a mate? It swims upside down.

DUMB CROOKS

Many people are worried about the growing threat of crime, but the good news is that there are plenty of crooks who are their own worst enemies. Want proof? Check out these news reports.

CAREFUL, THIS FINGER'S LOADED

MERCED, California— "A man tried to rob a bank by pointing his finger at a teller, police said.

"Steven Richard King just held up his finger and thumb in plain sight and demanded money. The Bank of America teller told Mr. King to wait, then just walked away. Mr. King then went across the street to another bank…jumped over the counter, and tried to get the key to the cash drawer. But an employee grabbed the key and told him to 'get out of here.'

"Police officers found Mr. King sitting in the shrubs outside the bank and arrested him."

—*New York Times*, April 1997

STRANGE RESEMBLANCE

OROVILLE, California— "Thomas Martin, former manager of a Jack In the Box restaurant, reported that he'd been robbed of $307 as the store was closing. He provided police sketch artist Jack Lee with a detailed description of the suspect. When Lee put his pad down, he observed that the drawing looked just like Martin. When questioned, Martin confessed."

—*Parade* magazine, December 1996

KEYSTONE KROOK

OAKLAND, California— "According to the Alameda County District Attorney's office, in 1995 a man walked into an Oakland bank and handed the teller a note reading: *This is a stikkup. Hand over all yer mony fast.*

"Guessing from this that the guy was no rocket scientist, the teller replied, 'I'll hand over the cash as long as you sign for it. It's a bank policy: All robbers have to sign for their money.'

"The would-be robber thought this over, then said, 'I guess that's OK.' And he signed his full name and address.

It's impossible to snore in the weightlessness of space.

"That's where the cops found him a few hours later."

—*Jay Leno's Police Blotter*

SHAKE YOUR BOOTIES

WICHITA, Kansas— "Charles Taylor was on trial for robbing a shoe store at knifepoint, accused of taking a pair of tan hiking boots and $69. As he listened to testimony in court, he propped his feet on the defense table. He was wearing a pair of tan boots.

"'I leaned over and stared,' the judge told a reporter later. 'I thought, surely nobody would be so stupid as to wear the boots he stole to his own trial.' But when an FBI agent called the shoe store, he found out that the stolen boots were size 10, from lot no. 1046—the same size and lot number as the boots Taylor was wearing, The jury found Taylor guilty, and officers confiscated the boots. 'We sent him back to jail in his stocking feet,' the judge said."

—**From wire service reports, March 1997**

NEXT WEEK HE'S COMING BACK FOR BRAINS

"In March 1995, a twenty-six-year-old inmate walked away from his community release facility in South Carolina. He was recaptured a week later when he went back to pick up his [pay]."

—*Knuckleheads in the News,* by John Machay

OH, JUST BAG IT

"Not wishing to attract attention to himself, a bank robber in 1969 in Portland, Oregon, wrote all his instruction on a piece of paper rather than shouting.

"This is a hold-up and I've got a gun,' he wrote and then held the paper up for the cashier to read.

"The bemused bank official waited while he wrote out, 'Put all the money in a paper bag.'

"This message was pushed through the grille. The cashier read it and then wrote on the bottom, 'I don't have a paper bag,' and passed it back. The robber fled."

—*The Book of Heroic Failures,* by Stephen Pile

VIDEO TREASURES

How many times have you found yourself at a video store staring at the thousands of films you've never heard of, wondering which ones are worth watching? It happens to us all the time—so we decided to offer a few recommendations for relatively obscure, quirky videos you might like.

DREAMCHILD (1985) *Drama*
Review: "A poignant story of the autumn years of Alice Hargreaves, the model for Lewis Carroll's *Alice in Wonderland*. Film follows her on a visit to New York in the 1930s, with fantasy sequences by Jim Henson's Creature Shop." (*Video Hound's Golden Movie Retriever*) *Stars:* Coral Brown, Ian Holm, Peter Gallagher. *Director:* Gavin Millar.

THE STUNT MAN (1980) *Mystery / Suspense*
Review: "Nothing is ever quite what it seems in this fast-paced, superbly crafted film. It's a Chinese puzzle of a movie and, therefore, may not please all viewers. Nevertheless, this directorial tour de force by Richard Rush has ample thrills, chills, suspense, and surprises for those with a taste for something different." (*Video Movie Guide*) *Stars:* Peter O'Toole, Steve Railsback, Barbara Hershey. *Director:* Richard Rush.

SUGAR CANE ALLEY (1984. French, with subtitles) *Drama*
Review: "Beautifully made drama about an 11-year-old boy and his all-sacrificing grandmother, surviving in a Martinique shantytown in the 1930s. Rich, memorable characterizations; a humanist drama of the highest order." (*Leonard Maltin's Movie & Video Guide*) *Stars:* Gary Cadenat, Darling Legitimus. *Director:* Edwin L. Marian.

SMILE (1975) *Satire*
Review: "Hilarious, perceptive satire centring around the behind-the-scenes activity at a California 'Young American Miss' beauty pageant, presented as a symbol for the emptiness of American middle-class existence." (*Leonard Maltin's Movie & Video Guide*) *Stars:* Bruce Dern, Barbara Feldon. *Director:* Michael Ritchie.

WRONG IS RIGHT (1982) *Comedy*
Review: "Sean Connery, as a globe-trotting television reporter, gives what may be the best performance of his career, in this outrageous, thoroughly entertaining end-of-the-world black comedy, written, produced, and directed by Richard Brooks. An updated version of Network and Dr. Strangelove." (Video Movie Guide) *Stars:* Sean Connery, Robert Conrad. *Director:* Richard Brooks.

MIRACLE MILE (1989) *Thriller*
Review: "A riveting, apocalyptic thriller about a mild-mannered misfit who...standing on a street corner at 2 a.m., answers a ringing pay phone. The caller...announces that bombs have been launched for an all-out nuclear war....A surreal, wicked farce sadly overlooked in theatrical release." *(Video Hound's Golden Movie Retriever) Stars:* Anthony Edward, Mare Winningham. *Director:* Steve DeJamatt.

TIME BANDITS (1981) *Fantasy*
Review: "This subversive kid's adventure teams a youngster with a criminally minded pack of dwarves on the run from the Supreme Being through holes in time. A highly imaginative, quirky mix of Monty Python humour, historical swashbuckler, and kid's gee-whiz adventure." *(Seen That, Now What?) Stars:* Sean Connery, David Warner. *Director:* Terry Gilliam.

DEFENSE OF THE REALM (1985) *Thriller*
Review: "A British politician is accused of selling secrets to the KGB through his mistress and only a pair of dedicated newspapermen believe he is innocent....They discover a national cover-up conspiracy. An acclaimed, taut thriller." *(Video Hound's Golden Movie Retriever) Stars:* Gabriel Byrne, Greta Scacci. *Director:* David Drury.

NIGHT MOVES (1975) *Mystery*
Review: "While trying to deal with his own sour private life, a P.I. is hired by a fading Hollywood star to track down her reckless daughter, involving him in art smuggling, murder, and sex on Florida's Gulf Coast. This incisive psychological drama manages to be both intelligent and entertaining." *(Seen That, Now What?) Stars:* Gene Hackman, Jenifer Warren. *Director:* Arthur Penn.

LITTLE SHOP OF HORRORS

*In this chapter, we feed you the story of one of the most
unlikely—but most popular—cult films of all time.*

ALL SET TO GO

A few days after he finished work on a film called *A
Bucket of Blood* in 1959, director Roger Corman had lunch
with the manager of Producers Studio, the company that rented
him office space. The manager mentioned that another company
had just finished work on a film, and the sets were still standing.

"I said, just as a joke, 'If you leave the sets up, I'll come in for
a couple of days and see if I can just invent a picture, because I
have a little bit of money now and some free time," Corman
recalled years later. "And he said, 'Fine.' The whole thing was
kind of a whim. I booked the studio for a week."

TO B OR NOT TO B

Corman, 32, had only been directing films for five years (*The
Monster from the Ocean Floor* and *Attack of the Crab Monsters* were
two early titles). But he was already developing a reputation for
making profitable movies very quickly on minuscule budgets—a
skill that would later earn him the title "King of the B films."

He had filmed *A Bucket of Blood*, a "beatnik-styled horror
comedy" in only five days, a personal record. He bet his friend at
Producers Studio that he could make this next film in 48 hours.

COMING UP WITH A SCRIPT

Corman called scriptwriter Chuck Griffith, who'd written *A
Bucket of Blood*, and told him to write a new variation of the same
story. The only limitations: it had to be written for the existing
sets, and Corman had to be able to rehearse all the scenes in three
days...and then film them in two.

Griffith took the assignment. He and Corman went bar-
hopping to brainstorm and outline for the film. It was a long
night: Griffith got drunk, then got into a barroom brawl. Somehow, he and Corman still managed to come up with a story about
a nerdy flower shop employee and his man-eating plant.

DEJA VU

Griffith turned in the final script a week later. It was essentially a warmed-over version of *A Bucket of Blood*.

• In *A Bucket of Blood*, a well-meaning sculptor accidentally kills his landlord's cat, then hides the evidence by turning it into a sculpture, which he titles "Dead Cat." When the sculpture brings him the notoriety he's always sought, he starts killing people and making them into sculptures, too.

• In *Little Shop of Horrors*, a well-meaning flower shop employee becomes a local hero after he accidentally creates a man-eating plant (which he names Audrey Jr., after his girlfriend) by cross-breeding a Venus flytrap with a buttercup. He then begins killing people to keep the plant—and his fame—alive.

LOW BUDGET

• The filming took place between Christmas and New Year's Eve 1959. Corman spent a total of $23,000 on the film, including $800 for the finished script and $750 for three different models of Audrey Jr.: a 30-centimetre [12-inch] version, a 1.8-metre [6-foot] version, and a full-grown 2.4-metre [8-foot] version.

• Corman pinched pennies wherever he could. Jack Nicholson, 23 years old when Corman hired him to play a masochistic dental patient named Wilbur Force, remembers that Corman wouldn't even spend money making copies of the script: "Roger took the script apart and gave me only the pages for my scenes. That way he could give the rest of the script to another actor or actors."

• Corman also paid a musician named Fred Kat $317.34 for the musical score—but as John McCarty and Mark McGee write in *The Little Shop of Horrors* book,

> Katz simply used the same score he'd written for *A Bucket of Blood*, which has also been used in another Corman film, *The Wasp Woman* and would be used yet again in Corman's *Creature from the Haunted Sea*. Whether or not Corman was aware he was buying the same score three times is unknown.

• Even if a shot wasn't perfect, Corman would use it if he could. In the first day of shooting, Jackie Haze and Jack Nicholson accidentally knocked over the dentist's chair, spoiling the shot and breaking the chair. When the property master said it would take

---

A shark's teeth are nearly as hard as steel.

an hour to fix the chair so they could reshoot the scene, Corman changed the script to read, "The scene ends with the dentist's chair falling over."

• Corman was legendary for getting as much work out of his actors and writers as he could. One example: Chuck Griffith, who wrote the script, also played a shadow on a wall, the man who runs out of the dentist's office with his ear bitten, and the thief who robs the flower shop. He also directed the Skid Row exterior shots and provided the voice for Audrey Jr. (Griffith's voice wasn't supposed to make it into the final film—he was just the guy who stood off camera and read the plant's lines so the actors would have something to react to. Corman had planned to dub in another actor's voice later. "But it got laughs," Griffith says, "so Corman decided to leave it the way it was.")

• Corman also saved money by filming all of the Skid Row exteriors actually in Skid Row, and using "real bums to play the bums." Griffith, who directed the scenes, paid them 10¢ per scene, using the change he had in his pocket.

THAT'S A WRAP

• Corman finished all of the interior shots in the required two days, then spent a couple more evenings filming the exterior shots. To this day, *Little Shop of Horrors* is listed in the *Guinness Book of World Records* for "the shortest shooting schedule for a full-length, commercial feature film made without the use of stock footage."

• In this original release, *Little Shop of Horrors* was only a modest success. It didn't develop its cult following until the late 1960s, when it became a Creature Feature classic on late-night TV. It was adapted into an off-Broadway musical in 1982, which was itself adapted into a new $20 million film in 1987.

• "*Little Shop of Horrors* is the film that established me as an underground legend in film circles," Corman says. "People come up to me on the street who have memorized parts of the dialogue. I suppose you could say it was *The Rocky Horror Picture Show* of its time."

Short people have fewer back problems than tall people do.

BRAND NAMES

Here are some origins of commercial names.

ADIDAS. Adolph and Rudi Dassler formed Dassler Brothers Shoes in Germany in 1925. After World War II, the partnership broke up, but each brother kept a piece of the shoe business: Rudi called his new company Puma; Adolph, whose nick name was "Adi," renamed the old company after himself—*Adi Dassler*.

PENNZOIL. In the early 1900s, two motor oil companies—Merit Oil and Panama Oil—joined forces and created a brand name they could both use: Pennsoil (short for William Penn's Oil). It didn't work—consumers kept calling it Penn-soil. So in 1914 they changed the **s** to a **z**.

DIAL SOAP. The name refers to a clock or watch dial. The reason: It was the first deodorant soap, and Lever Bros. wanted to suggest that it would prevent B.O. "all around the clock."

WD-40. In the 1950s, the Rocket Chemical Company was working on a product for the aerospace industry that would reduce rust and corrosion by removing moisture from metals. It took them 40 tries to come up with a workable Water Displacement formula.

LYSOL. Short for lye solvent.

MAZDA. The Zoroastrian god of light.

NISSAN. Derived from the phrase *Nissan snagyo*, which means "Japanese industry."

ISUZU. Japanese for "50 bells."

MAGNAVOX. In 1915 the Commercial Wireless and Development Co. created a speaker that offered the clearest sound of any on the market. They called it the *Magna Vox*—which means *great voice* in Latin.

FAMOUS FOR
BEING NAKED

We know—this sounds a little off-colour. Butt—er—we
mean but—it's just another way to look at history.

LADY GODIVA, wife of Earl Leofric, Lord of Coventry, England, in the 1100s
Famous for: Riding horseback through Coventry, covered only by her long blonde hair.
The bare facts: Lady Godiva was upset by the heavy taxes her husband had imposed on poor people in his domain. When she asked him to give the folks a break, he laughingly replied that he'd cut the taxes if she would ride through the town naked. To his shock, she agreed. But she requested that townspeople stay indoors and not peek while she rode through the streets. Legend has it that they all complied except for one young man named Tom, who secretly watched through a shutter—which gave us the term "peeping Tom."

ARCHIMEDES (287–212 B.C.), a "classic absent-minded professor" and one of the most brilliant thinkers of the Ancient World
Famous for: Running naked through the streets of ancient Syracuse, screaming "Eureka!"
The bare facts: Archimedes' friend, King Hieron II of Syracuse, Sicily, was suspicious that his new crown wasn't solid gold. Had the goldsmith secretly mixed in silver? He asked Archimedes to find out. As Peter Lafferty recounts in book, *Archimedes:*

> Archimedes took the crown home and sat looking at it. What was he to do? He weighed the crown. He weighed a piece of pure gold just like the piece the goldsmith had been given. Sure enough, the crown weighed the same as the gold. For many days, he puzzled over the crown. Then one evening…the answer came to him.
>
> That night, his servants filled his bath to the brim with water. As Archimedes lowered himself into the tub, the water overflowed onto the floor. Suddenly, he gave a shout and jumped out. Forgetting that he was

naked, he ran down the street to the palace shouting
"Eureka" ("I have found it!")

Archimedes, presumably still wearing his birthday suit, explained
his discovery to the king: "When an object is placed in water," he
said, "it displaces an amount of water equal to its own volume."

To demonstrate, he put the crown in a bowl of water and
measured the overflow. Then he put a lump of gold that weighed
the same as the crown into the bowl. "The amount of water was
measured," writes Lafferty, "and to the king's surprise, the gold had
spilled less than the crown." It was proof that the goldsmith really
had tried to cheat the king. The secret: "Silver is lighter than
gold, so to make up the correct weight, extra silver was needed.
This meant that the volume of the crown was slightly larger than
the gold, so the crown spilled more water."

Archimedes became famous for his discovery. We can only
guess what happened to the goldsmith.

RED BUTTONS, popular red-headed actor of the 1940s and
1950s
Famous for: Being the first person ever to appear naked on TV.
The bare facts: In the early 1950s, Red did a guest spot on the
"Milton Berle Show," which was broadcast live. One skit featured
Berle as a doctor and Buttons as a shy patient who wouldn't dis-
robe for his exam. Buttons wore a special "breakaway" suit—the
coat, shirt, and pants were sewn together so they'd all come off
when Berle yanked on the shirt collar. As he explained in *The
Hollywood Walk of Shame:*

> When my character refused to get undressed, Milton
> was supposed to grab my shirt front and rip the entire
> thing off—and I'd be left standing there in old-fash-
> ioned, knee-to-neck piece underwear.
>
> Well, Milton reached for my shirt and accidental-
> ly grabbed me under the collar. And when he yanked
> at my breakaway suit, everything came off—including
> my underwear! We were on live television and there I
> stood—nude in front of a studio audience and all the
> people watching at home. When I realized what had
> happened, I got behind Milton, who was as shocked
> as I was, but had the presence of mind to announce
> the next act and have the curtain closed.

Buttons said he turned "as red as my hair."

THE SPIDER DANCE

Here's an interesting little tale about a classic folk dance.

DANCE FEVER
Over the last 2000 years there have been occasional instances of mass hysteria that scientists call "epidemic dancing." Entire towns or provinces will begin a wild, spontaneous dancing, often accompanied by hallucinations.

Perhaps the most serious outbreak took place in July 1374, in the French town of Aix-la-Chapelle. As Frederick Cartwright writes in *Disease and History*,

> The sufferers began to dance uncontrollably in the streets, screaming and foaming at the mouth. Some declared they were immersed in a sea of blood, others claimed to have seen the heavens open to reveal Christ enthroned with the Virgin Mary....Streams of dancers invaded the Low Countries, moved along the Rhine, and appeared throughout Germany....In the later stages, the dancers often appeared to be entirely insensible to pain, a symptom of hysteria.

Today, scientists and historians speculate the dancing was caused by eating rye bread contaminated with "ergot," a fungus that infects bread cereals. One of the chemical compounds created by ergot is lysergic acid diethylamide—LSD. So the dancers were essentially high on LSD. And long after the effects of the drug had worn off, mass hysteria kept them going.

We know about the hallucinogenic effects of LSD today—but until a few decades ago, no one had any idea what caused the mysterious outbreaks. In the 16th century, when a similar incident took place near Taranto, Italy, the townspeople blamed the *tarantula*, a local spider named after the town.

The tarantula was known for its painful bite, which was thought to be deadly. So when the dancers survived, the Tarantans were surprised. "In due course," John Ayto notes in *The Dictionary of Word Origins*, "the dancing came to be rationalized as a method of counteracting the effects of the spider's bite, and so the dance was named the *tarantella*."

Italians don't dance away their spider bites anymore, but they still have a lively folk dance called the *tarantella*.

THE AUSTRALIAN FLAG

A little bit like the U.K.'s and an awful lot like New Zealand's, our Australian flag is a hotch-potch of different cultures. So should we add a kangaroo to it? Or maybe ditch the Union Jack? And why are there only six stars?

A LITTLE BACKGROUND
After Australia's federation in 1901 (when the six self-governing colonies were united under one federal government), the Australian flag was chosen following a nation-wide competition. Over 30,000 designs were received and the winners were five finalists with identical designs, including a 14-year-old boy called Ivor Evans.

When designing the flag, young Ivor wanted to maintain Australia's links with the past, so he chose the Union Jack to represent our ties with England. At the same time he also wanted to include the Southern Cross because he liked the idea that it was the brightest constellation in the Southern Hemisphere and thought it reflected Australia's bright future. Awww, how sweet! Young Ivor scored a cool 200 pounds for his troubles—an absolute fortune in those days and the equivalent of four years' wages!

WHAT DOES IT ALL MEAN

• The famous Union Jack (in the top left-hand corner of our flag) shows Australia's ties to Great Britain.

• The five white stars on the right represent the stars of the Southern Cross, a constellation that can be seen in the Australian night sky.

• The big white star under the Union Jack is known as the Star of Federation. It has seven points, one each for the six states plus one for the territories of Australia.

THE GREAT FLAG DEBATE
Should we keep it or ditch it? Should we adopt the aboriginal flag or design a new one with a whacking big kangaroo on it? Over the past 15 years, more than 50,000 original designs for a new flag have been put forward. This goes to show that a lot of people are

---

Longest word in Japanese: Chi-n-chi-ku-ri-n. It means "very short person."

keen for a change! Yet others are still very attached to our old one. It's a touchy subject and you can rest assured you haven't heard the last of it yet!

Some of the suggestions...

• Adopt the aboriginal flag or incorporate parts of it into a new Australian flag. The aboriginal flag is black at the top (representing the people) and red at the bottom (representing the earth) and has a large yellow sun in the middle linking the two halves together. It's a popular choice by indigenous Australians.

• The winner of the Peoples' Vote in the 1998 Ausflag Professional Design Competition was a Qantas-type big yellow Skippy the kangaroo hopping from one side of the flag to the other towards a big white star on a sky-blue and red background. It's a great design and even passes the cringe test!

• Adopt the famous 'Boxing Kangaroo' flag—a reflection of Australia's love of sport! With the bottom half green and the top half gold with a mean-looking kangaroo in the middle wearing red boxing gloves, this would be a popular choice with most sporting fans—Aussie, Aussie, Aussie, Oi, Oi, Oi!

* * *

A UNIQUE BUSINESS CONCEPT

Entrepreneur: Jun Sato, a 25-year-old man who lost his job in the recession that plagued Japan in the late 1990s
Idea: The Three-minute Beating
Description: Frustrated by his inability to find another job and figuring others were as exasperated by the economic downturn as he was, Sato made up his own job: He dresses up in protective padding, and lets passersby beat him (with boxing gloves) for three minutes at a time. Price: $1,000 yen, or about $10. "I enjoy being used as a punching bag," he told the Reuters news service, "It's another way to experience life."

THE CURSE
OF DRACULA

*In every film about Dracula, there's a curse. But did the curse extend
beyond the screen…and actually affect the people involved with
bringing the character to life? Don't dismiss the idea. Read
these stories…and then decide.*

Horace Liveright. The stage producer who brought *Dracula*—and later *Frankenstein*—to America made a
fortune doing it. But he was a terrible businessman and
spent money as fast as it came in. He made more than $2 million
on *Dracula* alone, but was so slow to pay author Bram Stoker's
widow, Florence, the royalties she was due that he lost control of
the stage rights in a dispute over a delinquent payment…of a mere
$678.01. He died drunk, broke, and alone in New York in
September 1933.

Helen Chandler. She was only 20 when she signed on to play the
female lead Mina Murray in the 1931 film version of *Dracula*, but
she was already close to the end of her film career. It was tragically
shortened by a bad marriage and addictions to alcohol and sleeping pills. By the mid-1930s she was no longer able to find work in
Hollywood, and in 1940 she was committed to a sanitarium. Ten
years later she was severely burned after smoking and drinking in
bed, in what may have been a suicide attempt. She died in 1965.

Dwight Frye. In the 1931 film, Frye played Renfield, the character who goes insane after meeting Dracula and spends the rest of
the movie as Dracula's slave. He performed so well in that part
that he was offered a similar role in the movie version of *Frankenstein*, as Dr. Frankenstein's hunchback assistant Igor.

Unfortunately for him, he took it—and was promptly typecast
as the monster's/mad scientist's assistant for the rest of his career.
He didn't get a chance to play any other type of role until 1944,
when he was cast as the Secretary of War in the film *Wilson*. Not
long after he won the part, Frye had a heart attack on a Los
Angeles bus and died before he was able to appear in the film.

Carl Laemmle, Jr. As president of Universal Pictures, he did more than anyone else to establish Universal as the horror movie studio of the 1930s. He left the studio after it was sold in 1936 and tried to establish himself as an independent producer. He never succeeded. A notorious hypochondriac, Laemmle eventually did come down with a debilitating disease—multiple sclerosis—in the early 1960s. He died in 1979—40 years to the day after the death of his father.

Bela Lugosi. Worn out by years of playing Dracula in New York and on the road, Lugosi was already sick of the vampire character by the time he began work on the film version; the indignity of being paid less than his supporting cast only made things worse. Reporter Lillian Shirley recounted one incident that took place in Lugosi's dressing room between scenes:

> I was with him when a telegram arrived. It was from
> Henry Duffy, the Pacific Coast theatre impresario,
> who wanted Mr. Lugosi to play Dracula for sixteen
> weeks. "No! Not at any price," he yelled. "When I am
> through with this picture I hope never to hear of
> Dracula again. I cannot stand it…I do not intend that
> it shall possess me. No one knows what I suffer for
> this role."

But like a real vampire, Lugosi was trapped in his role. *Dracula* was a box-office smash when it premiered in 1931 and Universal, eager to repeat its success, offered Lugosi the part of the monster in Frankenstein. It was the first in a series of planned monster movie roles for Lugosi that Universal hoped would turn Lugosi into "the new Lon Chaney," man of a thousand monsters.

Stubborn Kind of Fellow
Foolishly, Lugosi turned down the role of the Frankenstein monster because there was no dialogue—Frankenstein spoke only in grunts—and the makeup would have obscured his features, which he feared would prevent fans from knowing that he was the one under all that makeup.

The role went instead to an unknown actor named William Henry Pratt…who changed his name to Boris Karloff and within a year eclipsed Lugosi to become Hollywood's most famous horror star of the 1930s.

It takes about 21 pounds of milk to make 1 pound of butter.

"Thereafter," David Skal writes in *V Is for Vampire*, "Lugosi was never able to negotiate a lucrative Hollywood contract. *Dracula* was the height of his Hollywood career, and also the beginning of its end." His last good role was as the monster keeper Igor in the 1939 film *Son of Frankenstein*, considered to be the finest performance of his entire career.

Count on Him

Lugosi played Count Dracula for a second and final time in the 1948 Universal film *Abbot and Costello Meet Frankenstein*, his last major-studio film. After that he was reduced to appearing in a string of low-budget films, including the Ed Wood film *Bride of the Monster* (1956). Wood also had cast Lugosi in his film *Plan 9 From Outer Space* (1958), but Lugosi died on August 16, 1956 (and was buried in full Dracula costume, cape, and makeup)...so Wood recycled some old footage of Lugosi and hired a stand-in, who covered his face with his cape so that viewers would think he was Lugosi. When he died, Lugosi left an estate valued at $2,900.

...LAST, BUT NOT LEAST

Florence Stoker. Mrs. Stoker was nearly broke when she sold Universal the movie rights to *Dracula*, a sale that, combined with the royalties from the novel and the London and American plays, enabled her to live in modest comfort for the rest of her life. But she never did get rich off of the property that would bring wealth to so many others. When she died in 1937, she left an estate valued at £6,913.

Then again, Mrs. Stoker may have been luckier than she knew: After her death it was discovered that when Bram Stoker was issued a copyright for *Dracula* in 1897, he or his agents neglected to turn over two copies of the work to the American copyright office as was required by law; and the Stoker estate failed to do so again in the 1920s when the copyright was renewed in the U.K. Since Stoker failed to comply with the requirements of the law, *Dracula* was technically in the public domain, which meant that anyone in the United States could have published the novel or adapted it into plays, movies or any other form without Mrs. Stoker's permission and without having to pay her a cent in royalties.

MR. MOONLIGHT

Some facts about our night-light in the sky, from astronomer (and BRI member) Richard Moeschl.

It takes 29 days, 12 hours, 44 minutes, and 3 seconds for the moon to go through all of its phases (from one full moon to the next). This is close to the length of a month—which is why the word *month* means "moon."

The light that comes from the moon is sunlight reflected off the moon's surface. It takes 1 1/4 seconds for the light to travel to Earth.

The moon is smaller than any planet in the solar system, but relative to the size of the planets they orbit, our moon is the largest of the moons.

The moon is 3,457 kilometres [2,160 miles] in diameter—about a quarter of the Earth's diameter.

If the Earth was as big as a fist, the moon would be the size of a stamp—placed 3 metres [10 feet] away.

The average temperature on the Moon is –175° to –165°C [–283° to 266°F].

Since the moon spins once on its axis every 27 1/3 days—the same amount of time it takes to go around the Earth once—we end up seeing only one side of the moon (about 59% of its surface).

The side of the moon we always see is called "the near side." The side we never see from Earth is "the far side." That's probably where Gary Larsen got the name of his comic strip.

There is no sound on the moon. Nor is there weather, wind, clouds, or colours at sunrise and sunset.

If you weigh 54 kilograms [120 pounds] on Earth, you would weigh 9 kilograms [20 pounds] on the Moon—1/6 of your Earth weight.

A 1-metre [3-foot] jump on Earth would carry you 5.7 metres [18 feet, 9 inches] on the moon.

Astronauts have brought over 382 kilograms [843 pounds] of moon samples back to Earth.

The moon is moving away from the Earth at the rate of about 3 millimetres [1/8 inch] a year.

The German language has about 185,000 words. French has less than 100,000.

THE WRITING ON THE WALL

At some time, all bathroom readers have found themselves in a public toilet with nothing to read. Your eye starts to wander…and then you spot—graffiti! Here's a tribute to that emergency reading material.

You might be surprised to learn that graffiti is not something new. The term comes from the Italian word for "scribbling"…and it was coined by archeologists to describe wall-writing found in ancient ruins. It has been discovered in the catacombs of Rome, the Tower of London, medieval English alehouses, and even Mayan pyramids.

Some of the earliest examples of graffiti were preserved on the walls of Pompeii when Mt. Vesuvius erupted in 79 A.D. As you can see from the following examples, it hasn't changed much in nearly 2,000 years:

Appolinaris, doctor to the Emperor Titus, had a crap here

NO ONE'S A HANDSOME FELLOW UNLESS HE HAS LOVED

Whoever loves, goes to hell. I want to break Venus' ribs with blows and deform her hips. If she can break my tender heart, why can't I hit her over the head?

HULLO, WE'RE WINESKINS

Artimetus got me pregnant

In Nuceria, near Porta Romana, is the district of Venus. Ask for Novellia Primigenia

He who sits here, read this before anything else: If you want to make love ask for Attice. The price is 16 asses.

LOVERS, LIKE BEES, ENJOY A LIFE OF HONEY

Wishful thinking

O Chius, I hope your ulcerous pustules reopen and burn even more than they did before

IN NUCERIA VOTE FOR LUCIUS MUNATIUS CAESARNINUS: HE IS AN HONEST MAN

Romula tarried here with Staphylus

Brain food: You can think 625 thoughts on the caloric energy of one Cheerio.

A RECORD OF HISTORY

People have been studying and collecting graffiti for centuries. Hurlo Thrumbo, an English publisher, put out the first printed collection in the 1700s. In the early 1900s, German sociologists collected scrawls from public toilets and turned them into the first academic study of graffiti. In America, the Kinsey researchers collected bathroom messages as part of their study of men's and women's sex habits. But it wasn't until the 1960s, when graffiti became an outlet for the counterculture and anti-Vietnam protest movement, that academics really started to pay attention.

Now these "scribblings" are regarded as important adjuncts to the "official" history of a culture. They provide a look at what the average person was thinking and give evidence of the social unrest, political trends, and inner psychology of a society.

COLLECTING INFO

After decades of study, experts have decided that graffiti fit into four major categories.

• **Identity graffitists:** Want to immortalize themselves or a part of their lives (a romance, an accomplishment)

• **Opinion or message graffitists:** Want to let the world know what they think: "UFOs are real—the Air Force doesn't exist."

• **Dialogue graffitists:** Talk back to other graffitists. "I've got what every woman wants"…(*underneath:*) "You must be in the fur coat business."

• **"Art" graffitists:** The most recent trend, with spray cans of paint used to create intricate designs signed with pseudonyms. Either vandalism or modern design, depending on your point of view.

THE GRAFFITI HERO

The most famous graffitist in history was Kilroy. Beginning in World War II, the line "Kilroy was here" started showing up in outrageous places. Kilroy left his signature on the top of the torch of the Statue of Liberty, on the Marco Polo Bridge in China, and even on a Bikini atoll where an atomic bomb was to be tested. The original Kilroy was an infantry soldier who was sick of hearing the Air Force brag about always being first on the spot. But the phrase has appeared for so many years in so many places that "Kilroy was here" has become synonymous with graffiti.

The water we drink is 3 billion years old.

MORE WRITING ON THE WALL

A sampling of contemporary graffiti, collected since the 1960s.

Q: How do you tell the sex of a chromosome?
A: Pull down its genes.

If Love is blind, and God is love, and Ray Charles is blind, then God plays the piano.

Mafia: Organized Crime
Government: Disorganized Crime

Flush twice, it's a long way to Washington.

Death is just nature's way of telling you to slow down.

How come nobody ever writes on the toilet seats?

Things are more like they are now than they have ever been before.

I can't stand labels, after all, I'm a liberal.

Although the moon is smaller than the earth, it's farther away.

Free Chile!
...Free tacos!
...Free burritos!

Only Jackie knows what her Onassis worth.

Did you ever feel like the whole world was a white wedding gown, and you were a pair of muddy hiking boots?

Standing room only. [written on top of a men's urinal]

The chicken is an egg's way of producing another egg.

If you think you have someone eating out of your hands, it's a good idea of count your fingers.

The typical Stanford undergrad is like a milkshake: thick and rich.

Blessed is he who sits on a bee, for he shall rise again.

Please remain seated during the entire program.
　　　—The Management

There are those who shun elitism. Why?
...Because it is there.
...It's the elitist thing to do.

Please do not throw cigarette butts in the toilet, as they become hard to light.

You can lead a horticulture, but you can't make her think.

A light-year (the distance light travels in a year) is about 6 trillion miles.

MOTHERS OF INVENTION

*There have always been women inventors—even if they've
been overlooked in history books. Here are a few
you may not have heard of.*

MELITTA BENTZ, *a housewife in Dresden, Germany*
Invention: Drip coffeemakers
Background: At the beginning of the 20th century, people made coffee by dumping a cloth bag full of coffee grounds into boiling water. It was an ugly process—the grounds inevitably leaked into the water, leaving it gritty and bitter.

One morning in 1908, Frau Bentz decided to try something different: she tore a piece of blotting paper (used to mop up after runny fountain pens) from her son's schoolbook and put it in the bottom of a brass pot she'd poked with holes. She put coffee on top of the paper and poured boiling water over it. It was the birth of "drip" coffeemakers—and the Melitta company. Today, Melitta sells its coffeemakers in 150 countries around the world.

LADY ADA LOVELACE, *daughter of British poet Lord Byron*
Invention: Computer programming
Background: The forerunner of modern computers—called the "analytical engine"—was the brainchild of a mathematical engineer named George Babbage. In 1834 Babbage met Lady Lovelace, and the two formed a partnership, working together on the engine's prototype. In the process, Lovelace created the first programming method, which used punch cards. Unfortunately, tools available to Babbage and Lovelace in the mid-1800s weren't sophisticated enough to complete the machine (though it worked in theory). Lovelace spent the rest of her life studying cybernetics.

LADY MARY MONTAGU, *a British noblewoman*
Invention: smallpox vaccine
Background: In 1717, while travelling in Turkey, she observed a curious custom known as *ingrafting*. Families would call for the services of old women, who would bring nutshells full of "virulent"—live smallpox—to a home. Then it would be "ingrafted" into a patient's open vein. The patient would spend a few days in bed with a slight illness but was rendered immune to smallpox.

The biggest pumpkin ever recorded weighed 884 pounds.

This technique was unknown in England, where 30% of smallpox victims died. Montagu convinced Caroline, Princess of Wales, to try it on her own daughters. When it worked, she anonymously published *The Plain Account of the Inoculating of the Small-pox by a Turkish Merchant.* Despite vehement opposition from the church and medical establishments, the idea took hold. Lady Montagu lived to see England's smallpox death rate drop to 2%.

MARGARET KNIGHT, *an employee of the Columbia Paper Bag Company in the late 1800s*

Invention: The modern paper bag

Background: Knight grew so tired of making paper bags by hand that she began experimenting with machines that could make them automatically. She came up with one that made square-bottomed, folding paper bags (until then, paper sacks all had V-shaped bottoms). But her idea was stolen by a man who'd seen her building her prototype. A court battle followed in which the main argument used against Knight was her "womanhood." But she proved beyond a doubt that the invention was hers and received her patent in 1870. Knight was awarded 27 patents in her lifetime, but was no businesswoman—she died in 1914 leaving an estate of only $275.05.

BETTE NESMITH GRAHAM, *a secretary at the Texas Bank & Trust in Dallas in the early 1950s*

Invention: Liquid Paper

Background: Graham was a terrible typist…but when she tried to erase her mistakes, the ink on her IBM typewriter just smeared. One afternoon in 1951, while watching sign painters letter the bank's windows, she got a brilliant idea: "With lettering, an artist never corrects by erasing but always paints over the error. So I decided to use what artists use. I put some waterbase paint in a bottle and took my watercolour brush to the office. And I used that to correct my typing mistakes." So many other secretaries asked for bottles of "Mistake Out" that in 1956 she started a small business selling it. A year later, she changed the formula and founded Liquid Paper, Inc. In 1966 her son, Michael Nesmith, made more money as a member of the Monkees than she did with Liquid Paper. But in 1979, she sold her company to Gillette for $47 million.

The human brain can hold 500 times the info found in a set of the *Encyclopedia Britannica.*

MISSED IT BY *THAT MUCH*

Often success and disaster are a lot closer than we'd like to think. Here are some classic "near misses."

AN ASSASSINATION
Theodore Roosevelt: On October 14, 1912, the former president was on his way to give a speech in Milwaukee when a man named John Schrank drew a revolver, pointed it at Roosevelt, and pulled the trigger. Roosevelt staggered but didn't fall. No blood could be detected, but Roosevelt's handlers begged him to go to the hospital. He refused and delivered a 50-minute speech to a cheering throng. However, when he pulled the 100-page speech out of his vest, he noticed a bullet hole in it. It turned out that the bullet had ripped through the paper and penetrated 10 centimetres [4 inches] into Roosevelt's body, right below his right nipple. If the written speech hadn't slowed the bullet down, he would have been killed. After speaking, Roosevelt was treated for shock and loss of blood.

A PLACE IN HISTORY
Elisha Gray: Gray was an electrical genius who independently developed his own telephone. Incredibly, he filed a patent for the invention on February 14, 1876—the *exact same day* that Alexander Graham Bell did—but a few hours *after* Bell. "If Bell had been a few hours late," says one historian, "what we know of as the Bell System would have been the Gray System." Gray was successful with other inventions, but was bitter for the rest of his life about not receiving credit for the telephone.
James Swinburne: Leo Baekeland patented the first modern plastic on June 14, 1907; he called it "Bakelite." A day later, a Scottish electrical engineer named James Swinburne filed a patent for almost exactly the same thing. He'd been experimenting with the same chemicals on his own halfway around the world, and had come up with the substance completely independently. Unlike Gray, though, he made peace with his near-miss and wound up chairman of the Bakelite company.

In the 1600s in Europe, "fashion" wigs were often made of plaster of Paris.

A CAREER-ENDING "INJURY"

Frank Sinatra: "Gangster Sam Giancana once ordered a hit on Frank Sinatra. He was going to have Sinatra's throat cut to ruin his voice. But on the night the hit was supposed to go down, Giancana was enjoying an intimate moment with [his girlfriend] Phyllis McGuire, who played Sinatra records to heighten the romantic mood. After listening for a while, Giancana decided he couldn't in good conscience silence that voice. He cancelled the hit." (The Portland *Oregonian*, August 29, 1997)

MILITARY DEFEAT

George Washington: "On Christmas night, 1776, Washington was preparing to cross the Delaware with his army to attack the British. The commander of forces at Trenton, Colonel Rall, was German. He was drinking and playing cards when he received a note from a British loyalist warning him of the attack. But the note was in English, which Rall couldn't read, and he was groggy anyway, so he put it in his pocket. At dawn, Washington attacked and because the British were unprepared, he won. As Rall lay dying on the battlefield, the note was translated into German and Rall admitted if he'd read it, 'I would not be here.'" (From *Oh Say Can You See?*)

THE PRESIDENCY

John Janney: "In 1840, Janney was Chairman of the Whig Party Convention in Virginia. This convention nominated William Henry Harrison for President. John Janney and John Tyler were the nominees for Vice President. When the vote of the convention was a tie, Janney, as Chairman, did the "honourable" thing and voted for Tyler. Harrison won the election but died soon after, and John Tyler became President. John Janney lost the presidency by one vote—his own." (From *Dear Abby*, December 17, 1996)

Sen. Ben Wade: When Lincoln was shot in 1865, Andrew Johnson became president. In 1867 the Republican Congress tried to impeach him, but was one vote shy of the two-thirds majority needed to remove him from office. Wade, as president of the Senate, would have become the 18th American president. He became the second man in history to miss the U.S. presidency by one vote.

World record: On September 26, 1970, John Kenmuir licked 393 stamps in four minutes.

THE RUBBISH BIN
OF HISTORY

*Think your heroes will go down in history for something they've done?
Don't count on it. These folks were VIPs in their time…but they're
forgotten now. They've been swept into the Rubbish Bin of History.*

FORGOTTEN FIGURE: Fanny Elssler, Viennese ballerina
CLAIM TO FAME: A superstar of the 1840s, Elssler
toured America for two years and inspired what newspapers
referred to as "Elssler Mania." Wherever she went, "The Divine
Fanny" drew hordes of admirers. They rioted outside her hotel in
New York and mobbed her carriage in Baltimore. In Washington,
Congress adjourned so law-makers wouldn't miss her performance.
Poems and songs were written about her. At the end of her tour,
she went back to Europe and (as far as we know) never returned.

FORGOTTEN FIGURE: Peter Francisco, American soldier
CLAIM TO FAME: Every war has its working-class heroes. During the Revolutionary War, this 19-year-old, known as the
"strongest man in the Colonies" and "the American Samson," was
the people's favourite. They told stories of Private Francisco's
exploits—like the time in 1780, during retreat, when he "lifted a
1,100-pound [500-kilogram] cannon and carried it to the rear";
the time when he was ordered by a British cavalryman to drop his
musket and he used his bayonet to "lift the hapless horseman from
the saddle"; the time in 1781 at Guilford Courthouse when, "with
his thigh laid open by a bayonet, Francisco chopped down 11
British troops before collapsing." By the end of the war, he had
become the most famous regular soldier in the Continental Army.
After the war, he was rewarded with a job as sergeant at arms for
the Virginia legislature.

FORGOTTEN FIGURE: Belva Ann Lockwood (née Bennett),
pioneering crusader for women's rights
CLAIM TO FAME: One historian writes: "Lockwood's entire
career was a living example of women's potential, even in the stifling atmosphere of the 19th century." In 1873, at age 43, she

became an attorney; and in 1879, she was the first woman to plead a case before the United States Supreme Court. She persuaded male law-makers in Washington to pass a bill awarding equal pay to women employed by the federal government. In 1884 and 1888, she ran for President as the candidate of the National Equal Rights Party and won Indiana's electoral votes—something no woman candidate has done since (at least, not yet).

FORGOTTEN FIGURE: Dr. Mary Edwards Walker, Civil War soldier, the only woman to receive the Congressional Medal of Honour

CLAIM TO FAME: Achieved national prominence during the Civil War, serving as a nurse and later as a spy and surgeon (she was the first woman to hold a medical commission). In the field she dressed like male officers, wearing gold-striped trousers, a felt hat encircled with gold braid, and an officer's greatcoat. She always wore her hair in curls, though, so that "everyone would know that I was a woman." For her service to the sick and wounded, President Andrew Johnson awarded Walker the Congressional Medal of Honour; she was the first and only woman in history thus recognized.

"Immediately after the war," writes one historian, "her attire was so notorious that she was arrested on several occasions for 'masquerading as a man.' However, Walker was never prosecuted, since a grateful Congress had passed a special act granting her the right to wear trousers, in recognition of her wartime services."

Walker avidly campaigned for women's political rights…and for their right to wear pants. She also campaigned against cigarettes; she always carried an umbrerlla "with which she batted offending cigarettes from the mouths of startled men."

She wore her medal proudly, but in 1917, when Walker was 85, a government review board revoked it (along with the medals of 911 other Civil War veterans) on the grounds that "nothing in the records show the specific act or acts for which the decoration was originally awarded." When asked by the Army to return her medal, she replied, "Over my dead body!" "She wore the medal every day, and was wearing it when she took a bad fall on the Capitol steps" on her way to petition Congress for one of her reform causes. A few months later she died…and when she was buried, the medal was still pinned securely to her Prince Albert coat.

The fingerprints of humans and koalas are virtually identical.

BOND ON FILM

Sean Connery is so closely associated with the role of James Bond that it's hard to believe he was initially a longshot for the part. Here's the story of how Ian Fleming's 007 thrillers found their way onto film.

BOND-AGE FILMS
In the late 1950s Albert R. "Cubby" Broccoli and Harry Saltzman, two movie producers, teamed up to turn Ian Fleming's Bond novels into action films. *Thunderball* was their choice for the first Bond film, but it was tied up in a lawsuit between Fleming and some other writers. So they settled on *Dr. No*. They shopped the idea around to every film studio in Hollywood...and were rejected by nearly everyone. Finally, United Artists agreed to back the film—as long as they didn't have to spend a lot of money. *Dr. No's* budget was set at a paltry $1 million.

Casting Call
The first task was to find the right James Bond. Broccoli and Saltzman knew what kind of actor they were looking for: a top-notch British performer who was willing to work for low-budget wages, and who would commit to making several sequels (in the unlikely event that *Dr. No* was successful).

But as Broccoli and Saltzman quickly realized, no actor like that existed. Broccoli's friend Cary Grant was one of the first people to say no; many others followed. Stage actor Patrick McGoohan rejected the role on moral grounds (too violent); and up-and-coming British actor Richard Johnson refused to commit to a multipicture deal, fearing it would hurt his career. (Both men later ended up playing James Bond knock-offs on TV and in film.) Ian Fleming suggested either David Niven or Roger Moore; Niven wasn't interested, and Moore was already committed to *The Saint*, a TV detective/spy series.

SERENDIPITY
Not long after it was announced that Dr. No was being made into a film, the *Daily Express*, which ran the James Bond comic strip, held a readers' poll to see who should be cast as Bond. The winner was Sean Connery, a little-known Scottish actor and former Mr.

Universe contestant. Connery was beginning to build a following in Great Britain, and had recently been interviewed by the paper.

At about the same time, Cubby Broccoli and his wife saw the Disney film *Darby O'Gill and the Little People*, in which Connery played a "farmer and country bumpkin." Neither of the Broccolis was particularly impressed with Connery's acting, but Cubby Broccoli liked his accent, and Mrs. Broccoli thought he had the raw sex appeal that the Bond part needed.

Coincidentally, a short time later, film editor Peter Hunt sent Broccoli several reels of a film he was working on called *Operation Snafu*, with the recommendation that one of the stars—Sean Connery again—would make a great Bond.

TOUGH GUY

Connery's career prior to the Bond films was nothing to brag about, but he still played hard to get. When Broccoli asked him to test for the part, he refused, telling Broccoli "Either take me as I am or not at all."

"He pounded the desk and told us what he wanted," Broccoli recounted years later. "What impressed us was that he had balls." The producers finally tricked him into auditioning on film by telling him they were experimenting with camera setups.

Mr. Right

Connery came from a working-class background and he showed up at the audition wearing grubby clothes, but by the time he finished his screen test Broccoli and Saltzman knew the search for Eton-educated Bond was over. "He walked like he was Superman," Broccoli recalled, "and I believed we had to go along with him. The difference between him and the other young actors was like the difference between a still photo and film. We knew we had our Bond." Connery remembers getting the part somewhat less romantically:

> Originally, they were considering all sorts of stars to play James Bond. Trevor Howard was one. Rex Harrison was another. The character was to be a shining example of British upper-crust elegance, but they couldn't afford a major name. Luckily, I was available at a price they could afford.

Casting an unknown in the lead part did not go down well at

the studio—one executive rejected him and told the producers to,
"see if you can do better." Connery did not impress Ian Fleming,
either. "I'm looking for Commander James Bond," he complained,
"not an overgrown stuntman." But Connery stayed.

THE BOND THEME

Composer Monty Norman created the musical score for *Dr. No*,
and while Broccoli and Saltzman were happy with his work on the
rest of the film, they didn't like his theme song. So they hired a
new composer named John Barry. They told him they needed a
song exactly 2-1/2 minutes long to fit into the soundtrack where
the old song had gone. Without even seeing the film, Barry composed the "James Bond Theme," one of the most recognizable
themes in Hollywood history. He was paid £200 for his effort.

BOND MANIA

Dr. No premiered in 1962 and was a smash hit. The film earned
huge returns for Broccoli, Saltzman, and United Artists and
launched the most successful film series in history. By 1997 a total
of 20 Bond films had been made, including seven with Sean Connery, one with George Lazenby, one with David Niven, seven with
Roger Moore, two with Timothy Dalton, and two with Pierce
Brosnan, who signed on for two more through the 21st century.

    Dr. No and the second Bond film, *From Russia with Love*, also
launched a "Bond mania" complete with 007 toys, board games,
spy kits, decoder rings, cartoons, toiletries, clock radios, and even
lingerie. The fad peaked in 1965, but continued well into the
1970s, inspiring numerous TV knock-offs such as *The Man from
U.N.C.L.E.*, *I Spy*, and *The Avengers*.

For the Boys

But the success of *Dr. No* went beyond launching a spy fad or a
film series, as Suzanna Andrews writes in the *New York Times*.

> *Dr. No* also marked the beginning of the big-budget
> "boy" movies that today dominate the film industry,
> movies marked by action, special effects, and, men
> who never fail. In spirit and style, Bond is godfather
> to such movies as *Lethal Weapon* and *Die Hard*, and
> many films that star Sylvester Stallone or Arnold
> Schwarzenegger.

UNTIMELY END

James Bond's creator, Ian Fleming, did not live to see the full impact of the genre he created: In 1964, after only two Bond films had been completed, he died from a massive heart attack brought on by years of heavy drinking and a 70-cigarette-a-day smoking habit. He was 56.

In his lifetime Fleming earned nearly $3 million in book royalties; but his heirs would lose out on many of the profits his work generated after he died. Less than a month before his death, Fleming, who suspected the end was near, sold 51% of his interest in the James Bond character to reduce the inheritance taxes on his estate. He collected only $280,000, even though it was worth millions.

* * * * *

FOOD NOTES

Ian Fleming made James Bond into a connoisseur of fine wine, women, weapons, and food, but Fleming's own tastes left a lot to be desired, especially when it came to food. As his friend and neighbour on Jamaica, Noel Coward, recounted years later,

> Whenever I ate with Ian at Goldeneye (Fleming's Jamaican hideaway) the food was so abominable I used to cross myself before I took a mouthful....I used to say, "Ian, it tastes like armpits." And all the time you were eating there was old Ian smacking his lips for more while his guests remembered all those delicious meals he had put into the books.

BOND'S FIRST MARTINI

> "A dry Martini," [Bond] said. "One. In a deep champagne goblet." "Oui, Monsieur."
>
> "Just a moment. Three measures of Gordon's, one of vodka, half a measure of Kina Lillet. Shake it very well until it's ice cold, then add a large thin slice of lemon peel. Got it?"
>
> "Certainly, Monsieur." The barman seemed pleased with the idea.
>
> —*Casino Royale*, 1953

As a boy, young Ian Fleming also gave his mother the nickname "M."

THE DISCOVERY OF THE PLANETS

As early as kindergarten, we're taught that there are nine planets. but 200 years ago, even scholars were sure there were only six planets. Here's how we got the three new ones.

THE END OF THE SOLAR SYSTEM

People have always known about Mercury, Venus, Mars, Jupiter, and Saturn. Early civilizations named the days of the week after each of these planets, plus the sun and moon. The Greeks watched them move through the night sky, passing in front of the stars that make up the constellations of the zodiac, and called them *planetes*—which means "wanderers."

As recently as the 1700s, people still believed that the planet Saturn was at the farthest extent of the solar system. That there might be other planets wasn't even a respectable idea. But as technology and science became more sophisticated, other members of the solar system were discovered.

URANUS

In 1781 a self-taught astronomer, William Herschel, was "sweeping the skies" with his telescope. By March, he had reached the section that included the constellation Gemini, and he spotted an object that appeared as a disk rather than a glowing star. Because it moved slightly from week to week, Herschel thought it was circular...and came to the shocking conclusion that it wasn't a comet, but an unknown planet. People were astonished.

Finding a Name

No one since ancient times had named a planet. Herschel felt that it should be called "Georgium Sidus" (George's Star) in honour of his patron, George III—the king of England who reigned during the American Revolution. Some people wanted to name it "Herschel" after its discoverer. But one influential astronomer suggested they call it "Uranus," after the Greek god of the heavens. That made sense, since this new planet was certainly the limit of the skies of the solar system. Or so they thought.

In 1995, 8,000 kids were poisoned by eating cigarette butts.

NEPTUNE

The newly found planet had a slight variation in its orbit, almost as if something were tugging at it. Could there be another planet affecting Uranus? A century earlier, Isaac Newton had come up with laws describing the effects that the gravitational forces of planets have on one another. Using Newton's laws, two young scientists set out independently in 1840 to find the unknown planet whose gravitational forces might be pulling on Uranus. One of the scientists was a French mathematician, Jean Leverrier. The other was an English astronomer, John Couch Adams. Both hoped the unknown planet would be where their calculations said they could find it.

The Hidden Planet

Adams finished his calculations first, in September 1845. The following August, Leverrier completed his. Neither had access to a large telescope, so they couldn't verify their projections—and no one would make one available to them. Finally, Leverrier travelled to the Berlin Observatory in Germany, and the young assistant manager, Johann Gottfried Galle, agreed to help search for the planet.

That was September 23, 1846. That night, Galle looked through the telescope, calling out stars and their positions while a young student astronomer, Heinrich Louis d'Arrest, looked at a star chart, seaching for the stars Galle described. Finally Galle called out an eighth-magnitude star that d'Arrest couldn't locate on the charts. They had found the unknown planet! It had taken two years of research—but only a half hour at the telescope. The honour of the discovery belongs to both Adams and Leverrier, who had essentially discovered the new planet with just a pen and a new set of mathematical laws. The greenish planet was named after Neptune, god of the sea.

VULCAN

Leverrier was on a roll. He started looking for other planets...and became convinced that there was one between the Sun and Mercury. He called his planet "Vulcan," the god of fire, because it was so close to the Sun. Leverrier noted that, like Uranus, Mercury experienced disturbances that caused it to travel farther in one point in its orbit. Since Neptune was one of the causes of similar pulls on Uranus, it made sense that another planet was affecting Mercury.

Leverrier never found Vulcan, but people believed it was there until 1916, when Einstein's general theory of relativity was published. Einstein gave a satisfactory explanation for the discrepancies in Mercury's orbit, so scientists no longer needed Vulcan. It thereby ceased to exist...until decades later, when Gene Roddenberry, creator of *Star Trek,* appropriated the planet and made it the home of Spock.

PLUTO

The discovery of Neptune did not completely account for the peculiar movements of Uranus. Once again, scientists considered the pull of another planet as a cause and set out to find "Planet X." Using the telescope at his observatory in Flagstaff, Arizona, Percival Lowell searched for Planet X for 10 years. After he died in 1916, his brother gave the observatory a donation that enabled it to buy a telescope-camera. The light-sensitive process of photography allowed astronomers to capture images of dim and distant stars that they couldn't see, even with the aid of a telescope.

In 1929 the Lowell Observatory hired Clyde Tombaugh, a young self-taught astronomer from Kansas, to continue the search for Planet X. Lowell had suggested that the unknown planet was in the Gemini region of the sky. Using an instrument called the blink microscope, Tombaugh took two photographs of that area of the sky a few days apart and placed them side by side under the microscope. If something moved in the sky, as planets do, it would appear as a speck of light jumping back and forth as Tombaugh's eyes moved from one photograph to the other, looking through the microscope.

That's just what happened. The observatory announced the discovery of the ninth planet on March 13, 1930. An 11-year-old girl, the daughter of an Oxford astronomy professor, chose the name Pluto—the god of the underworld—for the new planet.

For years before his death, Tombaugh repeatedly declared that there were no more planets in our solar system. If there were, he said, he would have found them.

OOPS!

More goofs, blunders, and dumb mistakes.

CHURCH MUSIC

"A funeral in 1996 in an English church ended with Rod Stewart singing:

> If you want my body,
> And you think I'm sexy,
> C'mon baby let me know.

The vicar admitted that when he was recording the deceased's last request—a hymn—he'd apparently failed to erase the entire cassette tape."

—*Fortean Times*, 1996

UNPLUGGED

"In 1978 workers were sent to dredge a murky stretch of the Chesterfied-Stockwith Canal. Their task was to remove all the rubbish and leave the canal clear.... They were disturbed during their tea-break by a policeman who said he was investigating a giant whirlpool in the canal. When they got back, however, the whirlpool had gone...and so had a 1 1/2-mile [2.4-kilometre] stretch of the canal.... A flotilla of irate holidaymakers were stranded on their boats in brown sludge.

Among the first pieces of junk the workers had hauled out had been the 200-year-old plug that ensured the canal's continued existence. 'We didn't know there was a plug,' said one bewildered workman.... All the records had been lost in a fire during the war."

—*The Book of Heroic Failures*, by Stephen Pile

YIKES!

"Defense lawyer Phillip Robertson, trying to make a dramatic point in front of the jury at his client's recent robbery trial in Dallas [Texas, USA] pointed the pistol used in the crime at the jury box, causing two jurors to fling their arms in front of their faces and others to gasp. Though Robertson was arguing that his client should be sentenced only to probation, the horrified jury gave him 13 years."

— "The Edge," in the *Portland Oregonian*, September 10, 1997

THE WRONG NOTE

"A 61-year-old woman and her daughter made a deposit at the drive-up window of an Albuquerque, New Mexico, bank Thursday, and were waiting for a receipt when police cars surrounded them and officers ordered them out of their vehicle at gunpoint. It turned out the New Mexico grandmother had accidentally held up the bank; she'd handed in a deposit slip on which a prankster had scrawled a hold-up message. The FBI said investigators believe someone wrote the note on the deposit slip and left it in a pile inside the bank, where the woman picked it up and used it, unaware of what was written on the back."

—*Washington Post,* May 24, 1997

A PAIR OF BIRDBRAINS

"Each evening, birdlover Neil Symmons stood in his backyard in Devon, England, hooting like an owl—and one night, an owl called back to him.

"For a year, the man and his feathered friend hooted back and forth. Symmons even kept a log of their 'conversations.'

"Just as Symmons thought he was on the verge of a breakthrough in interspecies communication, his wife had a chat with next-door neighbour Wendy Cornes.

"My husband spends his night in the garden calling out to owls,' said Mrs. Symmons.

"'That's odd,' Mrs. Cornes replied. 'So does my Fred.'

"And then it dawned on them."

— **"The Edge,"** in the *Portland Oregonian,*
August 29, 1997

GOVERNMENT EFFICIENCY

"In 1977, a government clerk in Australia made a slight error in paperwork. As a result, a $300,000 police headquarters was built in St. Arnaud's (population 3,000) instead of in St. Alban's (population 40,000). Part of the new construction was a 50-car parking lot. It is currently being used by the two cars and two bicycles of the St. Arnaud's police department."

—*Encyclopedia Brown's Book of Facts,* by Donald Sobol

FAIR GO, OZ

*"He's got kangaroos in the top paddock" (crazy) may not be
understood by a visitor who is "short of a sheet of bark" (dense)
or who "has come down in the last shower" (naive).*

A visitor would be "flat out like a lizard drinking" to absorb
Australia's colourful language. At first they might feel as
lost as "an orphan bandicoot on a burnt ridge" or "all
alone like a country dunny." Words like "fair go," "digger," and
"furphy" have been in circulation for nearly a century. New words
like "Australian salute" and "un-Australian" are likely to stay for
centuries. Some words like "Sydney-sider" and "larrikin" have
made a U-turn in meaning.

FAIR GO
Meaning: exhortation to reasonableness and tolerance.
History: Australia's most loved saying, its credo, started with a
favourite gambling game, now illegal except in casinos. Before
the spin of the coins for the game of Two-up, the ringmaster called
"All set—a fair go." First recorded in 1911.
Usage: "Give him a fair go, Wally, it's not his fault he is born
stupid."

DIGGER
Meaning: ANZAC soldier
History: A name given to goldminers in Victoria about 1850.
Also used for New Zealand kauri gum diggers who served in World
War I. In 1917 it is recorded as meaning any ANZAC (Australia
and New Zealand Army Corps) private. They were also called
"dinkums." Their strong spirit and mateship in war earned them
mythical hero status.
Usage: "They're good blokes, diggers, they saved this country.
Don't you go knockin' them."

AUSTRALIAN SALUTE
Meaning: movement of the hand slowly backwards and forwards
in front of the face to brush away flies—usually unsuccessful.
History: Recorded use from 1972.
Usage: Most often viewed when politicians make big statements

---

The most widely used surname in the world is Li. About 87 million people have it.

on television in the outback. "That galah pollie, all he can do out here in the bush is make an Aussie salute." (Politicians, by the way, are keen idiomatic speakers, accusing one another of "having more front than a round house," of being too feeble "to go two rounds with a revolving door," or of having integrity as "scarce as rocking horse shit.")

FURPHY
Meaning: rumour or false report.
History: From gossip around the water-carts in early Victorian history. First recorded use is in 1915. The manufacturer's name, J. Furphy & Sons Pty. Ltd. of Shepparton, was emblazoned on the carts. John Furphy was a strong Methodist who last century inscribed the tanks with the saying "Good better best, never let it rest, until your good is good and your better best." The company is now run by Furphy's fifth-generation descendants and still makes water-tanks on wheels—for fire fighting.
Usage: "The story my mate told about the cyclone being so strong it bent the beam of his torch isn't a furphy—I was there!" (For more examples consult any edition of Hansard; the pollies love to use it!)

LARRIKIN
Meaning (1890s): petty thug, criminal, member of a rowdy street gang.
History: From British dialect in Cornwall and Worcestershire— "larrikan" meaning mischievous youngster. Today it has the complimentary meaning of a spirited extrovert who has little time for the niceties of society.
Usage (today): "Geez, he's a funny bastard. He's a real larrikin and he can tell some ripper yarns."

SYDNEY-SIDER
Meaning (historical): A convict.
History: There never were any convicts sent to Victoria after its separation from New South Wales, while Sydney was originally a convict settlement. It was therefore natural to talk of a convict, as late as 1892, as being on the Sydney-side.
Usage (today): "You can always flatter a Sydney-sider, mate. Just tell him he comes from a bigger and better city than Melbourne."

WEIRD GAME SHOWS

According to experts, the most important aspect of a game show is…the game. So what were the designers of these ridiculous shows thinking?

TV Champions (Japan). A different bizarre contest each week. One week contestants chug "rancid, evil-smelling soy bean gruel," another week they "allow themselves to be locked in cages and sworn at."

The Game of the Goose (Spain). Contestants move around a game board; each space represents a different challenge. One challenge: release a semi-nude model from an exploding bed. Another: try to escape from a box that's slowly filling with sand.

Dream House (U.S.). Young married couples move from room to room, competing to win furniture. Grand prize: An entire mobile home, "put anywhere in the USA."

Finders Keepers (U.S.). "Each day, the show is filmed on location at a different contestant's house. The film crew hides a prize in the contestant's living room, sets up cameras, and then lets viewers watch the contestant tear the room apart looking for it."

Italian Stripping Housewives (Italy). "A strange game show takeoff on strip poker. Wives strip while their husbands gamble."

100 Grand (U.S.). Hollywood's response to the quiz show scandals of the 1950s: Contestants spend part of the show in an isolation booth writing their own questions. Amazingly, the first time the show aired, one contestant missed every single question. *"100 Grand* aired twice before sinking into oblivion."

Endurance (Japan). "Contestants are literally tortured. One of the stunts, for example, involves dragging contestants across gravel until they are injured." In another, they crawl through a cage of scorpions. When a contestant fails, the studio audience shouts, "Go Home!"

Gonzo Games (U.S.). A gentler version of Endurance. "Overanxious contestants vie to see, for instance, who can attach the most clothespins to their face." In another test of strength, "contestants stand on a barbecue grill until the pain forces them off."

The market value of the raw materials in a 170-lb. man's body, at 1997 prices: About $25.

GREAT MOMENTS IN TELEPHONE HISTORY

Everyone's got a telephone—but it seems the only thing anyone knows about it is that Alexander Graham Bell invented it. In our Encyclopedia Bathroomica, we talk about how the phone works. Here's a little history to go along with it.

FEB. 14, 1876. Beating a competing inventor by only a few hours, Alexander Graham Bell arrives at the U.S. patent office and patents the telephone in his name. Three days later, he builds the first telephone that actually works. Hoping to earn a page in the history books, he memorizes lines from Shakespeare to use in the world's first telephone conversation. But when the magic moment arrives, he spills acid on himself and barks out "Mr. Watson, come here. I want you."

Fall 1876. Bell offers to sell the rights to his invention to the Western Union Telegraph Co. for $100,000. He is laughed out of the office.

• Stage fright becomes a significant obstacle in expanding telephone sales. To reassure the public, Bell takes out ads claiming that "Conversations can be easily carried on after slight practice and with occasional repetitions of a word or sentence."

1877. Charles Williams of Somerville, Massachusetts, becomes the first American to install a telephone in his house. (But since no one else had a phone, he couldn't call anyone. So he installed a telephone in his office, where his wife could reach him during the day.)

1877. A woman named Emma Nutt becomes the first female telephone operator in the United States. Initially the phone company preferred to hire young boys as operators, but eventually had to phase them out because of their foul language and penchant for practical jokes.

1879. In the middle of a measles epidemic in Lowell, Massachusetts, a physician, worried about what would happen if the town's operators succumbed to the disease, suggests to the local phone company that it begin issuing the nation's first phone numbers to telephone subscribers. At first the public resists the idea, attacking phone numbers as being too impersonal.

1881. Thomas Edison comes up with a new way to answer the telephone. "Originally," writes Margaret Cousins in *The Story of Thomas Edison,* "people wound the phone with a crank, which rang a bell, and then said: 'Are you there?' This took too much time for Edison. During one of the hundreds of tests made in his labouratory, he picked up the phone one day, twisted the crank and shouted: "Hello!" This became the way to answer the telephone all over [the world], and it still is."

* * * * *

GREAT MOMENTS IN EMERGENCY DIALLING

In 1995, a woman in Devizes, England, was awakened from a sound sleep by a phone ringing.

> Upon answering it, she was greeted by moans, groans, and yelling. The woman dismissed the call as a prank and hung up.
>
> A short while later the phone rang again. This time the woman heard outright screaming, followed by a female shouting, "Oh my God!" Terrified, the woman hung up. There was no mistaking it: the voice on the other end belonged to her daughter, who lived about a hundred miles away.

The woman phoned the police. They sent squad cars to the daughter's house, broke down the door, and stormed the bedroom.

> There they found the daughter making love to her boyfriend on the bed.
>
> Apparently, during two wild moments of passion, the daughter's big toe accidentally hit the speed-dial button on the phone, which was on a nightstand by the bed.
>
> "This is a warning for other people," a police spokesman said. "If you're going to indulge in that sort of thing, move the phone."

—Knuckleheads in the News

The average lightning bolt is only an inch in diameter.

THE LEANINGEST TOWER ON EARTH

*The Leaning Tower of Pisa is one of the most recognizable
buildings in the world, a visual symbol of Italy itself.
Here's a look at its unusual history.*

CIVIC RIVALRY
In 1155, builders in Venice, Italy, finished work on a bell tower next to the Cathedral of San Marco. Legend has it that citizens in the seaport town of Pisa—determined not to be outdone by the Venetians—decided to build their own bell tower next to the Cathedral of Pisa.

Work began in 1173. The plans called for a seven-storey marble tower with more than 200 columns, plus a belfry with seven large bells at the top. The building would be 56 metres [184 feet] tall but only 16 metres [52 feet] in diameter.

The entire building was supposed to stand on a foundation less than 683 metres [2240 feet] deep. But as it turned out, the ground—largely sandy soil and waterlogged clay—was too spongy to support it.

BACK AND FORTH
By the time the second floor was finished, the building had already begun leaning slightly to the north. But rather than start over, the builders just lengthened the northern walls on the third floor and shortened the southern ones, levelling off the top of the building in the process. That way, they figured, the rest of the building would be level, too.

STOP AND GO
As luck would have it, political unrest in Pisa forced builders to stop work on the building for 90 years. That meant the clay soil beneath the tower was allowed to compact and strengthen over time. Soil experts now believe that if it hadn't, the tower would have collapsed when the upper floors were added.

But they didn't. Six more storeys were successfully added between 1270 and 1278. This time, however, the added weight

---

The Elvis Presley hit "Hound Dog" was written in about ten minutes.

caused the building to lean to the *south*, the direction it still leans today. The builders applied the same solution to the fifth floor that they'd used on the third, only in reverse: they lengthened the southern walls and shortened the northern ones, giving the building a slight banana shape. Once again, the top was level.

FINAL ADDITION
Political unrest halted construction again, this time until 1360. By now the building was terribly off-centre, but builders added the belfry anyway—again making the southern walls taller than the northern ones, to level out the roof. One hundred and eighty-seven years after it was begun, the tower was finally finished.

But the tilt was only beginning. Over the next six centuries, the building moved a tiny amount each year. By the early 1990s, it was more than 4 metres [14 feet] off-centre.

SAVING THE TOWER
By 1990, the Leaning Tower of Pisa had already become one of the world's great tourist attractions. So the Italian government just appointed a commission to figure out how to keep it from falling over.

The commission wasn't much help—except to the government, which was able to take credit for actively trying to save the tower. After that, whenever scientists speculated that the tower was falling, the government just appointed another commission. The only one that had any lasting impact was the 1933 commission…which made things worse. They drilled 361 holes in the ground surrounding the tower and filled them with 1,800 tons of concrete. Instead of stabilizing the ground, the concrete added weight to the tower's foundation, causing it to tip six times faster.

THE FINAL FIX
In 1989, the Italian government appointed its 15th commission. This time, it actually helped. In 1992, scientists began implementing a three-phase plan to halt the tilting:
1. In April 1992, five steel bands were strapped around the second floor of the building (judged to be weakest part). The belts act like girdles—when a masonry building collapses at the base, the part that gives way bursts *outward*, not inward. The bands hold everything in place.

The single most common object involved in choking is toothpicks.

2. In the summer of 1993, scientists began placing 75 8-ton weights on the north side of the tower, hoping that by compressing the earth to the north, the building would stop leaning so much to the south. By November, the tower had actually straightened up about 6 mm [1/4 of an inch].

3. In 1995, the scientists began removing clay soil from beneath the tower, extracting the water, and replacing it all in a process they called "controlled subsistence." The goal: to have the tower resting on a drier, firmer soil base that will be better able to support the building.

THE END?

In April 1997, John Burland, the British soil mechanics expert who devised the plan, announced that the Leaning Tower of Pisa had finally stopped its tilt. However, in 2001, the tower was continuing to increase its tilt at about 1.2 mm per year. Has the tower been saved? Only time—a lot of it—will tell.

TOWER FACTS

• Six of the tower's eight floors are without safety rails. More than 250 people have fallen to their deaths since 1174.

• According to Italian officials, there's little danger anyone will be hurt if the tower does come crashing down. They predict that a collapse won't be sudden—that there will be plenty of rumbling and groaning in the building ahead of time to warn people. The point was moot for years; the building was closed to the public in 1990—though after extensive safety improvements, it reopened in 2001.

• Restoration officials get an average of two letters a week with suggestions on how to keep the tower upright. Some of the weirdest: building an identical tower to lean against the first one; building a huge statue of a man who looks like he's holding the tower up; tying helium balloons to the roof; anchoring the top of the tower to a hillside several miles away with a large steel cable.

• Of course, officials could tear the tower down, stone by stone, and rebuild it—this time perfectly vertical—on a strengthened foundation. But there's no chance of that—the tower brings in $300 million a year from tourists. "Let's face it, the tower would have no significance if it were straight," caretaker Spartacom Campani admitted in 1983. "Its lean is Pisa's bread-and-butter."

IT'S SO BAD, IT'S...

*...Well...funny, anyway. Here's some dialogue
from B-grade sci-fi films. No kidding, someone actually
got paid to write this stuff.*

Scientist: "They took five death row inmates and injected them with a genetic code of sorts, taken from different species of fish, primarily salmon. It essentially fuses with the genetic material already existing."

Astonished Listener: "Fish-men!?"

Scientist: "You could say that. The goal was to create an amphibious soldier, but...something went wrong."

—Humanoids from the Deep

Dr. Wagner: "But you're sacrificing a human life!"

Dr. Brandon (mad scientist): "Do you cry over a guinea pig? This boy is a free police case. We're probably saving him from the gas chamber."

Dr. Wagner: "But the boy is so young, the transformation horrible..."

Dr. Brandon: "And you call yourself a scientist! That's why you've never been more than an assistant."

—I Was a Teenage Werewolf

Teenager: "You know something? Those things, whatever they are—they're smarter than all of us put together."

—The Eye Creatures

Dr. Durea: "Oh, she's a lucky young woman, [Dr.] Groton. We have desperate need of her blood. She has survived decapitation and is manufacturing the right type of vital fluid for us. We are not butchers, Groton! We don't have this young lady here to merely drain her body and cast her aside! No. We are scientists! And we must have others to experiment with!"

—Dracula vs. Frankenstein

Rule of thumb: The right rear tire on your car will wear out before the others do.

First Scientist: "You say you made a close examination of this light?"

Second Scientist: "Not as close as I would have liked. It was being guarded by a…a sea serpent! A hideous beast that defies description!"

First Scientist: "Oh, doctor, if I didn't know you were a scientist of high standards, I'd say you were a victim of the ridiculous 'Phantom' stories that are running wild around the village!"

—The Phantom from 10,000 Leagues

Steve (the hero scientist): "Who are you? What do you want?"

Evil alien brain: "I am Gor! I need your body as a dwelling-place while I am here on your planet Earth!"

Steve: "Why me?"

Gor: "Because you are a recognized nuclear scientist. Because you have entrée to places on Earth I want to go. I chose your body very carefully, even before I knew about Sally—a very exciting female!"

Steve: "Leave Sally out of this!"

Gor: "Why? She appeals to me! There are some aspects of the life of an Earth savage that are exciting and rewarding! Things that are missed by the brains on my planet, Arous."

—The Brain from Planet Arous

Dr. Marvin (hero scientist): "General, we saw a strange thing this afternoon. We saw what appeared to be a flying saucer."

General Hanley: "A flying saucer!?"

Carol Marvin (scientist's new wife): "It nearly ran us off the road."

Hanley: "You're sure of that?"

Dr. Marvin: "Both Carol and I are subject to the same atmospheric disturbances that may have affected other observers, but there is a quantitative difference, when you're a scientist."

Dr. Marvin: "What do you want with me?"

Alien: "Arrange for your world leaders to confer with us in the city of Washington D.C."

Dr. Marvin: "They may not listen! I'm only a scientist!"

—Earth Versus the Flying Saucers

A horse expends more energy lying down than it does standing up.

HOW A
MICROWAVE WORKS

*We gave you a brief history of the microwave oven
on page 251. Now here's the rest of the story—
the science that makes it work.*

WHAT ARE MICROWAVES?

Here's the first thing you should know about
"microwaves": Like visible light, radio waves, and
X-rays, they are waves of electromagnetic energy. What makes the
four waves different from each other? Each has a different length
(*wavelength*) and vibrates at a different speed (*frequency*).

• Microwaves get their name because their wavelength is
much shorter than electromagnetic waves that carry TV and
radio signals.

• The microwaves in a microwave oven have a wavelength of
about 10 centimetres [4 inches], and they vibrate 2.5 billion times
per second—about the same natural frequency as water molecules.
That's what makes them so effective at heating food.

• A conventional oven heats the air in the oven, which then
cooks the food. But microwaves cause water molecules in the food
to vibrate at high speeds, creating heat. The heated water
molecules are what cook the food.

• Glass, ceramic, and plastic plates contain virtually no water
molecules, which is why they don't heat up in the microwave.

MICROWAVE MECHANICS

• When the microwave oven is turned on, electricty passes
through the magnetron, the tube which produces microwaves.
The microwaves are then channelled down a metal tube (*wave-
guide*) and through a slow rotating metal fan (*stirrer*), which scat-
ters them into the part of the oven where the food is placed.

• The walls of the oven are made of metal, which reflects
microwaves the same way that a mirror reflects visible light. So
when the microwaves hit the stirrer and are scattered into the

Female spiders spin better webs than males do.

food chamber, they bounce off the metal walls and penetrate the food from every direction. Some ovens have a rotating turntable that helps food cook more evenly.

• Do microwave ovens cook food from the inside out? Some people think so, but the answer seems to be no. Microwaves cook food from the outside in, like conventional ovens. But the microwave energy only penetrates a couple of centimetres into the food. The heat that's created by the water molecules then penetrates deeper into the food, cooking it all the way through. This secondary cooking process is known as "conduction."

• The metal holes in the glass door of the microwave oven are large enough to let out visible light (which has a small wavelength), but too small to allow the microwaves (which have a larger wavelength) to escape. So you can see what's cooking without getting cooked yourself.

YOU CALL THAT COOKING?

According to legend, shortly after Raytheon perfected its first microwave oven in the 1950s, Charles Adams, the chairman of Raytheon, had one installed in his kitchen so he could taste for himself what microwave-cooked food was like. But as Adams's cook quickly discovered, meat didn't brown in the oven, french fries stayed limp and damp, and cakes didn't rise. The cook, condemning the oven as "black magic," quit.

When sales of microwave ovens took off in the late 1980s, millions of cooks discovered the same thing: Microwaves just don't cook some foods as well as regular ovens do. The reason: Because microwaves cook by exciting the water molecules in food, the food inside a microwave oven rarely cooks at temperatures higher than 100°C [212°F], the temperature at which water turns to steam.

Conventional ovens, on the other hand, cook at temperatures as high as 287°C [550°F]. High temperatures are needed to caramelize sugars and break down proteins, carbohydrates, and other substances and combine them into more complex flavors. So microwave ovens can't do any of this, and they can't bake, either.

Some people feel this is the microwave's Achilles' heel. "The name 'microwave oven' is a misnomer," says Cindy Ayers, an executive with Campbell's Soup. "It doesn't do what an oven does."

"It's a glorified popcorn popper," says Tom Vierhile, a researcher with *Marketing Intelligence*, a newsletter that tracks microwave sales. "When the microwave first came out, people thought they had stumbled on nirvana. It's not the appliance the food industry thought it would be. It's a major disappointment."

Adds one cooking critic: "Microwave sales are still strong, but time will tell whether they have a future in the American kitchen." In the meantime, Uncle John isn't holding his breath—he's too busy heating up leftovers.

MICROWAVE FACTS

• Have you heard that microwave ovens are dangerous? In 1968 the Walter Reed Hospital tested them to see if the microwaves leaked out. They did—and the government stepped in to set the first federal standards for microwave construction. Today all microwaves sold in the U.S. must be manufactured according to federal safety standards.

• If you microwave your foods in a square container and aren't happy with the results, try cooking them in a round one. "Food cooks better in a round container than in a square one," says Jim Watkins, president of the company that makes Healthy Choice microwave food products. "No one really knows why."

• Irregularly shaped foods, such as a leg of chicken that is thick at one end and thin at the other end, cook unevenly.

• Food that has been cut up will also cook faster than a single, large piece of food, for the same reason: the microwaves penetrate completely through smaller pieces of food, but not through larger pieces.

• Aluminum foil reflects microwave energy the same way mirrors reflect light energy. That's why you can't use foil in a microwave...unless, for example, you're using it to shield some food items on a plate while others are being cooked. But be careful: if too much food is shielded with foil, the microwaves can overload the oven and damage the magnetron.

MYTH-CONCEPTIONS

Common knowledge is frequently wrong.
Here are a few examples of things that
most people believe…but just aren't true.

Myth: Watching TV in a dark room is bad for your eyesight.
Fact: As Paul Dickson and Joseph C. Goulden write in *Myth-Informed:* "The myth was created in the early 1950s by an innovative Philadelphia public relations man named J. Robert Mendte, on behalf of a client who manufactured lamps."

Myth: For every cockroach you see in your house, there are 10 more you didn't see.
Fact: According to studies conducted by the Insects Affecting Man and Animals Labouratory of the U.S. Department of Agriculture, the number is actually closer to 1,000 to 1.

Myth: Flamingos are naturally pink.
Fact: Flamingos are grey when chicks. They turn pink as adults because the sea creatures they eat turn pink during digestion. The pigment is then absorbed by the bird's body and colours its feathers. If flamingos are fed a different diet, they're white.

Myth: Johnny Weissmuller's famous Tarzan yell was his own voice.
Fact: His voice was combined with a high C sung by a soprano, and a hyena's howl recorded on tape and played backward.

Myth: All your fingernails grow at the same rate.
Fact: If you're right-handed, nails on your right hand grow faster; if you're left-handed, nails on your left will.

Myth: Tonto's nickname for the Lone Ranger, Kemo Sabe, means "faithful friend."
Fact: In Apache *Kemo Sabe* means "white shirt," and in Navaho it means "soggy shrub." But George Trendle, who created the Lone Ranger, didn't known that. He took the name from a summer camp he went to as a boy.

Only 1% of people suffering from night blindness are females.

Myth: The artist Vincent van Gogh cut off his entire ear.
Fact: The famous episode followed two months of hard work, hard drinking, and an argument with his best friend, Paul Gauguin. Van Gogh was despondent and cut off only a small part of his earlobe.

Myth: Hens cannot lay eggs without a rooster.
Fact: Almost all eggs we buy in the store are unfertile eggs, laid by hens with no help from a rooster.

Myth: More women in the U.S. have had face lifts than any other type of cosmetic surgery.
Fact: Nope, the cosmetic surgery performed most frequently on women in the U.S. is liposuction. The second most popular process: collagen injections.

Myth: John Kennedy is one of many presidents buried in Arlington National Cemetery in Virginia.
Fact: Actually, there are only three. William Howard Taft (27th president) and Woodrow Wilson (28th president) are the others.

Myth: The largest pyramid in the world is in Egypt.
Fact: The Quetzalcoatl pyramid southeast of Mexico City is 54 metres [177 feet] tall, with a base covering 18 hectares [45 acres] and a volume of 3.4 million cubic metres [120 million cubic feet]. Cheops, the largest in Egypt, though originally 147 metres [481 feet] tall, has a base covering only 5.26 hectares [13 acres] and a volume of only 2.5 million cubic metres [90 million cubic feet].

Myth: Giraffes have more vertebrae in their necks than other mammals.
Fact: They're the same as the rest of us. Although giraffes have the longest neck of any animal—3 to 4 metres [10 to 12 feet]— they have the same number of vertebrae as all mammals, including humans. The giraffe's neck bones are farther apart, though.

Myth: Air fresheners remove offending odours from the air.
Fact: Not even close. Actually, they either cover smells up with a stronger scent, or make your nose numb so you can't smell the bad stuff. The only way you can get *rid* of odours is with expensive absorption agents like charcoal or silica gel.

LOVE POTION #9

People have been looking for aphrodisiacs since the beginning of recorded time. Most of the concoctions they've come up with are pretty weird and basically worthless. But some, it turns out, may actually work.

ORIGIN OF THE TERM

The word *aphrodisiac* comes from Aphrodite, the Greek goddess of love and beauty (also known as *Kallipygos*, or "Beautiful Buttocks" in Greek).

• Aphrodite was originally supposed to be the embodiment of pure beauty and heavenly love. But over the years she came to represent great prowess in sexuality and seduction as well.

• Eventually, according to the *Dictionary of Word and Phrase Origins*, her name was used "to describe any drug or other substances used to heighten one's amatory desires."

APHRODISIACS IN HISTORY

As sex therapist Dr. Ruth Westheimer says—and history proves—"an aphrodisiac is anything you think it is."

• In the Middle Ages people believed that "eating an apple soaked in your lover's armpit is a sure means of seduction." Others drank the urine of powerful animals to increase sexual powers.

• A 15th-century Middle Eastern book entitled *The Perfumed Garden for the Soul's Delectation* suggested that lovers eat a sparrow's tongue, and chase it down with a cocktail made of honey, 20 almonds, and parts of a pine tree.

• People once thought that eating any plant that looks phallic would increase male virility—carrots, asparagus, and mandrake root were especially popular. Bulbs and tubers—e.g., onions—which people thought resembled testicles, were also believed to increase sexual potency, And peaches, tomatoes, mangoes, or other soft, moist fruits were considered aphrodisiacs for women.

• In *Consuming Passions*, Peter Farb and George Armelagos write that during the 1500s and 1600s, "Europe was suddenly flooded with exotic plants whose very strangeness suggested the existence of secret powers." For example:

> Tomatoes brought back from South America were at first thought to be the forbidden fruit of Eden, and were known as "love apples." And when potatoes first

arrived in Europe—the sweet potato probably brought back by Columbus and the white potato somewhat later—they were immediately celebrated as potent sexual stimulants....A work dated 1850 tells the English reader that the white potato will "incite to Venus."

• In the 20th century, everything from green M&Ms to products like Cleopatra Oil and Indian Love Powder have been passed off as aphrodisiacs. Even in 1989, a British mail-order firm called Comet Scientific was offering an aerosol spray that it claimed made men "irresistible to women."

DANGEROUS APHRODISIACS
• Spanish fly, one of the most famous aphrodisiacs, is also one of the most dangerous. It has nothing to do with Spain or flies. It's really the dried, crushed remains of an insect known as the "blister beetle." Although it can constrict blood vessels, and thus may appear to be a sexual stimulant, it's actually a deadly poison. It can do irreparable damage to the kidneys.
• For thousands of years, people (especially in the Far East) have believed that by eating part of a powerful animal, a man can absorb its sexual vitality. This has led to the ingestion of such weird stuff as dried and powdered bear gallbladders, camel humps, and rhinoceros horns. (In fact, animal horns have been considered sexual stimulants for so long that the term "horny" became slang for "a need for sex.") It has also had a drastic effect on some endangered species. *U.S. News & World Report* noted in 1989 that "with a kilo of rhino horn fetching $42,800 in Taiwan, poachers have slaughtered rhinos so relentlessly that barely 11,000 survive." And in North America, poachers have killed thousands of black bears to get their golf ball sized gallbladders.

THE REAL THING
Traditionally, scientists have dismissed aphrodisiacs as frauds. But new research into medicinal herbs and pheromones (chemical messengers) has produced some interesting results. Experts now believe that some aphrodisiacs may really work. Here are seven "maybe's."

1. Yohimbe: The bark of a West African tree thought for centuries to produce passion in African men. Research has found that the chemical yohimbine can in fact excite men by increasing blood flow. The drug was approved by the FDA 10 years ago as a prescription treatment for impotence.

2. Oysters: Traditionally considered an aphrodisiac because of their association with the sea and their resemblance to female sex organs. However, now we also know that they're very rich in zinc—a mineral necessary to male sexual health. A man deficient in zinc is at high risk for infertility and loss of libido.

3. Chocolate: Contains PEA, a neurotransmitter that is a natural form of the stimulant amphetamine. It has been shown that either love or lust increases the level of PEA in the bloodstream and that with heartbreak, the levels drop automatically.

4. Caffeine: Research has shown that coffee drinkers are more sexually active than non-drinkers, but no one's sure if that's because of something in the caffeine, or just because it keeps people awake, and therefore interested, after bedtime.

5. DHEA: This hormone has been called the "natural aphrodisiac" by doctors. It's been shown in studies that blood levels of DHEA predict sexual thoughts and desire. DHEA became a food-supplement fad when it was hyped in the media as a way to increase energy and maybe even prevent cancer or heart disease (as well as boosting the libido).

6. Cinnamon: According to Dr. Alan Hirsch, director of the Smell and Taste Research Foundation, the aroma of cinnamon has the ability to arouse lust. As reported in *Psychology Today*, "Hirsch fitted male medical students with gauges that detected their excitement level, and then exposed them to dozens of fragrances. The only one that got a rise was the smell of hot cinnamon buns."

7. Androstenone: This is a pheromone. Scientists conducting research with animals found that androstenone produced by boars had a very positive effect on the sexual receptivity of sows. Androstenone is also found in human sweat.

FINAL THOUGHT

"Power is the great aphrodisiac."
—**Henry Kissinger**

WHAT HAPPENED AT ROSWELL?

The "incident at Roswell" is probably the biggest UFO story in history. Was it a military balloon…or an alien spacecraft? You be the judge…

THE FIRST FLYING SAUCERS

In 1947, a U.S Forest Service pilot name Kenneth Arnold was flying over the Cascade Mountains in Washington State in search of a missing plane when he spotted what he claimed were nine "disc-shaped craft." He calculated them to be moving at speeds of nearly 2,000 kilometers [1,200 miles] per hour, far faster than any human-built aircraft of the 1940s could manage.

When he talked to reporters after the flight, Arnold said the crafts moved "like a *saucer* skipping over water," and a newspaper editor, hearing the description, called the objects "flying saucers." Thus, the expression "flying saucer" entered the English language, and a UFO craze much like the one that followed Orson Welles's 1938 broadcast of *War of the Worlds* swept the country. "Almost instantly," Dava Sobel writes in his article *The Truth About Roswell*, "believable witnesses from other states and several countries reported similar sightings, enlivening wire-service dispatches for days."

THE ROSWELL DISCOVERY

It was in this atmosphere that William "Mac" Brazel made an unusual discovery. On July 8, 1947, while riding across his ranch 42 kilometres [26 miles] outside of Roswell, New Mexico, he came across some mysterious wreckage—sticks, foil paper, tape, and other debris. Brazel had never seen anything like it, but UFOs were on his mind. He'd read about Arnold's sighting in the newspaper and had heard about a national contest offering $3,000 to anyone who recovered a flying saucer. He wondered if he'd stumbled across just the kind of evidence the contest organizers were looking for.

Brazel gathered a few pieces of the stuff and showed it to his neighbours, Floyd and Loretta Proctor. The Proctors didn't know what it was, either. And neither did George Wilcox, the county sheriff. So Brazel contacted officials at the nearby Roswell Army

Air Force base to see if they could help.

The next day, an Army Intelligence Officer named Jesse Marcel went out to Brazel's ranch to have a look. He was as baffled as everyone else. "I saw…small bits of metal," he recalled to reporters years later, "but mostly we found some material that's hard to describe." Some of it "looked very much like parchment" and some of it consisted of square sticks as much as 1.2 metres [4 feet] long. Much was metallic.

The stuff was also surprisingly light—Brazel later estimated that all the scraps together didn't weigh more than 2.3 kilograms [5 pounds]. Marcel and his assistant had no trouble loading all the debris into their cars and driving it back to the Roswell base. The next day, Marcel took it to another base, in Fort Worth, Texas, where it was examined further.

SUSPICIOUS FACTS
Was the Wreckage from Outer Space?
• Brazel and the Proctors examined some of the debris before surrendering it to the military. Although it seemed flimsy at first, it was extremely resilient. "We tried to burn it, but it wouldn't ignite," Loretta recalls. "We tried to cut it and scrape at it, but a knife wouldn't touch it….It looked like wood or plastic, but back then we didn't have plastic. Back then, we figured it doesn't look like a weather balloon. I don't think it was something from this Earth."

The Military's About-Face
• The morning after the military took possession of the wreckage, the media relations officer at Roswell hand-delivered a news release to the two radio stations and newspapers in town. The release stated that the object found in Brazel's field was a "flying disc," which in the 1940s was synonymous with "flying saucer." It was the first time in history that the U.S. military had ever made such a claim.

• A few hours later, though, the military changed its story. It issued a new press release claiming that the wreckage was that of a weather balloon carrying a radar target, not a "flying disc." But it was too late—the newspaper deadline had already passed. They ran the first news release on the front page, under the headline

AIR FORCE CAPTURES FLYING SAUCER
ON RANCH IN ROSWELL REGION

Other newspapers picked up the story and ran it as well; within 24 hours, news of the military's "capture" spread around the globe.

• Interest in the story was so great that the next day, Brig. Gen. Roger Ramey, commander of the U.S. Eighth Air Force, had to hold a press conference in Fort Worth in which he again stated that the recovered object was only a weather balloon and a radar target that was suspended from it. He even displayed the wreckage for reporters and allowed them to photograph it.

Mr. Brazel's Unusual Behaviour

• Mac Brazel refused to talk about the incident for the rest of his life, even with members of his immediate family, except to say that "whatever the wreckage was, it wasn't any type of balloon." Why the silence? His son Bill explains: "The Air Force asked him to take an oath that he wouldn't tell anybody in detail about it. My dad was such a guy that he went to his grave and he *never* told anyone."

• Kevin Randle and Donald Schmitt, authors of *UFO Crash at Roswell,* claim that shortly after Brazel made his famous discovery, "His neighbours noticed a change in his lifestyle....He suddenly seemed to have more money...When he returned, he drove a new pickup truck...he also had the money to buy a new house in Tularosa, New Mexico, and a meat locker in Las Cruces." Randle and Schmitt believe the military may have paid Brazel for his silence.

TRUST ME

Today, if the government announced it had captured a UFO—even if it was mistaken—and tried to change its story a few hours later by claiming it was really a weather balloon, nobody would buy it. But people were more trusting in the years just following World War II. Amazingly, the story died away. As Dava Sobel writes:

> The Army's announcement of the "weather balloon" explanation ended the flying saucer excitement. All mention of the craft dropped from the newspapers, from military records, from the national consciousness, and even from the talk of the town in Roswell.

Even the *Roswell Daily Record*—which broke the story in the first place—was satisfied with the military's explanation. A few days later, it ran a headline that was even bigger than the first one:

GENERAL RAMEY EMPTIES ROSWELL SAUCER

THE NAKED TRUTH

Here's the latest BRI collection of "Nudes in the News."

THE NAKED USHERETTE

RIO DE JANEIRO, Brazil— "During a screening of *The Exorcist* at La Pampa Cinema in 1974, the audience was distracted by an usherette scampering backward and forward across the screen pursuing a rat with a mop. To cries of "Get them off!' she started to disrobe. It was while dancing naked in front of the screen that she noticed the auditorium being cleared by armed police. Explaining her behaviour, the usherette said later: 'I thought the audience was calling for me. I was as surprised as anyone.'"

—*Star Billing,* by David Brown

WHAT, NO DERBYS?

SEDGLEY, England— "Last May, police investigated claims that smartly dressed men were stripping off their suits and dancing naked in woodland near Penn Common, on the edge of the Black Country. 'We just do not know what these men are up to,' said Superintendent Malcolm Gough.

'It's been going on and off for about a year now, although it seems to stop after November,' said resident Judy Bardburn. She added: 'People who have seen them say that all they wear are black shoes and black socks.'"

—*Fortean Times* #90

COUNTRY COMFORT

NASHVILLE, Tennessee— "When singer-songwriter Kristi Lockwood said she was looking for a little exposure, she meant it.

Wearing only cowboy boots and a cowboy hat…Lockwood strolled down the city's famous Music Row, stunning other onlookers.

'Yeah, I saw Lady Godiva walking around,' said George McLain, who works at a recording company. 'She looked at us, and said "Hi guys." It was pretty amazing.'

The singer admitted she was doing it all for the publicity. She said she'd been in Nashville for three years, 'working real hard on my voice and getting good feedback on my songs, but nobody was paying much attention.'

The police did. After getting a few calls, they found Lockwood, covered her, cited her for indecent exposure, and took her home."

—*Nashville Banner*, **February 15, 1996**

GEN. BUTT NAKED
MONROVIA, Liberia— "In the annals of Liberia's civil war, nothing tops the tale of Gen. Butt Naked. Nude except for lace-up leather shoes and a gun, the general would lead his Butt Naked Battalion—which was famed for its fearlessness and brutality—into battle. Why no clothes? The general says he believed 'it ensured protection from his enemies.'

As the war wound down, so did Gen. Butt Naked's commitment to kill, until he gave it up and became an evangelical preacher. Today he wears a suit and tie as he roams the battered capital with a microphone preaching peace and reconciliation."

—**Wire service reports, August 3, 1997**

NAKED LUNCH
MELBOURNE, Australia— "Daring shoppers escaped the heat by taking off their clothes today in an Australian music store. About 50 patrons crowded Gaslight Music for its annual Nude Day promotion.

"The nude customers won free compact discs and were served buffet lunch by a waiter and waitress and entertained by a pianist and an orator, all wearing only a smile…as the media looked on."

—*Reuters News Service*, **October 18, 1994**

NAKED LUNCH II
STOCKHOLM, Sweden— "A tourist in Stockholm could not catch the restaurant waiter's eyes, so he stepped outside, took all his clothes off and reentered, shouting: "You Swedes only pay attention to nudes. Now will you serve me?" He was arrested for indecent behaviour."

—*The World's Greatest Mistakes*, **by Steve Brummett**

THE ENGLISH QUEEN

*Did you think the push for an Australian republic was something
new? Judging from this poem written by Henry Lawson
in 1892, this movement has been around for a long time.*

There's an ordinary woman whom the English call "the Queen:"
They keep her in a palace, and they worship her, I ween;
She's served as one to whom is owed a nation's gratitude;
(May angels keep the sainted sire of her angelic brood!)
The people must be blind, I think, or else they're very green,
To keep that dull old woman whom the English call "the Queen,"
Whom the English call "the Queen,"
Whom the English call "the Queen"—
That ordinary woman whom the English call "the Queen."

The Queen has reigned for fifty years, for fifty years and five,
And scarcely done a kindly turn to anyone alive;
It can be said, and it is said, and it is said in scorn,
That the poor are starved the same as on the day when she was born.
Yet she is praised and worshipped more than God has ever been —
That ordinary woman whom the English call "the Queen,"
Whom the English call "the Queen,"
Whom the English call "the Queen"—
That cold and selfish woman whom the English call "the Queen."

The Queen has lived for seventy years, for seventy years and three;
And few have lived a flatter life, more useless life than she;
She never said a clever thing or wrote a clever line,
She never did a noble deed, in coming times to shine;
And yet we read, and still we read, in every magazine,
The praises of that woman whom the English call "the Queen,"
Whom the English call "the Queen,"
Whom the English call "the Queen"—
That dull and brainless woman whom the English call "the Queen."

The first golf course to have 18 holes was St. Andrews in Scotland, in 1764.

She lived a 'virtuous life', tis true, but then there's nothing in
The useless life of one who ne'er had heart enough to sin.
She's lived a blameless life, they say—she thinks it not a crime
To take her thousands while the poor are starving half the time.
And when they blow the final trump, we rather think Faustine
Will stand as good a show as she whom the English call "the Queen,"
Whom the English call "the Queen,"
Whom the English call "the Queen"—
That pure and selfish woman whom the English call "the Queen."

The Prince of Wales is worshipped next (it is a funny thing)
For he will be the loafer whom the fools will call 'the King'.
They keep the children of "the Queen", and they are not a few;
The children of "the Queen" and all her children's children too.
The little great-grandchild is great because the nation's green
And Grandmama's the person whom the English call "the Queen,"
Whom the English call "the Queen,"
Whom the English call "the Queen"—
The dull, yet gilded dummy whom the English call "the Queen."

And yearly, on the Queen's birthday they praise her and rejoice,
And even far across the sea is heard the toady's voice.
They gammon Christianity, and go to church and pray,
Yet thrust HER in the sight of God, an idol of to-day.
And she is praised and worshipped more than God has ever been —
That ordinary woman whom the English call "the Queen,"
Whom the English call "the Queen,"
Whom the English call "the Queen"—
The selfish, callous woman whom the English call "the Queen."

YOU CALL THAT ART?

*It's interesting to study the paintings of the great masters—
but sometimes it's even more fun to study the work
of the great fakers. Like these folks.*

HANS VAN MEEGEREN

Background: At the end of World War II, Dutch authorities began investigating the sale of Dutch national treas-
ures to Nazi officials. They learned that Hans Van Meegeren, a
struggling Dutch artist, had sold a priceless 17th-century Vermeer
called *Christ and the Adulteress* to Nazi leader Hermann Goering
for $256,000. Once the painting was repossessed and authenticat-
ed as a work painted during Vermeer's "middle period," Van
Meegeren was arrested and charged with collabourating with the
Nazis—a crime punishable by death.

The Truth: Van Meegeren defended himself by saying that there
was no Vermeer "middle period," and that he had faked all six of
the paintings attributed to those years of the artist's life. Van
Meegeren also claimed to have painted two works by Dieter de
Hoochs, and one by Terborch.

The judge didn't believe him. But to be sure, he sent the
artist back to his studio (under guard) and told him to "paint
another Vermeer." Van Meegeren quickly created something he
called *The Young Christ Teaching at the Temple*. It was, by all
appearances, painted in the style of Vermeer.

What Happened: The judge dropped the treason charges. But as
each of the paintings Van Meegeren took credit for were tested
and proven to be fakes, he was arrested again—this time for for-
gery and fraud. He was convicted and sentenced to a year in
prison; he died from a heart attack one month after the trial.

DAVID STEIN

Background: In the mid-60s, a 31-year-old art collector named
David Stein walked into the shop of one of New York's top art
dealers with three watercolour paintings by Russian painter Marc
Chagall. The dealer bought all three for $10,000.

The Truth: Stein had painted all three "Chagalls" that morning
before lunch. He made the new canvases look old by soaking them

---

First two kitchen utensils: the ladle and the apple corer, in that order.

in Lipton's tea, and forged letters of authentication at the frame shop while waiting for the paintings to be framed.

What Happened: As Stein put it, "I should have stuck to dead men." By pure coincidence, Marc Chagall happened to be in New York that very same day…and the art dealer who bought the paintings had an appointment to meet with him. The dealer brought the paintings to the meeting, and Chagall immediately denounced them as fakes. Stein was arrested and spent nearly four years in American and French prisons. But the bust was such a boost to his reputation that when he got out of prison, he was able to make a living from his own original paintings.

PAVEL JERDANOWICH

Background: In the spring of 1925, the Russian-born Jerdanowich submitted a painting called *Exaltation* to a New York art exhibit. The red and green colours were unusual for the period, and the face of the woman in the painting was distorted, but art critics admired the work, and Jerdanowich was invited to exhibit at a New York show in 1926. He did—this time displaying a painting called *Aspiration* and explaining that he was the founder of the "Disumbrationist" school of painting. The following year, he showed two more paintings, *Adoration* and *Illumination*. Jerdanowich's groundbreaking work caused a storm, and he was hailed as a visionary.

The Truth: "Pavel Jerdanowich" was actually Paul Jordan Smith, a Latin scholar who hated abstract and modernist trends in art. When an art critic criticized his wife's realistic paintings as "definitely of the old school" in 1925, he set out to prove that critics would praise any painting they couldn't understand. "I asked my wife for paint and canvas," he recounted after admitting the hoax. "I'd never tried to paint anything in my life." The Disumbrationist School was born.

What Happened: Smith admitted the ruse to the *Los Angles Times* in 1927, but the confession only fuelled interest in his work. A Chicago gallery owner displayed the paintings in 1928, and later called the show "the most widely noticed exhibition I have ever heard of."

HAR-HAR! RAH-RAH!

Palindromes are phrases or sentences that are spelled the same way backward or forward. Some people spend their whole lives making new ones up. Here are some of Uncle John's favourites.

A dog! A panic in a pagoda!

I'm a boob, am I?

Dog doo! Good god!

"Do orbits all last?" I brood.

Ed, I saw Harpo Marx ram Oprah W. aside.

An admirer! I'm Dana!

Oh no! Don Ho!

Emil, a sleepy baby, peels a lime.

Party boobytrap.

He spots one last sale. No stops, eh?

Neil, an alien.

Go hang a salami! I'm a lasagna hog!

Tarzan raised Desi Arnaz' rat.

All erotic, I lose solicitor Ella.

Madame, not one man is self-less; I name not one, Madam.

Ron, I'm a minor.

Stressed was I ere I saw desserts.

So, Ed, I vow to do two videos.

Yo! Bozo boy!

Wonton? Not now.

Sis, ask Costner to not rent socks "as is."

Cigar? Toss it in a can, it is so tragic.

Too far, Edna, we wander afoot.

Diana saw I was an aid.

Mad? Am I, madam?

Angola balogna.

Tennis set won, now Tess in net.

Stella wondered: "No wallets?"

Star comedy: Democrats.

I Love Me, vol. I

Now, Ned, I am a maiden won!

Ma is a nun, as I am.

Did I do, O God, did I as I said I'd do? Good, I did!

Amoral aroma.

Alan Alda stops race car, spots ad: "Lana—L.A."

CURSES!

We've all heard of one curse or another. Usually, we laugh about them. But perhaps sometimes there's a good reason for believing.

THE CURSE OF TOSCA
Curse: Nasty things happen to actors during performances of this opera.

Origin: Unknown, but productions have been plagued with problems at least as far back as the 1920s.

Among Its Victims:
• During a production at the Met in the 1920s, the knife with which Tosca "murdered" Scarpia at the end of Act II failed to retract. Singer Antonio Scotti was stabbed.
• In 1965 at Covent Garden, Maria Callas's hair caught fire while she was singing the title role. It had to be put out by a quick-thinking Tito Gobbi, who was playing Scarpia.
• In a production in Rome in 1965, Gionni Raimondi's face was scorched during the firing squad scene.
• In 1993, Elisabeth Knighton Printy jumped off the wrong side of the stage in St. Paul, Minnesota, and plunged more than 9 metres [30 feet] to the ground, breaking both her legs.

Status: Ongoing. Last reported incident was in 1995, when Fabio Armiliatu, starring in a Roman production, was hit in the leg by debris from blanks fired in the execution scene. He was taken off in a stretcher. Two weeks later he returned to the stage; he fell and broke his other leg in two places while standing in the wings at the end of the first act.

THE *SPORTS ILLUSTRATED* JINX

Curse: If you appear on the cover of *Sports Illustrated* magazine, you're in for a slump or a defeat.

Origin: Unknown. For decades, sports stars have claimed that making *SI's* cover was the fastest way to a slump.

Among its Victims:
• Studying the records of 58 baseball players going back to 1955

(because there are sufficient records to check in baseball), researchers found that "there was a distinct tendency for batting performance to decline…about 50 points from immediately before appearing on the cover until three weeks after the appearance."

Status: Scientists say that if there is anything to the *SI* jinx, it's because it spooks players and thus is self-fulfilling. Also: "This extra attention and effort might cause more injuries, fatigue, or other interruptions to the hitter's natural flow, with the result that performance suffers."

THE OSCAR CURSE

Curse: Winning the gold statuette can ruin, rather than help, an actor's career.

Origin: Luise Rainer won back-to-back Oscars for *The Great Zeigfield* (1936) and *The Good Earth* (1937). Two years and five horrible movies later, she was considered a has-been. Hollywood columnist Louella Parsons wrote that it was "the Oscar curse." Parsons said her Ouija board had warned, "Beware, beware, the Oscar will get you if you don't watch out."

Among its Victims:
• Rita Morena and George Chakiris (Best Supporting Actor and Actress, 1961, *West Side Story*). Disappeared from films after winning.
• Richard Dreyfuss (Best actor, 1978, *The Goodbye Girl*). His weight rose to 82 kilograms [180 pounds], he stopped bathing, and he started binging on booze and drugs.
• Michael Cimino (Best Director, 1979, *The Deer Hunter*). Followed Oscar with three losers: *Heaven's Gate*, *Year of the Dragon*, and *The Sicilian*.
• Linda Hunt (Best Supporting Actress, 1983, *The Year of Living Dangerously*). Last seen in the short-lived sci-fi TV series, *Space Rangers*.

Status: Considered credible in Hollywood. High expectations that can't always be fulfilled accompany an Oscar. It's also attributed to salary demands, type-casting, greedy agents or studio bosses, and stars who believe their own press and become hard to work with.

WORD GEOGRAPHY

*A few more words that were derived from the
names of real places.*

SUEDE
From: Sweden
Explanation: *Gants de Suede* is French for "gloves of
Sweden." It was in Sweden that the first leather was buffed to a
fine softness, and the French bought the *gants de Suede*. Suede
now refers to the buffing processes—not to any particular kind
of leather.

TURKEY
From: Turkey
Explanation: *Turk* means "strength" in Turkish. The turkey bird is
a large European fowl named after the country of its origin. Amer-
ican colonists mistakenly thought that a big bird they found in the
New World was the same animal—so they called it a turkey.

CHEAP
From: Cheapside, a market in London
Explanation: The Old English word was *ceap* (pronounced
"keep"), which meant "to sell or barter." Because *Cheapside* was a
major market where people went to barter for low prices, the word
gradually took on a new pronunciation…and meaning.

MAYONNAISE
From: Port Mahon, Spain (according to legend)
Explanation: The *-aise* suffix is French for "native to" or "originat-
ing in." *Mahonnaise* was supposedly created to celebrate a 1756
French battle victory over the British on the Spanish isle of Port
Mahon.

COFFEE
From: Kaffa, Ethiopia
Explanation: According to legend, coffee beans were first discovered in the town of Kaffia. By the thirteenth century, the Kaffa
beans had travelled, becoming *qahwah* in Arabia, *café* in Europe,
and finally *coffee* in the New World.

If an octopus is hungry enough, it will eat its own arms.

COLOGNE
From: Cologne, Germany
Explanation: Scented water that was produced there beginning in 1709 was named for the city.

DENIM
From: Nimes, France
Explanation: The tough cloth used in jeans was also made in Nimes. It was called *serge di Nimes*—later shortened to *di nimes*, which became *denim*.

SLAVE
From: Slavonia, Yugoslavia
Explanation: After large parts of Slavonia were subjugated by Europeans in the Middle Ages, a *Slav* become synonomous with someone who lived in servitude. Eventually *Slav* became *Slave*.

LIMERICK
From: Limerick, Ireland
Explanation: The town was popularly associated with humourous verses that had five lines, the first two rhyming with the last, the middle two rhyming with each other. The poems became an English fad in the mid-19th century, and people naturally identified them with the town's name.

HAMBURGER
From: Hamburg, Germany
Explanation: People in the immigration-port city of Hamburg—called Hamburgers—liked to eat raw meat with salt, pepper, and onion-juice seasoning, a treat brought to them via Russia that we call *steak tartare* today. A broiled version using chopped meat eventually became popular in America.

TURQUOISE
From: Turkey/Europe
Explanation: Another Turkish origin. Turquoise comes from a number of places, but was probably first imported to Europe from Turkey. So it was called *turquoise*, which means "Turkish stone."

OH, WHAT A
TANGLED WEB

*Some cultures consider the spider a sign of good luck: "If you wish
to live and thrive, let a spider run alive." This old English rhyme
may be a recognition of the important role spiders play in insect
control. In fact, that's what webs—those amazingly beautiful
tapestries strung between branches, leaves, doorways, etc.—
are for. They're deadly traps. Here's some info on the
spider webs to make them even more interesting.*

WEB CONSTRUCTION
- Only about half of all spiders spin webs.
- All spider webs are made of silk.
- Although it's only about .003 millimetre [.00012 inch] in diameter, a spider's silk is stronger than steel of equal diameter. It is more elastic than nylon, more difficult to break than rubber, and is bacteria and fungi resistant.
- These qualities explain why at one time web was used to pack wounds to help mend them and stop bleeding.
- Spiders have 1–6 kinds of spinning glands, each producing a different type of silk. For instance, the cylindrical gland produces silk used for egg sacs (males often lack this) and the aciniform gland produces silk used for wrapping prey. Some spiders have glands that produce very fine silk. They comb and tease the fine strands until it's like velcro—tiny loops and hooks which entrap insect feet.
- Silk is extruded through special pores called *spinneretes* which consist of different sized "spigots." Silk starts out as a liquid. As the liquid silk contacts the air, it hardens. The spider may need different silk for different purposes. By changing how fast the liquid is extruded or by using a different silk gland, it can control the strength and quality of the silk.
- Why doesn't a spider get stuck on its own web? The spider weaves in non-sticky silk strands and only walks on those. Also, spiders have a special oil on their legs which keeps them from sticking.

THE WELL-BRED SPIDER

• A spider can often be identified by the type of web it weaves. The ability to weave is inherited, so specific types of spiders build specific types of webs. In addition, individual spiders sometimes develop a personal style; sort of like a signature.

• The spider is a hunter and its web is a snare, designed to hold its prey. So the design of its web and the place where the spider builds it depends on the kind of insects it is trying to catch.

• The determining factor: There are more insects, especially crawling ones, closer to the ground. Strong flying insects are usually higher, so the web is stronger.

WEB-SPINNERS

There are five different types of webspinners.

Cobweb spiders: (example: black widows)

• Use "trip lines" to snare prey. From their web, several vertical lines are drawn down and secured tautly to a surface with globs of "glue."

• Some unfortunate insect becomes stuck to the glue and breaks the line. The tension of the elastic trip lines, once released, flings the victim up to the spider waiting in its web.

• Cobweb weavers usually build only one web and so, with time, the web becomes tattered and littered with bits of debris.

Sheet-builders: (example: filmy dome spiders)

• Construct a horizontal mat beneath a horizontal trip line, much like a trampoline under an invisible wire.

• Flying or jumping insects that are stopped midair by the line are flung to the net below.

• As the prey struggles to regain its balance, the agile spider pounces and inflicts a deadly bite.

Web-casting spiders: (example: ogre-faced spiders)

• Use "web snares" much differently than others: Instead of attaching the web to a bush or wall, the spider carries it.

• The spider uses it much like a fishing net and casts it on passing prey. Each night it hunts. Afterwards, it may either tuck the web away until the next day's hunt, or spin a new one.

Angle lines: (example: the bola spider)
• It first suspends itself from a trapeze line and hangs there upside down. Then it sends down a single line baited with a glob of glue.
• When an insect moves by, the bola takes careful aim and casts the line towards the moving insect. If successful, it will reel in its prize.

Orb weavers: (the most familiar webs)
• Spin the largest and strongest webs. Some span more than one metre. Natives of New Guinea and the Solomon Islands used the webs of the orb weaving spiders as fishing nets. They were reportedly strong enough to hold a fish weighing as much as half a kilogram [one pound].
• These webs are especially tailored to capture flying insects—which is why they're vertically suspended.
• Orb weavers weave such intricate webs that they are often the focus of behavioural studies. For example: two orb weavers went along on *Sky Lab II* on July 28, 1973. Researchers were interested to know the effects of zero gravity on weaving. After some adjustments, the spiders were able to weave fairly normal webs. One curious difference: the space webs were symmetrical while earth webs tend to be asymmetrical.

WEB FACTS

Experimenters have covered the eyes of web-spinning spiders and discovered that it did not keep them from finding their prey in the web. The secret: a web spinner uses its web as a giant feeler. Based on vibrations it feels in the web, a spider can determine the size and energy of prey, environmental conditions, and even the presence of another spider.
• Male spiders of some species use vibrations to communicate to the female. They strum the female's web—and must send just the right vibration to convince the female that they are mates...and not dinner.

F.Y.I.: In old English, the word "cob" meant spider.

OOPS—FALSE ALARM!

*With people so nervous about bomb threats these days,
it's inevitable that there are going to be some pretty bizarre
false alarms. At the BRI, we've been keeping a file on them.
Here's what we've collected so far.*

A LIQUOR PROBLEM

Background: In 1978, security personnel at Pan American Airlines suspected that either maintenance crews or flight attendants were stealing miniature liquor bottles, which cost 35¢ apiece, from aeroplanes. So they attached a clock device to the liquor cabinet to record the times of the alleged thefts.

False Alarm: "While airborne," write Nash and Zullo in *The Misfortune 500*, "a flight attendant heard the ticking and thought it was a bomb. She alerted the captain, who re-routed the plane to the nearest airport, where passengers were quickly evacuated by emergency exits. The unscheduled landing cost Pan Am $15,000."

DIAL B FOR BOMB

Background: In November 1995, a Royal Jordanian Airlines plane en route to Chicago was forced to land in Iceland when it received a bomb threat.

False Alarm: It turned out that the culprit was a Chicago woman who was trying to keep her mother-in-law, a passenger on the plane, from visiting her.

HIT OR MISSILE

Background: On October 17, 1995, Joanna Ashworth heard a thud outside her Level Plains, Alabama, USA home. "She opened the door," reported the local Daleville *News Ledger*, "and saw a white object sticking out from the roof of the shed behind her home." It was an 18-inch [46-centimetre] missile. She called the police.

Level Plains officer Lt. Ralph Reed arrived shortly after 6 a.m. and climbed a ladder to look at the missile. He saw markings that could have been military, so he decided to leave it where it was. "My mother didn't raise no fool," Reed said. "I wasn't gonna touch it."

Reed contacted officials at nearby Fort Rucker, who decided

to evacuate people from the area. They closed the roads nearby and called the bomb squad from Fort Benning in Georgia.

False Alarm: Fort Benning's Ordnance Explosive Detachment (OED) arrived four hours later. For about half an hour, they carefully worked on getting the object out of Ashworth's roof. Then they announced to the press that it was a cardboard model that could be purchased at any toy store.

Local police vowed to get to the bottom of things. "The investigation is not closed," Lt. Reed said, as the story made national news. A few days later a 14-year-old dropped by the police station to let them know it was his rocket. He'd shot it off at a nearby playground and had been wondering what happened to it.

BRITISH FARCE

Background: According to the *Fortean Times*: "A suspicious-looking cardboard box was found outside a Territorial Army centre in Bristol (England) in 1993."

False Alarm: "The TA called the police, who in turn called an Army bomb-disposal unit, who blew up the box—to find it full of leaflets on how to deal with suspicious-looking packages."

ANIMAL CRACKERS

Background: On May 28, 1996, an employee at the Wal-Mart Superstore in Enterprise, Alabama, found a suspicious-looking box in the parking lot. Police were called. Taking no chances, they roped off the area, then called the bomb squad at Fort Benning, Georgia.

False Alarm: A few hours later, their Ordnance Explosive Detachment (the same ones who showed up in Level Plains) arrived by helicopter. They X-rayed the package and determined that it contained suspicious-looking wires. The store and surrounding area were evacuated. Then the package was blown up. It turned out to contain a dead armadillo.

* * * * *

"My licence plate says PMS. Nobody cuts me off."

—*Wendy Liebman*

The farthest planet from the sun? Due to Pluto's erratic orbit, until 1999, it was Neptune.

RUMOURS: BASED ON A TRUE STORY

*Some rumours are straight fiction, but some have a kernel of truth
at the core—which makes them a little more believable.
Have you heard any of these?*

Rumour: After World War II the Japanese renamed one of
their cities Usa, so products manufactured there could be
exported with labels that read, "made in USA."

Hidden fact: There really is a town in Japan called Usa, just as
there are Usas in Russia, Tanzania, and Mozambique.

The truth: Usa predates the war. The town is very small, so it
doesn't show up on every map of the country—which may contribute to the notion that it suddenly "popped up" out of nowhere.
But even if a country wanted to pull such a stunt, U.S. Customs
regulations wouldn't allow it: Imported goods must be stamped
with the *country* of origin, not the city.

Rumour: In the 1960s the U.S. military forced the recall of
U.S.S. Nautilus plastic submarine models. The models were so
accurate that the government feared Soviet spies would buy them
and learn our submarine secrets.

Hidden fact: In 1961 Vice Admiral Hyman Rickover *did*
complain that a model kit of the Polaris nuclear submarine, made
by the Revell Toy Company, revealed too much—including
detailed floor plans of the engine and missile compartments.
(Defense contractors that made the real submarine's missiles even
used the models to demonstrate how their weapons systems
worked.)

The truth: The military complained...but the model was never
recalled. Super-accurate models annoy the military even today; In
1986 the Testor Model Company offered a surprisingly accurate
model of the F-19 Stealth fighter—even before the U.S. Air Force
acknowledged the plane existed.

A HISTORY OF THE YO-YO

*What's it like being in the yo-yo business? They say it has
its ups and downs. Here's a brief history of
one of the world's most enduring toys.*

WHODUNNIT?

• The yo-yo is believed to be the second-oldest toy in the world, after dolls. No one knows for sure when or where it was invented: some think China, others the Philippines.

• Most yo-yo experts agree that a version of the yo-yo was used as a weapon in the Philippines as far back as prehistoric times. Hunters wrapped 6-metre [20-foot] leather straps around heavy pieces of flint and hurled the rock at prey. If a hunter missed, he could pull the rock back and try again. (The name "yo-yo" comes from a Filipino expression that means "come come" or "come back.")

• Even when it fell into disuse as a weapon, the yo-yo retained an important role in Filipino culture: people used yo-yo contests to settle disputes. Yo-yoing became the national pastime of the islands. "To this day," says one game historian, "young, rural Fil-ipinos spend weeks creating their own custom yo-yos out of rare wood or a piece of buffalo horn."

YO-YOS IN EUROPE

• The ancient Greeks played with yo-yos as far back as 500 B.C. They even portrayed yo-yoers in their art. In *World on a String*, Heliane Zeiger writes that terra-cota yo-yos and a "piece of deco-rated pottery showing a youngster in a headband and tunic, play-ing with a yo-yo—both from the classical period in Greece—are currently on display in the Museum of Athens."

• "In 1790," Zeiger continues, "the yo-yo made its way from the Orient to Europe, where it became popular among the British and French aristocracies…and inherited some new names. In England the yo-yo was known as the *bandalore, quiz,* or *Prince of Wales's toy.* (A painting from the 1700s shows King George IV, then Prince of Wales, whirling a bandalore.)"

• "In France, the yo-yo picked up the nicknames *incroyable, l'emi-grette,* and *jou-jou.*" One contemporary account of the French

Revolution notes that several French noblemen were seen
yo-yoing in the carts hauling them off to the guillotine."
And Napoleon's soldiers amused themselves with yo-yos
between battles.

Coming to America
Bandalores appeared in the United States in the 19th century. For
about 100 years, they occasionally popped up as local fads in areas
on the East Coast...then faded in popularity each time. They
never disappeared completely but didn't attain greater success
until the early 20th century.

ENTER DONALD DUNCAN
The turning point for the yo-yo came in 1928, when a businessman named Donald Duncan happened to see Pedro Flores, owner
of the Flores Yo-Yo Corporation, demonstrating yo-yos in front of
his store. Duncan was impressed with the huge crowds that had
gathered to watch the tricks. He figured that a mass-produced yo-
yo, if heavily promoted, would make a lot of money—so in 1929
he and Flores began manufacturing yo-yos on a larger scale. A year
later Duncan bought Flores out for $25,000 and renamed the com-
pany after himself.

No Strings Attached
Yo-yo historians disagree on whether Flores or Duncan deserves
credit for the innovation, but the yo-yos that Duncan manufactured in 1929 boasted an important new feature: the yo-yo string
was looped loosely *around* the axle (the centre post between the
two halves of the yo-yo), rather than being firmly secured to it.
This allowed a Duncan Yo-Yo to spin freely at the end of the
string. It transformed the yo-yo from a device that could only to
up and down to one that could perform an endless number of
tricks.

Duncan started out with just one model—the O-Boy Yo-Yo
Top—but by the early 1930s had a whole line of yo-yo products...
and a trademark on the name "yo-yo." Legally, his company was
the only one in the United States that could call its toy a yo-yo.

SALES HYPE
But it took more than a technical innovation to make the yo-yo a
national fad. It took promotion—and Duncan was a promotional

genius. He immediately created...

• **The "Yo-Yo Champion."** Many Filipinos living in the United States had played with yo-yos since they were kids. Duncan hired 42 of them (including his former business partner, Pedro Flores), gave them each the title "Champion," and sent them on tour to demonstrate yo-yos all over the country. At its peak, the company had one demonstrator on the road for every 100,000 people in America.

• **The yo-yo contest.** To drum up local support, Duncan sponsored neighbourhood yo-yo contests all over the country, awarding new yo-yos, "All American Yo-Yo Sweaters," baseballs, gloves, bicycles, and other prizes to winners.

HELP FROM HEARST

But Duncan's most productive effort came one afternoon in 1929, when he walked uninvited into the San Simeon mansion of newspaper press baron William Randolph Hearst, talked his way past the butler, and made a quick sales pitch to Hearst, telling him how he could use yo-yo contests to boost newspaper circulation.

Duncan's idea was simple: Hearst's newspapers would publicize his yo-yo competitions, and in exchange for the free publicity, Duncan would require all entrants to sell three Hearst newspaper subscriptions as the price of admission to the contests. Hearst knew a good idea—and a good product—when he saw one. He took Duncan up on the offer. The promotions worked; in 1931, for example, one month-long effort in Philadelphia helped sell three million yo-yos.

Picture Perfect

To make newspaper coverage of his product as exciting as possible, Duncan arranged to photograph as many actors, professional athletes, and other celebrities playing with yo-yos as he could. He got lucky: two of the first stars who agreed to the photos were Douglas Fairbanks and Mary Pickford—then Hollywood's biggest stars. Their superstar status guaranteed that other celebrities would enthusiastically follow suit.

Some celebrity endorsements went beyond mere photographs: he got Bob Hope to perform yo-yo tricks for U.S. troops during World War II, and talked a young singer named Bing Crosby into singing promotional songs for the company, including this one:

You would've been a scholar in the Middle Ages—barely 5% of the people were literate.

What is the dearest thing on earth,
that fills my soul with joy and mirth? My yo-yo.
What keeps my senses in a whirl,
and makes me break dates with my best girl? My yo-yo.

THAT'S A LOT OF YO-YOS

These promotional efforts paid off. By the early 1930s, annual sales had shot from thousands of yo-yos to millions. The yo-yo craze spread all over the world. Demand became so great that in 1946 Duncan had to build a huge plant in Luck, Wisconsin, to keep up. The factory could turn out 3,600 yo-yos an hour—but at times Duncan still couldn't fill all the orders…even running the plant 24 hours a day.

Still, long-term sales were unpredictable. In boom years, the demand for yo-yos was insatiable. Other years, the demand declined by as much as 90%.

UPS AND DOWNS

The biggest yo-yo craze in history took place in the 1960s. In 1962 alone, according to news reports, 45 million were sold in America—despite the fact that there were only 40 million kids in the country. This should have been the Duncan Yo-Yo Company's finest hour—but it was their undoing. Why?

1. To meet the demand, they expanded and got too far into debt.

2. They stuck with wood when they should have switched to plastic. Wood had to dry for as long as six months, so they couldn't increase production fast enough.

3. They lost their "yo-yo" trademark. There was so much money to be made selling yo-yos that competitors challenged the trademark in court. As proof that the term had become generic, they pointed to a billboard Duncan itself had erected near its factory: *Welcome to Luck, Wisconsin, Yo-yo Capital of the World.* If there was a yo-yo *capital*, that must mean yo-yos were made elsewhere, too. In 1962 a Federal Court of Appeals ruled that the trademark was invalid because the word yo-yo was the name of the toy itself.

These problems, combined with increasing costs and competition from Frisbees, skateboards, and other toys, sent the company into a tailspin. In 1965 the Duncan Co. filed for bankruptcy.

Three years later, the Flambeau Plastics Corporation bought the rights to the Duncan name and began cranking out plastic yo-yos. The Duncan name survives to this day (its yo-yos still have an 80% to 85% market share), and yo-yo fads still come and go; Donald Duncan, Jr. is even still in the business, producing yo-yos for the educational market under the name Playmaxx. But for purists, the end of the era came in 1965.

YO-YO FACTS

• Donald Duncan applied his promotional genius to other products: he also invented the Eskimo Pie, originated the Good Humour ice cream truck, co-patented the first four-wheel hydraulic automobile brake, and was the first person to successfully market the parking meter to cities and towns. (At one point, his parking meter company manufactured 80% of all meters in the United States.)

• In the early 1900s Hubert Meyer of Toledo, Ohio, patented an edible yo-yo.

• The Lego company built yo-yos for sale in the 1930s, but like Duncan, it sometimes found itself with huge inventories and low demand. One year it had so many unsold yo-yos in its warehouses that it sawed them in half and used them for wheels on toy trucks and cars.

• In 1984 astronaut David Griggs brought a yo-yo on board the Space Shuttle as part of NASA's "Toys in Space" experiments. His finding: yo-yos don't "sleep" in space—they just reach the end of their string and bounce right back up.

• The world's record for yo-yoing was set by John Winslow of Gloucester, Virginia. He started on November 23, 1977 and didn't stop for five days—120 hours.

• The world's largest yo-yo, Big-Yo, is 127 cm [50 inches] tall and 80 cm [31 1/2 inches] wide, and weighs 115 kg [256 pounds]. The string is 2 cm [3/4 inch] braided Dacron rope. In 1980 the "You Asked for It" TV show launched it off Pier 39 in San Francisco. But the string accidentally got wet before the launch and Big-Yo kept spinning in a "sleeper" position until its axle overheated and the string burned through. The yo-yo plunged nine metres [30 feet] into San Francisco Bay and frogmen had to keep it from drifting away until it could be retrieved and towed to shore.

There are 31,557,600 seconds in a year.

CELEBRITY SUPERSTITIONS

They're only human, after all.

John Madden: As Oakland Raiders coach, he wouldn't let his team leave the locker room until running back Mark van Eeghen belched.

Confederate General Stonewall Jackson: Jackson always charged into battle with his left hand held over his head, for "psychic balance."

Alfred Hitchcock: The cameo appearance he made in each film he directed was for good luck.

Michael Jordan: Always wears his North Carolina shorts under his uniform. "As long as I have these shorts on...I feel confident," he says.

The Barrymores: Lionel, Ethel, and John always gave each other an apple on the night of a show's premiere.

Jimmy Connors: Wouldn't compete in a tennis match without a little note from his grandma tucked into his sock.

Jack Lemmon: Whispered "magic time" as filming started.

Thomas Edison: Carried a staurolite, a stone that forms naturally in the shape of a cross. Legend has it that when fairies heard of Christ's crucifixion, their tears fell as "fairy cross" stones. Also a lucky piece for Theodore Roosevelt and Woodrow Wilson.

Greta Garbo: Wore a lucky string of pearls.

Mario Andretti: Won't use a green pen to sign autographs.

Kichiro Toyoda: A fortune-teller told him it was good luck to change his product's name to *Toyota* and only use car names beginning with "C" (Celica, Camry, etc.).

John Wayne: Considered it lucky to be in a movie with actor Ward Bond.

John McEnroe: Thinks it's bad luck to play on a Thursday the 12th. Carefully avoids stepping on a white line on the tennis court.

Randy Johnson: Eats pancakes before pitching.

Flush away! The average toilet will last about 50 years before it has to be replaced.

ADVANCE OSTRAYA FAAAAIIIRRR!

"Australians all let us rejoice. For we are young and freeee…"
Ahh, the rousing Australian national anthem. Every Monday morning,
the echo of half a million school kids at assemblies around the country
can be heard mumbling their way through the anthem but who really
knows the words? And what does "girt by sea" really mean?

What you probably didn't know …
- That until 1984 our official national anthem was "God Save the Queen," composed by Henry Carey.

- "Advance Australia Fair" has only been our anthem since 1984.

- Unlike America, we don't have a pledge of allegiance to our country.

- That our national anthem has an official SECOND VERSE! (which was actually a third verse—the second verse was cut)

- There are FIVE verses altogether!

- Our unofficial anthem is "Waltzing Matilda."

- "Advance Australia Fair" was written by Scotsman Peter Dodds McCormick in 1878.

- Peter was paid one hundred pounds for it.

- That the first line was originally "Australia's sons let us rejoice" but it was seen as not politically correct and changed to "Australians all let us rejoice."

- That a referendum was held in 1984 to give the people of Australia a vote on what the anthem would be. There were a number to choose from, including "God Save the Queen," "Advance Australia Fair," "Song of Australia" and "Waltzing Matilda."

Now, with fine voice please be upstanding and sing with me:

Australians all let us rejoice.
For we are young and free;
We've golden soil and wealth for toil,
Our home is girt by sea;
Our land abounds in Nature's gifts
Of beauty rich and rare;
In history's page, let every stage
Advance Australia fair!
In joyful strains then let us sing,
"Advance Australia fair!"

(the second verse that was officially
dropped, thank goodness!)

When gallant Cook from Albion sail'd,
To trace wide oceans o'er,
True British courage bore him on,
Till he landed on our shore.
Then here he raised Old England's flag,
The standard of the brave;
With all her faults we love her still,
"Britannia rules the wave!"
In joyful strains then let us sing
"Advance Australia fair!"

(the official second verse)

Beneath our radiant Southern Cross,
We'll toil with hearts and hands;
To make this Commonwealth of ours
Renowned of all the lands;
For those who've come across the seas
We've boundless plains to share;
With courage let us all combine
To advance Australia fair.
In joyful strains then let us sing
"Advance Australia fair!"

(the forgotten fourth and fifth verses)

While other nations of the globe
Behold us from afar,
We'll rise to high renown and shine
Like our glorious southern star;
From England, Scotia, Erin's Isle,
Who come our lot to share,
Let all combine with heart and hand
To advance Australia fair!
In joyful strains then let us sing
"Advance Australia fair!"

Shou'd foreign foe e'er sight our coast,
Or dare a foot to land,
We'll rouse to arms like sires of yore
To guard our native strand;
Britannia then shall surely know,
Beyond wide ocean's roll,
Her sons in fair Australia's land
Still keep a British soul.
In joyful strains then let us sing
"Advance Australia fair!"

The two lines that connect the bottom of your nose to your lip are called the philtrum.

FAMILIAR PHRASES

More unusual origins of everyday words.

PARTING SHOT
Meaning: A final cutting remark or severe look at the end of an argument.
Origin: Unlikely as it seems, this term apparently evolved from the term *Parthian shot* or *Parthian shaft*. In about 1 B.C. in Western Asia, Parthian warriors were known for firing arrows *backwards* as they were retreating from an enemy.

TO LICK SOMETHING (OR SOMEONE) INTO SHAPE
Meaning: Improve something/someone; make them presentable
Origin: Comes from the old belief that bear cubs were born featureless, as "shapeless masses of flesh and fur" and needed constant licking from their parents to achieve their final shape.

NO-MAN'S LAND
Meaning: Any desolate or dangerous place.
Origin: A thousand years ago in London, retribution for criminal acts was swift and severe. Most crimes were punishable by death. It was customary to transport condemned men just outside of the north wall of the city, where they would be hanged, impaled, or beheaded, and their bodies disposed of. Long after the surrounding territory was settled, no one laid a claim to the land where the executions had been held. Since no one owned it, it was designated as *no-man's land*.

TAKE WITH A GRAIN OF SALT
Meaning: Be skeptical; examine something carefully before accepting a statement's accuracy.
Origin: In ancient times, salt was rare and people thought it had special powers. Among other uses, they sprinkled it on food suspected of containing poison. It became customary to eat a questionable dish only if it was accompanied with a dash of salt.

Pour leftover cola into your toilet. Our resident plumber says it'll give it a nice shine.

Q&A:
ASK THE EXPERTS

*More random questions, with answers from
leading trivia experts.*

A LOT OF BULL

Q: *Do animals see colour?*
A: We often act as if they do, but the truth is, most don't.
"Apes and some monkeys perceive the full spectrum of colour, as
may some fish and birds. But most mammals view colour only as
shades of grey." So, for example, "bulls don't charge because a cape
is red. They charge because of the *movement* of the cape." (From
The Book of Answers, by Barbara Berliner)

CARROT TRICK

Q: *What are the "baby carrots" sold in plastic bags at supermarkets?*
A: "Take a closer look. Right there on the bag, it says clearly:
'baby-cut.' These aren't now and never were baby carrots. In the
early 1990s, a carrot packer…thought of a clever way to use his
misshapen culls. Mechanically he cut them into short pieces, then
ground and polished them until they looked like sweet, tender
young carrots.

"Baby-cut packers today don't rely on culls…They use a
hybrid carrot called 'Caropak' that grow long and slender; it
doesn't taper much and has little or no core. In the processing
shed, the carrots are cleaned, cut into pieces, sorted by size, peeled
in abrasive drums, then polished. Bagged with a little water and
kept cold, they stay crisp and bright orange." (From the *S.F.
Chronicle*)

THREAD OF TRUTH

Q: *Is fibreglass really made of glass?*
A: "It is, literally, tiny strands of glass that are anywhere from
.0004 inches [.01 mm] to two-millionths of an inch [0.00005 mm]
in diameter. They can be from six inches [15 cm] to more than a
mile [nearly two kilometres] long.

"It's made by either of two processes. The longer, thicker

fibres are made by melting glass marbles, then drawing melted strands through holes in a platinum bushing. Shorter, thinner fibres are made by an *air-stream* or *flame blowing* process that pulls bits of melted glass into tiny fibres. As the glass fibres cool, they are sprayed with a polymer that protects their surface and keeps the fibres strong." (From *Everything You Pretend to Know and Are Afraid Someone Will Ask*, by Lynette Padwa)

THAT JUMPY FEELING
Q: *How far can a kangaroo jump?*
A: "One large kangaroo, at a single desperate bound, is reported to have cleared a pile of timber 10-1/2 feet [over three metres] high and 27 feet [over eight metres] long." (From *Can Elephants Swim?*, compiled by Robert M. Jones)

STEEL AWAY
Q: *What makes stainless steel stainless?*
A: "Stainless steel is coated with a thin, transparent film of iron oxide and chromium. This prevents soap, food, water, and air from getting to the metal below and eating it away. Since its coating is smooth, stainless steel is [also] very sanitary. Bacteria, fungi, and dirt have nowhere to hide and are easily washed away...[Ironically, the metal] was developed in 1913 by British metallurgist Harry Brearly, who was searching for a better lining for cannons." (From *The Book of Totally Useless Information*, by Don Voorhees)

QUESTION WITH A-PEEL
Q: *Are most of a potato's nutrients in the peel?*
A: "In most cases, the vitamins are spread evenly throughout the potato. But eating the peel is still a good idea. Certain minerals that your body needs, such as calcium and zinc, are found in larger amounts in the peel.... In baked potatoes, the peel does contain more than its share of vitamins. Baking causes vitamins and other nutrients to pile up in the peel.... [However], potatoes are members of the nightshade family. The stems, seeds and skins of this family are poisonous—some more so than others.... While the flesh of the potato (the white part) is okay, the leaves and skin contain [a small amount of] substances called glycoalkaloids.... That's why you should never eat potato eyes—that's where the glycoalkaloids concentrate." (From *Know It All*, by Ed Zotti)

Research reports: An average 4-year-old child asks 437 questions a day.

NEAR-DEATH EXPERIENCES

Death may be lurking closer than you think. Judging from these stories, it might be a good idea to have a box of groceries on hand, just in case. Here are a few classic "near misses."

TUNA SURPRISE

"During a robbery at a grocery store in Chicago, employee Vincente Arriaga was shot by the robber at a distance of 20 feet [6 metres]. According to a report in the *Chicago Sun-Times*, the bullet barely broke Arriaga's skin because it was slowed down as it passed through a box of Tuna Helper he was holding."

—*News of the Weird*,
January 10, 1996

A STIRRING STORY

"Someone fired a .45 caliber bullet into Ava Donner's kitchen. Luckily, she was holding a spoon. Donner was stirring a pot of macaroni and cheese when a bullet hit the stem of the stainless steel spoon, ricocheted off the refrigerator and landed on the kitchen counter... 'If it had been an inch [a couple of centimetres] either way, it would have been in her chest,' said Donner's husband. Police suspect the shot was fired by youths target shooting in a nearby vacant lot."

—*San Francisco Chronicle*,
February 26, 1996

RADAR RANGE

"Two members of the British traffic police were in Berwickshire with a radar gun, checking for speeding motorists, when suddenly their equipment locked up with a reading of over 300 miles [480 km] per hour. Seconds later a low flying Harrier jet flew over their heads and explained the mystery. When the policemen complained to the RAF, they were informed they were lucky to be alive. The jet's target-seeker had locked onto their radar gun as 'enemy' radar...which triggered an automatic retaliatory air-to-surface missile attack. Luckily for the traffic cops, the Harrier was unarmed."

—*Pilot* magazine

REEL QUOTES

Here are some of our favourite lines from the Silver Screen.

ON INTELLIGENCE
Doc: "This kid is so dumb he doesn't know what time it is."
Golfer: "By the way, what time is it?"
Doc: "I don't know."
—**W.C. Fields,** *The Dentist*

ON MARRIAGE
"If love is blind...marriage must be like having a stroke."
—**Danny De Vito,** *War of the Roses*

"What's marriage anyhow? Just a tradition started by cavemen and encouraged by florists."
—**Olivia de Haviland,** *The Strawberry Blonde*

"Marriage is forever—like cement."
—**Peter Sellers,** *What's New Pussycat?*

ON SEX
"I like my sex the way I play basketball: one on one, and with as little dribbling as possible."
—**Leslie Nielsen,** *The Naked Gun*

ON RELIGION
Luna: "Do you believe in God?"
Miles: "Do I believe in God? I'm what you'd call a theological atheist. I believe that there is intelligence to the universe, with the exception of certain parts of New Jersey. Do YOU believe in God?"
Luna: "Well, I believe that there's somebody out there who watches over us."
Miles: "Unfortunately, it's the government."
—**Woody Allen's** *Sleeper*

ON RELATIONSHIPS
"She dumped me cause she said I wasn't paying enough attention to her, or something. I don't know, I wasn't really listening."
—**Jeff Daniels,** *Dumb & Dumber*

"A guy'll listen to anything if he thinks it's foreplay."
—**Susan Sarandon,** *Bull Durham*

"I'm not livin' with you. We occupy the same cage, that's all."
—**Elizabeth Taylor,** *Cat on a Hot Tin Roof*

No surprise: People laugh least in the first hour after waking up in the morning.

THE DISAPPEARANCE OF THE MARY CELESTE

One of the most famous unexplained disappearances ever recorded is the case of the Mary Celeste. In 1872 it was found drifting aimlessly in the Atlantic, in seaworthy condition and fully provisioned. But the entire crew had vanished without a trace. To this day, no one knows what happened.

BACKGROUND

On November 5, 1872, the *Mary Celeste* set off from New York carrying a cargo of 1,701 barrels of commercial alcohol. Her captain was Benjamin Spooner Briggs, a well-known seaman who allowed no drinking on his ship and regularly read the Bible to his men. The crew had been carefully chosen for their character and seamanship, especially because the captain had brought along his wife and two-year-old daughter. He was looking forward to a safe and pleasant voyage.

DISAPPEARANCE

One month later, on December 5, Captain Morehouse of the *Dei Gratia*—another cargo ship bound for Gibraltar—noticed a vessel on the horizon. It looked like it was in trouble, so he changed course to see if he could be of assistance. After calling out to the ship and getting no reply, Morehouse lowered a boat and sent two men to board. It was immediately evident that the ship, which turned out to be the *Mary Celeste*, was deserted. The men looked for underwater damage, but the vessel was not leaking, and was in no danger of sinking. There was evidence that the *Mary Celeste* had encountered bad weather, but on the whole she was in perfectly good condition and should have had no problem continuing her journey.

Stranger yet, there were six months' worth of provisions aboard and plenty of fresh water. All of the crew's personal possessions were intact—even the ship's strongbox. In fact, absolutely nothing was missing except some of the ship's papers and the ship's lifeboat. Captain Briggs, his family, and the crew had obviously abandoned the ship in hurry…but why? What could have

A bee has 5,000 nostrils. It can smell an apple tree that's 2 miles away.

frightened them so much that they'd desert a seaworthy vessel for an overcrowded yawl and take their chances in the stormy Atlantic?

INVESTIGATION
Still puzzled by the disappearance of the crew, Captain Morehouse decided to claim the *Mary Celeste* as salvage. He put three men aboard her and proceeded with both ships to Gibraltar.

Officials in Gibraltar were suspicious of Morehouse when he showed up with a "salvage" ship in such good condition, still carrying valuable cargo. They investigated and discovered that:

• The *Mary Celeste*'s hull was perfectly sound, indicting she had not been in a collision. Nor was there any evidence of explosion or fire.

• The cargo of commercial alcohol seemed to be intact and complete.

• A phial of sewing machine oil was standing upright, spare panes of glass were found unbroken, and the furniture in the captain's cabin was in its proper place—all indications that the ship hadn't endured particularly rough weather.

• The fact that the crew had left behind all their possessions— even their tobacco—indicated that they had left the ship in a panic, afraid for their lives, but the investigators could see no reason for this.

• The most mysterious item aboard was a sword found under the captain's bed. It seemed to be smeared with blood, then wiped. Blood was also found on the railing, and both bows of the ship had strange cuts in them which could not be explained.

THE OFFICIAL WORD
Solly Flood, Attorney General for Gibraltar, found the bloodstains suspicious and was convinced there had been violence aboard the *Mary Celeste*. However, the Vice Admiralty Court issued a verdict clearing Morehouse and his crew of any suspicion. After the ship's owners paid Morehouse a reward, the *Mary Celeste* was given a new crew, and went on to Italy, where her cargo was delivered. She continued to sail for 12 years but was known as a "hoodoo ship," so most seamen refused to set foot on her.

Rather than sell the first story he wrote, Charles Dickens traded it for a bag of marbles.

WHAT HAPPENED?

The mysterious disappearance of the *Mary Celeste's* crew had people all over the world imagining possible scenarios.

•Some believed a mutiny had occurred—the crew murdered the captain and his family, then took the ship. But if that were true, why did they abandon their prize?

•Perhaps an outbreak of disease panicked those left alive. But why would they subject themselves to the close quarters of the smaller boat, where the crowding would *guarantee* that everyone caught the disease?

•The most outrageous explanation offered was that the ship had been attacked by a giant squid several times, until everyone was killed. But a squid wouldn't have been interested in the ship's papers. And a Squid wouldn't need the ship's lifeboat.

•Because the story of the *Mary Celeste* got so much publicity, phony survivors started popping up and selling their stories to newspapers and magazines. But they all checked out false—no one who claimed to have been on board had their facts straight.

ONLY ONE EXPLANATION?

The mystery of the *Mary Celeste* has puzzled people for over a century. In all that time, say experts, only one feasible explanation has been proposed. This postulates that four things happened, in succession:

1. The captain died of natural causes while the ship was caught in bad weather.

2. A crew member misread the depth of the water in the hold, and everyone panicked, thinking the ship was going down.

3. They abandoned ship in such a hurry that they took no food or water.

4. Everyone in the lifeboat either starved or drowned.

Is that what happened? No one will ever know.

QUEEN OF THE NILE

*She's one of the most famous queens in history…but
how much do you really know about her?*

For centuries, people have been enthralled by stories of
Cleopatra. She was a tragic heroine in Shakespeare's *Antony
and Cleopatra*; a scheming vamp in *Cleopatra*, Theda Bara's
classic 1917 silent film; a buxom babe in Elizabeth Taylor's 1963
film flop. But most people know very little about the real Queen
of the Nile. And much of what they *think* they know is false.

Belief: There was only one Cleopatra.
Truth: There were seven Queen Cleopatras in the Egyptian
dynasty that began with King Ptolemy I in 323 B.C.; Cleopatra,
who reigned from 15 B.C.–30 B.C. was the seventh and last. Her
eldest sister was Queen Cleopatra VI, and her daughter (who
never became queen) was also named Cleopatra.

Belief: She was Egyptian.
Truth: She was considered Greek. Cleopatra was one of king
Ptolemy I's direct descendants; *he* had been a Greek staff officer of
Alexander the Great before becoming king of Egypt following
Alexander's death. Like the Egyptian pharaohs before them, the
Ptolemaic dynasty adopted incestuous brother-sister marriages as a
way to keep their bloodline "pure"; historians believe it's unlikely
Cleopatra had any Egyptian blood at all. For that matter, she was
the first Ptolemaic ruler who could even *speak* Egyptian.

Belief: She was one of the most beautiful women in the world.
Truth: At best, she had ordinary features; at worst, she was decid-
edly unattractive. "Her coins," Lucy Huges-Hallett writes in
Cleopatra: History, Dreams and Distortions, "minted on her orders
and therefore more likely to flatter than otherwise, show a strong,
bony face with a hooked nose and a jutting chin, pretty neither by
the standards of Cleopatra's day not by those of ours." The ancient
Roman historian Plutarch describes her as being not particularly
good-looking, although her intellect, beautiful voice, and strong
character made her desirable and enjoyable company.

Belief: ~~She was a great seductress.~~
Truth: This is based on her well-known affairs with Julius Caesar and Marc Antony. But in the days of ancient Rome, affairs between rulers were a common means of cementing alliances. Caesar is known to have had liaisons with several other queens and at least one king (one of his contemporaries described him as "every woman's man and every man's woman"); Mark Antony was also a notorious womanizer. Cleopatra, on the other hand, was completely celibate for more than half her adult life and is believed to have had only two lovers: Caesar and Marc Antony.

Belief: Caesar and Marc Antony were madly in love with her.
Truth: It is possible Caesar fell in love with Cleopatra (no one knows); but he really stayed in Egypt to get his hands on her fortune. And historians say he made her queen of Egypt because he didn't want to appoint a Roman who might become his rival.

Cleopatra's relationship with Marc Antony was also based on politics. At their first meeting, when they supposedly fell in love, they made a deal: Antony agreed to kill Cleopatra's sister so she'd have no challenge to her authority; Cleopatra became a loyal ally. Then he went back to Rome and his wife. When his wife died, he didn't marry Cleopatra—he hooked up with the sister of a political rival. Years later, he finally visited Cleopatra and the twins he'd fathered with her. Coincidentally, he also needed her treasure and her navy at the time.

Antony did commit suicide and die in Cleopatra's arms, but it wasn't for love; he was despondent because they'd been defeated in battle. Cleopatra committed suicide, too. For love? No. The Romans told her she was going to be paraded in disgrace through Rome in chains, and she couldn't take that.

Belief: She committed suicide by getting herself bitten by an asp.
Truth: Nobody knows for sure how she killed herself. "Plutarch had read the memoirs of her private physician, but even he was not sure," Huges-Hallett writes in *Cleopatra: History, Dreams and Distortions*: "It seems likely to have been the bite of a snake brought to her in a basket of figs, but it may be that she had some poison ready prepared and hidden in a hollow hair comb, or that she pricked herself with a poisoned hairpin. The only marks found on her body were two tiny scratches on her arm."

LUCKY FINDS

Here are three more stories of people who found
something valuable. It could happen to you...

A HIDDEN VALUE
The Find: An 1830 painting
Where It Was Found: At an auction
The Story: In the mid-1990s, Wanda Bell paid $25 for an old print depicting the signing of the Declaration of Independence. One day, as she was cleaning the print, she noticed something underneath it. She removed it...and found an oil painting of a man. Bell was curious to know more about it. In August 1997, she heard that an "antiques roadshow" was offering free appraisals with experts from Sotheby's, so she took the painting there. Their assessment: It's an early portrait painted by a famous New England artist named Sheldon Peck. Estimated value: $250,000.

A ROLL OF FILM
The Find: The pilot show of *I Love Lucy*
Where It Was Found: Under a bed
The Story: In 1949, CBS offered Lucille Ball her own TV show, to be based on her successful radio program, *My Favorite Husband*. She agreed—as long as they'd let her real-life husband, Desi Arnaz, co-star. CBS called the idea preposterous. "Who'd believe you were married to a Cuban bandleader?" they said.

Lucy was determined. She and Desi decided to create a live show and take it on the road to prove that audiences would accept them together. "Desi moved quickly to assemble a first-rate vaudeville act," write Steven Coyne Sanders and Tom Gilbert in their book, *Desilu*.

> He called in an old friend, the renowned international Spanish clown Pepito, to devise some physical-comedy sketch material. Pepito rigorously coached the couple, as Desi recalled, "eight to ten hours a day" at the Coronado Hotel in San Diego.

The stage show was a huge success, so CBS agreed to film a sitcom pilot. The synopsis: "Ricky goes to a TV audition. Pepito the

Clown, due to an accident, fails to appear and Lucy takes his place for the show." It was filmed on March 2, 1951.

I Love Lucy, of course, became one of the most successful TV programs in history. But along the way, the pilot episode was lost. Fans and TV historians tried over the years to locate it, but it appeared to be gone for good. Then one day in 1989, Pepito's 84-year-old widow (he'd died in 1975) looked under a bed in her Orange County home and came across a can of film labelled "Lucy-Desi-Pepito" audition. It was the long-lost *Lucy* pilot. Desi, it turns out, had given it to Pepito as a thank-you for his help. The film, with an estimated value of over $1 million, was quickly turned into a TV special and home video.

A LUCKY MISTAKE
The Find: A unique coin
Where It Was Found: At a flea market
The Story: In 1970, Guy Giamo came across an interesting 1969 penny at a Northern California flea market. "What made it intriguing," reported the *San Francisco Chronicle,* "was that it seemed to be a 'double die' stamping, a Bureau of the Mint manufacturing error that gave the legends *Liberty* and *In God We Trust* a blurred, double-image look."

There are a lot of double-dies from 1955, worth more than $500 apiece. But double-die coins are easy to fake, and many are counterfeit. Giamo bought it anyway Cost: about $100.

In 1978, he sent it to the U.S. Mint to find out if it was real. A few months later a Secret Service agent called and said simply: "The Treasury Department has determined your coin to be counterfeit, and it will be confiscated and destroyed." "That's it? Giamo asked. "Affirmative," the agent replied, and hung up.

But that's not the end. A year later, Giamo was surprised by another call from the Treasury Department. "What the hell do you want now?" he asked bitterly. "We have a coin for you," he was told. Someone had re-examined his penny before it was melted down, and decided it was genuine. "We goofed," they told him.

Giamo's coin is the only double-die 1969-S penny in existence. Its estimated value: as much as $50,000.

STRANGE CELEBRITY LAWSUITS

*Here's a "strange lawsuits" for celebrity junkies—
people who read* People *magazine.*

THE PLAINTIFF: Elton John
THE DEFENDANT: The *Sunday Mirror*, an English
newspaper
THE LAWSUIT: In 1992, the *Mirror* claimed that John had
been spitting out chewed hors d'oeuvres at a Hollywood party,
calling it a "new diet." The singer had recently gone public about
his bulimia; he sued because "the story implied he was a sham"...
and because he wasn't even at the party.
THE VERDICT: The singer was awarded $518,000 in damages.
The *Mirror* issued a formal apology admitting the story was bogus.

THE PLAINTIFF: Catherine Deneuve, French movie star
THE DEFENDANT: Outspoken Enterprises, Inc., a San
Francisco magazine publisher
THE LAWSUIT: For five years, Outspoken Enterprises published
Deneuve magazine. By 1996, it had 200,000 readers—making it
one of the largest magazines for lesbians in the United States. The
editor claimed the title was inspired by "the name of her first
love," not the actress. But Catherine Deneuve didn't believe it. In
January, 1996, she sued for trademark infringement.
THE VERDICT: The suit was apparently dropped when the
magazine voluntarily changed its name to *Curve*.

THE PLAINTIFFS: French sexpot Brigitte Bardot and her
neighbour, Jean-Pierre Manivet
THE DEFENDANTS: Jean-Pierre Manivet and Brigitte Bardot
THE LAWSUIT: Not surprisingly, it's about sex. In 1989, Bardot
and Manivet lived next to each other on the French Riviera. Bardot owned a female donkey, Mimosa, and a mare, Duchesse;
Manivet had a male donkey named Charly. Bardot, an animal
activist, agreed to let Charly graze with her animals. But when
Charly "began to show male instincts toward the old mare," he

lost his rights—Bardot had him castrated. Manivet was out of town at the time; when he returned, he sued Bardot for 4,500 francs (about $950) in damages, plus 10,000 for "moral prejudice." Bardot countersued, claiming Manivet's publicity about the case had harmed her image.

THE VERDICT: Everyone lost. The court ruled it was within Bardot's rights to "fix" the donkey, but not to protect her "image."

THE PLAINTIFF: Richard Belzer, of TV's *Homicide: Life on the Street*
THE DEFENDANTS: Hulk Hogan and Mr. T., professional wrestlers
THE LAWSUIT: In 1985, Belzer hosted a cable talk show called *Hot Properties*. Hogan and Mr. T. appeared on one program as guests. According to news reports, the interview was "merely awkward" until Belzer asked them to show him some wrestling moves.

"I'm going to make him squeal," Hogan chuckled as he stood up. Mr. T. urged "the Hulkster" to show Belzer a "Pipsqueak Sandwich."

While the band played Chopin's funeral march in the background—and a Manhattan studio audience, including 50 children in wheelchairs, who had been invited to the show, watched in horror—Hogan demonstrated his "front chin lock." After a few seconds, the comedian collapsed. He recovered briefly—long enough to break for a commercial—and then he was taken by ambulance to Mount Sinai Hospital where nine stitches were taken in his scalp.

Belzer sued the two wrestlers for $5 million.
THE VERDICT: In 1988, the case was settled out of court.

THE PLAINTIFF: Michael B. Mukasey, stepfather of singer Mariah Carey
THE DEFENDANT: Mariah Carey
THE LAWSUIT: in 1993, Mukasey filed suit claiming that Carey had promised to let him market "singing dolls that looked like her." Underlying the lawsuit: His contention that he deserved a share of her earnings because "he helped her achieve stardom by...providing transportation to rehearsals and paying for dental work."
THE VERDICT: Case dismissed.

Pound for pound, spiders, flies, and grasshoppers all contain more protein than beef does.

THE HISTORY OF ROCK: QUIZ #2

Now it's time to find out how much you know about
oldies from the 1960s. See page 466 for the answers.

1. The Jefferson Airplane's "White Rabbit"—inspired by *Alice in Wonderland*—was one of the rock classics of the 1960s. What prompted singer Grace Slick to write it?

a) The rest of the group locked her in a room and told her not to come out until she'd written some songs.

b) She read *Alice* to her niece and couldn't get over how "psychedelic" the story was.

c) She went to a Halloween party and saw Janis Joplin dressed as Alice.

2. "Summer in the City" was the Lovin' Spoonful's biggest hit, a #1 song in 1966. It was co-written by Spoonful leader John Sebastian and…

a) Tommy Gershwin, nephew of composer George Gershwin. He adapted it from an unpublished piece of music his uncle had left him.

b) Mark Sebastian, John's brother. According to legend, Mark submitted the lyrics as a poem in his high school English class…and got an "F" on them. John didn't think they were so bad and put them to music

c) Grace Slick. She'd just finished "White Rabbit" and was looking for something new to work on.

3. Roy Orbison hit #1 in 1964 with "Pretty Woman." How did he come up with the idea for the song?

a) His wife announced she was going to buy groceries.

b) His wife announced she was pregnant.

c) His wife announced she was leaving him.

Cost, per day, of fighting the Revolutionary War: $20,411. World II: $409.4 million

4.   In 1962, Frankie Valli and the Four Seasons were rudely inter-
rupted while recording their soon-to-be #1 song, "Walk Like a
Man." What happened?

a) The studio was robbed. The thieves took their money,
jewellery—and all the instruments.

b) The building was on fire—fire fighters were smashing down
the studio door as the group desperately tried to finish the
recording.

c) A gang of fans broke down the door and chased the group
all over the studio—finally cornering them in the men's
room. Police had to rescue them.

5.   In 1969, a group called Steam hit #1 with a pop tune called
"Na Na Hey Hey Kiss Him Goodbye." How did they wind up with
that title (which is also the chorus)?

a) One of the musicians was a Native American whose tribal
name was "Nah nah hay-hay."

b) They couldn't think of any words, so they just stuck in
some nonsense syllables.

c) One of the musician's kids, a three-year-old, came up with
it.

6. In 1964, jazz trumpeter Louis Armstrong became the oldest
artist ever to have a #1 song when his version of "Hello, Dolly"
topped the charts. Why did he record the song?

a) "Dolly" was his first wife's name.

b) It was a publicity gimmick. He cut a deal with David Merrick, the show's producer: if Armstrong's record made the Top
10, Merrick said he'd pay the trumpeter an extra $100,000.

c) Someone gave it to Armstrong at the recording session.
He'd never heard of the musical or the song, but thought it
was decent enough to record.

7. Which of these classic 1960s rock songs was made up sponta-
neously—right in the middle of a live performance?

a) "When a Man Loves a Woman," by Percy Sledge

b) "All You Need Is Love," by the Beatles

c) "My Boyfriend's Back," by the Angels

ANZAC DAY

ANZAC Day is a day that is very dear to the hearts of all Australians. It is a day when we remember those that have died in war, those that have served their country, and celebrates the freedom that we Australians take very much for granted.

Anzac Day is celebrated on 25th April—the anniversary of the first major military campaign of World War 1 fought by Australian and New Zealand troops. ANZAC stands for Australian and New Zealand Army Corps, and services are held around the country and abroad to pay tribute to the lives of Australians lost in war. April 25th was officially named Anzac Day in 1916 but the first Anzac Day was not commemorated in Australia until 1942 when a small service was held at the Australian War Memorial.

WORLD WAR I AND GALLIPOLI

When World War I began on 4th August 1914, Australia was a young nation—a Federal Commonwealth barely fourteen years old. The Prime Minister, Joseph Cook, committed 20,000 volunteer soldiers to the war effort and hoped to establish Australia's reputation as a nation of the world. This was to be the first time that our soldiers fought as Australians and the attention of the nation was very much on them. The troops were sent to Egypt under the control of the British and formed part of the allied alliance. After four and a half months of training near Cairo, the Australian and New Zealand troops left with British and French troops to sail to Turkey. A strategy had been formulated, at the request of another ally, Russia, to take control of a stretch of water called the Dardanelles, capture the Gallipoli peninsula, overtake Constantinople (Istanbul) and open up the way to the Black Sea for allied naval boats.

At 06.00 hours on 25th April 1915, the first Anzac troops landed on the beaches of Gallipoli, now known as Anzac Cove, to an unexpected welcome of heavy artillery fire. Instead of finding flat, open beaches as they had expected, they were landed at an incorrect position and faced steep cliffs covered with prickly bushes defended by a strong Turkish army. The British had formulated their plans based on inaccurate information and out-of-date tourist maps so instead of landing the troops at a position where they could gain a strong hold, the troops found themselves under constant barrages of enemy fighting. Over the next two days over 20,000 soldiers landed at Anzac Cove and thousands of Australians died, but what followed was a story of courage and endurance in the face of terrible conditions and this courage is at the heart of the Anzac story.

What had been planned as a quick attack to knock Turkey out of the war soon developed into a stalemate with heavy casualties and great hardship on both sides. The Gallipoli campaign dragged on for eight months and finally on 20 December 1915, the survivors were evacuated. Over 8,000 Australians and nearly 2,500 New Zealanders were killed at Gallipoli and thousands more were wounded. This campaign had a profound effect on Australians at home and April 25th quickly gained acceptance as the day on which Australians remembered the sacrifices of those that had fought and died in war.

The Anzac story is not based on glorious military victories and successes, rather than on triumphs against the odds and the bonds of mateship that rose out of necessity. The word Anzac today means so much more than the military campaign where the term was first used. It stands for valour, hardship and mateship, and embodies what it means to be a soldier and a digger. It is not that Gallipoli was any worse than other wars that Australians have been involved in but it was the first real test of our country as a nation and it helped to shape the new Australia. In the words of the official Gallipoli historian, CE Bean, "Anzac stood and still stands for reckless valour in a good cause, for enterprise, resourcefulness, fidelity, comradeship and endurance that will never own defeat." So every year on April 25th, we remember those that gave their lives to protect our freedom and way of life.

They shall grow not old ... as we that are left grow old,
Age shall not weary them, nor the years condemn,
At the going down of the sun, and in the morning,
we will remember them.

LEST WE FORGET

In Denmark, Danish pastries are called "Vienna bread."

ANZAC BISCUITS

There are a number of theories on the origins of ANZAC biscuits but it is certain they came about during World War I in 1914 or 1915. Some say that the soldiers made them originally with whatever provisions they had at hand to relieve the boredom of their battle rations. Others say that they came about due to the resourceful women on the "home front" in an endeavour to make a treat for their loved ones that would survive the long journey by post to the war front. There is even the suggestion that they originated from Scottish Oatmeal cakes but we don't like that theory as we want to claim them as totally ours. Whatever the origin, they have won the hearts of all Australians the globe over as our national biscuit.

Feeling hungry? Here's the recipe for you to whip up a batch.

INGREDIENTS
- 1 cup plain flour
- 1 cup rolled oats
- 1 cup desiccated coconut
- 1 cup brown sugar
- 1/2 cup butter
- 2 tbsp golden syrup
- 1 tsp bicarbonate of soda
- 2 tbsp boiling water

METHOD
- Combine the flour, oats, coconut and sugar in a bowl.
- Melt the butter and golden syrup in a saucepan over a low heat.
- Mix the bicarbonate of soda with the water and add to the butter and golden syrup.
- Pour the liquids into the dry ingredients and mix well.
- Spoon small dollops of the mixture onto a greased tin leaving space between the dollops to allow for spreading.
- Bake in a moderate oven, 180C/350F for 15-20 minutes.
- Cool on a wire rack and seal in airtight containers.

In Nepal, Mt. Everest is known as "Gauriosankar."

THE EIFFEL TOWER, PART II

Room with a view: Among amenities that Gustave Eiffel designed for the tower was a penthouse apartment at the top, complete with a grand piano and spotlights for shining on other Paris monuments. He built it for his own use.

EIGHTH WONDER OF THE WORLD

Most advances in architecture and engineering are incremental. If, for instance, you wanted to build the world's first ten-storey building, you'd expect to study the construction techniques of eight- and nine-storey buildings first.

But Gustave Eiffel didn't have that luxury. No one had ever built an iron tower like his of *any* size—let alone one that was twice as tall as the tallest building on earth.

AN ENGINEERING GENIUS

To accomplish his task, Eiffel devised some incredibly ingenious techniques:

- Unlike other massive engineering projects of the day, he had nearly all of the parts used in the tower prefabricated off-site in his workshops. This meant that when they arrived at the tower, the parts could be quickly riveted into place with a minimum of fuss.

- The rivet holes themselves were predrilled to a tolerance of one-tenth of one millimetre, making it possible for the twenty riveting teams to drive an average of 1,650 rivets a day.

- None of the girders used in the tower was permitted to weigh more than three tons. This made it possible to use smaller cranes to lift everything into place. As Joseph Harris writes in *The Tallest Tower*:

    > Eiffel had learned that using small components was faster and safer, even if this method did require more riveting, for cranes could be smaller and more mobile. The chances of accidents were reduced, and if one did occur the consequences were less serious. Use of bigger girders would have slowed the entire operation

---

The word mattress originally meant "place to throw things."

and required more expensive and complicated
construction methods.

Thanks to these and other safety measures, the Eiffel Tower—the
world's tallest construction site—was also one of the safest. Of the
hundreds of people who worked on the tower, only one, a riveter's
assistant named Dussardin, fell to his death.

THE PIERS

In the early days of the project there were actually four construction sites at the Eiffel Tower, one for each foot, or "pier." These
piers did not join together until the 55-metre [180-foot] level—
and once this point was reached, they had to be set *perfectly* level
with one another to create a perfectly horizontal platform on
which the remaining 244 metres [800 feet] of the tower could be
built. If the piers were even slightly out of alignment, the tiniest
discrepancy at the base of the tower would be magnified at the
top: it would appear to lean.

Eiffel knew there was no way he could *guarantee* the piers
would be vertical when finished—the margin for error was too
great. So he installed temporary hydraulic pistons in the base of
each of the feet. That way, as work on the tower progressed, he
could "fine-tune" the entire tower into perfect alignment by
slightly raising or lowering each foot. When the tower was properly aligned, workers could drive iron wedges into the piers to secure
them permanently.

As it turned out, Eiffel had little to worry about. Even at the
55-metre [180-foot] level, the worst of the four massive piers was
less than 6.5 centimetres [2 1/2 inches] out of alignment. All four
were easily adjusted and secured in place. Even today, the tower is
perfectly vertical.

FINIS

The Eiffel Tower was a marvel—not just for its ingenuity of
design, but also because it was completed ahead of schedule and
under budget. The Exposition was scheduled to open on May 6;
work on the tower was finished on March 31.

Eiffel & Company earned back its money in record time.
During the six months of the Exposition alone, the tower earned
back more than $1.4 million of its $1.6 million construction cost;
that, combined with the $300,000 subsidy provided by the French
government, pushed the tower into the black even before the

Exposition closed.

The tower was such a magnificent structure that it won over many of its earlier critics. Among them was French Prime Minister Tirard. He had opposed the project at its inception, but awarded Eiffel the medal of the Legion of Honour after it was finished. The tower, a symbol of France's unrivalled technical expertise, became the symbol of France itself.

Not everyone who hated the tower experienced a change of heart. Guy de Maupassant, the novelist best known for *The Necklace*, was said to eat regularly at a restaurant on the tower's second floor. His reason: It was the only place in Paris where he was sure he wouldn't see the tower. (Even some of the characters in his novels hated the tower.)

TOWER FACTS

• Every seven years, the Eiffel Tower receives a fresh coat of more than 300 tons of reddish-green paint. Why reddish-green? Because, tower officials say, it is the colour that clashes least with the blue sky over Paris, and the green landscape of the Champ de Mars below.

• The positions of the Eiffel Tower's four "feet" correspond to the "cardinal" points of a compass: they point exactly north, south, west, and east.

• In 1925 the City of Paris wanted to decorate the tower with electric lights as part of an arts exposition being held nearby, but the cost, estimated at $500,000, was too high. When automaker Andre Citroën learned of the project, he offered to pay for it himself—in exchange for the right to put his company name and corporate symbol in lights as well. The City agreed. "The Eiffel Tower," Blake Ehrlich writes in *Paris on the Seine*, "became the world's largest electric sign, its outlines traced in lights." The lights were so popular that the tower remained lit with various designs until 1937.

• Sad fact: The Eiffel Tower is the most popular landmark for suicides in France. In an average year, four people commit suicide by jumping off the tower or, occasionally, by hanging themselves from its wrought iron beams. The first person killed in a jump from the tower, in 1911, was not an intentional suicide—the man was a tailor named Teichelt who had sewn himself a "spring-loaded bat-wing cape" that he thought would enable him to fly. It didn't.

A wolf's howl can be heard as far as seven miles away; a bullfrog's croak—one mile away.

THE FIRST CENTREFOLD

Whether you approve of the magazine or not, Playboy *represents a significant part of Australian and American culture. One of its trademarks is the centrefold. Here's the tale of the first one.*

THE BARE FACTS

In the late 1940s, Marilyn Monroe was still an unknown actress, struggling to pay rent. One day in 1948 she borrowed a car to get to an audition, but had an accident on the way. As bystanders gathered, she announced she was late for an appointment and had no money for a cab. Tom Kelley, a photographer, gave her $5 and his business card.

A year later when Marilyn needed money, she went to Kelley's studio to ask if he had any work for her. He did—he was doing a photo shoot for poster advertising Pabst Blue Ribbon Beer and his model had failed to show up. Marilyn happily stepped in and took the job.

A few weeks later Kelley called Monroe with more work. A Chicago calendar manufacturer named John Baumgarth had seen the Pabst poster and wanted a few "tasteful" nude pinup shots. According to Anthony Spoto in *Marilyn*:

> [She] accepted at once. Two nights later she returned to Kelley's studio and signed a release form as "Mona Monroe."
>
> A red velvet drape was spread on the studio floor, and for two hours Marilyn posed nude, moving easily from one position to another as the photographer, perched ten feet [three metres] above her on a ladder, clicked away.

Baumgarth paid Kelley $500 for all rights to the photos from the session, and Kelley gave Marilyn $50. They never met again.

PIN-UP GIRL

Baumgarth did nothing with the photos until 1950, when Marilyn began to get attention for her role in *The Asphalt Jungle*. He decided to use her picture on a pinup calendar. It was only meant to be a giveaway for service stations, tool dealers, contractors, etc. But in April 1952, *Life* magazine included a tiny reproduction of the

About 75% of all the gold mined each year is made into jewelry.

calendar in a cover story they did on Marilyn. As a result, the picture became world-famous. And Marilyn became infamous.

"Marilyn blunted the potential effect on her career," says Spoto, "by giving interviews in which she explained that she had desperately needed money. The public bought it. But the saga of the pinup calendar wasn't over."

PUBLIC EXPOSURE

Just as the furor surrounding Marilyn's pinup shot was dying down, Baumgarth got a visit from a fellow Chicagoan who wanted to use it. According to Russell Miller in *Bunny, the Real Story of Playboy*:

> Because of the risk of prosecution for obscenity, Baumgarth believed there was probably no other use to which the pictures could be put. He was surprised, therefore, when [a young man] showed up at his office, without an appointment, on the morning of June 13, 1953, and asked if he could buy the rights to publish the Monroe nude pictures in a magazine he was planning to launch.

The man was Hugh Hefner; the magazine was *Stag Party* (soon to be renamed *Playboy*). Baumgarth not only sold Hefner the magazine rights, but threw in the colour separations as well—which saved the struggling Hefner—who'd barely scraped up enough money for the 48-page first issue—a bundle.

Hefner knew his magazine was finally on its way. Monroe—featured that year in *How to Marry a Millionaire*—was now a star. And Hefner could announce that she would be his first "centre-fold." In December 1953, the premiere issue of *Playboy* hit the stands, with Marilyn beckoning from the front cover. Due in part to the famous pinup, *Playboy* was an instant success. Ironically, this exposure made the photos even more famous—and more valuable. Spoto concludes:

> More than any other portraits of a nude woman in the history of photography, those of Marilyn Monroe taken in 1949 became virtual icons, everywhere recognizable, ever in demand. Landmarks in the union of art with commerce, the photographs have appeared in calendars, playing cards, keychains, pens, clothing, accessories, linens and household items; for decades, entrepreneurs have become wealthy by claiming or purchasing rights to their dissemination.

THE ACME ANTI-CASTRO SPY KIT

Like the Coyote and Road Runner, the CIA was obsessively trying to kill Fidel Castro in the 1960s. But like Coyote, they just couldn't seem to do it. Was it because Castro was so wily…or because the CIA was so imcompetent? Here are some examples of how the anti-Castro super-spies spent their time and the taxpayers' money.

CONCOCTING WEIRD PLOTS
Seven plots against Castro that the CIA actually considered.

1. Use agents in Cuba to spread rumours that the second coming of Christ is imminent and that Castro is the anti-Christ.

2. Surprise him at the beach with an exploding conch shell.

3. Put thallium salts in his shoes or cigars during an appearance on "The David Susskind Show," to make his beard and hair fall out.

4. Put itching powder in his scuba suit and LSD on his mouth-piece so he would be driven crazy and drown.

5. Offer him exploding cigars designed to blow his head off.

6. Shoot him with a TV camera that has a machine gun inside.

7. Spray his broadcasting studio with hallucinogens.

EMBARGOING BASEBALLS
In its war against Fidel Castro during the 1960s, the CIA literally tried to play hardball politics. "The CIA tried to cut off the supply of baseballs to Cuba. Agents persuaded suppliers in other countries not to ship them. (U.S. baseballs were already banned by the trade embargo the U.S. had declared.)" The bizarre embargo was effective. Some balls got through, "but the supply was so limited that the government had to ask fans to throw foul balls and home runs back onto the field for continued play."

—Jonathan Kwitny, *Endless Enemies*

Charles Darwin's cousin invented the IQ test.

CONSULTING JAMES BOND

How out-of-control was the CIA in its anti-Castro frenzy? They even took Ian Fleming's jokes seriously. This anecdote from Deadly Secrets, *by Warren Hinkle and William Turner, says it all.*

"It was, even by Georgetown standards, one helluva dinner party. It was the spring 1960. The hosts were Senator and Mrs. John F. Kennedy. The guest of honour was John Kennedy's favourite author, Ian Fleming.

"Kennedy asked Fleming what his man James Bond might do if M. assigned him to get rid of Castro. Fleming had been in British intelligence....He was quick to answer. According to his biographer, John Pearson, Fleming thought he would have himself some fun...

"[He] said there were three things which really mattered to the Cubans—money, religion, and sex. Therefore, he suggested a triple whammy. First the United States should send planes to scatter [counterfeit] Cuban money over Havana. Second, using the Guantanamo base, the United States should conjure up some religious manifestation, say a cross of sorts in the sky which would induce the Cubans to look constantly skyward. And third, the United States should send planes over Cuba dropping pamphlets to the effect that owing to American atom bomb tests the atmosphere over the island had become radioactive; that radioactivity is held longest in beards, and that radioactivity makes men impotent. As a consequence the Cubans would shave off their beards, and without bearded Cubans there would be no revolution.

"Fleming was staying at the house of British newsman Henry Brandon. The next day CIA director Allen Dulles called Brandon to speak to Fleming. Brandon said his guest had already left Washington. Dulles expressed great regret. He had heard about Fleming's terrific ideas for doing in Castro and was sorry he wouldn't be able to discuss them with him in person.

"It is testimony to the resounding good sense exercised by the CIA during the Secret War that all three of Fleming's spoof ideas were in one form or another attempted—or at least seriously considered."

FAMOUS FOR 15 MINUTES

Here's another instalment of our feature based on Andy Warhol's comment that "in the future, everyone will be famous for 15 minutes."

THE STAR: Shawn Christopher Ryan, 7-year-old resident of Castro Valley, California
THE HEADLINE: *Second-Grader Smells Smoke, Saves Sixteen*
WHAT HAPPENED: At 4 a.m. on February 9, 1984, Shawn awoke and smelled smoke. He ran into his mother's room, saw that her mattress had caught fire (she'd fallen asleep smoking), and woke her up. He helped her escape, then ran back into the apartment building and knocked on every door, waking up and saving all 16 neighbours. For a few weeks, he was a national hero. He was honoured at the state capitol by the Governor of California, received a commendation from President Reagan, and was lauded on the floor of the U.S. House of Representatives.
AFTERMATH: Ryan wasn't in the news again until 1995, eleven years later. Ironically, it was because he pleaded guilty to the murder of two acquaintances (alleged drug dealers) while they were all high on methamphetamine. "I can't explain it," he said. "I'm not the kind of person to take a life, not for any reason." He was sentenced to 32 years in prison.

THE STAR: Diane King, a 33-year-old night-shift manager at a Portland, Oregon, Taco Bell
THE HEADLINE: *Good Samaritan Gets Heave-ho from Taco Bell*
WHAT HAPPENED: On August, 16, 1995, a fight broke out in a Taco Bell parking lot, leaving one teenager dead and one lying motionless in the street. King, a former nurse's aide, rushed to help. She left another employee in charge of the restaurant, even though she knew it was against company policy. Later, she explained, "I was worried he might die out there." When the police arrived, she went back to work. A few weeks later, she was fired. Newspapers reported the story as an example of both corporate insensitivity and a screwed-up society that discourages good samaritans.

In the 1800s, you could buy ketchup flavored with lobster, walnuts, oysters, or anchovies.

AFTERMATH: Hundreds of people offered King jobs and money. *People* magazine ran a story on the incident. Oprah Winfrey flew King to Chicago for a show titled "Would You Help a Stranger in Distress?" Finally, Taco Bell—which had tried to reinstate King without admitting it had done anything wrong (she refused)—ran a full-page apology in the Portland *Oregonian*. "Sometimes big corporations make mistakes," it said. "In this case, we did, and we've learned it." King ignored them and took a job at a convenience store. She also filed a $149,500 suit against Taco Bell for "shock, outrage, and emotional distress." No word on the outcome.

THE STAR: Nicholas Daniloff, Moscow bureau chief for *U.S. News and World Report*

THE HEADLINE: *U.S. Reporter Held Hostage by Soviets*

WHAT HAPPENED: In 1986 Gennadi Zakharov, a member of the Soviet Union's mission to the United Nations, was arrested in New York for spying. A few weeks later, the Soviets retaliated, arresting Daniloff in Moscow and charging *him* with espionage—with a possible death penalty. His arrest was front-page news. President Reagan and Secretary of State Schultz called it "an outrage," but swore they'd never trade a spy (Zakharov) for a hostage (Daniloff). The matter was so serious that it jeopardized the upcoming Summit meeting in Iceland between Reagan and Gorbachev. The United States even announced it was expelling 25 members of the Soviet delegation to the U.N. because they worked for the KGB.

Some fancy manoeuvering followed. Daniloff was released. The United States waited awhile (so it didn't seem like there was any connection) then released Zakharov in exchange for a Russian dissident and allowed some of the expelled U.N. workers to stay. Daniloff was welcomed home—but a *day* after his release, he was already old news. The Reagan administration changed the subject. Their new focus—it was to avoid scrutiny of the deal they'd made, political pundits suggested—was details of the Summit meeting.

AFTERMATH: Daniloff surfaced again in 1988 when he toured the country promoting his autobiography, *Two Lives, One Russia* (published on the second anniversary of his imprisonment). He became a professor at Northeastern University in Boston and a respected expert on Russia.

THE STAR: Lucy De Barbin, Dallas clothes designer who claimed to be Elvis's lover and mother of his child

THE HEADLINE: *Dallas Designer's Daughter Royal Descendant?*

WHAT HAPPENED: In 1987 De Barbin revealed her secret 24-year affair with Elvis in a book entitled *Are You Lonesome Tonight?: The Untold True Story of Elvis Presley's One True Love—and the Child He Never Knew.* She said they kept their involvement a secret so it wouldn't mess up his career. Later, she kept it quiet to protect Lisa Marie and the daughter she had with Elvis, Desir'ee. "I was so afraid of what was going to happen [if the secret got out]," she told a reporter. "I thought if one person found out, everybody would know." She didn't even tell Elvis they had a child, she said, although she hinted at it in a phone conversation just before the King's death: "I just said things like, 'I have a wonderful secret to tell you' and 'Her name is Desir'ee,' things like that. And he said, 'I hope what I'm thinking is true.'" De Barbin's publisher, Random House, believed her. And several experts confirmed that a poem the King had reportedly written for De Barbin was in his handwriting. But neither the public nor the Presley estate bought the story.

AFTERMATH: De Barbin never produced blood samples to prove that her daughter was Elvis's. Apparently, she offered no real evidence that they'd been lovers. The Presley estate claimed that because the book was not a success (it actually was), they didn't need to bother suing De Barbin.

THE STAR: Matthias Jung, a German tourist in Dubrovnik, Croatia

THE HEADLINE: *Brazen Tourist Has Dubrovnik All to Himself*

WHAT HAPPENED: Dubrovnik, Croatia, was one of the world's loveliest towns and a major tourist resort. But for seven months, from autumn 1991 to spring 1992, the Serbs bombarded it with mortar shells. Tourism fell off, then disappeared. In August 1995, tourists warily started returning—only to be greeted with more shelling. They all fled, except one—Jung, a 32-year-old shopkeeper from Hanover. He wasn't a thrill-seeker; he just wanted peace and quiet for his vacation.

AFTERMATH: After a while, things got *so* quiet that Jung admitted he was bored and went north.

In a single day, a pair of termites can produce as many as 30,000 offspring.

MYTH-SPOKEN

*Everyone knows that Captain Kirk said, "Beam me up, Scotty" in
every episode of* Star Trek *and that Bogart said, "Play it again,
Sam" in* Casablanca. *But everyone's wrong.
Here are a few common misquotes.*

Line: "Beam me up, Scotty."
Supposedly Said By: Captain Kirk
Actually: That line was *never* spoken on *Star Trek*. Not
once. What Kirk usually said was, "Beam us up, Mr. Scott," or
"Enterprise, beam us up." According to Trekkies, he came pretty
close just once. In the fourth episode, he said, "Scotty, beam me
up."

Line: "Don't fire till you see the whites of their eyes."
Supposedly Said By: Colonel William Prescott to American sol-
diers at the Battle of Bunker Hill, as they lay in wait for the
British
Actually: Sounds like another American myth. There's no record
of Prescott ever saying it, but there are records of both Prince
Charles of Prussia (in 1745) and Frederick the Great (in 1757)
using the command.

Line: "You dirty rat."
Supposedly Said By: James Cagney in one of his movies
Actually: Every Cagney impressionist says it, but Cagney never
did. He made over 70 movies but never spoke this line in any of
them.

Line: "Nice guys finish last."
Supposedly Said By: Leo Durocher in 1946, when he was manager of the Brooklyn Dodgers.
Actually: While being interviewed, he waved toward the Giants'
dugout and said, "The nice guys are all over there. In seventh
place." When the article came out, reporters had changed his
statement to "The nice guys are all over there in last place." As it
was repeated, it was shortened to "Nice guys finish last." Durocher
protested that he'd never made the remark but couldn't shake it.
Finally he gave in, and eventually used it as the title of his
autobiography.

Karate was invented in India.

Line: "Gerry Ford is so dumb he can't walk and chew gum at the same time."

Supposedly Said By: President Lyndon Johnson

Actually: This remark was cleaned up for the public—what Johnson really said was, "Gerry Ford is so dumb he can't fart and chew gum at the same time."

Line: "How I wish I had not expressed my theory of evolution as I have done."

Supposedly Said By: Charles Darwin, on his deathbed

Actually: The Christian evangelist, Jimmy Swaggart, announced in a speech in 1985 that Darwin had spoken the words as he lay dying, and asked that the Bible be read to him. But it was an old lie started shortly after Darwin's death by a Christian fanatic who was speaking to seminary students. Darwin's daughter and son both deny that their father ever had any change of heart about his scientific theory. According to his son, his last words were, "I am not the least afraid to die."

Line: "I rob banks because that's where the money is."

Supposedly Said By: Infamous bank robber Willie Sutton

Actually: According to Sutton, it was a reporter who thought up this statement and printed it. "I can't even remember when I first read it," Sutton once remarked. "It just seemed to appear one day, and then it was everywhere."

Line: "Play it again, Sam."

Supposedly Said By: Humphrey Bogart, in the classic film *Casablanca*

Actually: This may be the most famous movie line ever, but it wasn't in the movie. Ingrid Bergman said, "Play it, Sam. Play 'As Time Goes By.'" And Bogart said "If she can stand it, I can. Play it!" But the only person who ever used "Play it again, Sam" was Woody Allen—who jokingly called his theatrical homage to Bogart *Play It Again, Sam* because he knew it was a misquote.

Line: "Elementary, my dear Watson."

Supposedly Said By: Sherlock Holmes, in Arthur Conan Doyle's books

Actually: Holmes never said it in any of the stories. It was a movie standard, however, beginning in 1929 with *The Return of Sherlock Holmes*.

BOND(S)—JAMES BONDS

Every 007 fan has their own opinion of which actor—Sean Connery, George Lazenby, Roger Moore, Timothy Dalton, or Pierce Brosnan—made the best James Bond…but do you know how each actor landed the role? Here are their stories.

SEAN CONNERY (See page 316 for the whole story.)
The role of James Bond turned Connery from a nobody into an international sex symbol in less than five years—but as Connery's fame grew with each Bond film, so did his frustration with the part. He worried about being typecast, he hated reporters, and he was annoyed by the crowds of fans that followed him wherever he went. And since his image was inextricably linked with the Bond character, he was angry that Cubby Broccoli and Harry Saltzman wouldn't make him a full partner in the 007 films and merchandising deals. He left the series in 1967 after making *You Only Live Twice*, his sixth Bond film.

GEORGE LAZENBY
In 1967 a friend asked George Lazenby, a part-time actor, to substitute for him on a blind date when his girlfriend suddenly came back to town.

The blind date "was supposed to be some up-and-coming agent, which was why he wanted to go out with her," Lazenby recounted years later, "but I didn't care. I was running a health studio in Belgium." Some months later, the agent remembered Lazenby and contacted him when the search for Connery's replacement in *On Her Majesty's Secret Service* got underway. "I got the part," Lazenby remembers, "and my friend's career fizzled."

So did Lazenby's: After fighting with the producers, the director, and co-star Diana Rigg during the making of *On Her Majesty's Secret Service*, he either quit or was fired, depending on who you ask.

When it premiered in 1969, *On Her Majesty's Secret Service* was panned by the critics and was a box-office disappointment; today it is considered one of the best of the Bond films.

Alexander the Great introduced the eggplant to Europe.

SEAN CONNERY (II)

Panicked by the drubbing *On Her Majesty's Secret Service* took at the box office, Broccoli and Saltzman paid a reluctant Sean Connery $ 1.25 million plus a huge share of the profits to return to the series in the 1971 film *Diamonds Are Forever.*

Connery needed the boost—most of his post-Bond films were box-office flops—but he quit the series again after just one film, turning down a reported $5 million for *Live and Let Die.* The role went instead to his old friend Roger Moore. (Burt Reynolds was also considered, but Broccoli insisted on an Englishman.)

Connery returned for a seventh and last time in the 1983 film *Never Say Never Again.*

ROGER MOORE

Moore was one of Ian Fleming's original choices for the Bond role, and he finally got his shot in *Live and Let Die.* Unlike Lazenby, Moore succeeded—largely by complementing, not imitating, Connery's interpretation of the role. As Raymond Benson writes in *The James Bond Bedside Companion,*

> From *Live and Let Die* on, the scriptwriters tailored the screen-plays to fit Roger Moore's personality. As a result, James Bond lost much of the *machismo* image which was so prominent in the sixties. It seems Bond never gets hurt in any of the subsequent films—the Roger Moore Bond uses his wits rather than fists to escape dangerous situations.

Moore's departure from Connery's Bond was so dramatic that it inspired a Beatles-vs.-Rolling Stones-type rivalry among 007 fans over who was the best Bond. "People who saw their first Bond with Sean never took to Roger," says 007 marketing executive Charles Juroe, "and people who saw their first Bond with Roger never took to Sean. Roger's movies grossed more than Sean's." Moore made a total of seven Bond films between 1973 and 1985, tying Sean Connery. His last was *A View to a Kill.*

TIMOTHY DALTON

First choice for Moore's replacement was Irish actor Pierce Brosnan, star of the recently cancelled American TV series "Remington Steele." Brosnan was given the unofficial nod for the role, but when word of the deal leaked, it generated so much publicity for the failing "Remington Steele" that the show's ratings skyrocketed to fifth place in the Nielsens, their highest in history, promoting NBC to *un*-cancel the show and force Brosnan to serve out the remainder of his contract. With Brosnan out of the running, the job went to British actor Timothy Dalton, who appeared in *The Living Daylights* and *Licence to Kill*.

Dalton was considered by many 007 purists to be the best Bond since Connery; but he never dodged the stigma of being runner-up to Pierce Brosnan, and both films were box-office disappointments. In April 1994, amid rumours he was being fired, Dalton quit the series.

PIERCE BROSNAN

Two moths after Dalton quit, Brosnan finally won the nod to play 007 in *Goldeneye*, the 18th film in the series. "Most of today's biggest male stars were eliminated from consideration for the role," the *New York Times* reported in 1994. "Hugh Grant was thought too wimpy, Liam Neeson too icy. Mel Gibson...was deemed not quite right. Even Sharon Stone was talked about for the part of Bond." Brosnan turned out to be a wise choice: *Goldeneye* was the highest-grossing Bond film in history, with more than $350 million in ticket sales around the world. He signed on for three more films.

DAVID NIVEN

There will always be debates over which Bond movie is the best, but there isn't much disagreement over which one was the worst: *Casino Royale*, starring David Niven as James Bond. By the time Cubby Broccoli and Harry Saltzman bought the film rights to Ian Fleming's other novels, the rights to his first book, *Casino Royale*, had already been sold to someone else.

Work on the film version of *Casino Royale* did not begin until 1967, when Sean Connery's Bond image was already well established. Rather than compete against Connery directly, the producers decided to make a Bond spoof starring Niven, Peter Sellers, and Woody Allen.

Budgeted at $8 million, *Casino Royale* was the most expensive Bond film to date, as well as one of the messiest. Seven different writers wrote the screenplay, five different directors worked on various parts of the film, and seven of the characters are named James Bond. "What might have begun as a great idea ends up a total mess," Raymond Benson writes in *The James Bond Bedside Companion*. "The film should not be considered part of the James Bond series."

POISON GAS

One of the ways the U.S. intelligence community protected itself against adverse publicity and budget cuts in the early 1960s was by sending agents to Hollywood to act as "technical advisers" in spy films, thereby making the spy business appear vital and heroic to the public. *Dr. No* and other early Bond films were no exception: they had real-life secret agents working on the set.

The agents turned out to be quite useful, as Bond scriptwriter Richard Mailbum recalls:

> Before we got done, we had literally about ten technical agents, all telling us marvellous stories of what had happened to them all over the world which we incorporated into the plot. There were foreshadowings of things in the Bond films—the pipe that was a gun, and other gadgets. There were some things that we couldn't use, such as foul stuff smelling like an enormous fart that the OSS agents used to spray on people they wished to discredit.

* * * * *

PRESENTING—THE FEJEE MERMAID

Background: In 1842 P.T. Barnum began displaying the body of what he claimed was an actual mermaid, which he said had been found by sailors near the faraway island of "Feejee." (That's how Barnum spelled Fiji.) He put the mermaid on display in August 1842, printing up more than 10,000 handbills, leading up to opening day.

What Happened: The "mermaid," one of the biggest hoaxes of Barnum's long career, was actually "an ingenious sewing together of a large fish's body and tail with the head, shoulders, arms, and rather pendulous breasts of a female orangutan and the head of a baboon." But it did the trick—at the peak of New York's "mermaid fever," ticket sales at Barnum's Museum hit nearly $1,000 a week. "In truth, by the close of 1843," says a biographer, "with the help of…a dried up old mermaid, Barnum had become the most famous showman in America."

THE CURSE OF THE HOPE DIAMOND

The Hope Diamond is probably the most famous jewel in the Western world—and it carries with it one of the most famous curses. How much of it is legend, and how much of it is fact? Even historians can't agree.

BACKGROUND
In 1668, a French diamond merchant named Jean-Baptiste Tavernier returned from India with a magnificent 112.5-carat blue diamond. No one knew exactly where he'd found it—but rumours spread that it was stolen from the eye of a sacred Indian idol—and people said it was cursed.

Nonetheless, King Louis XIV bought the Great Blue and added it to his crown jewels. Four years later, he had it re-cut into the shape of a heart (which reduced it to 67.5 carats).

In 1774, the diamond was inherited by Louis XVI. His wife, Marie Antoinette, apparently wore it; she was also said to have loaned it on one occasion to the Princesse de Lamballe.

"When the French Revolution broke out, the Princesse de Lamballe was murdered by a mob and her head paraded under the window where Louis the XVI and his family awaited execution.

Marie Antoinette herself was executed in October 1793."

—*The Book of Curses,* by Gordon Stuart

THE HOPE DIAMOND
In 1792, in the midst of the French Revolution, the Great Blue diamond was stolen. It was never seen whole again.

"Thirty years later it emerged in Holland, owned now by an Amsterdam lapidary named Fals. His son stole the diamond and left Fals to die in poverty. After giving it to a Frenchman, named Beaulieu, Fal's son killed himself. Beaulieu brought it to London, where he died mysteriously."

—*The Book of Curses*

In 1830, an oval-shaped blue diamond weighing 44.5 carats turned up in a London auction house. Experts recognized it as a piece of the Great Blue, re-cut to conceal its identity.

A wealthy banker named Henry Philip Hope bought the jewel for about $90,000, and it became known as the Hope Diamond.

WAS IT CURSED?

Hope was warned about the gem's "sinister influence," but owning it didn't seem to have any effect on his life. He died peacefully.

However, in the early 1900s terrible things began happening again. Lord Francis Hope, a distant relative who'd inherited it, went bankrupt. Then his marriage fell apart. "His wife prophesied," says Colin Wilson in *Unsolved Mysteries*, "that it would bring bad luck to all who owned it, and she died in poverty."

She seemed to know what she was talking about. According to Colin Wilson, over the next few years:

• Lord Francis sold it to a French jewel dealer named Jacques Colot. He ultimately went insane and committed suicide.
• Colot sold it to a Russian prince. He lent it to his mistress, a dancer at the Folies Bergere. The first night she wore it, he shot her from his box in the theatre. The prince was reportedly stabbed by Russian revolutionaries.
• A Greek jewel dealer named Simon Manthadides bought it. He later fell (or was pushed) over a precipice.
• A Turkish sultan named Abdul Hamid bought it in 1908. He was forced into exile the following year and went insane.

TEMPTING FATE?

One wonders why anyone would want the diamond at this point. But French jeweller Jacques Cartier took possession. He quickly resold it to Edward McClean (owner of the *Washington Post*) and his wife, Evalyn. A fascinated public watched to see if the "curse" would affect them. Did it?

• According to some accounts, McLean's mother and two servants in his household died soon after he purchased the jewel.

> After her mother-in-law's death, Evalyn McLean had a priest bless the gem. In her autobiography she writes about the experience: "Just as he blessed it—without any wind or rain—this tree right across the street was

struck by lightning. My maid Maggie fainted dead
away. The old fellow was scared to death and my
knees were shaking. By the time we got home the sun
was out, bright as anything."

—*Vanity Fair* magazine

Over the next 30 years, Evalyn McLean's family was decimated.
Her father soon became an alcoholic and died. Her father-in-law
went insane. The McLeans' beloved 10-year-old son, Vinson, was
hit and killed by a car in front of their house. Their marriage
broke up and Edward McLean went insane; he died in a mental
institution. McLean's daughter Emily—who had worn the Hope
Diamond at her wedding—committed suicide.

AFTERMATH

Through all the tragedy and even her own gradual financial ruin,
Evalyn McLean scoffed at the "curse." She continued to wear the
Hope Diamond until her death in 1947. Two years later, her children sold it to the famous diamond dealer Harry Winston, to pay
estate taxes. He kept it (with no apparent ill effect) until 1958,
then decided to give it away. He put it in a box with $2.44 in
postage, paid $155 for $1 million insurance, and sent it to the
Smithsonian Institution via U.S. mail. "Letters of protest poured
in to the museum," writes Gary Cohen in *Vanity Fair*. "Some reasoned that the curse would be transferred to its new owners—the
American people."

> "Within a year, James Todd, the mailman who had
> delivered the gem, had one of his legs crushed by a
> truck, injured his head in a car crash, and lost his wife
> and dog. Then his house burned down. When asked if
> he blamed his ill fortune on the diamond, he said, 'I
> don't believe any of that stuff.'"

—*Vanity Fair* magazine

Today, the diamond is owned by the U.S. government. And we all
know what kind of luck the United States has had since 1959.

* * * * *

WHAT ABOUT LIZ? It's widely believed that Elizabeth Taylor
once owned the Hope. Not true. She owns a larger diamond, often
compared to the Hope, but now known as the Burton Diamond.

Pearls are made of calcium carbonate, the active ingredient in antacids.

READ ALL ABOUT IT!

We've all heard the expression "Don't believe everything you hear."
Here are a few more reasons not to believe everything you read, either.
Take a look at these newspaper hoaxes, for example:

BRITISH SCIENTIST FINDS LIFE ON THE MOON!
(*New York Sun,* 1835)
The Story: In 1835 the *Sun* reprinted a series of articles
from the *Edinburgh Journal of Science,* based on reports sent in by
Sir John Herschel, a respected astronomer. He was at the Cape of
Good Hope at the time, trying out a powerful new telescope.

In the first three instalments, Herschel wrote that with his
super-telescope, he could see amazing things on the moon: lakes,
fields of poppies, 38 species of forest trees, herds of buffalo with
heavy eyelids, bears with horns, two-footed beavers, etc.

In the fourth instalment (August 28, 1835), he made the
biggest revelation of all: he had seen furry, bat-winged people on
the lunar surface. He wrote:

> They averaged four feet [1.2 metres] in height, were
> covered, except in the face, with short and glossy
> copper coloured hair, and had wings composed of a
> thin membrane, without hair, lying snugly upon their
> backs from the top of their shoulders to the calves
> of the legs.

He said their faces looked like baboons' and officially named them
"Vespertilio-homo," or "bat-man."

Reaction: People were lined up at newsstands, waiting for the
next issue. Rival newspapers claimed to have access to the original
Edinburgh Journal articles and began reprinting the series. By the
fourth instalment, the *Sun's* publisher announced his paper had
the largest circulation in the world—about 20,000. A book about
the moon discoveries sold more than 60,000 copies. A committee
of scientists from Yale University arrived at the offices of the *Sun*
to inspect the source writings by Herschel (they were given the
runaround until they gave up). One group of society ladies even
began raising money to send Christian missionaries there.

The Truth: There was no *Edinburgh Journal of Science*—and the
Edinburgh Philosophical Journal (which is what they meant to

Food fact: "Exocannibals" eat their enemies. "Endocannibals" eat their friends.

quote) had gone out of business two years earlier. The whole thing was concocted by a young reporter named Richard Adams Locke, who said later that he'd written it as a "satire on absurd scientific speculations that had gotten out of hand." When the *Sun's* editors realized how out of control their scheme had gotten, they admitted it was a fake—and scolded other newspapers for copying the story without giving them credit.

CIVIL WAR WOES: LINCOLN DRAFTS 400,000 MEN!
(*Brooklyn Eagle*, May 18, 1864)

The Story: On the morning of May 18th, two New York newspapers, the *World* and the *Journal of Commerce*, reprinted an Associated Press dispatch in which President Abraham Lincoln, lamenting recent Union setbacks in the Civil War, called for a national day of "fasting, humiliation, and prayer," and announced the drafting of 400,000 additional troops to fight in the war.

Reaction: Wall Street was rocked by the pessimistic proclamation: Stock prices plummeted, and gold prices soared as panicked investors looked for safe places to put their money. According to one Lincoln confidant, the story "angered Lincoln more than almost any other occurrence of the war period."

The Truth: The story was planted by Joseph Howard, the city editor of the *Brooklyn Eagle*, who hoped to get rich by buying gold cheap before the story broke and selling it at inflated prices afterward. Howard wrote the fake AP report with an accomplice, then paid copy boys to deliver it to every newspaper in New York. Only two papers, the *World* and the *Journal of Commerce*, printed it without bothering to check if it was true. Howard and his accomplice were arrested two days after the story broke; they spent three months interned at an Army fort without trial before Lincoln personally ordered their release.

The Hidden Truth: As Carl Sifakis writes in *Hoaxes and Scams*,

> At the very time the phony proclamation was released, Lincoln had a real one on his desk, calling for the drafting of 300,000 men.
>
> When the president saw the impact of the false proclamation on the public and the financial markets, he delayed the real call up for 60 days until the situation cooled.

AUSTRALIAN
OF THE YEAR

*Every year on January 26th, Australians hold their breath in
anticipation of who will be named "Australian of the Year."
Over the years we have honoured sportsmen and women,
scientists, business people and people in the arts.*

YEAR	RECIPIENT	PROFILE
2001	Lieutenant-General Cosgrove	Head of the Australian Army
2000	Sir Gustav Nossal	Services to Medicine
1999	Mark Taylor	Cricketer
1998	Cathy Freeman	Athlete
1997	Professor Peter Doherty	Scientist/Contributions to HIV research
1996	Dr. John Yu	Paediatrician
1995	Arthur Boyd	Artist/Benefactor
1994	Ian Kiernan	Environmentalist/Clean up Australia
1993	No award given as dating changed to reflect the year awarded rather than the year of achievement	
1992	Mandawuy Yunupingu	Aboriginal Ambassador
1991	Archbishop Peter Hollingworth	Archishop/Advocate for social justice
1990	Dr. Fred Hollows	Opthamologist
1989	Allan Border	Cricketer
1988	Kay Cottee	Solo Yachtswoman
1987	John Farnham	Singer/Musician
1986	Dick Smith	Businessman/Adventurer
1985	Paul Hogan	Entertainer/Actor
1984	Lois O'Donoghue	Aboriginal Activist

Termites are blind.

Year	Name	Description
1983	Robert De Castella	Marathon Runner
1982	Sir Edward Williams	Australian Royal Commission into Drugs
1981	Sir John Crawford	Architect of Australia's post-war growth
1980	Professor Manning Clark	Historian
1979	Harry Butler	Conservationist/Naturalist
1978	Galarrwuy Yunupingu	Aboriginal Land Rights Leader
1977	Raigh Roe	Country Women's Association Leader
1976	Sir Edward Dunlop	Surgeon
1975	Professor John Cornforth	Scientist/Chemistry
1974	Sir Bernard Heinze	Orchestra Conductor/Musician
1973	Patrick White	Novelist
1972	Shane Gould	Olympic Swimmer
1971	Evonne Goolagong	Wimbledon Tennis Champion
1970	Cardinal Sir Norman Gilroy	First Australian-born Cardinal
1969	Lord Casey	Governor General of Australia
1968	Lionel Rose	World Champion Boxer
1967	The Seekers	Singing Group
1966	Jack Brabham	Motor Racing Driver
1965	Sir Robert Helpman	Ballet Dancer/Choreographer
1964	Dawn Fraser	Olympic Swimmer
1963	Sir John Eccles	Scientist/Nobel Prize for Medicine
1962	Jock Sturrock	Yachtsman
1961	Dame Joan Sutherland	Opera Singer
1960	Sir MacFarlane Burnet	Scientist/Nobel Prize for Medicine

Doctors, more than any other profession, are most likely to be late for a doctor's appointment.

WISE WOMEN

Some thoughtful observations from members of the stronger sex.

"If the world were a logical place, men would ride side-saddle."

—*Rita Mae Brown*

"Creative minds have always been known to survive any kind of bad training."

—*Anna Freud*

"Blessed is the man who, having nothing to say, abstains from giving worthy evidence of the fact."

—*George Eliot*

"If you just set out to be liked, you would be prepared to compromise on anything at any time, and you would achieve nothing."

—*Margaret Thatcher*

"If you don't risk anything, you risk even more."

—*Erica Jong*

"How wonderful it is that nobody need wait a single moment before starting to improve the world."

—*Anne Frank*

"It is not true that life is one damn thing after another. It's one damn thing over and over."

—*Edna St. Vincent Millay*

"The heresy of one age becomes the orthodoxy of the next."

—*Helen Keller*

"Regret is an appalling waste of energy; you can't build on it; it is only good for wallowing in."

—*Katherine Mansfield*

"In the face of an obstacle which is impossible to overcome, stubbornness is stupid."

—*Simone de Beauvoir*

"Spend the afternoon. You can't take it with you."

—*Annie Dillard*

"You can be up to your boobies in white satin, with gardenias in your hair and no sugarcane for miles, but you can still be working on a plantation."

—*Billie Holiday*

"You take your life in your own hands, and what happens? A terrible thing: no one to blame."

—*Erica Jong*

"Just remember, we're all in this alone."

—*Lily Tomlin*

RANDOM ORIGINS

*Once again, the B.R.I. asks—and answers—the
question: where did all this stuff come from?*

THE TELEPHONE BOOTH

Alexander Graham Bell invented the telephone, but it
was his assistant, Thomas Watson ("Come here, Mr. Watson"), who invented the phone booth. The reason: His landlady
complained that he made too much noise shouting into the phone
during his calls. Watson remedied the situation by throwing blankets over some furniture and climbing underneath whenever he
needed to make a call; by 1883 he'd upgraded to an enclosed
wooden booth with a domed top, screened windows, a writing
desk, and even a ventilator.

THE SLOT MACHINE

Other types of gambling machines date back as far as the 1890s,
but the first one to really catch on was a vending machine for
chewing gum introduced by the Mills Novelty Company in 1910.
Their machine dispensed three flavors of gum—cherry, orange,
and plum—depending on which fruits appeared on three randomly spinning wheels. If three bars reading "1910 Fruit Gum"
appeared in a row, the machine gave *extra* gum; if a lemon
appeared, it gave no gum at all (which is why "lemon" came to
mean something unsatisfactory or defective.) You can't get gum in
a slot machine anymore—the 1910 Fruit Gum machine was so
popular that the company converted them to cash payouts—but
the same fruit symbols are still used in slot machines today.

THE CINEMA MULTIPLEX

Invented by accident by theater owner Stan Durwood in 1963,
when he tried to open a large theater in a Kansas City, Missouri
shopping mall. The mall's developer told Durwood that the support columns in the building could not be removed to build a single large theater...so Durwood built two smaller theaters instead.
He showed the same movie on both screens—until it dawned on
him that he'd sell more tickets if he showed two different films. It
was a huge success; the national attention he got spurred a "multiplex boom" in other cities.

The world's first ski chair lift was modeled after a device that loaded bananas onto cargo ships.

MADE IN SWITZERLAND

If you've ever owned a Swiss Army knife, chances are you've asked yourself these two questions: Is there a Swiss army? And if so, do they really use these knives? The short answer is yes…and yes. The long answer is…

BACKGROUND. In 1891 Karl Elsner, owner of a company that made surgical instruments, got a rude shock—he found out that the pocket knives used by the Swiss Army were made in Germany. Outraged, he founded the Association of Swiss Master Cutlers. Their purpose: Swiss knives for Swiss soldiers.

Elsner designed a wood-handled knife that also contained a screwdriver, a punch, and a can-opener. He called it "the Soldier's Knife," and sold it to the Swiss Army.

But Elsner wasn't done yet—he also wanted to develop a better knife for officers. It took five years, but he finally found a way to put blades on both sides of the handle, using the same spring to hold them in place—something no one had done before. This made it possible to put roughly twice as many features on the knife. Elsner replaced the wood handle with red fiber (which lasted longer), then added a second blade and a corkscrew.

CHANGES.

Elsner had the market all to himself until 1908. Then a preacher named Theordore Wenger, from the French-speaking region of the country, started selling a similar product. The Swiss government, sensitive to regional favoritism, started buying half their pocket knives from him…and they still do. Today, the two companies are rivals. Elsner's company, Victorinox (after his mother, Victoria) calls its knife the "original" Swiss Army Knife. The Wenger Company calls its knife the "genuine" Swiss Army Knife. Each is allowed to put the Swiss White Cross on its knife—but no other company is.

Swiss Army knives became popular in the United States after World War II; returning G.I.'s brought them home by the thousands. Today, the U.S. is the world's largest market for them. And ironically, Victorinox, founded to prevent the Swiss Army from buying German pocket knives, is now the official supplier of pocket knives to the German Army.

Food for thought: "Caribbean" is derived from the same root as the word "cannibal."

A TOY IS BORN

Here are the origins of some toys you may have played with.

THE ERECTOR SET

Inventor: A.C. Gilbert, an Olympic pole-vaulter who owned the Mysto Company, which sold magic tricks and magicians' equipment

Origin: The market for magic tricks was pretty narrow, and Gilbert was hoping to break into the toy business. But he couldn't think of a product. Then one day in 1911, while riding a commuter train to New York City, Gilbert saw some new power lines being strung from steel girders. It suddenly occurred to him that kids might enjoy building things out of miniaturized girders. So he went home, cut out prototype girders from cardboard, and gave them to a machinist to make out of steel. "When I saw the samples," Gilbert wrote in his autobiography, "I knew I had something."

Selling It: Gilbert brought the prototypes to the big toy fairs of the year, in Chicago and New York…and walked out with enough orders to keep his factory busy for a year. So Gilbert took a chance and the following year, he made the Erector Set the first major toy ever to be advertised nationally. It sold so well that overnight, the Gilbert Toy Company became one of America's largest toy manufacturers.

THE BABY ALIVE DOLL

Inventor: The Kenner Products Company

Origin: Baby dolls that wet themselves were nothing new in the early 1970s, and they were popular sellers. So in 1972 Kenner decided to take the concept to the next level with a doll called Baby Alive. When someone held a spoon or a bottle up to the doll's mouth, she took in the food…and after "a suitable interval," she pooped it back out again. The baby's "food" consisted of cherry, banana, and lime "food packets" that were actually colored gel. "And to answer the obvious question," writes Sydney Stem in *Toyland*, "yes, what went in red, yellow, or green came out red, yellow or green."

Selling It: At the time, Kenner was owned by food giant General Mills—which meant that Kenner president Bernie Loomis had to get approval from the Chairman of General Mills before he could put the doll into production. He nearly blew it, Stem writes:

> Unfortunately, he forgot to put a disposable diaper on the doll before feeding it, and it extruded poo-poo gel all over his boss's arm. "Who in the world would ever want such a messy thing," asked the disgruntled chairman. As it turned out, there were fast hordes of children eager to own a defecating dolly. Baby Alive was the number-one-selling doll in 1973, and Kenner went on to sell three million of them.

RISK

Inventor: Albert Lamorisse, a French filmmaker
Origin: In 1957, a year after winning an Academy Award for his (now-classic) film, *The Red Balloon,* Lamorisse created the game he called La Conquête du Monde (Conquest of the World).
Sales Tales: La Conquête du Monde was a big hit in France, prompting U.S. game maker Parker Brothers to snap up the rights to the American version. They immediately ran into a problem: many of the executives at Parker Brothers were veterans of World War II and the Korean War, and they were uncomfortable with the game's title. So Parker Brothers ordered their R&D department to come up with a less warlike name. No luck—nobody could think of a name until a salesperson happened to hand the Parker Brothers president a piece of paper with the letters R-I-S-K written on it. A divine inspiration? No. According to company lore, R-I-S-K were merely the first letters of the names of each of Parker Brothers president's four grandchildren.
Historical Footnote: Risk was banned in Germany for years…until the object of the German version was changed from "conquering the world" to "liberating the world."

* * *

Koosh balls were invented when Scott Stillinger, an engineer, was looking for a safe ball to play catch with his small children. Foam balls bounced out of their hands, and bean bags were too heavy. So he made a ball from more than 2,000 rubber strings, joined together at the center.

MISTAKEN IDENTITY

Next time someone says, "Y'know, you remind me a lot of (someone's name)"
don't simply laugh it off—GET PARANOID! According to the BRI's
extensive files, a case of mistaken identity can lead to…

HARRASSMENT

Background: Slobodan "Dan" Milosovic (spelled with an 'o'), has lived in London, England, since 1980. Unfortunately for him, he has the same name—more or less—as Serbian ex-president Slobodan Milosevic (spelled with an 'e').
What Happened: During the Kosovo war, reporters assumed there was some connection between the two, and camped out on Milosovic's doorstep. They not only harangued him with questions, they even began quizzing his neighbors. Eventually, Milosovic had to file a complaint with England's Press Complaints Commission to protest all of the attention. "Milosovic was fed up with being hounded by the media," said the media.

LAWSUITS

Background: Kevin Moore, a 45-year-old Florida resident, was contacted some years ago by a woman named Anne Victoria Moore, who assumed she had finally located her ex-husband, also named Kevin Moore. He assured her she had made a mistake.
What Happened: Ms. Moore refused to believe him. At last report, Ms. Moore had spent more than eight months filing legal actions against Kevin Moore. First, she placed a claim on his house…then on his bank account…and then charged him with failure to pay child support. She persists, although numerous government agencies have informed her that this Kevin Moore is "11 years older than, six inches shorter than, and facially dissimilar to, her ex-husband."

UNEMPLOYMENT

Background: In 1990 Bronti Wayne Kelly, of Temecula, California, had his wallet stolen. The guy who stole it was then caught for shoplifting, and "pretended to be Kelly when he was arrested."
What Happened: Kelly wound up with a criminal record. And according to news reports, after losing his wallet in the theft, he

---

Stilts were invented by French shepherds who herded sheep in marshes near the Bay of Biscay.

also "lost his apartment, car and most of his belongings between 1991 and 1995 because no one would hire him....Every time potential employers did a background check, they found the shoplifting arrest... The same man apparently also pretended to be Kelly when he was arrested for arson, burglary, theft, and disturbing the peace." Today Kelly carries a special document that distinguishes him from the impostor, but—amazingly— "he cannot have the criminal record carrying his name erased unless the fake Kelly is found."

IMPRISONMENT
Background: In 1993, a "woman with long blonde hair" broke into the house of a Mississippi man named Darron Terry. He caught her in the act...but she escaped. Following the burglary, Terry looked through some photographs and identified Melissa Gammill, "a carefree single woman working at a mall food court." as the culprit. Three months later, Gammill was arrested.
What Happened: Gammill could not provide an alibi, because she couldn't remember where she'd been on the night of the burglary. She was charged with the crime, convicted, and sentenced to ten years in prison. Luckily for Gammill, her lawyer, Debra Allen, believed that her client was innocent and developed a hunch that a lookalike had actually committed the crime. She pursued her theory until she stumbled across a mugshot of Pauline Meshea Bailey, who looks so much like Gammill that their photographs are practically interchangeable. In April 1995, Terry admitted he'd mistakenly identified the wrong person, and Gammill was set free after serving 10 months in prison.

ASSASSINATION
Background: During World War II, England's prime minister, Winston Churchill, was targeted by Nazi agents for assassination. They were constantly on the alert, waiting for an opportunity to strike. In 1943, their moment came. At an airport in Lisbon, Portugal (a neutral country), they saw Churchill, famous as "a portly, cigar-smoking Britisher," board a commercial flight to England.

What Happened: According to Churchill in his 1950 memoir, *The Hinge of Fate*:

> The daily commercial aircraft was about to start from the Lisbon airfield when a thickset man smoking a cigar walked up and was thought to be a passenger on it. The German agents therefore signalled that I was on board. Although these neutral passenger planes had plied unmolested for many months between Portugal and England and had carried only civilian traffic, a German war plane was instantly ordered out, and the defenseless aircraft was ruthlessly shot down. Fourteen civilian passengers perished, among them the well-known British film actor, Leslie Howard.

The "portly, cigar smoking Britisher" was in reality one Alfred Chenhalls. "The brutality of the Germans was only matched by the stupidity of their agents," Churchill wrote. "It is difficult to understand how anyone could imagine that with all the resources of Great Britain at my disposal, I should have booked passage on a neutral plane from Lisbon and flown home in broad daylight."

THE DESTRUCTION OF AN ENTIRE CIVILIZATION

Background: When Hernán Cortés landed in Mexico with his 600 soldiers in 1519, the Aztecs were in control of most of present-day Mexico. They had been since around the year 1200.

Religion was a major part of Aztec life...and according to legend, the god Quetzalcoatl, who had light skin, light eyes, and a beard (just like Cortés) was supposed to return to earth. So when Cortés and his men started to march toward the Aztec capital city of Tenochtitlán (now Mexico City), word passed that Quetzalcoatl had come back.

What Happened: In the capital city, the Aztec king, Montezuma, received the visitors "in fulfillment of the ancient prophecy." The Spaniards were greeted with food, gold, and women. Montezuma is quoted as saying to Cortés, "Our lord, you are weary. The journey has tired you, but now you have arrived on the earth. You have come to your city....You have come here to sit on your throne, to sit under its canopy." Cortés, in reply, assured Montezuma he had come in peace. Actually, he had come to conquer, and quickly took Montezuma hostage. The Spaniards then proceeded to wipe the Aztec civilization out.

SALT OF THE EARTH

*A few facts you can use to spice up
your conversation at dinner tonight.*

SALT BECOMES YOU

• **Salt is life itself:** We each have about eight ounces of salt inside us. It's vital for regulating muscle contraction, heartbeat, nerve impulse transmission, protein digestion and the exchange of water between cells, so as to bring food in and waste out. Deprived of salt, the body goes into convulsion, paralysis and death.

• **Hypertension and salt:** Baby food makers have learned they can sell more if they salt it. Why? Because mothers are the ones who buy it and they like the taste better. Critics say babies don't need the salt and that hooking them on it early in life predisposes them to high blood pressure.

• **Salt can be poison:** It's healthy to eat about a third of an ounce of salt a day. If you eat more than four ounces at once, you'll die.

SALT SCIENCE

• Strangely enough, salt is made of two elements—sodium and chlorine—which, if put in your mouth by themselves, will either blow up (sodium) or poison you (chlorine). But merged into a compound—sodium chloride—they change into an essential of life. The salt taste comes from the chlorine—which is also vital for making the hydrochloric acid which digests food in our stomach.

• Scientists once thought the oceans were salty because rivers constantly washed salt out of soil and carried it to sea. But then they found pools of seawater trapped in underground sediments millions of years ago that show the ocean has always been about as salty as it is now.

• We can never run out of salt. There's enough in the oceans to cover the world 14 inches deep.

• Salt is the only mineral that can be mined by turning it into a liquid (by pumping water in). Then they pump out the brine and turn it back into a solid by evaporation.

• Salt is hygroscopic, which means it absorbs water. That's why you can't drink seawater; it will dehydrate you.

• Salt is one of the four things the tongue can taste (the others are sweet, sour and bitter). Only sweet and bitter are inborn; salt is an acquired taste.

• The hypothalamus at the base of the brain. It measures sodium and potassium in body fluids. When they get too high (from either not drinking enough water or eating too much salt), it triggers the sensation of thirst.

SALT MISCELLANY

• Only 5 percent of the salt we mine goes into food. The rest goes into making chemicals.

• When salt is made by vigorous boiling, it forms cubic crystals, but when it's naturally dried, it makes pyramid-shaped crystals. The pyramid-shaped crystals are particularly sought after for kosher use and in fine cooking.

• It takes four gallons of seawater to make a pound of salt.

• Salt is often found with oil and is often used by oil companies as an indicator of where to drill.

• For centuries, salt was served in a bowl, not a shaker. It couldn't be shaken, since it absorbs water and sticks together. The Morton Salt Co. changed that in 1910 by covering every grain with chemicals that keep water out—thus its famous slogan, "When it rains, it pours."

• The water in our bodies (we're 70% water) has the same saltiness as the seas from which we evolved. The amniotic fluid surrounding fetuses in the womb is essentially saltwater.

SALT SUPERSTITIONS

• In Scandinavia, knocking over salt is considered bad luck...*if* the salt gets wet.

• In some cultures people believe that since salt corrodes, it destroys evil. As protection, they wear a sachet of salt around their necks, and sprinkle it on brooms before sweeping their homes.

• Hebrews, Greeks, and Romans all salted their sacrifices.

• Bedouins won't attack a man if they've eaten his salt.

THE BARBADOS TOMBS

The island of Barbados is known for its tropical climate, its sandy beaches—and its restless dead. Here are two legendary, unexplained mysteries surrounding people who have been buried on the island.

THE CHASE FAMILY CRYPT

Background Col. Thomas Chase and his family were wealthy English settlers living on Barbados in the early 1800s. They owned a large burial crypt in the graveyard of Christ Church. In 1807, Thomisina Goddard, a relative of the Chases, died and was interred in the crypt. A year later, Mary Chase, Thomas Chase's infant daughter, died mysteriously. (It was widely believed that Thomas Chase beat her to death; he was known as a violent man who beat his children—a number of whom showed signs of mental illness.) She, too, was placed in the crypt. But unlike Thomisina, who was placed in a wooden coffin, Mary's body was placed in a heavy lead coffin. After her casket was interred, the vault was sealed shut with a massive marble slab.

A Mysterious Happening

A few months afterward, Dorcas Chase (Thomas Chase's teenage daughter) starved herself to death. Like her infant sister, Dorcas was placed in a heavy lead casket and brought to the crypt. But when the family unsealed and opened the vault, they saw that something peculiar had happened: Mary Chase's tiny coffin had moved to the opposite side of the crypt—and it was standing on one end. Thomisina Goddard's casket had not been moved.

The family was shocked, but assumed the crypt had been broken into by grave robbers. They returned Mary's casket to its proper place, laid Dorcas's coffin next to it, and sealed the crypt even tighter than before—this time pouring a layer of molten lead over the marble capstone.

A Moving Experience

Thomas Chase committed suicide a month later. As with Mary and Dorcas, his body was placed in a heavy lead casket. This time when the crypt was opened, all the coffins were still in place. The crypt was again tightly sealed; it would not be reopened again by

---

Genetically speaking, a guinea pig is more closely related to a cow than it is to a rat.

the family for another eight years.

In 1816 another child related to the Chase family died. This time when the vault was unsealed, the hinges on the doors were so rusty, they would not open; it took two strong men to finally pry them open wide enough to get the coffin inside. But when the family peered into the dark vault, they saw that the caskets had again been strewn about the crypt...except for Thomasina Goddard's, which was left untouched a second time.

The mourners were dumbfounded: the adult-sized lead coffins weighed more than 500 pounds each, and the child-sized ones weren't much lighter. It took four strong men to return each of the caskets to their proper places, and it seemed inconceivable that any natural forces could have tossed them around the tomb.

Keep on Moving

Less than a month after this latest interment, a woman visiting another grave heard groans and "loud cracking" noises coming from the Chase family crypt. Her horse became so agitated by the noises that it began foaming at the mouth and had to be treated by a veterinarian. And a week after that, something spooked several horses tied up outside Christ Church; they broke free, ran down the hill, and jumped into the sea, where they drowned.

By now the goings-on in the vault were public knowledge and the source of wild speculation; when the next member of the Chase family died, more than 1,000 people came to the funeral—some from as far away as Cuba and Haiti. They weren't disappointed: when the crypt was unsealed, all of the coffins were out of place, each one standing on end against the walls of the crypt—except for Thomasina Goddard's.

You Move Me, Governor

After this funeral, the governor of the island decided to investigate. He attended the next funeral, and once again the coffins had been strewn about. This time, he tested the crypt's walls for secret passages (there were none), had the floor of the crypt covered with sand to detect footprints and other marks, had a new lock installed in the crypt's door, and had the crypt sealed with a layer of cement to be sure the door would not be opened. To top it off, he and other officials stamped the wet cement with their signet rings, making sure that it couldn't be tampered with without being detected.

On April 8, 1820, the vault was reopened to inter another member of the Chase family. The cement was still in place, but when the family removed it, something heavy leaning against the door of the crypt prevented it from being opened. Several strong men tried to force the door open…and when they finally succeeded, something crashed down inside the crypt. They opened the door all the way…and saw that it had been held shut because one of the coffins had been leaning against it. This time *all* the coffins had been disturbed—including Thomasina Goddard's.

The governor and several others examined the crypt closely to try and find an explanation. There was none; there were no footprints in the sand and none of the jewelry on any of the bodies had been stolen. Completely mystified, the governor ordered that the bodies be removed from the crypt and interred in another crypt on the island. They were never disturbed again; they rest in peace to this day.

THE McGREGOR CRYPT
Background The Chase crypt wasn't the only one on Barbados to have strange things happen to it: In August 1943, a group of Freemasons unsealed a crypt containing the body of Alexander Irvine, the founder of freemasonry on Barbados. (Irvine's remains were interred in the 1830s in the same crypt as Sir Even McGregor, the owner of the crypt, who was laid to rest in 1841.)

Strange Happenings
The McGregor crypt was even more tightly sealed than the Chase crypt: the inner door was locked tight and cemented with bricks and mortar, which itself was covered with a huge stone slab. When they unsealed the crypt, the inner door of the tomb would not open. Peeking in through a hole, they saw that a heavy lead coffin was standing on its head, leaning against the inner door. The masons carefully moved it and opened the door—only to discover that Irvine's coffin was missing; McGregor's was the one up against the door. The mystery was never solved; the island's burial records confirmed that both men had been interred in the crypt nearly 100 years before, but no evidence was ever found to explain the missing coffin.

OFF YOUR ROCKER

We'll bet you didn't know your favorite rock singers could talk, too. Here are some of the profound things they have to say.

"I'm a mess and you're a mess, too. Everyone's a mess. Which means, actually, that no one's a mess."

—*Fiona Apple*

"It's really hard to maintain a one-on-one relationship if the other person is not going to allow me to be with other people."

—*Axl Rose*

"I only answer to two people— myself and God."

—*Cher*

"I'm not a snob. Ask anybody. Well, anybody who matters."

—*Simon LeBon, of Duran Duran*

"There's a basic rule which runs through all kinds of music, kind of an unwritten rule. I don't know what it is."

—*Ron Wood*

"I want to go out at the top, but the secret is knowing when you're at the top. It's so difficult in this business—your career fluctuates all the time, up and down, like a pair of trousers."

—*Rod Stewart*

"I can't think of a better way to spread the message of world peace than by working with the NFL and being part of Super Bowl XXVII."

—*Michael Jackson*

"Damn, I look good with guns."

—*Ted Nugent*

"We use volume to drive evil spirits out the back of your head, and by evil spirits I mean the job, the boss, the spouse, the probation officer."

—*David Lee Roth*

"I should think that being my old lady would be all the satisfaction or career any woman needs."

—*Mick Jagger*

"God had to create disco music so that I could be born and be successful."

—*Donna Summer*

"I can do anything. One of these days I'll be so complete I won't be a human. I'll be a god."

—*John Denver*

"Just because I have my standards, they think I'm a bitch."

—*Diana Ross*

LIFE AFTER DEATH

Plenty has been written about people who nearly die, get a glimpse of the "other side," and then somehow make it back to the land of the living. Here are four examples of another kind of "rebirth": people who were thought to be dead, but were actually quite alive.

DECEASED: 32-year-old Ali Abdel-Rahim Mohammad, of Alexandria, Egypt
NEWS OF HIS DEATH: In 1999 Mohammad blacked out while swimming off the coast of Alexandria. His body was recovered and taken to the morgue.
RESURRECTION: After about three hours in the morgue refrigerator, Mohammad was awakened by a loud banging sound—an attendant was trying to close the refrigerator drawer in which Mohammad had been placed. So the "corpse" reached up and grabbed the attendant's hand. According to one news account, "his firm grip sent the attendant and a family who had apparently come to identify the body of a loved one stampeding out of the morgue yelling, 'Help us!'"

DECEASED: Henry Lodge, a 63-year-old California man
NEWS OF HIS DEATH: In 1986 Lodge was fixing some fuses when he had a heart attack. He was pronounced dead, and his remains were transported to the Los Angeles morgue.
RESURRECTION: Just as the morgue's Dr. Philip Campbell was preparing to make an incision in the remains, Lodge opened his eyes and screamed, "HELP!" Lodge made a speedy recovery and was soon released from the hospital; Dr. Campbell took a leave of absence from work for "nervous exhaustion."

DECEASED: Xue Wangshi, an 81-year-old Chinese woman
NEWS OF HER DEATH: On December 2, 1995, Ms. Wangshi collapsed and stopped breathing. She was pronounced dead and sent to a nearby crematorium.
RESURRECTION: Workers put Ms. Wangshi on a conveyor belt that fed the deceased into the furnace, but in classic cliffhanger fashion, moments later they saw her move her right

---

The Chilean Pudu, the smallest member of the deer family, is no larger than a rabbit.

hand. So they stopped the conveyor belt, "and Mrs. Wangshi sat up."

DECEASED: Musyoka Mutata, 60, who lived in the village of Kitui in Kenya
NEWS OF HIS DEATH: In 1985 Mututa contracted cholera and was thought to have died. Funeral arrangements were made, and at the appointed hour pallbearers arrived in his home to take the body away for burial.
RESURRECTION: When the pallbearers sprayed Mutata with insecticide to ward off flies, he suddenly sat up and asked for a drink of water. According to newspaper reports, this was Mutata's second near-death experience: in 1928 his parents mistook him for dead after an illness, and when "his body, wrapped in sheets and blankets, was being lowered into its grave, the three-year-old let out a scream and was saved."
Update: Four months after his 1985 near-death experience, Mutata died again, this time for real. Rather than bury him right away, however, his family waited two days to be sure that he was really, really dead.

DECEASED: The entire Naua tribe, which until the turn of the century had made its home in the Amazon rain forest in Brazil
NEWS OF THEIR DEATH: No word on precisely when the tribe is thought to have gone extinct; the last known report on the tribe was a 1906 newspaper article titled, "Last Naua Woman Marries."
RESURRECTION: The Naua weren't dead—as far as anyone can tell, they were just hiding. After avoiding contact with the rest of the world for nearly a century, in August 2000, more than 250 members of the tribe emerged from deep in the rain forest to protest the Brazilian government's plan to incorporate the Naua native lands into a national wildlife park. It's too early to tell what will happen, but as the law stands now, the Naua are considered trespassers on their own land. "We thought there were no more Naua," one Brazilian government told reporters. "Our job now is finding them land. No humans are allowed in the park, just the forest and the animals."

UNDERWEAR
IN THE NEWS

*Here's a question you've probably never considered: When is
underwear newsworthy? We've got the answer because we've
been studying the news to find out. The answer is, when it's...*

ROYAL UNDERWEAR

In February 2000 Captain Nick Carrell, once a member of
the queen of England's elite bodyguard unit, "admitted
trying to steal Queen Elizabeth's underwear and being caught
red-handed by the monarch."

The incident occurred in 1992 during a fire at Windsor
Palace, when Carrell was helping remove belongings from the
queen's private apartments (which were threatened by the fire). "I
was planning to steal a pair of the queen's knickers," Carrell
admitted to London's *Sunday People* newspaper. "I was helping to
clear out her private apartment when I pulled open a chest of
drawers. I was amazed to see it was filled with the queen's underwear and I put out my hand to take a pair. Suddenly, I realized she
was standing right behind me, watching my every move. I don't
know what she thought, but she didn't say a word. It was all very
embarrassing."

LIFE-SAVING UNDERWEAR

"In 1994, fisherman Renato Arganza spent several days at sea
clinging to a buoy after his boat capsized off the Philippines. Once
rescued, he remarked that he had survived by eating his underpants."

DEADLY UNDERWEAR

In 1999, two women sheltering under a tree in London's Hyde
Park during a thunderstorm were killed when lightning struck the
tree. According to medical examiners, the two women died
because the metal underwire in their bras acted as an electrical
conductor. "This is only the second time in my experience of
50,000 deaths where lightning has struck the metal in a bra causing death," Westminster coroner Paul Knapman told the media. "I
do not wish to overemphasize any significance." (*In These Times*)

CELEBRITY UNDERWEAR

• "At the 1998 auction of Kennedy memorabilia, Richard Wilson paid $3,450 for a pair of JFK's long johns. Mr. Wilson plans to exhibit the underwear next to a slip and a pair of panties formerly owned by Marilyn Monroe." (*Presidential Indiscretions*)

• In the early 1990s, an upset young man paid a visit to Father Fambrini, pastor at Hollywood's Blessed Sacrament Church. The man confessed that he'd raided Frederick's of Hollywood's lingerie museum and stolen some celebrity undies. Now, consumed with guilt, he wanted to return them, but didn't have the courage…so he asked Father Fambrini to do it. Father Fambrini agreed and returned the two stolen items: a bra belonging to actress Katey Sagal, and "the pantaloons of the late actress Ava Gardner." ("The Edge," *Oregonian*)

LIFESTYLE-ENHANCING UNDERWEAR

• In 1998, Monash University's (Australia) Institute of Reproduction and Development announced the invention of air conditioned mens' briefs, which the Institute says will prevent heat buildup in the nether regions that is believed to inhibit fertility. Why not just ask infertile males to switch from snug-fitting briefs to looser, cooler boxer shorts? "Because," says the Institute's David de Kretser, "some men don't like the freedom."

• In 1998, Florida entrepreneur Victoria Morton announced that she'd invented a bra that she claims can increase a woman's breast size by repositioning body fat, and she doesn't mean just body fat on the chest. "If a woman has extra tissue anywhere above her waist," Morton explained in a press release, "even on her back, she can use this bra to create bigger, firmer breasts." (*Universal Press Syndicate*)

ARTISTICALLY INSPIRED UNDERWEAR

American artist Laurie Long wasn't just offended when she learned that some vending machines in Japan dispense panties worn by schoolgirls, she was also inspired: She stocked a vending machine with her own used panties, "which have labels describing what she did while she wore them." (*Stuff* magazine)

NUDES & PRUDES

It's hard to shock anyone with nudity today. But stupidity is always a shock. These characters demonstrate that whether you're dressed or naked, you can still be dumber than sin.

NUDE... "Bernard Defrance, a high school teacher near Paris, told his students that each time they stumped him with a riddle, he'd shed a piece of clothing—starting with his trademark bow tie. As it turns out, the kids were too smart for him. During one round of the game in November, the 51-year-old Defrance was left standing naked before his class. He was later suspended."

PRUDES... "In 1934, eight men were fined $1 apiece for bathing 'topless' at Coney Island. 'All of you fellows may be Adonises,' said the presiding magistrate, 'but there are many people who object to seeing so much of the human body exposed.' A year later, a mass arrest of 42 topless males in Atlantic City, New Jersey, fattened the municipal coffers by $84. The city fathers declared: 'We'll have no gorillas on our beaches.'"

NUDE... "A 41-year-old Allentown man known to police as 'The Naked Bandit' pleaded guilty to robbing a string of convenience stores while in the nude, authorities said on Thursday. 'His logic was that the last time he did some robberies, he had clothes on and was identified by his clothes,' said Lehigh County District Attorney James Anthony." (*Reuters*)

PRUDES... "Matt Zelen dived into the pool to start the 100-yard butterfly, then remembered something: He'd forgotten to tie his racing suit. When the St. John's University junior felt his suit sliding off, he decided to kick it off and finish the race. Zelen, a contender for the 2000 Olympics, would have won the race by more than two seconds but he was stripped of more than just his suit—he was disqualified for violating a uniform code." (*Parade* magazine)

NUDE... "Police in Vinton, Louisiana, were bemused when a Pontiac Grand Am hit a tree and disgorged 20 nude occupants. It turned out that they were the Rodriguez family, Pentecostalists from Floydada, Texas. Police Chief Douillard commented, 'They were completely nude. All 20 of them. Didn't have a stitch of clothes on. I mean, no socks, no underwear, no nothin'. Five of them were in the trunk. The Lord told them to get rid of all their belongings and go to Louisiana.'"

PRUDE... "The Mayor of North Platte, Nebraska, kept his promise to walk naked down the street. Mayor Jim Whitaker said he'd walk 'naked' if the Paws-itive Partners Humane Society raised $5,000. When his plan drew national attention—and angry calls— Whitaker revealed that he actually planned to walk a dog named 'Naked' instead of walking in the buff himself."

NUDE... "A bare-breasted mermaid perched on a rock is causing a stir along Lyse Fjord in Norway. 'One man jumped off a boat and swam over to me,' Line Oexnevad, 37, said of her job as a siren. 'Most people just look and cheer.' Ms. Oexnevad, naked except for a blonde wig and a fish-tail, was hired as a tourist attraction."

PRUDES... "At the turn of the century (1900, that is), Boston, Massachusetts, refused to accept shipments of navel oranges from Los Angeles, terming the fruit's name 'indelicate and immodest.'" ("Only in L.A.," the *Los Angeles Times*)

NUDE... "Police arriving at the scene of a two-car collision in Los Angeles found a totally nude woman behind the wheel of one car. The 35-year-old L.A. resident reportedly told police that when she began her drive, she thought she was a camel in Morocco, and when she saw the palm trees lining the downtown streets, she was sure of it...." (*Bizarre* magazine)

PRUDE... "Animal control workers in California recently received a call from a woman who insisted she needed to get a marriage license for a male and a female cat 'before they breed.'" ("Only in L.A.," the *Los Angeles Times*)

A 'TOON IS BORN

Here are the stories of how three popular cartoons were created.

THE JETSONS
Background: In 1960, Hanna-Barbera studios broke new ground with America's first prime-time cartoon series, *The Flintstones*. Airing at 7:30 on Friday nights, it became one of the Top 20 programs of the 1960–61 season. It did so well, in fact, that ABC wanted a second prime-time cartoon the following year.
Inspiration: So Hanna-Barbera just reversed the formula. "After *The Flintstones*, it was a pretty natural move," says Joseph Barbera. "The space race was on everybody's mind in the early 1960s...so we went from the cave days to the future, the exact opposite direction....if *The Flintstones* featured the likes of Stony Curtis, Cary Granite, and Ann Margrock, the Jetson family could go see Dean Martian perform in a Las Venus hotel such as the Sonic Sahara, the Riviera Satellite, or the Flamoongo.
On the Air: *The Jetsons* originally aired at 7:30 PM on Sunday night—traditionally a kids' time slot in the days before cable TV. But against *Walt Disney's Wonderful World of Color* (NBC) and *Dennis the Menace* (CBS), it flopped. *The Jetsons* was canceled after one season; only 24 episodes were made.

The following year (1963), however, ABC scheduled *Jetsons* reruns as a regular Saturday morning cartoon show (pre-cable). That's where it belonged. The show was so popular with kids that for the next 20 years, the same 24 episodes ran over and over again on Saturdays.

REN & STIMPY
Background: Fresh from his success animating *The New Adventures of Mighty Mouse* for television, in 1989 an animator named John Kricfalusi pitched the Nickelodeon channel an idea he had for a cartoon called "Your Gang."

Nickelodeon was interested in the show, but it insisted on buying all the rights to the characters, as part of its plan to create a stable of "evergreen" cartoons, like those at Walt Disney and Warner Brothers, that could be broadcast for decades to come.
Inspiration: Kricfalusi didn't want to sell the rights to his favorite

"Your Gang" characters. Instead, "he sold Nickelodeon a show about two ancillary 'Your Gang' characters with whom he was willing to part: a paranoid Chihuahua named Ren (inspired by a postcard of a chihuahua in a sweater), and an excretion-obsessed cat named Stimpy (which originated as a doodle and was named after a college friend)."

On the Air: When *Ren & Stimpy* debuted in August 1991, Nickelodeon had only six completed episodes to broadcast. But the show was such a surprise hit—Nickelodeon's Sunday morning ratings doubled on the strength of *Ren & Stimpy* alone—that Nickelodeon aired the six episodes over and over again for about a year until new episodes were ready. *The Los Angeles Times* reported: "*Ren & Stimpy* [has] started a national craze that helped turn Nicktoons into a major force in children's animation."

Meanwhile, however, Kricfalusi and Nickelodeon had a falling-out. The cable station said the cartoonist was too slow with new episodes; Kricfalusi said that Nick was meddling creatively. In 1992, Nick fired *Ren & Stimpy*'s creator and replaced him with a former partner. The show lost its edge and faded away. However, it's still considered the breakthrough series for modern TV animation. "All new shows that have any kind of style have to tip their hat to *Ren & Stimpy*," says animation historian Jerry Beck. *Beavis and Butt-head* actually owes its existence to the show. *Ren & Stimpy*'s success was the reason the channel was willing to pay for its own animated show.

BEAVIS AND BUTT-HEAD

Background: In the early 1990s, a defense industry engineer named Mike Judge grew tired of his job working for a company that made components for the F-18 fighter jet. So he quit and became a musician. After a few months of playing guitar in a bar band, he bought a $200 animation kit and began making cartoons to amuse himself.

Inspiration: "One day in the summer of 1990," *Newsweek* reported, "Judge was trying to draw this kid he remembered from junior high. It didn't much look like the kid, but when he came back to it a week later, it made him laugh, and that was enough. This was the birth of Butt-Head, with his short upper lip and massive gums. 'The guy I tried to draw, he had that laugh: "Huh-huh, huh-huh-huh,"' says Judge....'Actually, my hair is really unmanageable, so I may have gotten Butt-head's hair from myself.'"

Judge adds, "There were probably four or five guys who inspired Beavis, just a little Bic-flipping pyro kid. I've noticed that 13-year-old metal heads haven't changed much over the years."

A few years later, Judge decided to make an antisocial cartoon called "Frog Baseball" featuring Beavis and Butt-Head playing baseball using a live frog for the ball. "I was thinking of when I was a kid and bored," Judge said. "There's nothing to do. That's when kids start blowing up lizards. You're this 14-year-old guy with no car, you just have a bike and testosterone. It's a dangerous situation."

"My mom didn't like 'Frog Baseball' at all. I showed it once at this guy's house. He was having this cartoon viewing party, and everything else was very cartoony, standard stuff. When 'Frog Baseball' came on, this girl kept looking at the screen and then at me. She says, 'He isn't actually going to hit the frog, is he?' And then Butt-head hits the frog, and she says, 'God, you look so normal.'"

On the Air: Judge entered "Frog Baseball" in a "Sick and Twisted" cartoon festival, and a week later a company called Colossal Pictures bought it for the MTV series *Liquid Television*. But before they put it on the air, the channel tested it on a focus group to gauge their reaction. "The focus group was both riveted and hysterical from the moment they saw it," says Gwen Lipsky, MTV's vice president of research and planning. "After the tape was over, they kept asking to see it again. Then, after they had seen it again, several people offered to buy it from me."

MTV put Beavis and Butt-head on *Liquid Televison* for two weeks in March 1993. The reaction was so positive that in May it was back full-time. It quickly became MTV's most popular show, with ratings twice as high as any other show on the network.

* * *

AMAZING LUCK

"On February 2, 1931, a horse named Brampton was driving for the wire in a race in Dargaville, New Zealand, comfortably in the lead. But 40 feet from the finish line, the horse stumbled and fell, rolled over several times with his jockey clinging frantically to his back, and crossed the line as the winner."

WHO'D LOVE A PLATYPUS?

He looks suspiciously like a beaver in a duck costume (or vice versa). He's got a name that sounds like he's mates with Socrates or Aesop. No wonder he's such a shy little critter.

INTERESTING THINGS ABOUT THE PLATYPUS
- His real name is *Ornithorhynchus anatinus* (poor guy).
- He has one of the most waterproof coats in the world.
- He spends up to 12 hours a day in water as cold as 0°C.
- The girl platypus poohs and reproduces out of the same orifice (yuk!).
- He has a spur on his foot that is venomous enough to kill a dog.
- When first sightings of the platypus were reported back to Europe, they thought it was a hoax.
- He is found only in eastern Australia, especially in Tasmania.
- He growls like a puppy when in danger.

WHAT IS IT, AND WHERE DID IT COME FROM?
Apparently, there are two theories of where the platypus came from. The scientific theory is that the platypus (and his Aussie mate, the echidna) evolved from either marsupials or a bunch of early mammals. The other theory comes from Aboriginal folklore about a naughty little duck…

> Once upon a time, there was a duck whose name was… Duck. Duck lived with his friends in a sheltered river pond. All of them were in constant fear of Mulloka the Water Devil, and never strayed far from their pond. But one day, against the advice of her elders, Duck ventured downstream and eventually found herself on a patch of grass on the riverbank. Unaware that this was the territory of the lonely Water-rat, she climbed out. Hearing Duck, Water-rat emerged, threatened her with his spear and, dragging her underground, forced her to mate with him. By the time of egg-hatching, Duck was ashamed to have to lead out two extraordinary offspring. They had bills and webbed feet, but instead of two feet they had four and instead of feathers they had fur, while on each hind leg they had a sharp spike like Water-rat's spear. The first members of the platypus race were born.

I believe the second story…

AIR FORCE ONE

*You've heard of Air Force One, but what do you really
know about it? Here's a short history of what's now
considered the "flying White House."*

HOMEBOUND

Nowadays it's taken for granted that travelling around
the world is part of the U.S. president's job. But that
wasn't always the case: As late as the 1930s, it was considered the
president's duty not to leave the country—he was expected to
remain on U.S. soil for his entire term of office—and wasn't even
supposed to stray far from Washington, D.C. This tradition was
left over from the pre-telephone age, when the only way a
president could command the government on a moment's notice
in an emergency was to be physically in or near the nation's capital at all times. Leaving town literally meant leaving power, and
presidents aren't supposed to do that. For the first 130 years of the
Republic, not a single American president left the United States
while in office, not even once. (Well, okay, once. Grover Cleve-
land briefly sailed across the U.S.–Canada border in the 1890s.)

So in January 1943, when Franklin Roosevelt flew to North
Africa to meet with Winston Churchill and plan the Allied invasion of Southern Europe, he became only the fourth president to
leave the country (The others: cousin Teddy Roosevelt inspected
the Panama Canal in 1906 and Woodrow Wilson attended the
Paris Peace Conference at the end of World War I.)

SMALL WORLD

Franklin Roosevelt hated aeroplanes, but German submarines
were patrolling the Atlantic and sinking American ships, so the
Secret Service forbade him from travelling by sea. He flew in a
chartered PanAm Flying Boat seaplane called the *Dixie Clipper*.
That changed everything.

When Roosevelt's historic trip became publicized weeks later,
it turned out to be an important psychological boost not just for
the war effort, but also for the fledgling airline industry. If it was
safe enough for President Roosevelt to fly during the war, people
reasoned, it would safe enough for anyone else to fly in times of

---

On average, people who have asthma hear better than people who don't. Nobody knows why.

peace. Furthermore, Americans realized that with planes, the president could travel almost anywhere in the world in a matter of days and return just as quickly if need be. And thanks to radio and telephone communications, it was possible to remain in fairly close contact with the government at all times. Within weeks of Roosevelt's historic journey, the U.S. Army Air Corps (precursor to the Air Force) began making plans to provide a custom-made plane for the president's exclusive use. Since then, each president has had an official plane, and today the president's aeroplane is considered an extension of the White House.

THE NAME

• Technically speaking, although there is a special presidential aeroplane, it doesn't have the radio call sign *Air Force One*. The call sign is attached to the president himself; it is given to whatever Air Force plane in which he happens to be flying. Likewise, any plane in which the vice president flies is known as *Air Force Two*.

• In fact, before JFK, each presidential aircraft had its own name: President Roosevelt's plane was nicknamed the "Sacred Cow" by the White House Press Corp; President Truman's plane was the *Independence* (Truman named it himself, out of fear that it might otherwise become the "Sacred Cow II"); and President Eisenhower's was the *Columbine*.

• Then, in 1962, President Kennedy took delivery of a Boeing 707, the first presidential jet aeroplane—and never bothered to name it. With no other name to go by, the media began referring to the plane by its call sign. The term Air Force One has been used for presidential aircraft ever since.

• In 1971 Richard Nixon renamed his plane *The Spirit of '76* in advance of the U.S. Bicentennial, but the name never took hold.

MADE TO ORDER

• One of the perks of being president is that you get to have *Air Force One* remodelled to suit your own tastes. President Truman had his plane painted to look like a giant eagle, with stylized blue feathers, cockpit windows that looked like eyes, and a nose painted to look like a big brown beak. (The nose was later repainted yellow, out of fear the White House Press Corps might nickname the plane "Brown Nose.")

The average cigar smoker can smoke an average cigar in about an hour and a half.

• President Lyndon Johnson had all of the passenger seats unbolted and turned around so that they faced the rear of the plane—toward his compartment. He also ripped out the cherry wood divider separating his compartment from the rest of the plane and replaced it with clear Plexiglas, Jerry Ter Horst writes in *The Flying White House*, "so that he could keep an eye on everybody—and they on him."

• LBJ also installed a secret taping system, which, ironically, President Nixon ordered removed after he took office.

CODE NAME: PROJECT LIDA ROSE

The most extensive makeover for *Air Force One* came in the late 1950s and was proposed by Allen Dulles, director of the CIA. Not long after he inaugurated the super-secret, high-altitude U-2 spy plane program, Dulles proposed outfitting the president's aeroplane with hidden spy cameras for an upcoming trip to the Soviet Union.

Unlike U-2 spy planes, which flew at altitudes as high as 21,336 metres [70,000 feet], President Eisenhower's plane would be flying under 1,500 metres [5,000 feet], and was the only Western aircraft allowed into Russian airspace. Why not take advantage of the trip to take much closer pictures of Soviet defenses?

Whether or not Eisenhower was informed of the plan (many historians suspect he wasn't), it was approved, and his aircraft was fitted with a camera inside a hidden compartment in the fuselage. The controls were carefully disguised to look like the co-pilot's fresh-air vent, so that they would be undetectable even if a Soviet pilot was riding shotgun in the cockpit.

The cameras on board the presidential plane might well have provided the U.S. with the biggest intelligence coup of the Cold War—had they ever been put to use. But they weren't—on May 1, 1960, pilot Francis Gary Powers was shot down in his U-2 skyplane over Soviet airspace, and Nikita Khrushchev used the incident to scuttle Eisenhower's visit to the USSR. The cameras were removed when John F. Kennedy was elected president.

HELP YOURSELF

• Stealing objects stamped with the presidential seal has long been one of the perks of being invited to fly aboard *Air Force One*. Still, not every president has approved: President Carter was so offended by the practice that he ordered the plane's expensive engraved crystal ashtrays, candy dishes, and wine glasses removed and had them replaced with plastic containers and paper cups.

• Lyndon Johnson took the opposite approach—he filled the plane with expensive trinkets so that his guests would have something to steal. "It was useful to him to have people brag about flying with LBJ—and to have a souvenir with which to prove it," one aide remembers.

• True to form, when LBJ returned home to Texas on his last official trip aboard *Air Force One*, he reportedly stole everything that wasn't nailed down—and a few items that were, recalls pilot Ralph Albertazzie:

> When I took over the plane after it came back from Texas, I found an empty larder. We had no presidential china, no Air Force One silverware, no Air Force One cigarettes, no cocktail napkins [serviettes], no towels—not even any paper products like toilet tissue. They were all gone. Even LBJ's special executive chair—the one we called "the throne'—was unbolted from the floor and taken away. The presidential stateroom was bare of pillows, blankets, and everything else that bore the presidential seal. I couldn't believe my eyes.

* * * *

DRIVE-IN FOOD

The first drive-in restaurant was Kirby's Pig Stand, opened by J.G. Kirby on a highway between Dallas and Fort Worth in 1921. But it turns out that the idea of restaurant service to an automobile is almost as old as cars themselves.

It started as a way for the upper-class of Boston to show off. In 1904 Mrs. "Jack" Gardner of Boston, a social-climber famous for outrageous stunts like walking a lion around the city streets, organized a special "motoring event." She and four carloads of friends went to the Hotel Touraine, where, at her insistence, they were served oysters by waiters "compelled to run out with their trays to the autos." Next, the party motored to Adams House, where they were served soup in the street, and then to eight more establishments for eight more courses, the last of which was chop suey at a Chinese restaurant, for dessert.

PAUL IS DEAD!

*The biggest, most widely discussed rumour about rock bands and
performers ever was—appropriately—about the Beatles. In 1969,
millions of fans were convinced that Paul McCartney was dead,
and spent months trying to prove it. Here's the inside story.*

HAVE YOU HEARD THE NEWS?
Although no one knows precisely when or how it started,
sometime in 1969 a rumour began circulating that Paul
McCartney of the Beatles was dead. The idea really took off one
Sunday that September, when an Eastern Michigan University
student identifying himself as "Tom" called the "Russ Gibb Show"
on WKNR-FM.

The caller told Gibb he'd heard that McCartney had been
dead for some time, that the rest of the Beatles knew about it, and
that they had started inserting "hints" of McCartney's death into
their most recent record albums. Why were they keeping McCartney's death a secret? Maybe it was to let fans down easily—maybe
it was to make as much money as they could before the death
became public and the band had to dissolve.

But that was beside the point. The point was that Paul was
dead, the caller told Gibb, and the proof was in the music.

GETTING IT BACKWARD

Gibb had been in the radio business for some time, and this wasn't
the first dead-rock-star story he'd ever heard. Celebrity-death
rumours were as common as they were unfounded, and Gibb initially dismissed this one as being just as ridiculous as the others—
until Tom told him to play the Beatles' song "Revolution Nine"
backward to hear one of the "clues."

When Gibb played back the part of the song where the voice
says "Number Nine" over and over, he thought he could hear the
words, "Turn me on, dead man." He began to wonder if Paul
McCartney really was dead, and he shared his suspicions with his
listeners. Within minutes the switchboard was lit up with calls.
Everybody wanted to know if McCartney was really dead.

The Cambodian language has 72 letters in its alphabet, the most of any language.

PAPER TRAIL

The rumours might never have amounted to anything more, if someone named Fred LaBour hadn't been listening to the "Russ Gibb Show" that Sunday afternoon.

LaBour, a University of Michigan sophomore who wrote for his college newspaper, *The Michigan Daily*, was supposed to write a review of the Beatles' new *Abbey Road* album for an upcoming issue. But he was still looking for some kind of angle that would make the article more interesting.

As LaBour listened to Tom and Russ Gibb discussing whether Paul McCartney was dead, he knew he had his angle—turn the rumour into a full-length article, a satire that pretended to take the whole idea seriously. LaBour thought it would make an interesting and amusing read. He had no idea how right he was.

The next day, LaBour wrote up his "review" of *Abbey Road* and turned it in to John Gray, the arts editor for *The Michigan Daily*. Gray was so impressed that he decided to give it an entire page in the paper. "Just how long did it take you to come up with this masterpiece?" he asked.

"It only took an hour and a half," LaBour said, "and it's the best bull---- I ever wrote."

HOT OFF THE PRESSES

LaBour's article ran on page 2 of *The Michigan Daily* with the headline "McCartney Dead; New Evidence Brought to Light."

The article claimed that Paul had been dead for nearly three years:

> Paul McCartney was killed in an automobile accident in early November, 1966, after leaving EMI recording studios tired, sad, and dejected. The Beatles had been preparing their forthcoming album, tentatively titled *Smile*, when progress bogged down in intragroup hassles and bickering. Paul climbed into his Aston-Martin, sped away into the rainy, chill night, and was found hours later pinned under his car in a culvert with the top of his head sheared off. He was deader than a doornail.

The article claimed that the surviving Beatles decided "to make the best of a bad situation," because "Paul always loved a good joke," LaBour quoted John Lennon as saying. The surviving Beatles decided to replace Paul with a body double and continue as if he hadn't died. To that end, the group held a "Paul Look-Alike Contest" and found a living substitute in Scotland, a man named William Campbell.

Thanks to extensive voice training, lip-synching, and a moustache (which John, George, and Ringo also grew), Campbell had somehow managed to pass himself off as Paul McCartney for more than three years, despite the fact that the band had been inserting clues into their songs and onto their album covers all along. The *Abbey Road* album cover, for example, shows the four Beatles crossing the street: McCartney is the only one walking out of step, the only one who's barefoot ("the way corpses are buried in Italy," LaBour claimed), and is holding a cigarette in his right hand, when everybody knows he is left-handed. On top of that, the licence plate on one of the cars parked on the road reads "28IF"—which LaBour claimed was a coded way of saying that McCartney would be 28 if he were still alive.

CLUE ME IN

LaBour probably never intended for his joke to travel beyond the University of Michigan, but by the end of the day the story had spread to other nearby colleges, and from there to the rest of the country over the next several days. Wherever the rumour spread, people began studying the Beatles' recent album covers and listening to their albums backwards—and finding their own "clues," which only added to the story's credibility and caused it to spread even further.

"In terms of media coverage," Andru J. Reeve writes in *Turn Me On, Dead Man*, "the rumour reached an apex during the last two weeks of October. Major newspapers and network television had avoided comment up to this point, for they assumed that, like rumours of the past, the story would fade before the presses had a chance to warm up."

SILENT PARTNER

So did Paul McCartney: Recently married and burned out from the difficult *Abbey Road* recording session, McCartney was holed up with his wife and kids in Scotland and wasn't coming out for anything, not even to prove he wasn't dead. Like a lot of people, when he first heard the rumour, he figured it would soon pass.

But the rumour refused to die, and McCartney finally consented to giving Apple Records a written statement that he wasn't dead. But he still refused to make a public appearance. For many people, the fact that a written statement was all the Beatles' own record company could come up with was further proof that he really was dead.

WHEW!
It's probably fitting that *Life* magazine provided the most convincing evidence that death had not taken McCartney. *Life* sent a reporter and two staff photographers to McCartney's farm to "bring back any visual evidence of Paul's existence, even if he refused to be interviewed." McCartney not only refused, he heaved a bucket of water at them. Once he calmed down, however, McCartney let the photographers take some pictures of him with his family. *Life* ran one on the cover the next issue.

Amazingly, some skeptics saw the *Life* magazine article as further proof that McCartney was dead—when you hold the magazine cover up to a bright light, the car in the Lincoln Continental ad on the reverse side appears to be impaling McCartney. For most fans, though, seeing the pictures of Paul with his family was enough, and the rumour receded as quickly as it had spread.

FOR THE RECORD
The only unresolved question was whether the rumours were orchestrated or fuelled by the Beatles themselves, perhaps to increase sales of *Abbey Road*.

"One undeniable fact became apparent," Andru Reeve writes: "sales of Beatles albums did increase." Priced $2 higher than earlier Beatles albums, *Abbey Road* sold slowly at first—until about the time that the rumours started circulating. Then, Reeve writes, it "rocketed to number one and the other albums germane to the rumour (*Sgt. Pepper's*, *Magical Mystery Tour*, and the *"White Album"* resurfaced on the Billboard Top 200 LP chart after absences of up to a year and a half."

UNFINISHED MASTERPIECE: THE BEACH BOYS' *SMILE*

Today they're thought of as a golden-oldies pop band, but at their peak the Beach Boys were America's #1 rock band and considered the creative equivalent of the Beatles. Here's the story of the never-completed album that might have kept them on top.

UNFINISHED MASTERPIECE: *Smile*, by Brian Wilson, Van Dyke Parks and the Beach Boys

WHAT IT IS: An unfinished Beach Boys album. Considered by many who have heard bootleg tapes to be among the best albums in the history of rock 'n' roll, *Smile* might have had the same impact on the Beach Boys' career that *Sergeant Pepper's Lonely Hearts Club Band* had on the Beatles' (it was released a few months after Brian Wilson ended work on *Smile*.)

THE STORY: Before they'd even graduated from high school, the three Wilson brothers (Brian, Carl, and Dennis) their cousin Mike Love, and a friend named Al Jardine had hit it big with good-time pop music about Southern California surfing, cars, and girls.

The man behind the music was the oldest brother, Brian, who wrote most of their songs, arranged their harmonies, and worked with studio musicians to get exactly the right sound. In the Beatlemania mid-1960s, when it seemed like only British Invasion groups could make the charts, the Beach Boys successfully matched the Beatles, with hit after hit.

BATTLE OF THE BANDS

A rivalry developed between the Beach Boys and Beatles. When one group released a new album, it prompted the other to see if they could top it, a process that intensified as both bands' music became more serious and complex. Wilson, though, was at a disadvantage: The Beatles had two great songwriters, John Lennon and Paul McCartney (three if you include the less-prolific George). And they had a brilliant producer, George Martin. The Beach

---

The potato and the tomato are more closely related than the potato and the sweet potato.

Boys essentially had just Brian. "From the point of view of his family," David Leaf writes in *The Beach Boys and the California Myth*, "Brian was almost a benefactor rather than an artist. He wrote the hits and made the records, and the group sang them and toured and were rich and lived in the manner they had become accustomed to, all thanks to Brian Wilson."

For several years, Brian managed to write virtually all the songs on the three albums a year the band released, while also performing in concerts all over the world. But with such an unrelenting schedule something was bound to give, and in December 1964, Brian had a nervous breakdown on an aeroplane while en route to a concert tour. He recuperated, but he and the band decided to hire a replacement for him for touring, so Brian could stay home and work full-time in the studio, creating songs that would be ready for the boys to add their voices to whenever they returned from the road.

Brian made the studio his instrument and created a unique pop sound. But the new songs began to take the Beach Boys in a new direction, away from the surfing, cars, and girls that had made them America's #1 rock 'n' roll act. It was a direction the other members of the band weren't sure they wanted to go.

PET SOUNDS

In May 1966, the group released an album called *Pet Sounds*, which many critics consider the best Beach Boys album ever. It served as a wake-up call to the Beatles, a warning that their rivalry with the Beach Boys was escalating to a new level. Paul McCartney was floored by what he heard. "No one is educated musically until they hear *Pet Sounds*," he said later. "It is a total classic record that is unbeatable in many ways…. *Pet Sounds* was our inspiration for making Sergeant Pepper's. I just thought, 'Oh dear me, this is the album of all time. What are we going to do?'" For all the praise it received, *Pet Sounds* was a commercial disappointment. "What many critics consider to be one of the best and most important albums in rock history never was embraced by American record buyers," Leaf writes. "It never sold enough to become a gold record…It took many listenings for a fan to finally appreciate and absorb what Brian had accomplished. In terms of record sales, this was damaging, because the fan underground quickly passed the word to 'stay away from the new Beach Boys album, it's weird.'"

Pet Sounds' weak sales took its toll on Wilson. "*Pet Sounds* was not a big hit," Brian's ex-wife Marilyn says. "That really hurt Brian badly. He couldn't understand it. It's like, why put your heart and soul into something. I think that had a lot to do with slowing him down."

GOOD VIBRATIONS

The rivalry continued. The Beatles' "All You Need Is Love" inspired Brian Wilson to piece together a complex single called "Good Vibrations." Today "Good Vibrations" is considered a pop oldie, but in its day it was a revolutionary piece of music, a "pocket symphony," as Brian Wilson called it, that took more than six months of recording time and 90 hours of recording tape to create. Brian created 11 different versions of the song before he finally found one he liked, a process that caused production costs to balloon to more than $50,000, a fortune in the mid-1960s.

The expense was worth it. Unlike *Pet Sounds,* "Good Vibrations" was a huge hit. It sold 400,000 in the first four weeks alone and went on to become the Beach Boys' first million-selling single. "By the fall of 1966," Leaf writes, "the Beach Boys led by Brian Wilson, had musically gone past the Beatles....With 'Good Vibrations,' Brian surpassed everything current in popular music....It firmly established Brian as the foremost producer on the music scene."

"Jesus, that ear," Bob Dylan once remarked about Brian Wilson, "he should donate it to the Smithsonian."

SMILE

Brian Wilson's next project was an album tentatively titled *Dumb Angel,* which he told a friend would be a "teenage symphony to God." The album, a deeply personal statement, which was later renamed *Smile,* was poised to take the Beach Boys even deeper into the realm of "experimental" music, something that worried Brian Wilson's friend David Anderle. "I said, 'Don't have them as part of *Smile.* Do it on your own, man. Make it a Brian Wilson album." Perhaps out of loyalty to his brothers and his cousin Mike Love, Brian decided not to go off on his own. The band remained intact; *Smile* was slated as their next album.

By the time the other members returned from a concert tour of England, Brian had much of the background music for *Smile* finished; all the band would have to do was record the vocals.

Lyrics for many of the songs had been written by Van Dyke Parks, a composer and lyricist known for his obscure, Bob Dylan-esque style.

The other Beach Boys were anything but Bob Dylan-esque, so they began arguing with Brian as soon as they got into the studio. "When they came back from England," David Anderle says, "the last thing they wanted to do was become experimental. From where they were coming from, the Van Dyke Parks influence was not a healthy influence for them lyrically. They were hearing things they'd never heard before. It was not Beach Boys lyrics."

Mike Love was the most resistant. "Don't f*** with the formula," he groused during one recording session. The other members of the band dreaded another commercial disappointment like *Pet Sounds*.

FROWN

"The group resisted the experimentation," Leaf writes, "and resented the way Brian treated them as a musical instrument, but most of all, they didn't like Van Dyke Park's words. It was the fighting over Park's lyrics that eventually made Brian, who loved what Van had created, begin to question the songs."

As the arguments continued, Brian began to lose confidence, and *Smile* fell behind schedule. Pressure was mounting. Then, suddenly in February 1967, Van Dyke Parks left to sign a solo contract with Warner Bros., leaving Brian to finish the remaining songs alone and fend for himself against the rest of the band. Rather than fight for his ideas, he began to withdraw. "He really did back away from it, just back off and go to the bedroom or whatever," Anderle says. "He just wouldn't face up to it."

Capitol Records pushed *Smile's* release date back repeatedly; meanwhile, the Beatles, with much fanfare, came forth with Sergeant Pepper's Lonely Hearts Club Band. Brian bought a copy and put on the headphones. He played it over and over again into the night; and as he marvelled at the Beatles' accomplishment, what little self confidence he still had was shattered. He withdrew into his room and never finished his album. "*Smile* was destroying me," he explained in 1976.

"Had *Smile* been concluded and put out," David Anderle says, "I think it would have been a major influence in pop music. I think it would have been as significant if not a bigger influence than *Sergeant Pepper* was....That album was startling. And I think *Smile* would have been even more startling."

BEACHED BOYS

Within months after *Smile* bit the dust, the Beach Boys' reluctance to experiment caught up with them. The rock music world was changing all around them, and they weren't changing with it.

In June 1967, they cancelled their appearance at the Monterey Pop Festival at the last minute. The festival, which served as a springboard to superstardom for new artists like Janis Joplin, Jimi Hendrix, and The Who, was a major turning point in rock 'n roll, and the Beach Boys weren't a part of it. "Instead," Leaf writes, "they alienated the hip audience that had just begun to accept them because of music like *Pet Sounds* and 'Good Vibrations.' By not appearing, the Beach Boys quickly found themselves in exile as pop relics."

Within months of releasing "Good Vibrations," the Beach Boys had fallen so far out of step with where rock 'n' roll was heading that it had actually become fashionable to hate them. "In person, the Beach Boys are a totally disappointing group," *Rolling Stone* founder Jann Wenner wrote in December 1967. "The Beach Boys are just one prominent example of a group that has gotten hung up in trying to catch the Beatles. It is a pointless pursuit.... Their surfing work continued for about ten albums with little progress."

While reproduced and rerecorded versions of some of the *Smile* material appeared on subsequent Beach Boys albums over the next five years, it wasn't the same. The magical moment for what might have been the greatest rock album of all time was lost.

POST-MORTEM

"In the fall of 1989, I was working with a band who turned me on to the bootlegged recordings of Brian Wilson's legendary, aborted *Smile* sessions. Like a musical burning bush, these tapes awakened me to a higher consciousness in record making. I was amazed that one, single human could dream up this unprecedented and radically advanced approach to rock 'n' roll. How could a talent so great be so misunderstood and underappreciated?"

—**Record producer Don Was**

Among other things, the ancient Egyptians worshipped cabbages.

THE DARK SIDE OF PETER PAN

"All children except one, grow up. They soon know that they will grow up…this is the beginning of the end." The first paragraph of James Barrie's classic story, Peter Pan, *introduced its central theme. It sounds innocent, but a look at Barrie's life gives it a more sinister twist.*

I WON'T GROW UP

"All of James Barrie's life led up to the creation of *Peter Pan*," wrote one of his biographers.

A pivotal point came in 1866 when Barrie, the youngest in a Scottish family of 10 children, was six: his brother David, the pride of the family, died in a skating accident. Barrie's mother was devastated. To comfort her, little James began imitating David's mannerisms and mimicking his speech. This bizarre charade went on for years—and only got weirder: when James reached 13, the age at which David had died, he literally stopped growing. He never stood taller than 1.5 metres [5 feet], and didn't shave until he was 24. He always had a thin, high-pitched voice.

SUCCESS AND FAILURE

From childhood, Barrie's main interest had been creating stories and plays. After graduating from college, he moved to London to pursue a career as a writer, and soon his work was being published.

In the 1880s, his novels about a "wandering little girl"—his mother—captured the public's imagination and put him on the road to fame and wealth. He soon became one of England's most famous writers.

Despite his professional success, the gawky Barrie was painfully shy with women, and the thought of marriage terrified him. After a nightmare, he wrote in his journal: "Greatest horror, dream I am married, wake up screaming." But that didn't stop him from putting lovely actresses on a pedestal. Barrie became enamored of leading lady Mary Ansell, who appeared in his early plays. Motherlike, she nursed him through a life-threatening bout of pneumonia. And when he recovered, they decided to marry.

Minestrone means "big soup" in Italian.

It was a disaster. Barrie wasn't capable of an intimate relationship and was probably impotent as well—stuck, physically and emotionally in a state of perpetual boyhood. Eventually, Mary fell in love with a young writer named Gilbert Cannan and demanded a divorce. Barrie refused, because his marriage had provided him with the appearance of being normal. But when Mary threatened to tell the world that he was impotent and had never consummated their marriage, Barrie gave in.

THE LOST BOYS

In 1899, while still unhappily married, Barrie befriended young George, John, and Peter Davies and their mother, Sylvia, in London's Kensington Park. The boy's father, Arthur Davies, was too busy tending to his struggling career as a lawyer to spend much time with his family. So childless Barrie was only too happy to play with the Davies boys. He became a frequent caller at their home, and even rented a cottage nearby when they went on vacations in Surrey.

Barrie idolized the children's beautiful mother. But it was with the children that he could truly be himself. He met with them daily in the park or at their home. They played Indians together, or pretended to be pirates, forcing each other to "walk the plank." Barrie made up stories for the boys, featuring talking birds and fairies, and acted them out.

PETER IS BORN

In 1901 Barrie ordered a printing of only two copies of a photo-essay book of his adventures with the Davies boys. He entitled it *The Boy Castaways of Black Lake Island* and gave one copy to the boy's father (who promptly left it on a train). The next year, Barrie published these adventures in a novel called *The Little White Bird*. In a story-within-a-story, the narrator tells "David" (George Davies) about Peter Pan, a seven-day-old boy who flies away from his parents to live with fairies. All children start out as birds, the story goes, but soon forget how to fly.

Peter eventually flies home, and tearfully sees through the nursery window that his mother is holding a new baby and has forgotten him. Now Peter Pan can never go home and will never grow up.

England is only two-thirds the size of New England.

The Little White Bird was popular, and readers begged Barrie to give them more of that new character, Peter Pan.

Barrie knew exactly how to bring Peter Pan back. He had often taken the Davies boys to pantomimes—dazzling Christmas-time musical dramas put on for children. The plays always featured a young hero and heroine (both played by actresses), a Good Fairy, a Demon King, fight scenes, characters flying (on invisible wires) and a "transformation scene," in which the ordinary world became a fairyland. During the performances, Barrie carefully observed the boys' reactions. They seemed to love every moment.

So why not, Barrie thought, put Peter Pan in a similar children's play for the London stage?

THE DARLINGS

Barrie always acknowledged that the Davies boys' free-spirited youth was his inspiration for Peter Pan. "I made Peter by rubbing the five of you together, as savages with two sticks produce a flame," he wrote on the dedication page of the printed version of the play. More than that, however, the Davies family—loving mother, impatient father, and adorable sons—served as Barrie's model for the Darlings in the play. He even used their names:

• Mr. Darling was named after the eldest boy, George Davies.
• Jack Davies became John Darling.
• Michael and Nicholas became Michael Nicholas Darling.
• Peter Davies's name went to Peter Pan.

As for the author, he appears as Captain James Hook, whose right hand is gone. Barrie suffered paralysis of his right hand from tendonitis. Hook is relentlessly pursued by a crocodile who has swallowed a ticking clock, which biographers say was "a metaphor of Barrie stalked by cruel time." Porthos, his St. Bernard, became nurse-dog Nana, who exasperated the stuffy father (in real life, he was exasperated not with the dog, but with Barrie).

Barrie added a sister, Wendy, modelled after Margaret Henley, the deceased daughter of Barrie's friend, M. E. Henley. The six-year-old girl had called Barrie her "fwendy" (friend) and from that child-word, Barrie invented the name Wendy. It rapidly became one of England's most popular girls names.

Bees are born fully grown.

WILL PETER PAN FLY?

Peter Pan posed a radical departure for adult theatre. Barrie had an agreement with producer Charles Frohman to deliver a play manuscript. He offered Frohman another play gratis if he would only produce his "dream child," *Peter Pan*. "I'm sure it will not be a commercial success," Barrie said of *Peter*.

But Frohman, a wealthy American who liked risky ventures, said he would produce both plays. After reading the manuscript of *Peter Pan*, Frohman was so excited, he would stop friends on the street and force them to listen to passages from it. With an American staging now secured, it was easier for Barrie to find backing for a London opening.

The play was first performed at the Duke of York's Theatre on December 27, 1904, with an actress, Nina Boucicault, as Peter Pan. Having an actress play the boy—a tradition that continues to this day—began as a practical matter. The role was too demanding for a child; only an adult could handle all of the lines. And only an adult female could pass for a boy.

Peter Pan was an immediate hit, quelling Barrie's misgivings that an audience of adults wouldn't go for a play he'd originally written for children. One review compared Barrie's genius with that of George Bernard Shaw. Later, Barrie would cash in on the play's popularity by writing the novels *Peter Pan in Kensington Gardens* (1906) and *Peter and Wendy* (1911).

THE FATE OF THE LOST BOYS

But this story has no happy ending. Arthur Davies died of cancer, which left Barrie and Sylvia free to marry. Barrie went so far as to give her an engagement ring, but then she, too, died of cancer. Suddenly Barrie was the legal guardian of five boys, ages 7 to 17.

He devoted his life to them, imagining them as his own, but the boys felt he was overbearing in his possessiveness. Some biographers claim that the Davies brothers grew uncomfortable with their lives because they were always badgered about their relationship with the famous James Barrie. (On the other hand, he had little affection to bestow on his real family. Barrie was also named guardian of his brother's grandchildren when their parents died—but although he paid for their education, he refused to see them.)

Short people have been called "shrimps" longer than shrimps have.

George, the eldest Davies child and Barrie's favourite, died in World War I in 1915. Michael drowned in a pool at Oxford while being taught to swim by a close friend; there were rumours of a suicide pact. John married and distanced himself from Barrie. Peter Davies committed suicide as an adult in an attempt to escape, some say, from forever being called "Peter Pan."

Barrie ended up famous and rich, but a sad and lonely man. He was described as looking prematurely old and withered. Just before he died in 1937, he willed all proceeds from the copyright of *Peter Pan* to London's Great Ormond Street Hospital for Sick Children. Millions of dollars were realized from this bequest. Under British law, copyrights may extend no longer than 50 years before becoming public property. In this special case, Parliament made an exception and allowed the hospital to continue offering the world's best paediatric care because of the boy who never grew up.

* * * *

The Clapping Gamble

The play's most original and magical moment comes when the fairy Tinkerbell, in an attempt to save Peter's life, drinks poison that Captain Hook had intended for the boy. Boldy, Peter addresses the audience and calls on them to save the fairy's life. "Clap if you believe in fairies," he begs. Nina Boucicault, the first Peter, asked James Barrie, "Suppose they don't clap? What do I do then?" Barrie had no answer. The director told orchestra members to start the clapping if the audience sat on their hands. But the ploy was not necessary: the audience suspended disbelief with a vengeance and Nina-Peter wept openly with Tinkerbell's return to life.

* * * *

A "lost boy" was a Victorian
euphemism for one who died young.

The ancient Romans dyed their hair with bird droppings.

THE OTHER SIDE
OF PETER PAN

*Now that you know something about James Barrie and the origins
of Peter Pan, how does it change the way you perceive the story?
Here are some quotes from the original book.*

ALL CHILDREN, EXCEPT ONE, grow up. They soon know
that they will grow up, and the way Wendy knew was this. One
day when she was two years old she was playing in a garden, and
she plucked another flower and ran with it to her mother. I suppose she must have looked rather delightful, for Mrs. Darling put
her hand to her heart and cried, "Oh, why can't you remain like
this for ever!" This was all that passed between them on the subject, but henceforth Wendy knew that she must grow up. You
always know after you are two. Two is the beginning of the end.

* * * *

MRS. DARLING FIRST HEARD of Peter when she was tidying
up her children's minds. It is the nightly custom of every good
mother after her children are asleep to rummage in their minds
and put things straight for next morning, repacking into their
proper places the many articles that have wandered during the
day.

If you could keep awake (but of course you can't) you would
see your own mother doing this, and you would find it very interesting to watch her. It is quite like tidying up drawers. You would
see her on her knees, I expect, lingering humourously over some
of your contents, wondering where on earth you had picked this
thing up, making discoveries sweet and not so sweet, pressing this
to her cheek as if it were as nice as a kitten, and hurriedly stowing
that out of sight.

When you wake in the morning, the naughtiness and evil
passions with which you went to bed have been folded up small
and placed at the bottom of your mind; and on the top, beautifully
aired, are spread out your prettier thoughts, ready for you to put
on.

* * * *

Newborn babies don't have kneecaps.

SUDDENLY HOOK FOUND HIMSELF face to face with Peter. The others drew back and formed a ring around them.

For a long duck the two enemies looked at one another; Hook shuddering slightly, and Peter with the strange smile upon his face.

"So, Pan," said Hook at last, "this is your doing."

"Ay, James Hook," came the stern answer, "it is all my doing."

"Proud and insolent youth," said Hook, "prepare to meet thy doom."

"Dark and sinister man," Peter answered, "have at thee."

Without more words they fell to and for a space there was no advantage to either blade. Peter was a superb swordsman, and parried with dazzling rapidity....Hook, scarcely his inferior, forced him back, hoping suddenly to end all with a favourite thrust...but to his astonishment he found his thrust turned aside again and again.

... "Pan, who art thou?" he cried huskily.

"I'm youth, I'm joy," Peter answered... "I'm a little bird that has broken out of the egg."

This, of course, was nonsense; but it was proof to the unhappy Hook that Peter did not know in the least who or what he was, which is the very pinnacle of good form.

"To't again!" he cried despairingly.

He fought now like a human flail, and every sweep of that terrible sword would have severed in two any man or boy who obstructed it; but Peter fluttered around him as if the very wind it made blew him out of the danger zone.

* * * *

"PETER," WENDY SAID, "are you expecting me to fly away with you?

"Of course; that is why I have come."...

"I can't come," she said apologetically, "I have forgotten how to fly."

"I'll soon teach you again."

"O Peter, don't waste the fairy dust on me."...

Then she turned up the light, and Peter saw. He gave a cry of pain; ... "What is it?" he cried again.

She had to tell him. "I am old, Peter....I grew up a long time ago...I couldn't help it."

One third of the entire population of Sweden emigrated to the United States in the 1800s.

THE BIRTH OF THE COMPACT DISC

When CDs were introduced, we thought it was a conspiracy to make us replace our record collection with CDs. Well, maybe it was, but we have to admit that CD quality is pretty good. Here's the story of how they were invented.

AS SEEN ON TV

In 1974, the Philips Electronics company of the Netherlands started a revolution. They invented a laser video disc—the first product to make use of the "general induction laser" that had been developed at MIT in the early 1960s.

But LaserVision, as it was called, was a brand-new technology and it had a problem: poor error detection and correction—which resulted in inconsistent sound and picture quality. Philips built a prototype to show to several Japanese manufacturers, but the LaserVison player performed so poorly that only one of the Japanese companies—Sony—was willing to work with Philips to fix their new product.

At the time, Sony was a leader in both magnetic tape and digital recording technology. They had already built the world's first digital sound recorder—which used magnetic tape, weighed several hundred pounds, and was as large as a refrigerator...but it worked. And it gave Sony a head start in figuring out how to correct the problems that Philips was now experiencing with LaserVision.

DISC JOCKEYS

Sony put its digital magnetic tape system on the back burner and began developing a system that would record audio directly to a laser disc. It wouldn't be easy—on top of all the technical problems that had to be worked out, there was also strong opposition within the company to spending money on risky new technology.

Norio Ohga, the company's earliest and most enthusiastic proponent of digital sound recording, faced resistance from company founder Masaru Ibuka, and all but three of Sony's audio

---

engineers. Creatures of the analog age, they had little faith in the basic concept of digital technology—converting sound into numbers and then converting the numbers back into sound—and doubted it would ever improve on conventional analog recording. But Ohga, a former musician and aspiring symphony conductor, likened digital recording to "removing a winter coat from the sound," and insisted that the project be given the highest priority no matter what the cost.

STEP BY STEP
By the spring of 1976, most of the audio compact disc's bugs had been worked out, and the compact disc development team proudly presented Ohga with an astonishing technical marvel: a compact disc the same size as an LP record; but instead of having the same recording capacity as its vinyl counterpart, the CD could hold 13 hours and 20 minutes of sound.

So why aren't today's compact discs as big as an LP and capable of holding 13 hours of music? Because they'd cost too much to produce—something Ohga realized after taking one look at the prototype.

THE SIZE OF THINGS
Ohga sent his engineers back to the drawing board to come up with something that made more financial sense—a smaller CD that approximated the capacity of a vinyl record instead of its physical size. But exactly what size? The decision was still a few years off.

Back in the Netherlands, Philips Electronics was at work on its own version of a compact disc that was 11.5 centimeters across (about 4 1/2 inches) and capable of holding exactly 60 minutes of sound. Sixty minutes was a nice round number, and the discs were small enough to fit easily into players the size of automobile tape decks. But drawing from his background in classical music, Sony's Ohga pointed out a problem with the 11.5-centimeter standard that others had missed, as John Nathan writes in *Sony: The Private Life*:

Ohga was adamantly opposed on grounds that a 60-minute limit was "unmusical": at that length, he pointed out, a single disc could not accommodate all of Beethoven's Ninth Symphony and would require interrupting many of the major operas before the end of the First Act. On the other hand, 75 minutes would accommodate most important pieces of music, at least to a place where it made musical sense to cut them....The disc would have to be 12 centimeters to accommodate 75 minutes. In the end, Philips agreed to Sony's specifications.

FINAL TOUCHES

In March 1980, Sony and Philips tested their competing error-correction systems on discs that had been deliberately scratched, marked with chalk, and smeared with fingerprints. Sony's system worked better and was adopted by both companies.

Three months later, they submitted their prototype to the Digital Audio Disc Conference, which had been formed in 1977 to select a single worldwide standard for recording digital audio sound.

Two other companies submitted competing technologies: Telefunken, which recorded digital information mechanically, and JVC, which recorded digital sound electrostatically, the same way that a standard cassette recorder puts analog sound onto tape.

The Conference adopted both the Sony/Philips "Compact Disc Digital Audio System" and the JVC system, leaving Telefunken out in the cold. But the compact disc system quickly surpassed JVC's system because, unlike the JVC system, the compact disc's laser read the information on the CD without actually touching it—which meant that discs would last almost forever.

JUST SAY NO

While both companies continued work on perfecting their players, Sony's Norio Ohga and a Philips executive named Hans Timmer began preparing the recording industry for the introduction of CD technology. In May 1981, they brought Sony's prototype CD player to the International Music Industry Conference in Athens, Greece.

While they expected to dazzle the record company executives with CD technology, Ohga and Timmer also realized that they would encounter some opposition. But they were astonished by just how much opposition they did run into. The record companies had millions upon millions of dollars invested in LP record technology—all of which could become worthless if CDs ever took off. And because every compact disc manufactured was, in essence, a perfect "master" recording, counterfeiters could use them to make perfect bootleg recordings, something that had not been possible with LPs.

"Ohga must have been shaken, but he didn't show it," Timmer recalls. "He was calm and kept explaining that CDs would never scratch and that the sound was superior. But they shouted him down." Toward the end of Ohga's presentation, the executives stood up and began chanting, "The truth is in the groove! The truth is in the groove!"

"We barely escaped physical violence," Timmer says.

KEEP ON TRUCKIN'

Ohga was determined to continue developing CD technology, even if the entire industry was against him. Not that he had any choice: Sony's fortunes were now inextricably linked to the success of compact discs. Sony had taken a financial bath on its Betamax video recorders, which had been driven out of the marketplace by VHS-format, and the company sorely needed a hit product. Now they had invested tens of millions of dollars in CD technology. Compact discs had to succeed.

CD-DAY

On October 1, 1982, the world's first CD player—the Sony CDP 101—went on sale in Japan...and with it, the world's first CD albums, courtesy of CBS/Sony records.

The CDP 101 sold for $1,000 and compact discs sold for $16 to $18, twice the price of LPs. At those prices, the CDP 101 was a hit with audiophiles, but out of reach for most consumers. The *New York Times* wrote in March 1983:

> Some question whether the audio-disc will succeed. Even if prices come down—and industry experts expect they will—some analysts doubt whether consumers will be willing to sacrifice substantial investments in turntables and stacks of traditional recordings... The compact disc and player...is being likened in the music industry to the advent of stereophonic sound or the long-playing recording. Still, the CD's effect on record makers, manufacturers of audio

equipment, and—most importantly—the music-loving consumer will probably be more gradual than the two previous revolutions, according to analysts.

SUCCESS AT LAST

The analysts were wrong. In November 1984, Sony introduced a new CD player, the D-50, that was half the size of the CDP-101 and cost only $230. "The market came roaring back to life," John Nathan writes. By 1986, CDs players were selling at a rate of more than a million per year and consumers had purchased more than 45 million compact discs. And that was just the beginning: Sales doubled to 100 million CDs by 1988, and quadrupled to 400 million CDs in 1992, compared to 2.3 million LPs sold that year, making them the fastest-growing consumer electronic product ever introduced.

* * *

REALLY BAD, AWFUL, TERRIBLE JOKES

Yes, we know these jokes are bad and you'll groan when you read them…and then you'll tell them to someone else.

A man walks into a psychiatrist's office with banana up his nose and says, "What's the matter with me, Doc?" The psychiatrist says, "You're not eating properly."

Q: Why couldn't the sesame seed leave the gambling casino?
A: Because he was on a roll.

Upon seeing a flock of geese flying south for the winter, the bird watcher exclaimed, "Migratious."

Q: How many surrealists does it take to screw in a lightbulb?
A: To get to the other side.

Q: Did you hear about the dyslexic devil worshipper?
A: He sold his soul to Santa.

Q: What do you get if you don't pay your exorcist promptly?
A: Repossessed.

How much water in a cubic mile of fog? Less than a gallon.

THE ANSWER ZONE

ANSWERS TO "THE RIDDLER" ON PAGE 166

1. An echo.
2. Holes.
3. Mount Everest.
4. Envelope.
5. A ton.
6. A priest.
7. Only one...the last one.
8. Zero...Noah took animals on the ark, not Moses.
9. Only once. After the first calculation, you will be subtracting 5 from 20, then 5 from 15, and so on.
10. A secret.
11. You can't take a picture with a wooden leg...
    You need a camera!
12. Darkness.
13. Footsteps.
14. A coffin.
15. An umbrella.
16. Suicide.
17. The year 1961. It reads the same upside down.
    Won't happen again until the year 6009.
18. The letter "V."
19. "Are you asleep?"
20. A promise.

How many times do you breathe in a year? About 10 million.

ANSWERS TO "THE HISTORY OF ROCK: A QUIZ" ON PAGE 245

1.b. "Hound Dog" was written in 1952 by Jerry Lieber and Mike Stoller specifically for Willie Mae "Big Mama" Thornton. Her record went to #1 on the R & B charts in 1953. Then a lounge act named Freddie Bell and the Bellboys made a joke out of it in 1955. That's the version that Elvis copied.

How did he first hear it? In 1956, after "Heartbreak Hotel" had hit #1, Elvis was signed to do his first gig in Las Vegas. Later he'd be king of the town. But the first time around, he was fired—a two- week engagement at the Frontier Hotel was shortened to one week when audiences failed to respond to the hip wiggler. But Elvis still lucked out: he wandered into the lounge and watched Freddie Bell's group perform their humorous takeoff of "Hound Dog." He thought it was hilarious... and decided to do it himself.

Note: The Bellboys had already recorded the song, and Elvis may have picked up a copy of their record to refresh his memory before he recorded his own version.

2.c. Blackwell had just taken a job writing for a publisher called Shalimar Music when Moe Gayle, the head of the company, called him into his office with an unusual offer: Elvis Presley was interested in recording "Don't Be Cruel," but the deal was contingent on Blackwell giving up half his writer's credit (and thus half the royalties) to Presley. "Elvis Presley?" Blackwell answered. "Who the hell is Elvis Presley?"

Blackwell recalls: "I just felt that I was getting the shaft, man. It took them about two weeks to convince me. They pointed out that if Elvis did become big, I would make a good deal more money this way than not doing it at all. And if he didn't become big, I really wasn't losing anything...so I said okay."

It may have been an unjust arrangement, but it wound up an extremely lucrative one for Blackwell. "Don't Be Cruel" was released in July 1956 as the flip side of "Hound Dog." The double-sided hit reached #1 in August and stayed there for over two months; it was on the charts for six months, becoming the year's #1 record and Elvis's favorite early record. Blackwell was instantly established as a major songwriter. He went on to write "All Shook Up," "Great Balls of Fire," "Return to Sender," and many more hits.

3.a. Fats Domino wrote the song from real life: "I was walkin' down the street and I saw a little lady spankin' a baby. And I heard somebody say 'Ain't That a Shame.'" But Pat didn't relate to it —he objected to it because the grammar was bad.

"[When the record company asked me to record] 'Ain't That a Shame,' I balked," Boone says. "I said, 'Look, I just transferred to Columbia University, I'm an English major. I don't want to record a song called "Ain't That a Shame."' I mean, 'ain't' wasn't an accepted word. It is now in the dictionary, but I was majoring in English and I felt that this was going to be a terrible thing if it was a hit. I tried to record it 'Isn't That a Shame,' but it didn't work.'"

He finally gave in and used the original lyrics. It hit #1 on the charts. Domino's version was a hit, too—but with Boone taking the lion's share of sales away, it only reached #10.

4.a. In the mid-1950s, "respectable" people—including Mrs. Kern—thought doo-wop rock was a travesty. According to one account, she was so appalled and outraged by the Platters' treatment of the song that she explored ways of stopping it legally. Of course, when the Platters' record became a hit—and sold more copies of "Smoke Gets in Your Eyes" than anyone had before—her opinion changed. And she never turned down a royalty check.

5.c. Hard to believe, but although he may have been the most influential rock musician ever, Berry only had one #1 song—a novelty tune full of sophomoric sexual innuendo called "My Ding-a-Ling." He'd been using it to close his concerts and did it as "My Tambourine" on a live album in the mid-1960s. Then in 1972 he recorded it live again, in London. For some reason his record company released it as a single. As Bob Shannon and John Javna wrote in **Behind the Hits:** "It's kind of depressing for music fans that the biggest single Chuck Berry ever had was this...this...thing! But what the hell, at least Chuck got a hit out of it."

6.a. Radio stations found all kinds of reasons not to play it: it was too suggestive, he cursed on it (the part where he goes "We-ell-a" sounded like he was saying "Weh-hell-a"), he sounded black (most stations didn't play songs by black artists). But when the record was banned by BMI (Broadcast Music Inc., which licenses music for airplay) because it was "obscene," the record died.

Sun Records knew it could be a hit—and Jerry Lee Lewis

Where's the thickest skin on your body? Your foot. It's 3 times thicker than on your palms.

could be another Elvis—if it was handled right. So they took Lewis to New York to try to get him on "The Ed Sullivan Show." They flew to New York, but Sullivan wouldn't listen—Lewis didn't have a hit, and Sullivan didn't like that kind of music, anyway. So they called NBC and got the talent coordinator there to set up a meeting with the producer of "The Steve Allen Show" (a variety program that ran head to head with Sullivan's). Allen's biggest coup had been to introduce Elvis Presley as a guest after Sullivan had turned him down the first time. Now the Sun people hoped they could get Allen to do it again. They took Lewis with them to the meeting. When the TV execs asked to hear a record, Lewis stepped out and played in person. The NBC execs were blown away and scheduled him for that Sunday night.

What people at NBC never found out was that the song Jerry Lee was going to play— "Whole Lotta Shakin"—had been banned. Why? Because after NBC agreed to have Lewis on, the head of promotion for Sun Records called BMI and convinced them that if NBC didn't mind about the lyrics, why should they? He neglected to add that no one at NBC had actually heard the lyrics. But BMI gave in, and the way was clear for Jerry Lee's appearance.

On July 28, 1956, America was introduced to Jerry Lee Lewis and "Whole Lotta Shakin' Goin' On" on "The Steve Allen Show." Jerry went crazy, playing piano with his feet and inadvertently involving Allen himself. At one point he jumped off his piano stool to play standing up and sent the stool careening across the stage: Allen, who was stomping and clapping with the rest of the audience, tossed it back toward Jerry. Then Allen grabbed another piece of furniture and tossed it. Reportedly, he was about to throw a potted plant when Jerry finished playing. The exposure sent the record zooming up the charts. By the end of August it was a million-seller and Jerry Lee was the hottest new rocker in America.

7. b. Little Richard was so incensed by Boone's cover version of "Tutti Frutti" [which outdid Richard's on the charts], he purposely made the follow-up, "Long Tall Sally," too fast for Boone to sing. Nonetheless, Boone figured out how to adapt "Long Tall Sally" and gave Richard a run for his money. Little Richard's version did beat out Boone's—barely. Richard hit #7 in Billboard, Boone hit #8.

ANSWERS TO "THE HISTORY OF ROCK: QUIZ 2" ON PAGE 385

1. a. The story told in Grace Slick's biography is that members of the Great Society (Slick's first band) kept trying to get her to write music. Finally they practically locked her in a room and told her she couldn't come out until she'd written some songs. She emerged with several, including "White Rabbit," which was loosely based on a classical piece by Ravel called "Bolero." However, Slick has said repeatedly that "White Rabbit" isn't about, drugs. Her explanation: "We were talking about opening up, looking around, checking out what's happening. We were also talking about the fifties mentality, which was really bottled up." She added: "Feeding your head is not necessarily pumping chemicals into it."

Most of the imagery she use came directly from Lewis Carroll's two books, Alice's Adventures in Wonderland, and Through the Looking Glass (see page 79). Three examples from the book *Behind the Hits:*

1. "One pill makes you larger." Alice was about three inches tall and wandering around Wonderland when she spotted a caterpillar. It was about the same height as her, except that it was sitting on top of a mushroom, smoking a hookah. She asked it how she could get big again; as the caterpillar was walking away, it turned back and said, "One side makes you larger, the other side makes you smaller." Alice asked, "One side of what?" The caterpillar replied, "The mushroom." There weren't any pills in the story, but maybe they were magic mushrooms.

2. "When the men on the chessboard get up and tell you where to go." The premise of Through the Looking Glass: Alice is trying to get her cat to play chess with her; she falls asleep and dreams that she's a pawn on the chessboard and has to get to the other side to become a queen. Each chapter of Through the Looking Glass takes place on a different square of the chessboard, and the characters in it are characters in a game of chess. Occasionally they do tell her where to go (of course, she's lost). At one point, the White Knight guides her across a brook that turns out to be the space between the squares on the board.

3. "When logic and proportion have fallen softly dead." Everything is out of whack in Wonderland (although Carroll wrote a book about symbolic logic). What could be more illogi-

cal than the dialogue at the Mad Hatter's tea party? About proportion—Alice goes from three inches to 15 feet high. Hard to keep a sense of proportion with that happening. She mentions that it's rather uncomfortable to be so many different heights in one day.

By the way: The dormouse, who's sitting in a teacup at the Mad Tea Party, says, "Twinkle twinkle little bat. How I wonder where you're at." He doesn't say, "Feed your head."

2. b. In 1996 there was an amusing story coming from Lawrenceville Academy, a New Jersey prep school: People said that a student named Mark Sebastian —John's 15-year-old brother—had submitted the poem that became "Summer in the City" to his English teacher ...and had gotten an "F." It might well have been true—John Sebastian didn't particularly like the poem when he first saw it, either. But he did like the chorus—the part that went, "But at night there's a different world." Mark gave it to John and asked if he could do anything with it. John said he'd see. He put Mark's poem aside for a few months and in the interim came up with a little piano figure that he liked but didn't have a song for. Then one night as John was going to sleep, Mark's chorus, his own piano riff, and a set of new lyrics popped into his head.

"[Bassist] Steve Boone contributed a middle section," Sebastian says, and the song was done. His first impression of the song: certain notes sounded like car horns. "I said, 'Gee, this sounds sort of like Gershwin—sort of like "An American in Paris." Maybe we could put traffic on it.'"

The band went into New York's Columbia Studios for two nights. On the first, they did the entire instrumental track. The second night was for vocals...and sound effects. Sebastian says, "I remember this hilarious old sound man who'd never had a job with a rock 'n' roll band before looking at us quite puzzled as we auditioned pneumatic hammers to find the one that had the right intestinal tone to it." For car sounds, the old man brought in tapes of traffic jams and horns that he'd used when he worked in radio. The band listened to them for hours, then chose their favorites. John wanted the automobiles to start off softly, so the sound-effects man threw in a Volkswagen horn at the beginning.

The song was released in the summer, of course, and within a few weeks was #1 in America. It was the Spoonful's only #1 hit in their phenomenal string of seven consecutive Top 10 records between September 1965 and December 1966.

3. a. It started with a shopping trip. Roy and Billy Dees, a songwriter Orbison had been collaborating with, were sitting in the Orbisons' house when Orbison's wife, Claudette, announced she was going into town to buy some groceries. "Do you need any money?" Roy asked. Dees said, "A pretty woman never needs any money." Then he turned to Roy and said, "Hey, how about that for a song title?" Orbison liked the idea of doing a song about a "Pretty woman," but not the part about the money. After Claudette left, they began turning the phrase into a song. And when she returned, carrying bags of food, she was greeted by the debut performance of her husband's second #1 tune.

4. b. The Four Seasons and a bunch of side musicians were in a recording studio in the Abbey Victoria Hotel on Seventh Avenue in New York City, recording "Walk Like a Man." After a few takes, it was obvious to everyone in the studio that something was wrong. But Bob Crewe, the producer, refused to pay attention. "Another take," he kept saying. Here's the story of the unusual session, as told by a participant, guitarist Vinnie Bell:

> As we were recording, there was a sudden pounding on the door. And there was the smell of smoke. And plaster was starting to fall from the ceiling. And water was leaking in...while we're recording! And there's this pounding on the door of the studio, and Bob Crewe wouldn't unlock it—he kept saying, "We'll open it in a second, there's one more take." And the water's pouring onto us, and we've got electric guitars in our hands—we were afraid we were gonna be electrocuted. Finally, the [firemen] axed their way right through the door—and Crewe's trying to push them out! And then we could see the smoke pouring through. It seems that the floor above us in that hotel was on fire! It was barely audible from inside the studio, but you could hear fire engines and all that—the whole bit. And this guy was so intent on making the record—on getting another take—that he kept trying to push these guys out...until they knocked him on the floor.

And that was it for the recording session.

5. b. The story behind this record—which was certified gold in 1969 and still refuses to die—is almost unbelievable. Paul Leka was a producer at Mercury Records in 1969. He persuaded the label to sign a friend named Gary De Carlo, and they did a recording session together. They thought everything they recorded was good enough to be a hit, so they decided to record one really cheesy song for the B side of De Carlo's first single release. That way they'd save the good stuff for later.

The day of the B-side session, Leka ran into a friend he once wrote songs with. They remembered a tune called "Kiss Him Good-by" they'd written years earlier and decided to make that the stinker. The only problem: It was just two minutes long. They wanted to make it twice as long to make sure it never got on the air—no disc jockey would dare play a four-minute record—so they added a chorus...except they couldn't think of any words for it. So Leka just started singing "Na-na-na..." and someone else started singing "Hey-hey." And that was it. They didn't bother with lyrics because it was just a B-side.

To Leka's astonishment and embarrassment, when Mercury heard it, they decided to release it as an A-side. The musicians all agreed it should come out under an alias—and came up with Steam because at the end of the recording session, they'd seen a humongous cloud of steam coming out of a New York manhole cover.

6. c. Satchmo was making an album of show tunes, and David Merrick was trying to promote his new musical, so he encouraged performers to sing it. Armstrong had never heard of "Hello Dolly." And though he liked the tune, he was appalled that after all the innovative work he'd done in his career, his biggest hit was this silly, simple song.

7. a. Percy Sledge worked as an orderly at Colbert County Hospital in Alabama during the day and sang with a band called the Esquires Combo at night. One evening, the Esquires Combo was playing at a club in Sheffield, Alabama, and Sledge just couldn't keep his mind on the songs he was supposed to be singing. He was upset about a woman. Overcome by emotion, he turned to bass player Cameron Lewis and organ player Andrew Wright and begged them to play something he could sing to. Anything—it didn't matter what. The musicians looked at each other, shrugged, and just started playing. And Percy made up "When a Man Loves a Woman," one of the prettiest soul ballads ever written, on the spot.

The filaments for the first electric lamp were made of bamboo.

THE LAST PAGE

BATHROOM READERS,
We at the Bathroom Readers' Institute do not take your quest for good and plentiful bathroom reading lightly. We sit firmly and believe that it is your inalienable right to have quality reading material.

So we invite you to take the plunge. Sit down and be counted by joining the Bathroom Readers' Institute. Send a self-addressed, stamped envelope to:

BRI
P.O. Box 1117
Ashland, Oregon 97520, USA

You'll receive your attractive free membership card and a copy of the BRI newsletter (sent out irregularly via email), receive discounts when ordering directly through the BRI, and earn a permanent spot on the BRI honor roll!

Or contact us through our website at: **www.bathroomreader.com**

- Visit "The Throne Room"—a great place to read!

- Submit your favorite articles and facts.

- Suggest ideas for future editions.

- Order additional BRI books.

- Become a BRI member.

Well, we're out of space, and when you've gotta go, you've gotta go. We hope you've enjoyed this book as much as we have. And never forget:

Go with the flow!

The Atlantic Ocean is saltier than the Pacific.